© 2009 by Allison Downing

About the Author

JUSTIN FOX is editorial director of the *Harvard Business Review* Group. He was previously the business and economics columnist for *Time* magazine, the author of the popular Time.com blog the *Curious Capitalist*, and an editor and writer at *Fortune*. He appears regularly on CNN, CNBC, and PBS's *Nightly Business Report*. He lives in Cambridge, Massachusetts, with his wife and son.

THE
MYTH
OF THE
RATIONAL
MARKET

THE
MYTH
OF THE
RATIONAL
MARKET

A History of Risk, Reward,
and Delusion on Wall Street

JUSTIN FOX

HARPER
BUSINESS

NEW YORK • LONDON • TORONTO • SYDNEY

HARPER
BUSINESS

A hardcover edtion of this book was published in 2009 by Harper, an imprint of HarperCollins Publishers.

HarperCollins books may be purchased for educational, business, or sales promotional use. For information, please e-mail the Special Markets Department at SPsales@harpercollins.com.

FIRST HARPER BUSINESS PAPERBACK PUBLISHED 2011.

Designed by William Ruoto

The Library of Congress has catalogued the hardcover edition as follows:

Fox, Justin, 1964–
　The myth of the rational market : a history of risk, reward, and delusion on Wall Street / Justin Fox. — 1st ed.
　　p. cm.
　Includes bibliographical references and index.
　ISBN 978-0-06-059899-0
　1. Rational expectations (Economic theory) 2. Wall Street (New York, N.Y.) 3. Economics—Psychological aspects. 4. Economics—History. I. Title.
HB3731.F69 2009
332.6401—dc22   2008052718

ISBN 978-0-06-059903-4 (pbk.)

HB 02.05.2024

To Allison

CONTENTS

IT HAD BEEN WORKING SO EXCEPTIONALLY WELL

ON THE FOURTH THURSDAY OF October in 2008, eighty-two-year-old Alan Greenspan paid a visit to Capitol Hill to admit that he had misunderstood how the world works. Sitting at the witnesses' table in the hearing room on the first floor of the Rayburn House Office Building, the former Federal Reserve chairman started by reading a statement that tried to explain what had gone so wrong with financial markets over the past year. After asking Greenspan a few questions, the chairman of the House Committee on Government Oversight and Reform, California Democrat Henry Waxman, summed up. "In other words," he said, "you found that your view of the world, your ideology, was not right. It was not working."

"Precisely," replied Greenspan. "That's precisely the reason I was shocked, because I had been going for forty years or more with very considerable evidence that it was working exceptionally well."[1]

During those forty years—especially the nineteen during which Greenspan was the world's top central banker—financial markets grew to play an ever-larger and less-fettered role. The stock market boomed for most of Greenspan's years at the Fed. Bond markets boomed too, and expanded into new territory as Wall Street whizzes took mortgage loans and auto loans and credit card debt off the balance sheets of banks and repackaged them into asset-backed securities sold to investors around the world. The most dizzying growth came in over-the-counter derivatives, custom-made financial instruments (options, futures, swaps) that tracked the movements of other financial instruments. With them, traders could insure against or bet on moves in currencies or interest rates or stocks. In recent years it had even become possible to use derivatives to insure against loans gone bad. From 1987 to 2007, the face value of over-the-counter derivatives rose from $866 billion to $454 trillion.[2]

As Fed chairman, Greenspan had celebrated this financialization of the global economy. "These instruments enhance the ability to differentiate risk and allocate it to those investors most able and willing to take it,"[3] he said in 1999, referring to derivatives in particular. Greenspan had once expressed the worry, in 1996, that stock markets might be losing themselves in a frenzy of "irrational exuberance." When they kept rising after that, he took the lesson that the market knew more than he did.

This was Greenspan's ideology—and it had been widely shared in Washington and on Wall Street. Financial markets knew best. They moved capital from those who had it to those who needed it. They spread risk. They gathered and dispersed information. They regulated global economic affairs with a swiftness and decisiveness that governments couldn't match.

AND THEN, SUDDENLY, THEY DIDN'T. "The whole intellectual edifice collapsed in the summer of last year," Greenspan admitted at the October 2008 hearing.[4] That was when the private market for U.S. mortgage securities collapsed, beginning a fitful unraveling of asset market after asset market around the world. Distrust spread. Many previously thriving credit markets shut down entirely. Bank runs— long thought to endanger only actual banks—threatened any financial institution that ran on borrowed money. After Greenspan's successor at the Fed, Ben Bernanke, and Treasury Secretary Hank Paulson decided in September 2008 not to step in to avert such a run on Lehman Brothers, global finance virtually ceased functioning. It took a partial government takeover of the financial system—not just in the United States but in Europe—to bring back even a modicum of calm.

Greenspan struggled to explain what had gone wrong because the intellectual edifice around which he had built his thinking simply didn't allow room for the events of the preceding fourteen months. This was the edifice of rational market theory. The best-known element of rational market theory is the efficient market hypothesis, formulated at the University of Chicago in the 1960s with reference to the U.S stock market. The belief in the so-called rational market that took hold in the years that followed, though, was about more than just stocks. It held that as more stocks, bonds, options, futures, and other financial instruments were created and traded, they would inevitably bring more rationality to economic activity. Financial markets possessed a wisdom that individuals, companies, and governments did not.

The notion that financial markets know a lot has been around as long as financial markets themselves. In 1889, stock market chronicler George Rutledge Gibson asserted that when "shares become publicly known in an open market, the value which they there acquire may be regarded as the judgment of the best intelligence concerning them."[5] Hints of this same attitude could be found in the work of early economists such as Adam Smith—and even the religious thinkers of the Middle Ages. While some medieval ecclesiastical scholars argued that lawgivers should set a "just price" for every good to guarantee that producers earned a living wage and consumers weren't gouged, others, St. Thomas Aquinas among them, held that the just price was set by the market.[6]

All these early claims for the correctness and justness of market prices came with caveats—doses of realism, you could call them. George Gibson wrote that stock exchanges were prone to manias and panics and called for the regulation of "bucket shops" that urged customers to speculative excess.[7] Adam Smith thought corporations with widely dispersed ownership—the shares of which are what make stock markets go—were abominations. Thomas Aquinas made no claim that the market price was always right, just that it was hard to come up with a fairer alternative.

The twentieth-century version of rational market theory was different—both more careful and more extreme. It started with the observation that the movements of stock prices were random, and could not be predicted on the basis of past movements. This observation was followed by the claim that it was impossible to predict stock prices on the basis of any publicly available information (such as earnings, balance sheet data, and articles in the newspaper). From those starting points—both of which were, it turned out later, not entirely correct—flowed the conviction that stock prices were in some fundamental sense *right*.

Most of the scholars who backed this hypothesis early on didn't mean for it to be taken as a literal description of reality. It was a scientific construct, a model for understanding, for testing and engineering new tools. All scientific models are oversimplifications. The important test is whether they're useful. This particular oversimplification was undeniably useful, so useful that it took on a life of its own. As it traveled from college campuses in Cambridge, Massachusetts, and Chicago in the 1960s to Wall Street, Washington, and the boardrooms of the nation's corporations, the rational market hypothesis strengthened and lost nuance.

It was a powerful idea, helping to inspire the first index funds, the investment approach called modern portfolio theory, the risk-adjusted performance measures that shape the money management business, the corporate creed of shareholder value, the rise of derivatives, and the hands-off approach to financial regulation that prevailed in the United States from the 1970s on.

In some aspects the story of the rational market hypothesis parallels and is intertwined with the widely chronicled rebirth of pro-free-market ideology after World War II. But rational market finance was not at heart a political movement. It was a scientific one, an imposing of the midcentury fervor for rational, mathematical, statistical decision making upon financial markets. This endeavor was far from an unmitigated disaster. It represented, in many ways, the forward march of progress. But much was lost, most importantly the understanding—common among successful investors but absent from several decades of finance scholarship—that the market is a devilish thing. It is far too devilish to be captured by a single simple theory of behavior, and certainly not by a theory that allowed for nothing but calm rationality as far as the eye could see.

As far back as the 1970s, dissident economists and finance scholars began to question this rational market theory, to expose its theoretical inconsistencies and lack of empirical backing. By the end of the century they had knocked away most of its underpinnings. Yet there was no convincing replacement, so the rational market continued to inform public debate, government decision making, and private investment policy well into the first decade of the twenty-first century—right up to the market collapse of 2008.

This book offers no grand new theory of how markets truly behave. It is instead a history of the rise and fall of the old theory—the rational market theory. It is a history of ideas, not a biography, or even a collection of biographies. But it is full of characters—most of them economists and finance professors—who were actors in many of the great dramas of the twentieth century, from 1920s boom to 1930s Depression to war and then peace and prosperity, then 1960s boom and 1970s bust and so on. These characters weren't the lead actors, for the most part. But they were crucial to the plot. (A reference list of key players can be found on page 322.)

"The ideas of economists and political philosophers, both when they are right and when they are wrong, are more powerful than is commonly understood," wrote John Maynard Keynes, who plays a supporting role in the story to follow. "Indeed, the world is ruled by little else. Practical men, who believe themselves to be quite exempt from any intellectual influences, are usually the slaves of some defunct economist."

The defunct economist with whom this tale begins is Keynes's contemporary Irving Fisher.

THE
MYTH
OF THE
RATIONAL
MARKET

EARLY DAYS

CHAPTER 1

IRVING FISHER LOSES HIS BRIEFCASE, AND THEN HIS FORTUNE

The first serious try to impose reason and science upon the market comes in the early decades of the twentieth century. It doesn't work out so well.

It is 1905. A well-dressed man in his late thirties talks intently into a pay phone at Grand Central Depot in New York. Between his legs is a leather valise. The doors of the phone booth are open, and a thief makes off with the bag. It is, given what we know of its owner, of excellent quality. Finding a willing buyer will not be a problem.

The contents of the valise are another matter. Stuffed inside is an almost-completed manuscript that brings together economics, probability theory, and real-world business practice in ways never seen before. It is part economics treatise, part primer on what rational, scientific stock market investing ought to look like. It is a glimpse into Wall Street's distant future.

THAT SCIENCE AND REASON MIGHT be applied to the stock exchange was still a radical notion in 1905. "Wall Street and its captains ran the stock market, and they and their friends either owned or controlled the speculative pools," recalled one journalist of the time. "The speculative public hardly had a chance. The *right* stockholders knew when to buy and sell. The others groped."[1]

Times, though, were changing. Good information about stocks and bonds was getting easier for the "speculative public" to obtain. Corporations had become too big and too interested in respectability to be controlled by just a few cronies. The dark corners of Wall Street were being illuminated. Maybe the investing world *was* ready for a more scientific approach.

The stolen manuscript was never seen again, but its author, Yale University economics professor Irving Fisher, had a habit of overcoming setbacks that might cause a lesser (or more realistic) individual to despair. As he prepared to set off for college in 1884, his father died of tuberculosis, leaving the undergraduate to support his mother and younger siblings. Just as his academic career began to take off in the late 1890s, Fisher himself came down with TB, which incapacitated him for years. In 1904, finally healthy and working again, he watched as fire consumed the house just north of Yale's campus where he lived with his wife and two children.

And then the theft of his manuscript. Afterward, inured by then to disaster, Fisher went right back to work. He resolved always to close the door when he entered a phone booth, and he rewrote his book, this time making copies of each chapter as he went along. Published in 1906 as *The Nature of Capital and Income,* it cemented his international reputation among economists. It became, as one biographer wrote, "one of the principal building blocks of all present-day economic theory."[2]

Its impact on Wall Street was less immediately obvious. Stockbrokers and speculators did not rush out to buy the book. There's no evidence that investors began making probability calculations before they bought stocks, as Fisher recommended. But Fisher was at least as persistent as he was lacking in street smarts. His ideas began to have some impact in his lifetime, and after his death in 1947, they took off.

Books directly or indirectly descended from Fisher's work now adorn the desks of hedge fund managers, pension consultants, financial advisers, and do-it-yourself investors. The increasingly dominant quantitative side of the financial world—that strange wonderland of portfolio optimization software, enhanced indexing, asset allocators, credit default swaps, betas, alphas, and "model-derived" valuations— is a territory where Professor Fisher would feel intellectually right at home. He is perhaps not *the* father, but certainly a father of modern Wall Street.

Hardly anyone calls him that, though. Economists honor Fisher for his theoretical breakthroughs, but outside the discipline his chief claim to lasting fame is the horrendous stock market advice he proffered in the late 1920s. Read almost any history of the years leading up to the great crash of October 1929, and the famous Professor Fisher serves as a sort of idiot Greek chorus, popping up every few pages to assert that stock prices had reached a "permanently high plateau." He wasn't just talking the talk. Fisher blew his entire fortune (acquired through marriage, then increased through entrepreneurial success) in the bear market of late 1929 and the early 1930s.

Fisher's two historical personas—buffoon of the great crash and architect of financial modernity—are not as alien to each other as they might at first appear. In the early years of the twentieth century Fisher outlined a course of rational, scientific behavior for stock market players. In the late 1920s, blinded in part by his own spectacular financial success, he became convinced that America's masses of speculators and investors (not to mention its central bankers) were in fact following his advice. Nothing, therefore, could go wrong.

Irving Fisher had succumbed to the myth of the rational market. It is a myth of great power—one that, much of the time, explains reality pretty well. But it is nonetheless a myth, an oversimplification that, when taken too literally, can lead to all sorts of trouble. Fisher was just the first in a line of distinguished scholars who saw reason and scientific order in the market and made fools of themselves on the basis of this conviction. Most of the others came along much later, though. Irving Fisher was ahead of his time.

HE WAS NOT, HOWEVER, ALONE in his advanced thoughts about financial markets. In Paris, mathematics student Louis Bachelier studied the price fluctuations on the Paris Bourse (exchange) in a similar spirit. The result was a doctoral thesis that, when unearthed more than half a century after its completion in 1900, would help to relaunch the study of financial markets.

Bachelier undertook his investigation at a time when scientists had begun to embrace the idea that while there could be no absolute certainty about anything, uncertainty itself could be a powerful tool. Instead of trying to track down the cause of every last jiggling of a molecule or movement of a planet, one could simply assume that the causes were many and randomness the result. "It is thanks to chance—that is to say, thanks to our ignorance, that we can arrive at conclusions," wrote the great French mathematician and physicist Henri Poincaré in 1908.[3]

The greatest tool for building knowledge upon such ignorance was what was called the Gaussian distribution (after German stargazer and mathematician Carl Friedrich Gauss), the normal distribution, or simply the bell curve. A Gaussian array of numbers can be adequately described by invoking only the mean (i.e., the top of the bell) and what in the waning years of the nineteenth century came to be known as the standard deviation (the width of the bell). As scientists of the time were discovering, the bell curve popped up again and again in measurements of natural phenomena. The temptation to apply it to human endeavor was for some irresistible.

Bachelier used the assumptions of the bell curve to depict price movements on the Paris exchange. He began with the insight that "the mathematical expectation of the speculator is zero."[4] That is, the gains and losses of all the buyers and sellers on the exchange must by definition cancel each other out. This isn't strictly true—stocks and bonds have delivered positive returns over time—but as a logical framework for investing or speculating, Bachelier's diagnosis remains unsurpassed. The average investor cannot beat the market. The average investor *is* the market.

From this beginning, Bachelier realized, "it is possible to study mathematically the static state of the market at a given instant, i.e., to establish the law of probability of price changes consistent with the market at that instant."[5] It was a view of the market as a game of chance, like roulette or dice. And just as games of chance can be described mathematically (and had been since the 1500s), Bachelier sketched the probabilities of the exchange.

His work was so innovative that when Albert Einstein employed similar mathematical tools five years later to describe the random motion of tiny particles suspended in a fluid or a gas—called "Brownian motion," after the botanist who first noted it—he helped lay the foundations of nuclear physics. But while physicists, building upon Einstein's work, were putting together atomic bombs by the 1940s, practical application of Bachelier's insights would not emerge until the 1970s.

This is not simply a tale of ignored genius. There was a major limitation to Bachelier's work, of which he was well aware. His teacher, Henri Poincaré, made sure of that. While he celebrated the use of the bell curve in the physical sciences, Poincaré thought caution needed to be exercised in applying it to human behavior. The Gaussian distribution, or the bell curve, is the product of countless random and *independent* causes. "When men are brought together," Poincaré wrote, "they no longer decide by chance and independently of each other, but react upon one another. Many causes come into action, they trouble the men and draw them this way and that, but there is one thing they cannot destroy, the habits they have of Panurge's sheep."[6]

Panurge, a character from Rabelais's satirical *Gargantua and*

Pantagruel novels, got a flock of sheep to jump off a ship by throwing the lead ram overboard. In his examination of the Paris Bourse, Bachelier eluded the stampeding sheep only by limiting the application of his formulas. "One might fear that the author has exaggerated the applicability of Probability Theory as has often been done," Poincaré wrote in his grading report on the thesis. "Fortunately, this is not the case."

Bachelier contrived to see no more than an "instant" into the future, assuming that price changes in that instant would be unpredictable in direction but predictably small. That was as far as math could get him. "The probability dependent on future events," he conceded, is "impossible to predict in a mathematical manner." It is precisely this probability, he acknowledged, that most interests the speculator. "He analyzes causes which could influence a rise or a fall of market values or the amplitude of market fluctuations. His inductions are absolutely personal, since his counterpart in a transaction necessarily has the opposite opinion."[7]

That was that. Bachelier went on to a modestly successful career as a math professor, and published a well-received popular treatise on games, chance, and risk (*Le jeu, la chance et le hasard*). When he died in 1946, one year before Irving Fisher, no one on the trading floor was making use of his ideas. His colleagues, meanwhile, were nonplussed by his interest in markets. On a bibliography of Bachelier's writings found in the files of the great French mathematician Paul Lévy is scrawled the complaint, "Too much on finance!"[8]

IRVING FISHER WAS ABLE TO go where Bachelier did not because he had more than just mathematics and probability theory at his disposal. He was an *economist*. He was able to go where other economists did not because he, unlike all but a handful of them at the time, was a *mathematician*. And he was able to do something tangible with his insights because he was a wealthy resident of a country where, in the early decades of the twentieth century, financial markets were just beginning to grow into the vast bazaars that would steer the economy for the rest of the century and beyond.

At Yale, where he graduated first in the class of 1888 even while supporting his family with tutoring jobs and academic prizes, Fisher majored in mathematics. But he also took five courses in economics and sociology with the legendary William Graham Sumner. "Despite personal coldness and a crisp, dogmatic classroom manner, Sumner had a wider following than any teacher in Yale's history," wrote one historian. He was also, in this estimation, "the most vigorous and influential social Darwinist in America."[9]

In its most primitive form, social Darwinism was the belief that Charles Darwin's theory of evolution applied not just to plants and animals but to human affairs, and that the nineteenth-century rise of industrial capitalism in the United States and Great Britain was a Darwinian matter of the "survival of the fittest." Sumner's version was gloomier and more sophisticated than that. He worried that those who aimed to improve society ("social doctors," he called them) would inevitably screw it up. "They do not understand that all parts of society hold together," he wrote in 1883 in one of a series of *Harper's* articles later bundled into the classic tract *What the Social Classes Owe to Each Other*, "and that forces which are set into action act and react throughout the whole organism, until an equilibrium is produced by a readjustment of all interests and rights."[10]

The concept of equilibrium, in which competing influences balance each other out, lends itself naturally to mathematical treatment (all it takes is an equal sign) and was crucial to the early development of chemistry and physics. Hints of it had already appeared in economics—Scotsman Adam Smith's notion of an "invisible hand" steering selfish individuals toward societally beneficial results was the most famous example[11]—but attempts to build a unified theory of economics around it had foundered upon the imprecision of the field.

Economists were long stuck, for example, on the crucial question of what gave a product value. Was it the labor that went into producing it? Its abundance or scarcity? Its usefulness? Some combination of all three? In the 1870s, scholars in Austria, England, and Switzerland hit simultaneously upon an elegant answer, and a new era in economics—the neoclassical era, as it is called—began. "Value always depends upon degree of utility," wrote one of the neoclassical pioneers, Englishman William Stanley Jevons, "and labour has no connection with the matter, except through utility. If we can readily manufacture a great quantity of some article, our want of that article will be almost completely satisfied, so that its degree of utility and consequently its value will fall."[12]

From this basic building block of utility, one could conceivably build a coherent mathematical theory of economic equilibrium—which is what Jevons and a few of the other early neoclassical theorists set out to do. Yale's Sumner knew of these developments, and was enthusiastic about them. To get up to speed, he even hired a math professor to tutor him.[13] But he struggled, and when Fisher returned to the Yale campus in autumn 1888 for graduate study in mathematics, Sumner took the young man aside and urged *him* to examine the new mathematical economics.

Thus was launched the economics career of Irving Fisher. For his doctoral thesis he devised the most sophisticated mathematical treatment yet of economic equilibrium, and he also designed and built a contraption of interconnected water-filled cisterns that he described as "the physical analogue of the ideal economic market."[14] Many decades later, economist Paul Samuelson judged this work to be "the greatest doctoral dissertation in economics ever written."[15] It launched Fisher into a leading role among the world's still-sparse ranks of mathematical economists.

After getting his doctorate in 1893, Fisher married a daughter of the wealthiest family in his Rhode Island hometown. Her industrialist father (founder of a company that became one of the building blocks of Allied Chemical) paid for a year-long voyage through Europe for the newlyweds while building them a mansion just north of the Yale campus, where Fisher already had an offer to teach math and economics. On his European adventure Fisher met most of the founding fathers of neoclassical economics, and sat in on a few Poincaré lectures on probability in Paris. On his return, he brought his economic knowledge to bear on a matter of public policy for the first time.

The American Civil War of the 1860s had been followed by a decades-long decline in prices that left America's farmers feeling deeply victimized, a conviction that only hardened during the depression of the mid-1890s. A farmer who borrowed money to buy seed in 1895, when corn sold for as much as fifty cents a bushel, couldn't make his loan payments a year later when the price dropped to twenty-one cents.[16] The explanation for the deflation was that dollars were redeemable in gold, and there wasn't enough gold to go around. The less gold there was, the fewer dollars were in circulation. When fewer dollars chase the same goods, prices drop. The farmers were being crucified, presidential hopeful William Jennings Bryan said in his famous acceptance speech at the 1896 Democratic Convention, "on a cross of gold."

In Fisher's "ideal economic market," the complaints of Bryan and the farmers were beside the point. Markets automatically adjusted to changing price levels. "Multitudes of trade journals and investors' reviews have their sole reason for existence in supplying data on which to base prediction," Fisher wrote in 1896. "Every chance for gain is eagerly watched. An active and intelligent speculation is constantly going on, which, so far as it does not consist of fictitious and gambling transactions, performs a well-known and provident function for society. Is it reasonable to believe that foresight, which is the general rule, has an exception as applied to falling or rising prices?"[17] As farmers and their bankers could foresee that prices would drop, Fisher's reasoning went, interest rates on loans would drop too—so farmers wouldn't be any worse off.

THIS ASSUMPTION THAT PEOPLE COULD see clearly into the future was crucial to making equilibrium economics work. It was also crucially problematic. "You regard men as infinitely selfish and infinitely farsighted," Henri Poincaré wrote to mathematical economist Léon Walras in 1901. Infinite selfishness "may perhaps be admitted in a first approximation," Poincaré allowed. But the assumption of infinite farsightedness "may call for some reservations."[18]

The events that followed the publication of Fisher's gold standard argument were a textbook demonstration of the limits to foresight. Gold discoveries in Alaska and South Africa, coupled with the development of a new process for separating gold from ore, set the world on a decades-long inflationary path that no one had foreseen. The way people dealt with rising prices—or, more to the point, failed to deal with them—convinced Fisher that Bryan had been on to something in 1896.

In the midst of this reexamination, in 1898, a dire personal crisis arose for Fisher: the onset of tuberculosis, the same disease that had killed his father fourteen years before. Only after three years spent in clinics in Southern California, upstate New York, and Colorado Springs—and three more operating at half speed back in New Haven—did the young professor recover. He came away from the experience with an obsession for good health and a near-messianic fervor to better the world before his death. Fisher became a leading prohibitionist, coauthor of a bestselling hygiene textbook, a disciple of the corn-flakes-prescribing Dr. Kellogg of Battle Creek, an early backer of the League of Nations, and a prominent advocate of eugenics.

This last cause has since gotten a deservedly bad rap. But the intent was to improve the world, and the same could be said of Fisher's post-TB economics. Fisher became what his mentor William Graham Sumner would have mocked as a "social doctor," but he never strayed far from the bounds of neoclassical theory. His work on monetary policy led him to spend decades educating Americans about inflation and deflation and promoting government policies to keep prices stable. His take on the stock market exhibited a similar spirit.

This spirit was evident in *The Nature of Capital and Income*, the book Fisher lost at Grand Central in 1905 and rewrote in 1906. He kept it almost equation free to appeal to a broad readership, but his mathematical sensibility still permeated it. "If we take the history of the prices of stocks and bonds," Fisher wrote, "we shall find it chiefly to consist of a record of changing estimates of futurity, due to what is called chance." This was similar to Bachelier's depiction of Brownian motion at the Paris exchange. A half century later the concept was dubbed the random walk hypothesis, occasioning all manner of academic excitement. But the experiences of the previous decade had turned Fisher into enough of a realist that he immediately backpedaled from his bold statement. Stock and bond price movements weren't *entirely* random, he continued:

> Were it true that each individual speculator made up his mind independently of every other as to the future course of events, the errors of some would probably be offset by those of others. But, as a matter of fact, the mistakes of the common herd are usually in the same direction. Like sheep, they all follow a single leader.

Ah, those sheep again. But Fisher, ever the civic improver, hoped to make investors less ovine by getting them to use economics and probability theory. The value of any investment, he wrote, is the income it will produce. Money in the future is not worth as much as money today. People are impatient, and they must be compensated for the opportunity cost of not investing in some other productive endeavor. The current value, then, is the expected income stream discounted by a measure of people's preference for having the money now rather than later, also known as *interest*.

In 1906, sophisticated investors already consulted bond tables that listed the present, or "discounted," value of interest payments to be received in the future. The calculations behind these tables dated all the way back to the fourteenth century.[19] What was radically new in Fisher's work was his proposal to incorporate uncertainty into the equation—enabling investors to use the present-value formula to price not just bonds but stocks. At the time, investing in corporate shares was a new and suspect pursuit. Limited liability corporations, in which shareholders partake in the profits but are not liable for the company's debts if it goes under, had only recently become common in the United States and Great Britain. Bonds, along with real estate, were the chief means of investment. Stocks were for pure speculation.

To Fisher, this distinction made no economic sense. The fact that bond interest was guaranteed while stock dividends were not was only a difference of degree. Bond issuers could go bankrupt, after all, and inflation could eat into the value of even the "safest" bond. Yes, there was more uncertainty in valuing stocks than in bonds. But so what? And while Bachelier had distinguished between the fixed probability of games of chance (which could be rendered mathematically) and the "personal" probability involved in peering into an uncertain future (which, he said, could not), Fisher saw the difference as one of degree. Even the "objective" probability of dice throwing and coin flipping wasn't a sure thing, he argued. You could flip a fair coin a million times and it was possible, albeit highly improbable, that it would come up heads every time.

Fisher proposed that investors count the dividends they expected a stock to pay out in the future, and then plug that income estimate into a formula of the sort used to value bonds. This "riskless value" could then be adjusted by adding in an estimate of the chance that dividends might be larger than expected and subtracting the chance they might be smaller. This value could then be multiplied by a "measure of caution" (nine-tenths, Fisher suggested, without further explanation) to come up with a price.

It was all a lot of work, Fisher acknowledged. But that's how economic progress was achieved. Wrote Fisher:

> There was a time when business men did not use bond tables, when
> they did not calculate cost sheets, and even when life insurance

was contracted for in scornful disregard of any mortality tables. Just as these slipshod methods have been displaced by the work of expert accountants and actuaries, so should the mere guessing about future income conditions be replaced by making use of the modern statistical applications of probability.

Uncertainty could not be banished, Fisher was saying. But with enough data and the right mindset it could be tamed. The data were being churned out in abundance by 1906. The mindset took a bit longer.

AS NEW INDUSTRIAL GIANTS SUCH as Standard Oil, U.S. Steel, and General Electric grew to prominence in the decades before and after the turn of the century, their hankering for respectability and capital led them to disclose ever more about their finances. Data factories such as Moody's, Fitch, and Standard Statistics arose to assemble and disseminate this information. The *Wall Street Journal* was born in 1883, and soon afterward cofounder Charles Dow began compiling the stock price averages that for the first time allowed investors to discuss how "the market" was doing. The profession of stock market "statistician" was born—the number-crunching precursor of today's securities analyst.

The leaders of this information revolution were not interested in exploring the bounds of uncertainty and probability as Fisher advised. Instead, they hoped their number crunching could give them something more valuable—the ability to see into the future and forecast the cycles of the market.

That there were cycles seemed obvious to most. Securities markets as we understand them today (continuously operating, *indoor* exchanges) developed in the late 1700s as European governments began selling bonds on a regular basis, mainly to finance wars. There had been famous market manias and panics before—tulip mania in 1630s

Holland, and in the early 1700s the Mississippi Bubble in France and the South Sea Bubble in England. It was only in the 1800s that observers began to see a certain regularity in them. Near-clockwork regularity, it seemed. In England there were market panics in 1804–5, 1815, 1825, 1836, 1847, and 1857.

A famous early explanation for these cycles came from William Stanley Jevons, the mathematical economist, who proposed in the 1870s that the waxing and waning of spots on the sun—that occurred on an eleven-year cycle—was to blame. On this basis, Jevons predicted that a crash was due in 1879. When one came in October 1878 he figured he'd been close enough. After Jevons's death in 1882, though, a succession of British market downturns failed to follow his timetable. From then on, most academic economists shied away from hard-and-fast predictions about business fluctuations.

Market participants, though, grew ever more interested in forecasting the cycle's turns. By the early 1900s, two main schools of thought had developed. One proposed that the market's future could be divined through close examination of fundamental economic data. The other held that all the necessary omens could be found in the price moves of stocks themselves.

In the United States the most prominent member of the former school was Roger Babson, an 1898 graduate of the Massachusetts Institute of Technology and, like Irving Fisher, a veteran of the tuberculosis sanatorium of Colorado Springs. Babson had been an unsuccessful bond salesman in Boston before his battle with TB. Afterward he decided he might have better luck selling information about bonds rather than the bonds themselves. He started by digging up facts about obscure bond offerings and offering them to brokers. He then printed news about companies onto index cards that subscribers could file for easy access. This service evolved, after Babson sold it in 1906, into Standard Statistics (which after a later merger became Standard & Poor's). Another of Babson's businesses later became the National Quotation Bureau, a listing service for over-the-counter stocks that was the forerunner of the Nasdaq stock exchange.

That's how Babson got rich. But it was only after he sold off his various data services and set up shop as an investment guru that he became famous. The precipitating event was the panic of 1907, a stock market crash and series of bank failures that drove the U.S. financial system to near collapse. These events convinced Babson that the information about individual companies he had been trafficking in was less important than "fundamental data" about the economy as a whole. He developed a forecasting tool he called the "Babsonchart," a one-line composite of economic data through which he drew a smooth trend line.[20] He got the idea from one of his MIT professors, who was inspired by Isaac Newton's law of action and reaction.[21] For every period spent above the trend line, the economy—and with it the stock market—would later fall below the trend for a period such that the *area* below the trend line would equal that above.

This happens to be the definition of a trend line, which can only be drawn with certainty after the fact. Babson was merely stating a truism, but he nonetheless convinced himself, and many others, that with ever-better data his crack team of statisticians could make an ever-better approximation of the trend ahead of time. It was "folly" to try to predict the short swings of the stock market, Babson said at an American Statistical Association dinner in New York in April 1925, but "practically all the economic services have a clean record in the long-swing movements." By looking carefully enough at the information available on industrial production, crops, construction, railroad utilization, and the like, he reasoned, one could predict where the economy and thus the stock market were headed.

Another speaker at the dinner that night saw things very differently. William Peter Hamilton, editor of the *Wall Street Journal*, believed that the stock market predicted the economy, not the other way around. "The market represents everything everybody knows, hopes, believes, anticipates," Hamilton wrote three years before. He told the audience in New York that the market had "predicted" Germany's defeat in World War I eleven months before the armistice. This claim wasn't all that different from what Irving Fisher had written in 1896. Investors possessed foresight.

But Hamilton also believed—as Fisher had come to—that investors could behave like sheep as well. And he believed that their herd-like movements were at least partly predictable. He credited his view of the market to the man who had hired him at the *Journal*, cofounder Charles Dow. Dow created his famous daily average of the prices of twelve leading stocks in 1884. And from 1899 until his death in 1902, he wrote a series of front-page editorials in the *Journal* sharing the knowledge he had gained during a decade and a half of stock-average watching.

If you charted the movements of the averages over a few years, Dow claimed, you could see clear patterns emerge. "The stock market has three movements," he wrote on March 12, 1899. "It has a daily fluctuation . . . It has a longer swing working frequently through a period of about 20 to 40 days. It then has its main movement which extends over a period of years." In Dow's view, the key to success on Wall Street was to buy during upward main movements (bull markets) and sell during downward ones (bear markets). "When the public mind has a well defined tendency, either bullish or bearish, it is not easily changed," Dow wrote on April 24, 1899. "Scores or hundreds of people may change, but the mass press on in the same direction."

Dow himself was loath to declare *when* that direction had changed. As Hamilton put it, he had "a caution in prediction which is not merely New England but almost Scottish."[22] Hamilton, who authored the *Journal*'s daily stock market report during the years that Dow wrote his editorials, was bolder. After he took over the editorial writing in 1908, he repositioned the *Journal* from moderate, sometimes waffling voice of reason to fire-breathing defender of Wall Street and its ways. On occasion, he even took it upon himself to pronounce the onset of a bull market or a bear.

• • •

IRVING FISHER SAW THE "SO-CALLED business cycle" that obsessed Babson and Hamilton as a mere side effect of the difficulty people had in getting their heads around changes in the value of the dollar. They saw deflation or inflation and mistook it for real increases or decreases in the prices of goods, and adjusted their spending and borrowing fitfully and inconsistently, resulting in economic ups and downs.

Fisher's first remedy was education. He did his part by writing popular books and articles on the merits of stable money and accurate measurement of inflation and deflation. He initiated a national discussion among statisticians and economists over how best to put together indexes of consumer prices. He founded a company that provided weekly price indexes to newspapers around the country. He argued for linking business contracts and bond interest rates to inflation (it took a mere eighty-six years for the U.S. government to follow up on this suggestion by launching Treasury Inflation-Protected Securities, or TIPS, in 1997).[23]

As a side project, he also tried to bring indexing to the stock market. The Dow averages were and are merely that—*averages* of the prices of the selected stocks. This measure generates some deeply weird results. To use two modern Dow constituents as examples, General Electric was selling for $36 a share at the end of 2007 and Caterpillar for $72. As a result, Caterpillar had twice the impact on the average that GE did, even though Caterpillar's overall stock market value, or capitalization, was only 12 percent of GE's.[24]

Price *indexes* avoid this nonsense by weighting stocks—by volume of transacted shares or, most commonly, by market capitalization. In 1923, in response to campaigning by Fisher and a few other academics, Standard Statistics Co. launched a market-cap-weighted stock index to compete with the Dow. That was the genesis of the S&P 500.[25] It took far longer for Wall Street to warm to another stock market idea Fisher suggested, in passing, in 1912: that investors might want to buy and sell securities based on stock market indexes. The first index fund for retail investors arrived in 1976, and the first index-based *securities* a few years after that.[26]

Fisher also hoped to attack inflation and deflation by linking the dollar's value to a diverse basket of commodities, so it wouldn't be at the mercy of the vagaries of the gold-mining business. That never happened, but the creation of the Federal Reserve System in 1913 allowed for a more flexible relationship between the dollar and gold. The Fed, a belated offspring of the panic of 1907, was created to prevent such panics by making sure banks didn't run out of cash. It also had the power to manipulate the money supply (that is, create new dollars or take them out of circulation) and affect the price level.

Fearing that political pressure would inevitably tilt the Fed toward inflationary easy-money policies, Fisher was dubious at first. But in the 1920s the central bank adopted a stable-money approach much to his liking. Benjamin Strong, president of the Federal Reserve Bank of New York, could by virtue of his control of New York's open-market trading desk increase or decrease the money supply at will. In 1927, Strong's aggressive open-market purchases injected new money into circulation and kept a mild recession from worsening. It was the Fed's first soft landing, and it seems to have convinced Fisher that what he called the "dance of the dollar" was a thing of the past.

IT WASN'T THE ONLY GOOD news to come Fisher's way in the 1920s, a decade when success greeted him at every turn. Among his colleagues he was respected, although not much imitated. To the wider public he must have seemed an odd duck, but he could not be ignored. A tireless promoter of his own work, he went to great lengths to get his speeches reprinted in newspapers and always made time to talk to reporters. He was cited as an authority not just on economics but on politics, health, and even grammar. During a visit to Michigan, a local reporter asked him if the title of the 1923 hit song "Yes, We Have

No Bananas" was correct English. In typically earnest fashion, Fisher responded, "Yes, it would be correct, if the statement was preceded by the question 'Have you no bananas?' "[27]

By the second half of the 1920s, Fisher had also become a big financial success. Years before, he had devised a card-filing system to help him keep track of his many endeavors. Fisher's "Index Visible" filing cards, cut so that the first line of each was visible at a glance (similar to the Rolodex, which came along decades later), were a significant advance in information storage and retrieval. In 1913 he launched a company to manufacture and market his filing system, and in 1925 he sold it to office equipment maker Kardex Rand, which merged with typewriter titan Remington to create one of the hot technology stocks of the 1920s, Remington Rand.

Fisher's payment came in the form of shares and warrants (options to buy more shares at a preset price). As a believer in the glorious future of the company, where he stayed on as a board member, he borrowed money to buy even more shares. For a time it paid off. After decades of relying upon the generosity of his wealthy in-laws, Fisher became his family's breadwinner, boasting a net worth of more than $10 million ($128 million in 2008 dollars) by 1929. He dreamed of making enough money to endow a foundation that would carry on his pet causes—"the abolition of war, disease, degeneracy, and instability of money"[28]—even after his death. This sort of financial stake cannot help but skew one's view of the world, and it skewed Fisher's.

The tipping point seems to have been the arrival on Wall Street of the first popular investment guru to see the world as Fisher did. Edgar Lawrence Smith, a forty-something Harvard graduate with an odd résumé (he'd worked in banking, agriculture, and magazine publishing), signed on with a brokerage firm in the early 1920s to produce a pamphlet on bonds. As the firm specialized in bonds, Smith's initial plan had been to explain why they were better long-term investments than stocks. But Smith did his homework, and read a 1912 book coauthored by Fisher that argued that during inflationary times stocks were "safer" than even the highest-grade bonds. Bond yields are fixed while dividends rise with prices.[29] That seemed reasonable enough, but in the early 1920s prices were falling. Surely bonds would beat stocks in such an environment? Smith set out to investigate how stock and bond returns compared the last time prices *fell*, in the late 1800s. In doing so, he embarked on the first systematic reconstruction of stock market history.

Unlike those who followed in his footsteps in later years, Smith didn't try to examine how *every* stock had done over time. The advances of Irving Fisher and Remington Rand notwithstanding, this was still the precomputer era. Historical stock market research was pure drudgery. So Smith went with sampling. He assembled portfolios of ten stocks each and compared their performance to a similar sample of bonds over twenty-year stretches going back to 1866. In order to get results that were representative of an average investor's experience, Smith picked his portfolios using such "arbitrary" criteria as market capitalization, trading volume, and dividend yield.

It was a measure of the prevailing attitudes of the time that Smith felt obliged to caution readers repeatedly against using his "laboratory methods" in actual portfolio selection, which required the "highest degree of informed judgment."[30] Still, all his stock portfolios except one beat bonds. The 1924 book in which Smith reported his results, *Common Stocks as Long-Term Investments*, became a Wall Street sensation. On the strength of its success, he launched his own mutual fund company. Englishman John Maynard Keynes invited him to join the Royal Economic Society.[31] Decades of market experience have since proved Smith right: Stocks *have* outperformed bonds over time.

Fisher, not surprisingly, was a big fan of the book—too big a fan. He (and many others in the late 1920s) seemed to forget that just because stocks beat bonds over time doesn't mean they'll do it every year. Fisher also convinced himself that the Federal Reserve would keep downturns from getting out of hand—there hadn't been a major panic since 1907, after all—and that America's growing ranks of stock market investors had become so sophisticated that they no longer resembled sheep.

In December 1928, Fisher outlined his take on the market in a lengthy essay in the *New York Herald Tribune*'s Sunday magazine. The headline was "Will Stocks Stay Up in 1929?" and Fisher's answer was an emphatic *yes*. Parts of the piece sounded an awful lot like what would become standard advice a half century hence: The individual investor should be wary of "pitting his unaided judgment against the collective intelligence of the pools of professional traders," Fisher warned, but there was safety in diversification. "*The more unsafe the investments are, taken individually, the safer they are collectively,* to say nothing of profitableness, provided that the diversification is sufficiently increased," he wrote. Fisher admitted that neither he nor anyone else he knew of had "definitely formulated" this principle (that would have to wait until Harry Markowitz in 1952).

But then Fisher twisted his reasonably sound advice into a distinctly dodgy apologia for high stock prices: Because so many investors now held well-diversified portfolios, they were willing to venture into risky stocks that previously would have interested only speculators. "This enlightened process has created a tremendous new market for securities that in times past would have gone begging," Fisher wrote. "It constitutes a permanent reason why this plateau [of stock prices] will not sink again to the level of former years except for extraordinary cause."[32]

THROUGHOUT THE 1920S BOOM, ROGER Babson kept staring at his Babsoncharts and William Peter Hamilton at his Dow charts. After a mistaken bear market call in 1926, Hamilton had gone back to riding the bull in 1927 and 1928. Babson also turned bearish in 1926, announcing that the economy had been growing too fast for too long and that an "equal and opposite reaction" was due, although he allowed that it might take two or three years. For the next three years the market continued to rise, but Babson wouldn't back down. He became an object of mockery. "We could say that his worship of Isaac Newton was an eccentricity," recalled John Burr Williams, a young investment banker in Boston at the time, "and nothing was proved by his claim that action and reaction were always equal."[33]

In September 1929, Babson issued his most dire warning yet. "Sooner or later a crash is coming, and it may be terrific," he declared at the annual National Business Conference he hosted. "Wise are those investors who now get out of debt and reef their sails." That same day, Irving Fisher offered his rebuttal to the *New York Times*: "There may be a recession of stock prices, but nothing in the nature of a crash."[34] On October 15, speaking at a meeting of the Purchasing Agents Association in New York, Fisher hauled out his "plateau" metaphor again in what became one of the most infamous utterances of the twentieth century: Stock prices, he said, have reached "what looks like a permanently high plateau."[35]

The crash came two weeks later. Fisher initially argued that it was merely the "recession" he had said might transpire. "It is significant, that at this nadir of market despair and panic the market 'averages' had gone down only to those of February, 1928—well above the old plateau of stock market prices, from the level of which the market had ascended after 1923," he wrote in December 1929. "The worst panic in history had not destroyed this new price plateau!"[36] But the worst bear market in history, which followed in 1930 and 1931, did.

In 1932, Fisher acknowledged that there had been two big flaws in his precrash reasoning. First, he had assumed the Federal Reserve would do what it could to keep prices from falling and banks from failing. Instead, after Benjamin Strong's death in 1928, conservative bankers loath to accommodate what they considered speculative excess came to dominate the Fed. The Fed raised interest rates before the crash, in the face of criticism from business circles and some economists (including Fisher). Afterward, it failed to stave off sharp deflation and waves of bank failures. Second, Fisher admitted that he hadn't understood how deeply indebted Americans were—which led to disaster when the market crash and price deflation made it impossible for borrowers to pay back their loans.[37]

Fisher's theories of what caused the Depression were given little credence at the time, but they have become widely accepted among economists. His own investing behavior, though, was harder to explain away. Despite his talk of diversification, his own portfolio was tilted toward Remington Rand and a few start-ups. He held on to his Remington Rand stock as it dropped from $58 to $1, averting bankruptcy by borrowing from his still-wealthy sister-in-law, which seriously endangered *her* financial health as the market continued to tank in 1930 and 1931. (She forgave the debts in her will.) Fisher sold his New Haven house to Yale, on the condition that he and his wife could stay in it until they died.

Roger Babson emerged from the crash with his wealth mostly intact and his reputation as a forecaster restored. His legacy lives on at Babson College, the business-oriented school outside Boston he founded in 1919. But his subsequent forecasts were far from infallible, and his increasingly eccentric warnings of revolution and of nuclear attack on Boston didn't do much for his reputation. Dow theorist William Peter Hamilton spent much of 1929 attempting to assuage investors' fears and defend Wall Street from its ever-louder critics. A few weeks after the crash he bowed to reality and declared that a new bear market had begun. He then took ill with pneumonia, and died. Edgar Lawrence Smith was booted from his mutual fund post in 1931 and spent the next few decades spinning weird theories linking the business cycle to the weather.

This left the ever-resilient Irving Fisher, who in the 1930s watched his mathematical, rational ideas about economics and markets begin a slow but unstoppable renaissance. He may have made some grave mistakes in applying science to the stock market. But the idea that science *should* be applied to the market wasn't going away.

CHAPTER 2

A RANDOM WALK FROM FRED MACAULAY TO HOLBROOK WORKING

*Statistics and mathematics begin to find their
way into the economic mainstream in the 1930s,
setting the stage for big changes to come.*

THE COIN FLIP CAME TO stock market research in April 1925, at the same statisticians' dinner where Roger Babson and William Peter Hamilton described their forecasting methods. After they and the other speakers had finished, Frederick Macaulay stepped to the podium.

Macaulay was a late-blooming scholar—he had gotten his Columbia economics Ph.D. four years before at the age of thirty-nine—working on an investigation of market behavior for a new think tank called the National Bureau of Economic Research (NBER). He was also a mischievous sort.[1] To prepare for his presentation at the dinner he devised an experiment intended to mock the pretensions of the forecasters, in particular those of the *Wall Street Journal*'s Hamilton, who believed he could divine economic wisdom from the peaks and valleys of the Dow Jones averages. Macaulay (or, one suspects, a few underpaid assistants) flipped a coin several thousand times, counting each heads as a one-point price increase and each tails as a one-point decrease. He added up the increases and decreases and plotted the result. As he reported at the dinner, the product of his efforts looked eerily like a stock chart. "Everyone will admit that the course of such a purely chance curve cannot be predicted," he said.

Unlike so many future academic coin flippers, Macaulay did not think the story ended there. First, he could see that his method could lead to negative numbers, while stock prices can go to zero but no farther than that.[2] Second, real-world market randomness wouldn't necessarily follow the simple bell curve distribution of a coin flipathon. Stock prices often leap or fall distances bigger than a penny. Then there was the really big issue, one already noted by both Irving Fisher and Henri Poincaré: Human behavior isn't truly random. Men—and thus investors—at times act like sheep.

Macaulay knew firsthand about investor behavior. His father was the head of Sun Life of Canada, then and now among the world's biggest money managers, and his grandfather had run the company too.[3] The junior Macaulay never worked there, but he spent the middle part of the 1930s as partner in a small investment firm in New York, giving him a far closer view of the workings of Wall Street than most scholars were afforded.[4]

By the time he was asked to speak at yet another New York statisticians' dinner in 1934, Macaulay had moved on from the coin flip to a new metaphor for the market—a loaded pair of dice, with the load shifted from time to time. The day-to-day movements of stocks might be well described by the normal distribution, he said, echoing the earlier work of Bachelier, with which he does not appear to have been familiar, but the longer swings were something else entirely.[5]

In 1938, when he published the results of his long NBER research project on financial markets in book form, Macaulay explained why. "If the vagaries of individual conduct were always 'normally' distributed round a strictly rational 'mode,'" he wrote, "their curbing effects on the development of economics as a strictly logical social science might be small or negligible." The errors made by investors and speculators betting on the future via financial markets weren't random, though. They were "systematic" and "constant," the inevitable result of the "emotion, lack of logic and insufficiency of knowledge" that characterized all human decision making but especially decision making about the future. These systematic errors, Macaulay argued, were the main cause of the "violent social disturbances" known as the business cycle.[6] The cure he prescribed was more government planning of economic activity, so the future might hold fewer surprises.

THAT WAS A FASHIONABLE ENOUGH prescription by the late 1930s. But Macaulay's diagnosis was losing ground, at least among economists. The discipline was about to throw itself in a headlong rush into becoming a "strictly logical social science." Like physicists ignoring friction in building their models of the world, economists became more and more comfortable with ignoring widely recognized realities of human behavior in order to build better models of it. This process had begun in earnest as economists sorted through the wreckage of the great crash and the ensuing Depression looking for explanations of what had happened and tools to fight it. Even Macaulay became caught up in it.

Macaulay had begun his long investigation of financial markets in the spirit of his mentor, Columbia professor and National Bureau of Economic Research chief Wesley Clair Mitchell—who taught that economic truth could best be divined from close examination of data. Macaulay discovered during his years of poring through stock and bond prices that there were limits to what pure data gazing could reveal. "[T]he more he wrestled with these problems, the more critical he became of purely empirical relations," Mitchell wrote in the introduction to Macaulay's 1938 book, "and the more desirous of finding out why his different series behave as they do." In search of answers, Macaulay found himself turning to Irving Fisher's theories of interest and of stock values. He even devised a Fisheresque formula of his own to compare the value of bonds with different expiration dates.

Macaulay wielded his and Fisher's formulas not as evidence of the market's perfection but to show that the prices prevailing on financial markets didn't square with economic rationality. Subsequent generations of economists simply followed the formulas to their logical conclusions. In a fascinating little irony, Macaulay is known today only for his bond-price formula, called "Macaulay's duration," which quantitatively minded investors have been using since the early 1970s to make buying and selling decisions that presumably push prices closer to the rational ideal.

It was a development indicative of a much broader trend in economics. Equations were memorized and passed on. The accompanying words, and often the real-world data against which the formulas were tested, were forgotten. This increasing focus on the mathematical side of economics has been decried again and again over the years—mostly by journalists and other outsiders who found themselves no longer able to follow what was going on, but also by some economists. It wasn't just the product of orneriness, though. It happened for several good reasons.

One reason was that continuing advances in mathematics and statistics began to deliver more sophisticated and appropriate formulas than the ones the mathematical economists of the late nineteenth century had at their disposal. World War II, which brought economists and quantitative methods together in new and empowering ways, also played a big role. After that the rise of the computer was crucial. But the first big stimulus to the rise of mathematical economics may have been the implosion of the skeptical, empirical tradition to which Macaulay had belonged. An intellectual vacuum resulted, and math rushed in to fill it.

IN THE EARLY DECADES OF the twentieth century, there were two main schools of American economic thought. One was the orthodox strain descended from Adam Smith via the neoclassical revolution of the late nineteenth century. Its adherents saw economics as the study of rational individuals maximizing utility. Irving Fisher was a member of this group, but a lonely one. Few others shared either his mathematical bent or his urge to improve the world. Most leaned instead toward a laissez-faire approach to economic policy, and got their theories out of *Principles of Economics*, a textbook first published in 1890 by Cambridge University's Alfred Marshall that banished equations to an appendix and popularized the supply-demand graphs familiar to Econ 101 students today. "It's all in Marshall," the smug saying went. A growing parade of American scholars, though, objected that it *wasn't* all in Marshall. These dissidents came to be known as the institutionalists, because some emphasized the role of economic institutions (such as laws and customs) over individual decision makers. It was really a broader, more diverse movement than that, though.

The divide between the neoclassicists and the institutionalists reflected one that had riven science since the early 1600s. Before then, deduction—the practice of accepting certain axioms about the world and then using logic to derive answers from them—dominated Western thought. Observant Renaissance men like naturalist Francis Bacon noticed that the scientific answers deduced from the core principles of Aristotle and the Church didn't always square with real life. Bacon articulated a new philosophy of inductive reasoning, which amounted to observing nature and looking for patterns.

There was a crucial missing link to the inductive approach, as David Hume, the Scottish philosopher and mentor to Adam Smith, soon pointed out: Just seeing a phenomenon repeat itself doesn't guarantee that it will continue in the future. To assert that it will continue to repeat implies subscribing to some theory of why.[7] Ever since then, most sciences have been swinging back and forth between the poles of deduction and induction. At the turn of the twentieth century, economics in the United States appeared due for a turn in the latter direction, the direction of the institutionalists.

The institutionalist of most durable fame was Thorstein Veblen, author of acid critiques of capitalism that are still in print and coiner of such durable terms as "conspicuous consumption" and "technocracy." Veblen had studied with William Graham Sumner at Yale just as Irving Fisher had, but he seems to have taken different lecture notes. He excoriated neoclassical economics as abstract noodling with no connection to reality. Of *The Nature of Capital and Income,* the book that Fisher lost and rewrote in 1906, Veblen wrote that "what it lacks is the breath of life."[8]

Veblen was a crotchety philanderer with a habit of getting himself fired, meaning that he wasn't cut out to be the operational leader of an intellectual movement. His star student, Wesley Mitchell, was. Mitchell was in the first class of undergraduates at the University of Chicago, the John D. Rockefeller–funded experiment in scientific education that opened its doors in 1892. Veblen was a lowly instructor in an economics department dominated by neoclassicists. But he made a big impression on Mitchell, who stayed on at Chicago for his Ph.D., then went on to become the nation's foremost authority on the business cycle. Mitchell subscribed neither to Roger Babson's simplistic action-begets-reaction formula nor to Fisher's belief that the "dance of the dollar" explained all fluctuations. He seemed to subscribe to no theory at all. Instead, he saw the business cycle as a natural part of the workings of capitalism and hoped that close examination of the data would enable him to understand it better.

Mitchell's commitment to the drudgery-filled work of assembling better economic evidence so impressed Irving Fisher that he tried to lure the younger scholar to Yale, inviting the Mitchells up to New Haven one weekend in 1912 and throwing a dinner party in their honor. While the guests enjoyed a multicourse meal, their health-nut host slurped raw egg.[9] Mitchell turned Fisher down, choosing Columbia instead.

Just after World War I, a conservative AT&T statistician and a socialist economist approached Mitchell with a proposal to settle some of their arguments over economic policy by improving the quality of economic statistics.[10] The result was the National Bureau of Economic

Research, which opened its doors in New York in 1920 and went on to revolutionize the collection, dissemination, and understanding of economic data in the United States. Gross national product was one of the many measurement innovations it spawned.

Mitchell exerted a powerful attraction on younger economists. He was a New York City progressive intellectual of the first order, living in a Greenwich Village townhouse, married to a famed proponent of educational experimentation (Lucy Sprague Mitchell, founder of the Bank Street College of Education), and himself a cofounder of the New School for Social Research. When young Austrian Friedrich Hayek arrived in the United States for the first time in 1923, he was shocked to discover that his American peers no longer cared about Fisher or any of the country's other neoclassical greats. "The one name by which the eager young men swore was the only one I had not known . . . Wesley Clair Mitchell," he later wrote. "Indeed business cycles and institutionalism were the two main topics of discussion."[11] Fred Macaulay, Mitchell's student at Columbia and one of his first hires at NBER, was said to have "worshiped Mitchell as though he were a god."[12]

When the great crash and the Depression came, the moment seemed ripe for Mitchell and the institutionalists to seize control of American economics once and for all. The business cycle had asserted itself in all its ferociousness. Irving Fisher's talk of a "permanently high plateau" for stock prices proved to be nonsense, and near-complete shutdowns of the financial system—as occurred in the early 1930s—certainly weren't covered in Alfred Marshall's standard neoclassical textbook.

Far from rising to the occasion, though, Mitchell retreated. He spent the 1930–31 academic year thirty-five hundred miles away at Oxford University, and beyond that he did little but call for more study. One of his Columbia students became so distraught at his mentor's abdication that he wrote a paper exploring the historical and psychological reasons for it. (A sample: "Statistics offered Mitchell a means of escape from reality—for he was a realist who feared reality.")[13]

Some of Mitchell's fellow institutionalists were less reticent, and they headed to Washington to work in the Roosevelt administration. They too struggled, often battling each other. Most of the lasting economic innovations of the early Roosevelt years—from the founding of the Securities and Exchange Commission to the revamping of the Federal Reserve System—were the work of lawyers, bankers, and other practical sorts, not economists. The institutional economists envisioned themselves as technocrats, the business engineers that Thorstein Veblen argued would steer the economy more rationally than profit-driven "absentee owners" could.[14] It's hard to run a technocracy without a technology, though. While united by skepticism of the grand theories of neoclassical economics, the institutionalists had no grand theory of their own to explain economic behavior.

So a remarkable thing happened. In the broader intellectual environment of the 1930s, what had been discredited by the great crash and the Depression was the laissez-faire, promarket ethos that had preceded them. Economics graduate students shared this view. It was the Depression that had attracted most of them to economics. (Later it was claimed that this was the first time lots of smart people entered the discipline.) But in search of tools to understand and combat the crisis around them, these young scholars found that the institutionalist economists who had been most critical of laissez-faire had almost nothing to offer them. Marshall's *Principles of Economics* didn't say much about depressions either, but buried deeper in the neoclassical toolbox were ideas and approaches that did—mathematical ideas and approaches.

And so, almost in spite of themselves, the smart young things who entered the discipline in the 1930s began to create an economics that owed more to Irving Fisher than to Wesley Mitchell. Not that many of them would have called themselves Fisherites. Instead they went by the name "Keynesians," after John Maynard Keynes, the English speculator, political polemicist, art collector, and all-around bon vivant who would become the most famous economist of the twentieth century.

What was this Keynesianism? In part, it was a critique of free market verities that surpassed even Thorstein Veblen's in its stinging mockery. "Professional investment," Keynes wrote in a famous passage of his 1936 classic, *The General Theory of Employment, Interest, and Money,*

> may be likened to those newspaper competitions in which the competitors have to pick out the six prettiest faces from a hundred photographs, the prize being awarded to the competitor whose choice most nearly corresponds to the average preferences of the competitors as a whole; so that each competitor has to pick, not those faces which he himself finds prettiest, but those which he thinks likely to catch the fancy of the other competitors, all of whom are looking at the problem from the same point of view.

Market players thus spent their days "anticipating what average opinion expects the average opinion to be."[15] Who would want to leave the fate of the economy in the hands of people like *that?*

Keynes did not, however, make this withering assessment of financial markets the basis of either his investment strategy or his economics. As an investor, he succeeded by ignoring the daily beauty contests. He struck it truly rich for the first time in the 1930s, after years of vainly trying to time the market, by holding on through thick and thin to stocks he deemed good values.[16] And Keynesian economics was only tangentially about financial market irrationality.

Keynes was a product of Alfred Marshall's Cambridge, not just as a student but as son of one of Marshall's closest colleagues. Keynesianism was more a tweaking of Marshall's neoclassical teachings than a complete overturning of them. Through the 1920s, Keynes and Irving Fisher had been on a similar economic wavelength, sharing the belief that misguided monetary policies caused most economic problems.

During the Depression, Keynes took things a step further. The remedy Fisher prescribed was to print more money. Keynes despaired that this would amount merely to "pushing on a string," and argued that government needed to *spend* money to get the economy moving again. As a matter of economic policy, this was a big difference. In terms of economic theory, not so much. The doctrine that took Keynes's name came to consist of the mathematical economics of rational individual choice (that is, Fisher's economics), combined with a few less-than-elegant additions that attempted to represent the maladies of the national economy known as recession and depression.[17] "This was not a perfect bicycle," recalled one of the young Keynesians, Paul Samuelson, "but it was the best wheel in town."[18]

The perfect bicycle that was mathematical equilibrium economics remained intact. And as memories of the Depression faded, economists began returning to it. A complete return took a few more decades, but the beginnings were already apparent in the early 1930s—in, of all places, Colorado Springs.

IRVING FISHER AND ROGER BABSON both convalesced in the Colorado town's tuberculosis sanatorium around the turn of the century. Fred Macaulay landed in Colorado Springs for an extended stay a few years later.[19] The link between these men's mountain sojourns and their stock market research appears to have been coincidental. It was not so with Alfred Cowles III, who made Colorado Springs into the world's leading center of mathematical and statistical economic research during the 1930s.

Cowles fell ill with TB in 1915, when he was just two years out of Yale, and he was sent to Colorado. It was not until 1925 that he felt well enough to look much beyond his sickbed, at which point he turned to helping his father manage the family fortune. Cowles was the grandson and namesake of the quiet business genius behind the spectacular rise of the *Chicago Tribune* in the latter half of the nineteenth century. "He never, so far as known, made an investment that resulted in a loss," claimed a front-page obituary in the *Tribune* when the seniormost Alfred Cowles died in 1889.[20] The family remained Tribune Co.'s second-biggest shareholder after his death.

Those Tribune shares weren't publicly traded, but in the late 1920s a wealthy young man's fancy could not but turn to the stock market. Cowles found friends in Colorado Springs even more interested in stocks than he. One, a disabled World War I veteran and former tire salesman, published a newsletter that improbably established him as William Peter Hamilton's successor as tender of the Dow theory flame.[21]

Cowles approached the Wall Street bazaar more as disinterested outsider than fevered participant. "I was subscribing to many different services, and it seemed a little wasteful to me," he told an interviewer decades later. "Why not find which one was the best and just take that one? So I started keeping track records in 1928 of the twenty-four most widely circulated financial services."[22] In 1932, Cowles decided it was time to do something with all his data, but he didn't have the statistical background to proceed. After asking around, he got in touch with a mathematics professor who summered in Colorado Springs. The professor agreed to help, but he also recommended that Cowles contact an economist known for his interest in statistics and the stock market: Irving Fisher.

By this time, Fisher was in deep financial trouble, with his public reputation in tatters. That didn't stop him from working. In 1930 he had published *The Theory of Interest*, a polishing and rethinking of his earlier writings on financial economics that today is seen as his most important contribution to the field.[23] And the mathematical approach he favored had finally begun to gain traction, especially in Europe.

The wealth of 1920s America lured European scholars across the Atlantic. One of them, Norwegian future Nobelist Ragnar Frisch, persuaded Fisher to join him in launching an association of mathematically minded economists. Harvard's Joseph Schumpeter, an Austrian-educated scholar who didn't do much math himself but admired those who did, signed on as a cofounder. They dubbed their new group the Econometric

Society, and began to hold occasional small meetings where papers were presented. They didn't have the money to do much more.

A letter arrived in Fisher's mailbox from Cowles. Fisher, who had known Cowles's father and uncle at Yale, enlisted the newspaper heir as the society's patron. For Cowles, who had been something of an ineffectual dabbler, the role gave him purpose and focus. He became treasurer of the organization, circulation manager of its new journal, *Econometrica*, and even chief note taker at its meetings. He also founded the Cowles Commission for Research in Economics in Colorado Springs, hiring the math professor he had initially consulted and a couple of young statisticians to help him in his research. In future years, even after he had moved back to Chicago to take over the family's business interests and removed himself from the day-to-day activities of the Cowles Commission, he always proudly listed his profession in *Who's Who* as "economist."

He had every right to do so. At the meetings of the Econometric Society and the summer seminars of the Cowles Commission, the world's dispersed little band of mathematical economists became acquainted with one another and one another's ideas, forming the foundations of what would become an all-conquering intellectual movement—the triumphs and excesses of which will be described in the chapters to come.[24]

This work had all begun because of Cowles's interest in stock market forecasting. He presented his findings on that subject at a meeting of the Econometric Society in Cincinnati on the last day of 1932. With the help of his staff and a Hollerith (IBM) punch card calculating machine, Cowles had examined the individual stock picks of sixteen statistical services, the investment record of twenty-five insurance companies, the stock market calls of twenty-four forecasting letters, and the Dow theory editorials of the only forecaster Cowles mentioned by name: William Peter Hamilton.

Cowles's verdict, delivered in a paper titled, "Can Stock Market Forecasters Forecast?" was that no, they can't. An investor who had bought and sold when Hamilton instructed between December 1903 and December 1929 would have made 12 percent a year. Just buying and holding the Dow Jones industrial average would have delivered a return of 15.5 percent a year. Of the other forecasters, only a few had been able to beat the market and even those better-than-average performances were "little, if any, better than what might be expected to result from pure chance."[25] That last was no idle comment. Cowles and his helpers had assembled random market forecasts from shuffled decks of hundreds of cards. On the whole, the cards beat the pros. The headline in the *New York Times* the next day read, "Rates Luck Above Wall St. Experts: Alfred Cowles 3d Asserts That Turn of Card Is Preferable to Following Forecasters."[26]

Cowles himself was far from convinced that *no one* could forecast the market, and for several years he supported the work of economists and statisticians he thought might be able to do better than Wall Street's experts. In 1937, Cowles and one of his number crunchers found that, over periods ranging from twenty minutes to three years, stock indexes were more likely to keep moving in the same direction in the next period than to reverse direction (the opposite was true of longer periods). Before anyone could get excited about these patterns, they warned that "this type of forecasting could not be employed by speculators with any assurance of consistent or large profits."[27]

Cowles's last major stock market project was to extend the Standard Statistics stock index (what's now called the S&P 500) back in time to 1871, and tally up dividends paid over that period as well. The goal was "to portray the average experience of those investing in this class of security in the United States from 1871 to 1938." It was a vastly more exhaustive version of what Edgar Lawrence Smith had done in 1924. The verdict was the same: Common stocks had been a good long-haul investment, delivering an average annual increase in market value of 1.8 percent and an average dividend yield of 5 percent since 1871. Over that same period, high-grade bonds yielded an average 4.2 percent.[28] While the study attracted attention from researchers and a few Wall Streeters—and is still consulted by those calculating long-run stock market returns—it caused nothing like the public sensation that Smith's book did. It was 1939, and not many people were interested in buying stocks.

THERE WERE STILL LOTS OF people interested in debating whether financial markets had any socially redeeming value. John Maynard Keynes, Fred Macaulay, and most other 1930s intellectuals expressed the opinion that they did not. Holbrook Working, a Stanford University agricultural researcher and regular at the Cowles Commission's summer meetings, began building up a body of evidence that pointed in the opposite direction. It got little attention at the time, but it was to prove very much in tune with the future direction of economics.

Born and raised in Colorado, Working got his doctorate at the University of Wisconsin in 1921 on the strength of a dissertation about the statistical properties of the demand curve for potatoes. His first published paper, in 1923, examined whether changes in the money supply lead to changes in the price level. The answer was yes, which caught the approving attention of Irving Fisher.[29] Working soon returned to agricultural questions, landing a job in 1925 with Stanford University's Food Research Institute that he kept for the rest of his long career.

Of all financial markets, agricultural futures markets had long seemed to scholars to serve the most obvious economic function. Futures are contracts to buy or sell wheat or corn or some other commodity at a set price on a set date in the future. They allow millers of wheat, refiners of sugar, and other large purchasers to lock in prices and plan ahead—and they give farmers a similar level of security. "No trade deserves more the full protection of the law," Adam Smith wrote of corn futures trading in 1776, "and no trade requires it so much; because no trade is so much exposed to popular odium."[30]

In the United Kingdom, the loudest protests usually came from urban consumers, who blamed speculators for jacking up the price of food. In the United States, the farmers complained. Whenever prices for farm products dropped, they blamed futures traders, creating an antimarket constituency that didn't exist in the case of stocks. At the height of the agrarian rebellion of the 1890s, both the House and Senate passed bills that would have effectively banned all futures trading, although the two houses never resolved the differences between the two versions. In Germany the Reichstag banned futures trading in 1896.[31]

As they suffered the dust bowl conditions of the 1930s, American farmers raised their voices against futures trading once again. In response, Working began studying futures markets, initially in an attempt to figure out if speculators did in fact make big profits off the backs of farmers. The answer he came up with in 1931 was that they did not. By examining trading records from the Chicago Board of Trade, the main grain exchange, Working separated those traders he deemed "speculators" from the merchants and farmers who bought and sold out of necessity. Over the forty-two years of data he examined, Working found that the speculators had, as a group, lost money.[32]

Moving on, Working began to study the movements of futures prices. He found a few interesting patterns. "Wheat prices tend strongly to rise during a season following three of low average price and to decline during a season following three of high average price," he reported in 1931. "The relation is attributed partly to a tendency for price judgments of wheat traders to be unduly influenced by memory of prices in recent years."[33] Much of what Working saw in price movements, though, seemed random.

The phrase "random walk" appears to have been coined in 1905, in an exchange in the letters pages of the English journal *Nature* concerning the mathematical description of the meanderings of a hypothetical drunkard.[34] Most early studies of economic data had been a search not for drunken meanderings but for recognizable patterns and, not surprisingly, many were found. The purported link between the British business cycle and sunspots was one. Another famous example came in the mid-1920s when the young founder of Moscow's Business Cycle Institute, Nikolai Kondratiev, proposed that economic activity moved in half-century-long "waves."[35]

As the study of statistics progressed and the mathematics of random processes such as Brownian motion became more widely understood, those on the frontier of this work began to question these apparent cycles. In his November 1925 presidential address to Great Britain's Royal Statistical Society, Cambridge professor George Udny Yule demonstrated that random Brownian motion could, with a little tweaking, produce dramatic patterns that didn't look random at all.[36] A few years later, a mathematician working for Kondratiev in Moscow penned what came to be seen as the definitive debunking of the pattern finders. "Almost all of the phenomena of economic life," wrote Eugen Slutsky, "occur in sequences of rising and falling movements, like waves." No two such waves were ever *exactly* the same, but

> it is almost always possible to detect, even in the multitude of individual peculiarities of the phenomena, marks of certain approximate uniformities and regularities. The eye of the observer instinctively discovers on waves of a certain order other smaller waves, so that the idea of harmonic analysis . . . presents itself to the mind almost spontaneously.[37]

In other words, we *want* to see regular waves in economic data, and thus we do. Slutsky set out to create what seemed to be regular, predictable waves where in fact there were none. Just by adding random numbers together, he created multiple series that met every then-extant statistical standard of regularity.

Yule and Slutsky were making the same point as Fred Macaulay had with his coin tosses, but with a mathematical relentlessness absent from the economist's playful dinnertime address. Who were you going to believe, they seemed to be saying, the most advanced theories of statistics, or your easily deceived eyes?

A brief English-language summary of Slutsky's paper on patterns and randomness made the rounds among the Cowles crowd in the early 1930s, and a full translation appeared in *Econometrica* in 1937. At the 1936 summer research conference in Colorado Springs, one speaker stated that there was now a "school of economic thought" that "regarded economic time series as statistically equivalent to accumulated random series and hence essentially unpredictable."[38]

Working certainly was drawn toward the possibility that the futures price data he was studying might be random. "[F]ew people recognized this evidence as having any significant meaning for the theory of prices," he wrote later. "And no one, so far as I know, had any clear idea of what the meaning of the evidence might be. I, at least, was long at a loss to interpret the observations."[39]

Working interrupted his studies during World War II to teach American makers of planes, ships, tanks, and guns how to keep manufacturing defects in check without busting the bank. He did so using quality control methods developed in the 1920s at AT&T's Bell Labs, which used statistics to define the bounds within which manufacturing flaws should be tolerated. For Working, the years spent teaching the difference between acceptable error and unacceptable error seem to have led to an intellectual breakthrough.

"The most perfect expectations possible in economic affairs must be subject to substantial error because the outcome depends on unpredictable future events," he wrote in a paper that he presented at the annual meeting of the American Economic Association in Cleveland in December 1948. "Market expectations, therefore, have a certain *necessary inaccuracy.*" His concern was how much "objectionable inaccuracy" there might be, due to speculators overreacting to news or taking too long to digest it. Any sort of persistent errors on the part of speculators would lead to persistent, predictable market patterns:

If it is possible under any given set of circumstances to predict future price changes and have the predictions fulfilled, it follows that the market expectations must have been defective; ideal market expectations would have taken full account of the information which permitted successful prediction of the price change.[40]

Working wrote this at a time when most economists still agreed with Keynes's depiction of securities markets as a futile exercise in "anticipating what average opinion expects average opinion to be." Working praised Keynes's mocking account as a "gem," but he argued that perhaps it was time to focus not on markets' failures but on the extent to which they got things right. He proposed that Alfred Cowles's seemingly discouraging conclusion of 1932—that stock market forecasters can't forecast—be viewed in a more positive light: "Apparent imperfection of professional forecasting . . . may be evidence of perfection of the market," Working said. "The failures of stock market forecasters . . . reflect credit on the market."

This was the first clear statement of what came to be known as the efficient market hypothesis—in retrospect, a major landmark in twentieth-century thought. Others had made great claims for the ability of financial markets to assemble information and even anticipate future events. Others had remarked upon the apparent randomness of market price movements. Working was the first to put the two together.

Like so many intellectual landmarks, it passed mostly unnoticed at the time. The paper did catch the eye of the Harvard Business School professor who administered the Merrill Foundation for the Advancement of Financial Knowledge, funded by Merrill Lynch. Working received a grant to do more research. He picked Stanford student Claude Brinegar as his assistant, stationed him at a desk facing his own in his office at the Food Research Institute, and put him to work using "brute force" (Brinegar's phrase) and a Working-designed statistical measure to assess just how closely real futures markets resembled the unpredictable ideal.

Brinegar's conclusion in his 1953 Ph.D. dissertation, which was effectively Working's conclusion as well, was that futures markets displayed a slight tendency to overreact—that is, over one- or two-week periods you could make a little bit of money by betting that prices had jumped too far in one direction and were about to reverse—and a much more pronounced penchant for "price continuity" over periods of four to sixteen weeks. In other words, one could make some money by betting on the continuation of price trends. "The type of behavior that we have observed may well represent the closest approach to ideal that is obtainable," concluded Brinegar. "It may well be that if the market were any more 'perfect' it would not contain enough profit-making opportunities to sustain the speculative interest needed to keep it going."[41]

After that, Brinegar got a job in the oil industry, rising to chief financial officer at Union Oil of California and secretary of transportation in the Nixon administration. He had neither the incentive nor the time to get his work published where other economists studying financial markets might see it. His mentor, Working, meanwhile, remained a bit player as the random walk revolution swept through academia over the next two decades.

It was partly personality. Working was a taciturn fellow who came across as sour to those who didn't know him well. He was also too old-fashioned and too attached to empirical evidence to take his theories and run with them. Instead, he kept looking for new ways to test them. "He knew too much to accept any general theory," said economist Hendrik Houthakker, a colleague at Stanford in the 1950s. "As soon as anybody came up with a theory, he would know counterexamples." The 1950s and 1960s were a heyday for grand, sweeping theories in economics. There was little tolerance for counterexamples.

THE RISE OF THE
RATIONAL MARKET

CHAPTER 3

HARRY MARKOWITZ
BRINGS STATISTICAL MAN
TO THE STOCK MARKET

*The modern quantitative approach to investing
is assembled out of equal parts poker strategy
and World War II gunnery experience.*

HOLBROOK WORKING WAS FAR FROM the only economist
to contribute his number-crunching skills to the Allied cause in
World War II. Here's the kind of thing Milton Friedman spent the
war years doing:

> You have an anti-aircraft shell, and you can control its frag-
> mentation. You can score it in such a way that it will break up in
> pieces of specified size. What size pieces do you want? Would
> you rather have 600 small pieces or 20 big pieces? If they're big,
> when they hit the enemy aircraft they'll do real harm, but if
> you only have two pieces there's not much chance you'll hit it.
> There's a tradeoff.

This exercise wasn't just theoretical. Lives were at stake. In the
middle of the Battle of the Bulge in 1944, artillery officers flew
back to the United States to get the latest word on setting proxim-
ity fuses from this thirty-something economist with no military
background but some advanced training in statistics.[1] Friedman
was deputy director of Columbia University's Statistical Research

Group, a leading outpost of what later came to be called "operations research"— the use of statistical and mathematical theory to make better military decisions. The director was his close friend from graduate school at the University of Chicago, W. Allen Wallis.

Operations research (OR) originated in the 1930s in the United Kingdom and soon spread across the Atlantic. It played a crucial if generally underappreciated role in helping the Allies win World War II. After hostilities ended, veterans of the wartime OR effort began applying similar techniques to peaceful uses—such as stock market investing. In 1952, Harry Markowitz, a graduate student at Chicago, published a landmark marriage of operations research and investing advice in the *Journal of Finance*. His approach to what he called "portfolio selection" was all about balancing risk and return. It had a lot in common with those wartime calculations on bomb fragmentation.

"It's of the same exact form: How much power do you want to sacrifice in order to have a greater probability of hitting?" recalled Friedman, who was on Markowitz's dissertation committee. "This is exactly the same thing: How much return do you want to sacrifice in order to increase the probability that you will get what you planned for? The logical character of the problem was the same." Given this parallel, it should perhaps not be too surprising that three months after Markowitz published his initial findings in March 1952 an Oxford professor and World War II gunnery officer wrote an article for *Econometrica* outlining a similar "safety first" approach to asset selection.[2] The Oxford don, A. D. Roy, failed to pursue the matter after that. Markowitz kept at it.

SELECTING AN OPTIMAL PORTFOLIO OF stocks is more difficult than figuring out how many fragments you want your bomb to blow up into. In the example described by Friedman, it was possible to know through controlled experiments just how many pieces the shells were likely to break into. It is almost never possible to say with certainty what the eventual outcome of an economic choice will be or even what the odds might be. Early mathematical economists hadn't known how to incorporate this uncertainty into their equilibrium equations. So they ignored it, assuming that their economic actors possessed perfect foresight. This was a problem, given that perfect foresight is not just unrealistic but logically impossible.

This logical flaw became an obsession of Austrian economist Oskar Morgenstern. The Austrians are known for their free market bent, but the school of economic thought that developed in Vienna in the late nineteenth century also held a healthy respect for uncertainty, which Morgenstern chose to focus on. To illustrate why certainty could never exist in human affairs, Morgenstern concocted a tale of fictional detective Sherlock Holmes being pursued by Dr. Moriarty. Moriarty will kill Holmes if he catches him.

Holmes boards a train in London that is bound for Dover and makes one intermediate stop. He sees Moriarty in the station. Initially he assumes that the doctor will take a nonstop express to Dover to get there first and decides to get off the train at the intermediate station. But Moriarty might guess that's what Holmes would do, in which case Holmes should continue on to Dover. And so on. "Always, *there is exhibited an endless chain of reciprocally conjectural reactions and counter-reactions,*" Morgenstern wrote in a fit of italicizing in 1935. "*Unlimited foresight and economic equilibrium are thus irreconcilable with one another.*"[3]

Morgenstern sought an economics that incorporated limits to the ability to see into the future. He saw no hint of it in the work of his fellow economists, of whom he grew increasingly disdainful. The developments of the late 1930s, in which young Keynesians grafted a few kludgy imperfect-foresight formulas onto the body of perfect-foresight mathematical economics, aggravated him. He began consorting with the scientists and mathematicians of Vienna, one of whom steered him toward a 1928 paper about poker written by Hungarian mathematician John von Neumann.[4]

After emigrating to the United States in 1930, von Neumann became the brightest intellectual light at Princeton's Institute for Advanced Study, a place that also employed Albert Einstein. He helped plan the Battle of the Atlantic, design the atomic bomb, and invent the computer. In the late 1950s, dying of bone cancer likely brought on by witnessing one too many atomic test blasts, he peddled his doctrine of nuclear brinksmanship while rolling his wheelchair down the halls of power in Washington—providing at least part of the inspiration for Stanley Kubrick's Dr. Strangelove.

In the world of economists, von Neumann played the role of alien from a vastly more advanced species, alighting briefly to share his knowledge. A paper he wrote in the early 1930s on the mathematics of economic equilibrium utterly reshaped discussion of the subject.[5] The intellectual revolution unleashed by the paper he wrote about poker strategy in 1928 may have been even more significant.

There already existed a scholarly tradition of exploring the straightforward mathematics of games like chess. Poker is different. There is no *correct* set of moves, just an uncertain mix of bluffing and folding. Von Neumann set about replacing the intuition and judgment deemed essential to poker success with a mathematical, rational approach. It involved varying one's moves randomly, so the opponent can't pick up a pattern. That is, a player decides whether to hold or fold by flipping a coin. As some moves hold more promise than others, the player weights the random draw toward one move or another (think of Fred Macaulay's loaded dice, or a lopsided coin that lands heads 60 percent of the time). This strategy was no secret path to certain victory. It was simply a logically consistent way of playing the game—and of making decisions in the face of uncertainty.

Morgenstern arrived in the United States in 1938 after being forced out of Vienna by the Nazis, and landed a job at Princeton. He sought out von Neumann, and began pestering him to revisit his poker theory and explore its implications for economics. The result was the 641-page *Theory of Games and Economic Behavior*, coauthored by von Neumann and Morgenstern and published in 1944. As far as pure game theory went, the book added little to what von Neumann had written in 1928,[6] although it gave form and heft to von Neumann's big idea. It also solved the quandary faced by poor Sherlock Holmes and Dr. Moriarty. According to von Neumann's calculations, Holmes should choose randomly with a 60 percent probability of getting off at the intermediate station, while Moriarty should pick with a 60 percent probability of proceeding straight to Dover.[7] Got that?

For economists, the part of the book that made the biggest immediate impression was not game theory itself but the chapter outlining how one should weigh potential outcomes before deciding on a move. The gist of it: When outcomes are uncertain, think probabilistically. Assign a numerical value, a.k.a. utility, to each potential outcome, then decide how probable each is. Multiply probability by utility, and one gets what came to be called "von Neumann-Morgenstern expected utility." Rational people ought to maximize this value. It wasn't an entirely new idea. Mathematician Daniel Bernoulli outlined a similar approach in 1738 (his paper was published in English for the first time in *Econometrica* in 1954[8]). But this time around, there were lots of economists interested in learning more. Their chief teacher became Ukrainian-born Jacob Marschak, a professor of economics at the University of Chicago and research director of the Cowles Commission.

Alfred Cowles III had moved the organization (and himself) to Chicago in 1939 when he took over the family seat on the Tribune Co. board after his father's death. A few years later, he lured Marschak— who had turned down the same job when the commission was still in Colorado—from the New School for Social Research in New York. Marschak had learned statistics in Kiev from Eugen Slutsky, who had shown that apparent waves in economic data could be completely random. After a brief and spectacularly eventful career as a teenaged social-democratic politician during the years immediately following the Russian Revolution, Marschak fled to Germany, where he studied economics and met von Neumann. At Cowles, he gathered around him a spectacular assemblage of future Nobel winners ("I pick people with good eyes," he explained[9]) who together explored the cutting edge of mathematical economics.

Von Neumann and Morgenstern's book was on that cutting edge, and Marschak brought von Neumann to Chicago for a two-day seminar on game theory in 1945. Soon afterward, he wrote an article translating von Neumann and Morgenstern's concept of expected utility into language that would be understood by his fellow economists. "To be an 'economic man,'" Marschak summed up, "implies being a 'statistical man.'"[10]

IF EVER THERE WAS A statistical man, it was Harry Markowitz. A grocer's son from northwest Chicago, he sped through a special two-year undergraduate program at the University of Chicago and was pursuing a Ph.D. as a "student member" of the Cowles Commission. His statistics professor at Chicago was Leonard "Jimmie" Savage, a veteran of the wartime Statistical Research Group at Columbia, who was described by his sometime collaborator Milton Friedman as "one of the few people I have met whom I would unhesitatingly call a genius."[11] He studied the mathematics of tradeoffs with Tjalling Koopmans, a Dutch physicist-turned-economist and future Nobelist. During the war, Koopmans had developed the technique later dubbed "linear programming" to determine the most efficient use of merchant ships crisscrossing the Atlantic.[12] Markowitz's adviser, macroeconomics professor, and guide to the ideas of von Neumann and Morgenstern was Jacob Marschak. "When I first read the von Neumann axioms, I was not convinced," Markowitz recalled. "Somebody at Cowles said, 'Well, you ought to read Marschak's version of the von Neumann axioms.' I read Marschak's version, and I was convinced."

One day in 1950, Markowitz was sitting outside Marschak's office at the Cowles Commission waiting to talk to his adviser about possible dissertation topics. A stockbroker was waiting too. He struck up a conversation with Markowitz and suggested that the student write about the stock market.[13] When Markowitz shared this idea with Marschak, the professor reacted with enthusiasm—perhaps out of guilt at having steered the Cowles Commission's research so far away from its founder's original interest in the market. He gave Markowitz a copy of Cowles's 1932 forecasting paper and 1938 stock market history, and sent him off to the dean of Chicago's Graduate School of Business to get advice on what else to read.

The dean, Marshall Ketchum, recommended several books, among them Benjamin Graham and David Dodd's *Security Analysis* and John Burr Williams's *The Theory of Investment Value*. Graham was a successful New York money manager and lecturer at Columbia University, Dodd a professor at Columbia Business School. *Security Analysis*, first published in 1934, had become a seminal work on Wall Street. Markowitz read every word and every footnote, but found no inspiration. The book is a brilliant guide to bargain hunting, but isn't much help to someone looking for a general theory of investing.

Williams's *Theory* was more congenial in its approach. Williams had been a junior investment banker in Boston when the great crash came. He stayed on at his firm until 1932, and then enrolled in Harvard's economics Ph.D. program in hopes that he would learn to "understand the workings of the economy as a whole." His faculty adviser Joseph Schumpeter was worried that Williams's conservative political beliefs might rub others on the dissertation committee the wrong way and urged him to focus on a subject that no one would dare challenge him on.[14] The result was *The Theory of Investment Value*. "Rational men, when they buy stocks and bonds, would never pay more than the present worth of the expected future dividends," Williams wrote, " . . . nor could they pay less, assuming perfect competition, with all traders equally well informed."[15]

The book was thus a guide to valuing stocks on the basis of projected future dividends, much as Irving Fisher had outlined back in 1906. Williams left out the second part of Fisher's valuation equation: uncertainty. "No buyer considers all securities equally attractive at their present market prices whatever these prices happen to be," Williams wrote in the first page of the book, "on the contrary, he seeks 'the best at the price.'" Markowitz was dubious. Graham and Dodd exhorted their readers to hold a diversified portfolio, although they didn't go deeply into the hows or whys. As he read further in *The Theory of Investment Value*, Markowitz saw that even Williams assumed that investors would own many securities. Someone who was truly out to buy only "the best at the price" would only buy one stock—the best one. Yet only fools did that.

"Clearly, investors diversify to avoid risk," Markowitz said. "What was missing from Williams's analysis was the notion of the risk of the portfolio as a whole." Markowitz began contemplating an approach based upon von Neumann and Morgenstern's expected utility. An investor would make an estimate of the return he expected from a particular stock, then assess the probability that his estimate would turn out to be right. Markowitz expressed this estimate as the mean (the expected return) and the variance (a gauge of how spread out a distribution is). The higher the variance is, the greater the chance that a stock might do worse or better than expected. While this was not the understanding of risk prevalent on Wall Street, where risk meant the chance that things would go wrong, it was a reasonable starting point for a mathematical formula for diversification.

Markowitz contemplated this as he sat in the Chicago Business School library reading Williams's book. After deciding on variance, he got up and found a book on probability that "showed that the variance of a weighted sum of random variables (e.g., the return on a portfolio of securities) involves the covariances or correlations among the random variables," he recalled years later. Markowitz's translation: "It said that the riskiness of the portfolio had to do not only with the riskiness of the individual securities therein, but also to the extent that they moved up and down together." From there, Markowitz was a few equations away from separating an "efficient" portfolio—one that delivered the maximum potential reward for a given amount of risk—from an inefficient one. The terminology, and the math, came straight from his linear programming class with Tjalling Koopmans.[16]

Markowitz had not only a dissertation topic but an idea that would transform investing. Before he could get his degree, though, he had to put up with an unexpected razzing from Friedman at his dissertation defense. "Two minutes into the defense, Friedman says, 'Well, I don't find any mistake in the mathematics, but this isn't a dissertation in economics and we can't give you a Ph.D. in economics.'" Markowitz recalled. "This goes on and on, and at one point he says, 'Harry, you have a problem. It's not economics; it's not business administration; it's not mathematics.' And Marschak says, 'It's not literature.'"

Markowitz got his doctorate, and Friedman subsequently told him he was never in any danger of *not* getting it. But half a century later, Friedman stood by what he had said. "Every statement there is correct. It's not economics; it's not mathematics; it's not business. It is something different. It's finance."

THERE WASN'T A BIG MARKET for this new, quantitative version of finance in 1952. After finishing up at Chicago, Markowitz took a job doing linear programming at RAND—a think tank set up by the air force after the war that threw together mathematicians (von Neumann was a regular), physicists, economists, political scientists, and computer programmers to study the big questions of war and diplomacy. His portfolio theory article attracted the attention, though, of the same Merrill Foundation that had bankrolled Holbrook Working's research. Together with what was now called the Cowles Foundation—which Alfred Cowles had moved to Yale in the summer of 1955—the Merrill Foundation paid Markowitz to spend the 1955–56 academic year at Yale expanding his dissertation into a book. It was published in 1959 as *Portfolio Selection*.

Markowitz wanted the book to be a truly practical, if densely quantitative, guide to modern investing. To get it to that point, he had to face head-on some knotty questions that he had ignored in his original paper. The biggest conundrum was how a person was supposed to go about being a statistical man not in a game with clearly defined rules but in a messy, uncertain world. How was one to assign numerical probabilities to uncertain future events?

The answer—as Louis Bachelier had concluded back in 1900—is that there is no one way. Everyone's assessments of the future are of necessity personal and subjective. But rules *could* be devised for how to adjust those assessments in the face of new evidence, and the man who set them down in the early 1950s was Jimmie Savage, Markowitz's statistics professor. "Jimmie would say, 'The role of statistics is not to discover truth. The role of statistics is to resolve disagreements among people,'"[17] recalled Milton Friedman.

Savage set out his philosophy of probability in a 1954 book called *Foundations of Statistics,* paperback copies of which Markowitz still kept on hand at his office half a century later to give to visitors. Early in the book, Savage contrasts the proverbs "Look before you leap" and "You can cross that bridge when you come to it." "When two proverbs conflict in this way," he wrote, "it is proverbially true that there is some truth in both of them, but rarely, if ever, can their common truth be captured by a single pat proverb."[18] It was the job of statistical decision making to find the approximate common truth between the proverbial extremes.

Investing lore is full of proverbs, many of which conflict. Consider the age-old admonition, "Don't put all your eggs in one basket," and its late nineteenth-century opposite, probably first uttered by Andrew Carnegie but made famous by the Mark Twain character David "Pudd'nhead" Wilson, "Put all your eggs in the one basket, and— WATCH THAT BASKET."[19]

Markowitz was trying to use statistics to find the approximate common truth between these two extremes. In the sixteenth century,

Shakespeare's *Merchant of Venice*, Antonio, happily (if overconfidently) declared:

> *My ventures are not in one bottom trusted,*
> *Nor to one place; nor is my whole estate*
> *Upon the fortune of this present year;*
> *Therefore, my merchandise makes me not sad.* [20]

"Clearly, Shakespeare not only knew about diversification but, at an intuitive level, understood covariance," [21] Markowitz commented admiringly. Lots of people on Wall Street understood both concepts intuitively as well. Markowitz's aim was to create what Irving Fisher had first suggested in 1906—a system that assigned numbers to an investor's intuition and thus produced a consistent formula for portfolio building. He was trying to convert rules of thumb into science.

The Markowitz approach to portfolio selection has been contrasted with that of Gerald Loeb, cofounder of the once-great brokerage E. F. Hutton. In 1935, Loeb wrote *The Battle for Investment Survival*, a daredevil's guide to the market that still claims a following today. One of the book's core messages is that "once you attain competency, diversification is undesirable." [22] That certainly wasn't Markowitz's attitude, but neither did his work entirely contradict it. His measure of variance allowed investors to express their level of competence, or confidence in their own opinions. Someone who thought he knew as much about the future as Gerald Loeb thought he did would ascribe a small variance to his favorite picks. Plug that certainty into Markowitz's formula, and it yields an efficient portfolio consisting of just a few stocks.

Markowitz's book offered extensive guidance on how to follow Savage's axioms for weighing evidence in the face of uncertainty, but he wasn't trying to wrest the work of making stock market calls and risk judgments away from Wall Street. "My inclination, my assumption was that they would come from security analysts," he said. "I still

say, 'My job as an operations research guy is, you give me the estimates, and I'll compute the portfolios faster than the next guy.'"[23] For
all its pages and pages of mathematical notation, the book contained
several crucial concessions to practical reality.

Markowitz knew that his statistician's view of risk as the scatter
of potential outcomes around a mean wasn't necessarily the risk that
matters to an investor—who cares more about what could go wrong
than what could go unexpectedly right. He devised a measure he
called "semi-variance"—now usually called downside risk—to measure only the risk that an investment might do worse than expected.
You couldn't do all the things mathematically with semi-variance that
you could with variance, but Markowitz at least acknowledged that
it mattered.

He also acknowledged that different investors might want to maximize different things. His original portfolio selection formula aimed
for the highest possible arithmetic mean of expected wealth. That is,
you take all the possible outcomes of your investment (make a million dollars, end up broke, and so on), add them together weighted by
the probability that each will happen, and divide to get the average.
To get the geometric mean you multiply and take the root. This geometric mean gives a lot more weight to extreme outcomes. If there's
a chance that a bet will pay off spectacularly, the geometric-mean
approach will lead you to put lots of money in—unless there's also a
chance that it could wipe you out, in which case you wouldn't make
the bet at all (zero dollars times anything still equals zero). A former
Wall Street analyst studying finance at the University of North Carolina had proposed this geometric approach in a paper he presented at
a Cowles Foundation seminar in 1956. Markowitz devoted a chapter
to it in his 1959 book.[24]

Markowitz was trying to shape his advice to conform to Wall
Street reality. Few on Wall Street appreciated this. Markowitz tried
to sell executives at one smallish brokerage firm on his approach,
describing how they could keep track of their analysts' estimates over

the course of a few years, find out what the usual margin of error was and whether there were any systematic biases, then plug the average rate of error into a portfolio selection formula. The head of the firm was a veteran analyst who still made stock picks. No one could imagine testing *his* predictions for accuracy. "The reaction was, 'No thank you,'" Markowitz recalled.

That left academic students of the market—who came to embrace Markowitz's statistical approach with fervor, but didn't embrace it quite as Markowitz had envisioned. In the late 1960s, Markowitz took another break from RAND to prepare a new edition of his book and teach portfolio theory at UCLA. One of his students, Mark Rubinstein, assembled a bibliography of academic papers that referenced his work. When Markowitz began reading through them, he was taken aback. "People just didn't read my book," he told Rubinstein. "They read my paper, but they didn't read my book."[25] This was partly because economics and finance had reached that advanced stage in their academic development where only journal articles mattered. No one read books anymore. It was also because most finance scholars had ceased to care about the hard work of making judgments about risk and return in the stock market. Who needed judgment, after all, when everybody knew that stock price movements were completely random?

A RANDOM WALK FROM PAUL SAMUELSON TO PAUL SAMUELSON

The proposition that stock movements are mostly unpredictable goes from intellectual curiosity to centerpiece of an academic movement.

WHEN PAUL SAMUELSON ARRIVED AT the Massachusetts Institute of Technology in 1940, allowed to slip away from Harvard by an economics department chairman who valued neither math geeks nor Jews, the engineering-dominated school didn't even offer a Ph.D. in economics. Within a decade, MIT had built a department around Samuelson that left Harvard's in the shade.

One recent history of economic thought (Jürg Niehans's *A History of Economic Theory*) devotes twenty-four pages to Samuelson's ideas. Adam Smith only gets thirteen.[1] Samuelson's work on stock markets and the random walk takes up less than two of those twenty-four pages. He was "the last generalist in economics," as he liked to say, and for him financial market studies were just a side project that he at times seemed deeply ambivalent about. His intervention was, however, crucial to the triumph of the random walk. Here was one of the most important economists of all time, and *he* didn't think the relationship between coin flips and the stock market was a dinner-speech triviality.

The son of successful immigrant parents in Gary, Indiana, Samuelson arrived at the University of Chicago in 1932 and fell hard for the elegant logic of neoclassical economics. As a graduate student at Harvard, he became convinced that this logic was best expressed mathematically, and he embarked on a self-directed research program that made him probably the first American economist since Irving Fisher whose quantitative skills matched those of his peers in the hard sciences.

Samuelson thought equations clarified economic concepts often muddled by words. "The laborious literary working over of essentially simple mathematical concepts such as is characteristic of much of economic theory . . . involves . . . mental gymnastics of a peculiarly depraved type," he wrote in 1947 in the introduction to *Foundations of Economic Analysis*, an equation-filled rewording of his doctoral dissertation that became a core text of graduate economics education for years to come. At the same time, Samuelson could see that his equations didn't explain everything. Equilibrium theories alone, he concluded, certainly couldn't account for the Depression. Samuelson became a Keynesian, a leading purveyor of the "neoclassical synthesis" that paired *microeconomics*, the elegant study of the interactions of hyperrational firms and individuals, with less elegant *macroeconomic* explanations of the economy-wide phenomena like the business cycle. (The terms were coined by Ragnar Frisch, Irving Fisher's partner in launching the Econometric Society.)

Such juxtapositions came to typify Samuelson's approach. In matters of methodology and theory, he could be doctrinaire. But when it came to translating theory into practice, he was flexible. And while he loved the clarity of math, he was adept with words, too.

In his 1948 undergraduate textbook *Economics*, he described financial markets this way: The "ideal competitive market," he wrote, is characterized by "an equilibrium that is constantly being disturbed but is always in the process of re-forming itself—not unlike the surface of the ocean." Actual speculative markets, he conceded a few sentences later, often didn't look anything like that. They could be swept up in what he called "mass contagion" that drove prices far from their rational values. As he wrote of the bull market of the 1920s:

The most wonderful thing about a bull market is that it creates its own hopes. If people buy because they think stocks will rise, their act of buying sends up the price of stocks. This causes them to buy still further, and sends the dizzy dance off on another round. And unlike a game of cards or dice, no one loses what the winners gain. Everybody gets a prize! Of course, the prizes are all on paper and would disappear if everyone tried to cash them in. But why should anyone wish to sell such lucrative securities?[2]

Could a person take advantage of such mass delusions to make a killing? There can be no "foolproof system" to beat the market, Samuelson wrote in his textbook. But some approaches were better than others. He identified four classes of stock market players: (1) the buy and hold crowd, who do reasonably well as long as the economy grows; (2) "the hour-to-hour, day-to-day ticker watchers," who mostly "make money only for their brokers"; (3) the market timers who try to take advantage of the changing moods of the investing public, and are sometimes successful at it; and finally (4) those who study companies closely enough to take advantage of "special situations" of which the investing public is not aware. It is members of the last group who make the biggest money, Samuelson wrote, but they have to put in a lot of work or have privileged access to information.

For most of his career, Samuelson made an extracurricular pursuit of carving out a fifth method for himself—that of using economics and probability theory to gain an edge on the great majority of market players. He first became interested in stocks in the late 1930s, and first had serious money to play around with after the publication of *Economics*, which rode the postwar higher education boom to spectacular success (the first edition sold 121,453 copies, and about four million more have been sold since[3]). In the late 1940s, Samuelson subscribed to a $200-a-year newsletter touting warrants, the long-term options to buy stock at a preset price often issued in those days. He sensed even then that options, whose values were derived from those of the underlying stock, provided opportunities to math whizzes that plain-vanilla stocks and bonds did not. In 1954, when an MIT graduate student who was helping him with a revision of *Economics* needed a dissertation topic, Samuelson recommended that he write about options.[4]

In those days, Samuelson also made a habit of reading every article in every academic journal that arrived in the offices of the MIT-based *Quarterly Journal of Economics*. "That was a big waste of time," he joked later. But it is probably where he first came across the paper—presented in London the previous year by a prominent statistics professor—that propelled him down the path of market randomness.[5] The statistics professor was Maurice Kendall of the London School of Economics (LSE), and the paper was published in the first 1953 issue of the *Journal of the Royal Statistical Association*.

Kendall was a protégé of George Udny Yule, that exposer of false patterns and correlations from the 1920s. During World War II, when he wasn't busy crunching numbers for the British Chamber of Shipping or patrolling the streets and underground stations of London as an air raid warden, Kendall elaborated on Yule's pioneering efforts to separate true patterns in time series from statistical noise. Toward the end of the 1940s, he put his techniques to work on economic data, using a calculating machine newly acquired by the LSE—one of many advances in computing technology to factor in this saga. The most readily available data were stock prices and agricultural futures prices.

It was, Kendall said, "almost as if once a week the Demon of Chance drew a random number . . . and added it to the current price to determine the next week's price." By looking at price *changes* instead of prices themselves he saw only one pattern: the bell curve of normal randomness. "To the statistician there is some pleasure in the thought that the symmetrical distribution reared its graceful head undisturbed amid the uproar of the Chicago wheat pit," he continued. "The economist, I suspect, or at any rate the trade cyclist, will look for statistical snags before he is convinced of the absence of systematic movements."[6]

Kendall had circulated a preliminary version of his paper, so when he presented it at a December 1952 meeting of the Royal Statistical Society in London, the place was packed with economists ready to rumble. No one on hand appeared to be familiar with Holbrook Working's recent papers on market randomness, and most were dismayed by what Kendall had to say. "Economists . . . have been told to beware of a fearsome devil—serial correlation—and to look to statisticians to cast the devil out for them," complained LSE economics professor Roy Allen. "It seems now that the more statisticians work on the casting out of devils, the more they cast out everything else, including what the economists want."

Two young economists who had come down on the train from Cambridge professed not to be dismayed at all—just unimpressed. They both worked at Cambridge's Department of Applied Economics, England's leading outpost of statistical economics, and to them it was no surprise that the demon of chance was at work in the data Kendall had chosen. One of them, Hendrik Houthakker, punningly referred to the paper as "the backwash of the Yule tide" and complained that Kendall had taken on a "straw man."

The other, Sig Prais, explained why. "These are share and commodity markets which are the best examples of markets that are dynamically perfect," he said. "That is, any expected future changes in the demand or supply conditions are already taken into account by the price ruling in the market as a result of the activities of hedgers and speculators. There is, therefore, no reason to expect changes in prices this week to be correlated with changes next week." The insight that for Holbrook Working had been so hard-won came to the younger Prais naturally. He just claimed not to find it interesting. It was "particularly unfortunate," Prais concluded, that Kendall had chosen such markets to investigate rather than something more significant. (Years later, Prais still complained that Kendall's paper "seems to have become more important than it should be.")

This was the postwar British mindset. Government controlled the commanding heights of the economy, and the markets of London's City simply didn't seem all that important. Just as Oxford's A. D. Roy failed to pursue the portfolio selection theory he unveiled the same year, Kendall soon dropped the subject. If the beguiling idea of a "demon of chance" at work in the market were to resonate, it would have to do so where financial markets mattered—in the United States.

Like Prais and Houthakker, Paul Samuelson could immediately see the link between randomness and a well-functioning financial market, but unlike them he cared enough about investing to find it interesting. Not long after Kendall's talk, the Dutch-born Houthakker moved to the United States, initially to work at the Cowles Commission. "Let's work the other side of the street," Samuelson remembered urging him in a letter. And so Samuelson (and, before long, Houthakker) began to work that other side—the side already visited by Holbrook Working, where market randomness was not a disappointing triviality but an important fact. Before long, a historical document emerged that established their investigation as part of a great scientific tradition.

Sometime in 1955 or 1956, statistical theorist Jimmie Savage sent postcards to a few like-minded scholars. He had come across a fascinating book in the library: *Le jeu, la chance et le hasard (Games, Chance, and Risk)*, by somebody named Louis Bachelier. Had any of them, Savage wondered, heard of the guy or the book? Samuelson set to searching the libraries of Cambridge, Massachusetts, for the book. He found something far more interesting: Bachelier's 1900 doctoral dissertation, the *Théorie de la spéculation*.

Samuelson recognized almost immediately that Bachelier's densely mathematical description of market behavior was almost identical to Albert Einstein's description of Brownian motion—the random movement of microscopic particles suspended in a liquid or gas. The significance of this discovery to the subsequent development of quantitative finance cannot be overstated. Economists and finance professors could claim that one of their own—and they embraced the deceased French mathematician as such—had beaten the great Einstein to a major discovery.

Samuelson's first order of business after encountering Bachelier's work was to help his student incorporate the parts on options into his almost-finished dissertation. He then began thinking about whether Bachelier's formula actually fit real-life security markets. In his opinion it did not. One reason why not had been noted by Fred Macaulay at that statisticians' dinner in 1925. If stock price changes followed a true random walk, prices could become negative, a fate that the entire limited-liability structure of the modern corporation is designed to prevent. Another problem was that if price movements were truly random, the price of a pea might follow the same trajectory as that of a share of IBM stock. Instead, stock prices trended upward with the growth of a company and of the economy as a whole. The price of a pea did not. So it wasn't that "the mathematical expectation of the speculator was zero," as Bachelier had posited. The mathematical expectation of the speculator was the expected return of the stock or of the overall market, around which the actual return would fluctuate randomly.

It is conceivable that Bachelier and Poincaré were aware of these flaws in 1900, and didn't bother correcting them because Bachelier's formula was meant to look only an "instant" into the future. It didn't matter that Bachelier's Brownian motion would eventually lead prices where they could not go, because he had made explicit that it was not to be used for purposes of long-term prediction anyway. Beset by no such qualms, Samuelson revised Bachelier's formula. He introduced what he variously called "geometric," "economic," or "logarithmic" Brownian motion, which avoided negative prices by describing percentage moves of stock prices, not dollars and cents. And he depicted stock market investing as a bet in which the payoffs fluctuated randomly around the expected return.

W SAMUELSON BEGAN TALKING UP THESE ideas around MIT and in visits to other universities in the late 1950s. He didn't publish anything about them. Like John Maynard Keynes before him, Samuelson enjoyed playing the market, but he had doubts as to the social value of such activity. Before long, though, his reservations were irrelevant. In the spring of 1959, an astrophysicist and a statistics professor—each unaware of Samuelson's work and of each other's—published papers that marked the transformation of what had up to then been intermittent musings about the behavior of stock market prices into an intellectual movement.

The astrophysicist was M. F. M. Osborne, and he worked at the U.S. Naval Research Laboratory in Washington, D.C. Osborne had joined the lab in 1941, straight out of graduate school at UC–Berkeley, and spent World War II on such operations research tasks as figuring how best to track down submarines and blow them up. After the war he and his fellow scientists at the laboratory were set loose to study whatever interested them. Osborne's research topics included the aerodynamics of insect flight and the hydrodynamical performance of migrating salmon. To him, the stock market was just one more source of interesting data. After some study of the market, he concluded:

> It was a game of competitive gambling. In it some were smart and some were not so smart, and the players changed sides so often that it was a picture of financial chaos or bedlam. As I had some experience in molecular chaos as a physicist studying statistical mechanics, the analogies were very clear to me indeed.[7]

The analogy that was clearest to him was that of Brownian motion. As Samuelson had already noticed, straight arithmetic Brownian motion couldn't possibly fit the data. Instead, Osborne used the same percentage-change version as Samuelson had, then published his findings in the March–April 1959 issue of the journal *Operations Research*. As soon as the article came out, letters pointing out similarities to the stock market work of Bachelier, Maurice Kendall, and others came pouring in. Osborne hadn't known about any of that beforehand. The one academic work about the market that he cited was the 1937 article coauthored by Alfred Cowles that described the tendency of stock indexes to keep moving in the same direction for periods of up to three years, then reverse direction over longer periods.

When Osborne first started looking into the stock market, in fact, the study that most captured his attention was *Technical Analysis of Stock Trends*, by Robert Edwards and John Magee. "I just about wore out a copy of Magee and Edwards' book," Osborne wrote later. "There is a lot in it which enlightens what is otherwise a strange phenomenon indeed."[8] The book, first published in 1947, was in the tradition of stock-chart reading introduced a half century before by Charles Dow, but it focused more on individual stocks than the market as a whole, made use of trading volume data as well as price trends, and introduced many colorful new terms to the Wall Street vernacular, from the "island reversal" to the "bent neckline" to the "scallops."

These methods were a hit with small investors in the 1950s. Wall Street firms began hiring "technical analysts" to satisfy customers' yearnings for chartist guidance. "Don't get the idea that the chart method is black magic," Magee told John Brooks of the *New Yorker*. "It isn't. It's a science, or at least a quasi-science. The chartist regards the development of stock-chart formations as a natural phenomenon, the way a botanist regards the development of plants." It was this aspect of the chart readers' work that appealed to Osborne, who went on to author several papers on patterns that he had identified in stock prices. But while Osborne grounded his work in statistical theory, the chart readers did not. Most weren't capable of subjecting their naturalistic observations to even the most rudimentary tests of statistical significance. All they did was describe apparent patterns in stock prices, even though statistics professors had been demonstrating since the 1920s how easy it was to create seemingly regular patterns by adding together random numbers.

And so, as Osborne worked out his idea of Brownian stock market motion, University of Chicago statistics professor Harry Roberts was deciding that he had had just about enough of the chart readers' willful ignorance. Roberts wrote a paper that amounted to a reprise of Fred Macaulay's coin tossing experiment of 1925, citing the findings of Kendall and Working and displaying a few randomly generated stock charts to make the point that, by looking at stock price *levels*, technical market analysts were likely to see patterns where there were none. He recommended that they watch price *changes* instead, and he did not rule out the possibility that they might find something interesting there. While Roberts wrote the piece as if he were addressing the chart readers, he published it in March 1959 in a publication read almost exclusively by academics, the *Journal of Finance*.[9] Together with Osborne's article it announced that the moment of the random walk as a scholarly sensation had arrived.

The random walkers were at first a cozy little fraternity. Roberts put his student Arnold Moore to work examining the statistical properties of stock price movements. After Osborne's paper came out, Moore paid the astrophysicist a visit in Washington. He recommended to his professors that they bring Osborne to the Business School for a semester, but Osborne demurred because his large family made relocation problematic.[10]

Another early member of the gang was Houthakker. While serving on the Stanford faculty with Holbrook Working in the 1950s, he began to focus on the commodity price series that he had criticized Maurice Kendall for bothering to study. He brought this avocation with him to Harvard, where one day in 1960 Benoit Mandelbrot came calling. Mandelbrot was a mathematician who had emigrated from France to work at IBM's research center in Yorktown Heights, New York, studying—like Osborne at the Naval Research Laboratory— most anything that interested him. He had been looking at the mathematics of income distribution, and Houthakker invited him up to Harvard to speak about it.

When Mandelbrot arrived he saw a chart on Houthakker's blackboard of what appeared to be his income data. "Mandelbrot made a querulous joke—how should my diagram have materialized ahead of my lecture?—but Houthakker didn't know what Mandelbrot was talking about," recounted science writer James Gleick in his book *Chaos*. "The diagram had nothing to do with income distribution; it represented eight years of cotton prices."[11] Enthralled, Mandelbrot began sharing his discovery in visits to other universities. At the University of Chicago, he found an enthusiastic follower in Eugene Fama, another student of Harry Roberts studying market movements.

Holbrook Working rejoined the fray with a paper showing that Alfred Cowles's 1937 finding of patterns in stock movements was largely the result of a statistical error.[12] Oskar Morgenstern chipped in, too. His friend John von Neumann had suggested before he died in 1957 that Morgenstern use a statistical technique called spectral analysis, helpful in distinguishing between true cycles and randomly generated ones, to examine economic data. Morgenstern wasn't enough of a mathematician to do this himself, but he hired young British statistician Clive Granger and put him to work examining stock prices. In 1963, Morgenstern and Granger published a paper confirming that, according to their tests, stock prices moved in a short-term random walk (over the longer run, the movements didn't look quite so random).[13] Morgenstern had connections at *Fortune* that dated back to the magazine's coverage of game theory fifteen years before, and his was thus the first of the random walk papers to receive attention in the mainstream press. The headline of the brief item in the magazine's personal investing section in February 1963 was "A Random Walk in Wall Street."[14]

THE HEADQUARTERS OF THIS EARLY random walk movement was Samuelson's MIT. The university's new Sloan School of Industrial Management shared a building with the Economics Department. For a time in the late 1950s, professors from both came to share an obsession with commodities trading. "On the third floor of the economics department were the soybean bulls," recalled Samuelson; "the soybean bears were on the fourth floor of the Sloan School; possibly all of us succeeded in making losses."

Samuelson concluded that the main reason he and his colleagues didn't go broke in the process was that the father of one of them was a commodities broker who vetoed some of their craziest ideas. He was also impressed with the acumen displayed by his former student Paul Cootner, who received his economics Ph.D. at MIT in 1953 and returned six years later to teach finance at the Business School. Cootner put to use his own research into statistical relationships between futures price spreads and other factors. "These fundamentalist paradigms, in the hands of a sensitive and informed analyst, did seem to work," Samuelson said.[15]

Cootner became a ringleader of the random walkers, compiling an influential 1964 book of writings on the subject that included the first English translation of Bachelier's doctoral thesis. But as his commodity trading indicated, Cootner never believed market movements were entirely random. "My model is perfectly compatible with much of what I interpret Wall Street chart reading to be all about," he told a financial journalist in the mid-1960s. "Like the Indian folk doctors who discovered tranquilizers, the Wall Street witch doctors, without benefit of the scientific method, have produced something with their magic, even if they can't tell you what it is or how it works."[16] As a scientist, Cootner figured he could beat the witch doctors. At one speech in the 1960s, a Wall Streeter introduced him with the standard anti-economist crack, "If you're so smart, why aren't you rich?" To which Cootner reputedly replied, "If you're so rich, why aren't you smart?"[17]

This summed up the MIT attitude. Yes, the market's movements were hard to predict—if they weren't, any fool could get rich predicting them. But MIT professors weren't fools, and if anyone could beat the market, *they* could. Sloan School professor Sidney Alexander, another member of the soybean-trading crowd, devised a "filter" that bought stocks on the rise and sold those that were dropping. Alexander wrote two papers describing how his filter brought profits greater than could be ascribed to chance, although Chicago's Eugene Fama later pointed out flaws in Alexander's work. Houthakker, who spent a year as a visiting professor at MIT in the midst of the commodity mania, showed that by using stop orders—that is, automatically selling if the price of a futures contract dropped a certain percentage—one could consistently, if barely, beat the market. He also penned a cogent 1961 summary of just what the random walk crowd had proved. "The question whether prices in speculative markets move randomly has so far been answered mostly in the affirmative," he wrote. Then he continued:

It should be realized, however, that randomness can only be defined negatively; namely, as the absence of any systematic pattern. A particular test can detect only a particular pattern or class of patterns, and complete randomness can therefore only be disproved, not proved. The results just mentioned do show that any systematic pattern in price changes is not likely to be obvious or simple.[18]

As Samuelson liked to say, "There are no easy pickings." It was a conclusion most economists and even the more thoughtful stock market speculators could be comfortable with. It did not stand to reason that, just by looking at the past history of stock prices, one could find straightforward, durable ways to make money in the future. Whatever clear patterns did exist would disappear as clever chart-reading traders pounced upon and profited from them. This was the gist of the "random walk hypothesis," a term that appears to have first been used in 1963 by a skeptical economist[19] but was soon adopted by proponents. It was a statement not so much about the correctness of prices or the virtues of markets as about the difficulty of finding free meals on Wall Street.

In 1965, after a decade of talking up his "economic Brownian motion," Samuelson published something on the subject, albeit in an obscure in-house MIT publication. His "Proof that Properly Anticipated Prices Fluctuate Randomly" took an important step beyond the random walk hypothesis. It stated in mathematical form what Holbrook Working had argued in 1948—that randomness was characteristic of a perfectly functioning financial market.

In the finance literature, Samuelson's paper is often cited as the origin of the efficient market hypothesis. This must be chalked up to the now-universal convention in economics and finance that until something is said mathematically, it has not been said at all. Seventeen years before, Holbrook Working had not just posited that randomness and perfect markets went together. He had argued that actual securities markets approached this random ideal. Samuelson claimed nothing of the sort. In classic Samuelsonian fashion, he claimed strikingly little:

> One should not read too much into the established theorem. It does not prove that actual competitive markets work well. It does not say that speculation is a good thing or that randomness of price changes would be a good thing. It does not prove that anyone who makes money in speculation is ipso facto deserving of the gain or even that he has accomplished something good for society or for anyone but himself. All or none of these may be true, but that would require a different investigation.[20]

Samuelson had no interest in conducting this investigation. It just wasn't his style. The next year, he started writing a regular column for *Newsweek*. He was supposed to represent the liberal viewpoint on economic matters, but while he wrote clearly and entertainingly it was often hard to tell which side he was on. That was never a question with Milton Friedman, whom Samuelson helped recruit as his conservative counterpoint in *Newsweek*'s pages.

It was at Friedman's Chicago that the "different investigation" of whether real-world speculative markets got things right was undertaken in the mid to late 1960s. Even before that happened, scholars on multiple campuses were making it clear that, *in theory*, it would be awfully convenient if speculative markets functioned perfectly.

CHAPTER 5

MODIGLIANI AND MILLER ARRIVE AT A SIMPLIFYING ASSUMPTION

Finance, the business school version of economics, is transformed from a field of empirical research and rules of thumb to one ruled by theory.

FOUR YEARS AFTER JOHN VON Neumann and Oskar Morgenstern published their equation-filled guide to weighing potential rewards and losses in an uncertain future, economist Milton Friedman and statistician Jimmie Savage made a startling proposal. With just a few tweaks, they wrote, the von Neumann-Morgenstern utility theory could describe the way real people made economic decisions. At the very least, they argued, "individuals behave *as if* they calculated and compared expected utility and *as if* they knew the odds."

To head off the obvious objection that it was ridiculous to think that regular folks reason according to complex statistical rules, Friedman and Savage argued that billiards players couldn't write down the physics formulas that underlay their shot selections but nonetheless *acted* as if they did.[1] Friedman liked the analogy so much that he reprised it five years later, in a piece called "The Methodology of Positive Economics." This essay became a landmark, the most famous of several similar manifestos produced by mathematically inclined young economists in those days. These papers marked the definitive dismissal from the economic mainstream of the institutionalists and their skepticism of theory.[2]

Friedman was no extremist, at least not in his economic methods. A working-class kid from Rahway, New Jersey, who majored in math at Rutgers and hoped to become an actuary, he had been steered toward economics by two young instructors—one a Chicagoan disciple of Irving Fisher's monetary theories, the other (Arthur Burns) the protégé and eventual successor of institutionalist icon Wesley Mitchell at the National Bureau of Economic Research. Friedman split his grad school years between neoclassical Chicago and the more institutionalist Columbia. After getting his degree he worked for Mitchell at the NBER. And after the Cowles Commission's Tjalling Koopmans published a withering review of Mitchell's last book (a sample: "The movements of economic variables are studied as if they were eruptions of a mysterious volcano whose boiling caldron can never be penetrated."),[3] Friedman defended his former boss as a closet theorist.[4]

Still, when it came time to choose sides, Friedman didn't waffle. Empirical study was important, but theory had to come first. The institutionalists' major criticism of orthodox economic theory had long been that its assumptions were unrealistic, that man was not really "a lightning calculator of pleasures and pains," as Thorstein Veblen put it in 1898.[5] Friedman's gloriously liberating reply in 1953 was, *So what!?*

[T]he relevant question to ask about the "assumptions" of a theory is not whether they are descriptively "realistic," for they never are, but whether they are sufficiently good approximations for the purpose in hand. And this question can be answered only by seeing whether the theory works, which means whether it yields sufficiently accurate predictions.[6]

All scientific theories were unrealistic oversimplifications, Friedman wrote. It was by winnowing the complexity of reality down to patently unrealistic models that science progressed. There was no hard-and-fast rule as to how those models should be built. Sociologists, for example, concentrated on a very different set of human impulses than economists did. But the economists' "single-minded pursuit of pecuniary self-interest," as Friedman characterized it, had been a useful and durable simplifying assumption about human conduct. The controlled experiments of the physical sciences were impractical for social scientists, and going around asking people questions about their economic decisions was "about on par with testing theories of longevity by asking octogenarians how they account for their long life," Friedman wrote. Thus there was but one legitimate way to do economics: Build models based on rational behavior and then test their predictions against actual economic data.

In the late 1940s and early 1950s, there was still some debate over what constituted rational behavior. Friedman and Savage tried to explain, by means of what they called a "wiggly" utility curve, the people who buy both insurance and lottery tickets—behavior not countenanced in the decision-making models of von Neumann and Morgenstern. Herbert Simon of the Carnegie Institute of Technology suggested that real people didn't have the time and mental energy to make probability calculations and instead took mental shortcuts to arrive at choices.[7] French economist Maurice Allais argued that we value certainty, or near certainty, far more than the equations of von Neumann and Morgenstern allowed.[8]

Before long, though, economists tired of the debate. They were busy building models of economic behavior, and Friedman had taught them that closely examining the assumptions behind those models was a waste of time. They already had the statistical man of von Neumann and Morgenstern. Why confuse the picture?

The abstract high point of the economic theorizing enabled by such simplifying assumptions came from two young scholars who had worked at the Cowles Commission, Kenneth Arrow and Gerard Debreu.[9] In one paper written together and in several separate works in the 1950s, the two men rebuilt economic equilibrium theory from the ground up. What has since come to be known as "Arrow-Debreu equilibrium" (or the "Arrow-Debreu framework," the "Arrow-Debreu paradigm," or just plain "Arrow-Debreu") amounted to a mathematical proof of the existence of Adam Smith's invisible hand. This version was far more logically consistent and mathematically sophisticated than its predecessors. Crucially, it made room for economic actors who couldn't see perfectly into the future. What was needed to achieve equilibrium under uncertainty was what Arrow termed a "complete" securities market, in which one could bet on or insure against every possible future state of the world.

No such market existed, of course, and Arrow spent much of the rest of his career exploring ways that economic reality diverged from equilibrium theory. But the excitement generated by Arrow-Debreu and the other big theoretical breakthroughs of the era was contagious. It spread to almost every corner of economics, and even began making itself felt in the recalcitrant discipline of finance.

FINANCE WAS WHAT BUSINESS SCHOOL professors talked about when they talked about money. Until the late 1950s, the discipline's teachings were a mix of common sense, judgment, and tradition that had strikingly little to do with economics. This separation could be traced back to the founding of the leading business school, at Harvard, in 1908. The driving force behind the Harvard Business School's creation was himself an economist, but he was convinced that the new school should emphasize the practical and avoid contact with academics bearing theories. The second dean, who imported the famous "case method" of teaching from Harvard Law School, didn't even have a graduate degree.[10] "I see now why the Business School steers clear of theory," John Burr Williams wrote after getting both an MBA at Harvard's Business School and a Ph.D. from the Economics Department. "[I]t is because the B-School distrusts the theory that is now available."[11]

This distrust became a core principle of business school education, and not just at Harvard. Merton Miller, a young economics professor at the Carnegie Institute of Technology, agreed in exchange for a bigger paycheck to jump to Carnegie Tech's new Business School in the early 1950s. Before he was set loose on the business students, he sat through a class on finance taught in the Harvard case-method style.

When we took up case number one in the case book, I remember being struck that the solution was not obvious to me. After the instructor explained it, however, I said, Yeah. That's right; that makes sense. Then we came to case two, and I said, Okay, I remember how we solved case one, so the answer must be this. And of course, it was different. I couldn't sense any connection from one case to the next. Everything was, as they say on railway tickets, good for this train and this day only. For me, as an economist, it was very frustrating to have no sense of a theory of corporate finance to tie all this material together.[12]

Miller, the recent recipient of a Ph.D. from Johns Hopkins, started thinking about building such a theory. He was at the perfect place to do so. Carnegie Tech's Graduate School of Industrial Administration (GSIA)—established in 1949 with a $6 million grant from a member of the Mellon family—was a new kind of business school. Carnegie Tech (renamed Carnegie-Mellon University in 1967) had revamped its engineering programs in the 1940s to emphasize scientific and mathematical rigor over rule-of-thumb trade school instruction, and the plan was to do the same thing for management education. The Business School hired promising young economists, operations research experts, and behavioral scientists and set them loose on what was initially a tiny student body.

This pedagogy was a mixed blessing for master's-degree students, as the near-exclusive focus on theory sometimes left them flailing in the real world. "You look around wildly for something to program linearly, or perhaps a game theory situation," joked one 1953 alumnus about his post-Carnegie experience in small business. "You know that the cat on the hot tin roof has nothing on you."[13] But for the faculty, and the handful of students who stayed on for doctorates, the Carnegie GSIA was a spectacularly stimulating environment. The most stimulating faculty member of all was Herbert Simon, mentioned already as a skeptic of the von Neumann-Morgenstern utility theory. Simon soon despaired of gaining acceptance among economists for his ideas about "bounded rationality," and moved into psychology and computer science. It was thus left to two more conventional economists on the Carnegie faculty to remake the study of finance in the image of modern mathematical economics.

One was Miller. The other was Franco Modigliani, an Italian who after emigrating to the United States in 1939 studied with Jacob Marschak at the New School. They were an odd couple. Miller's politics leaned to the right, Modigliani's to the left. Miller was loyal to whatever team he associated himself with—be it the new finance he helped pioneer or, after he moved to the University of Chicago in 1961, the Chicago Bears. Modigliani's allegiances were difficult to parse. Years later, he even claimed that the two world-changing papers he wrote with Miller were "written with tongue in cheek, to really make fun of my colleagues."[14] What Modigliani and Miller did share was a belief that building mathematical models based on rational behavior was what economists did. They thought finance professors should do the same thing.

The question they took on together at Carnegie Tech was central to the study of corporate finance: How was a corporation to decide if an investment was worth pursuing? The practical approach, pioneered at chemical manufacturer DuPont in the second decade of the century, was to compare the expected rate of return on the investment to the "economic cost of capital" needed to finance it.[15] By the 1950s, this approach to capital budgeting was part of every business school's curriculum. There was a catch, though. Nobody really knew what the "economic cost of capital" was. The standard practice was to take the rate of interest the company paid on its bonds and then add a risk premium of a percentage point or two or three or four to account for the uncertainty of the investment. The choice of that risk premium was almost entirely arbitrary.

As a macroeconomist, Modigliani had been puzzling over this matter because corporate decisions about whether to hoard money or invest it in future growth affect the business cycle. Together with Miller he came up with a straightforward plan of intellectual attack: Assume that all the firm's owners, and all its potential owners, know what they are doing. "Under this approach," they wrote in 1958, "any investment project and its concomitant financing plan must pass only the following test: Will the project, as financed, raise the value of the firm's shares? If so, it is worth undertaking; if not, its return is less than the marginal cost of capital to the firm."

Conceptually this was a brilliant line of attack. Its practical implications were murkier. How was a company supposed to know ahead of time how the stock market would react to a new investment project? Modigliani and Miller never came up with an answer to that. Just asking the question, though, brought some dramatic insights.

First, it led Modigliani and Miller to conclude that it was irrelevant where a company got its money—whether by issuing bonds, selling shares, or reinvesting earnings. Their "proof " of this conclusion was that if two companies with identical earnings but different capital structures didn't command the same market price, "an investor could buy and sell stocks and bonds in such a way as to exchange one income stream for another stream, identical in all relevant respects but selling at a lower price."[16] If investors were the rational profit seekers of economic theory, that just couldn't happen. And Modigliani and Miller clearly believed that investors *were* rational, or at least close enough for their purposes.

It was a striking demonstration of how much the experience of the 1929 crash and subsequent Great Depression had already faded from memory. Yes, "speculative bubbles have actually arisen in the past," Modigliani and Miller wrote in another landmark paper three years later, but they "do not seem to us to be a dominant, or even a fundamental, feature of actual market behavior under uncertainty." As a result, they concluded, assuming that investors behave in a rational manner was "useful, at least as a first approximation, for the analysis of long-run tendencies in organized markets."[17]

In this second paper, Modigliani and Miller claimed that it was irrelevant to shareholders whether corporations paid out their leftover cash in dividends or held on to it. This was in some ways an even more radical claim than their initial argument that capital structure didn't matter. John Burr Williams had proposed that a stock was worth the discounted value of future dividends—not earnings, he emphasized, but dividends. Benjamin Graham and David Dodd, in their famous guide to value investing, argued that given two otherwise equivalent companies, "the one paying the larger dividend will always sell at the higher price."[18] Modigliani and Miller countered that in a "rational and perfect economic environment," stock prices "are determined solely by 'real' considerations—in this case the earning power of the firm's assets and its investment policy—and not by how the fruits of the earning power are 'packaged' for distribution."

This was the second of what came to be known as the "M&M propositions," which went on to have as great an impact on the study of finance as any pair of academic papers have ever had in any discipline. The first says it doesn't matter how a company raises its money, and the second says it doesn't matter whether it gives the money to shareholders. "The great thing about M&M," University of Chicago professor James Lorie would jokingly tell his students in the 1970s, "is that nothing really matters."[19] Miller himself explained the papers' significance like this: "The pizza delivery man comes to Yogi Berra after the game and says, Yogi, how do you want this pizza cut, into quarters or eighths? Yogi says, cut it into eight pieces. I'm feeling hungry tonight."[20]

The M&M propositions were thus either breathtakingly bold or trivially obvious—or both. Their greatest significance was that they made it acceptable to wield deductive logic in the study of finance. For older finance professors who had devoted their careers to empirical examinations of corporate behavior, this development was profoundly disturbing. Both M&M articles generated impassioned critiques, giving Modigliani and Miller the opportunity to respond in print—getting their arguments even more attention.

Those arguments proved compelling to younger scholars without a vested interest in the old ways of finance. They offered a systematic, logical way of studying financial problems at a time when systems and logic were in vogue. They also offered the promise that theory-wielding academics could one day tell executives what to do. That they eventually did. The M&M papers were precursors to the practical philosophy that decades later came to be known as "shareholder value" (dubbed that by a business school professor, of course). Just do what makes shareholders happy, M&M were saying, and you were doing the right thing as a corporate manager.

FOR ALL THAT, MODIGLIANI AND Miller never figured out how to calculate the cost of capital. That question, they wrote in 1958, "must be deferred to a subsequent paper." When Jack Treynor read these words in the library of the University of Denver in the summer of 1958, he sniffed opportunity.

Treynor was staying at his parents' Colorado vacation cabin on a break from his job with the Cambridge, Massachusetts, consulting firm Arthur D. Little. "Little's," as Treynor called it, aimed to be to management consulting what Carnegie Tech's Graduate School of Industrial Administration was to business schools. After World War II the firm, known mainly for its chemical engineering expertise, launched an operations research division to apply scientific methods to business questions. Treynor, a 1955 Harvard Business School grad with an undergraduate math background, ended up there. He started out programming computers but was soon working on financial consulting projects. He used cost-of-capital calculations in his work, and was not at all satisfied with the standard practice of arbitrarily adding percentage points to the bond interest rate. "That bothered me," Treynor recalled. "These projects often had a thirty-year life. By changing the discount rate one percent, you could make it a go or a no go. This clearly wasn't a very satisfactory answer."

What was needed to calculate the cost of capital was a theory of asset prices. As defined by Modigliani and Miller, a firm's cost of capital was the opportunity cost of *not* putting money into the shares of a different firm in the "equivalent return" class. They never really defined what that was supposed to mean.

It had long been argued that investment returns were a reward for taking risks. In the parable of the talents in the Gospel of Matthew, two servants who take intelligent risks with money their master has given them are rewarded, while one who buries the money in the ground because he is afraid of losing it is fiercely punished.[21] Later, in the sixteenth and seventeenth centuries, canon lawyers helped clear the way for the rise of capitalism by arguing that money lenders weren't violating the Bible's injunction against usury because the interest they received amounted to a payment for taking on risk.[22]

This risk-reward relationship made frequent appearances in economics through the centuries. While it was apparent that risk and return were related, it was equally apparent that some risks were rewarded more generously than others. Running across a busy freeway is certainly risky, but who's going to pay you to do it? Frank Knight, a leading figure in the University of Chicago Economics Department of the interwar years, addressed this question in his 1921 book, *Risk, Uncertainty, and Profit*. He concluded that you couldn't get paid just for taking a *risk*, because risk was a measurable quantity that could be insured against. Profit came when you proceeded in the face of *uncertainty*. This distinction has many merits, but Knight was proposing to throw out something that could be measured and replace it with something that couldn't—no help at all to someone trying to calculate the cost of capital.

Treynor looked instead to the work of the person who had gone to the greatest lengths yet to quantify investment risk, Harry Markowitz.[23] Markowitz's portfolio theory was meant to guide optimal decision making by investors, not to describe actual investor behavior. But if one took it as a description of investor behavior, it pointed in the direction of a useful and seemingly sensible answer to the question of what determined asset prices. The risk that mattered most was the market's risk, Treynor concluded, so investors should receive a risk premium on an asset "proportional to the covariance of the investment with the total value of all the investments in the market."[24] That is, the relevant risk was how sensitive a particular investment was to the movements of the total market. The more sensitive it was, the higher the premium. Just as in Frank Knight's theory, one was rewarded for taking risks that were impossible to diversify or insure away. But in Treynor's version these risks could be measured.

Treynor showed an early version of his work to the only academic economist he knew, John Lintner of nearby Harvard Business School. Lintner was dismissive, but a copy of the paper found its way through other channels (and without Treynor's knowledge) to Modigliani, who in 1960 had moved from Carnegie Tech to MIT. Modigliani read the paper, and invited Treynor to study economics and finance with him, which Treynor did for six months in 1962. While at MIT he further elaborated his theory of asset pricing, but he never submitted it for publication. For one thing, he thought there were other risk factors besides covariance that he needed to nail down. For another, he had to go back to work at Arthur D. Little. It was left to an assistant professor on the other side of the country to unveil what came to be known as the "capital asset pricing model." He too arrived at it by way of Harry Markowitz.

• • •

AFTER WRITING HIS BOOK ON portfolio selection, Markowitz had gone back to RAND, where he devised a computer simulation language, SIMSCRIPT, which is still in use today. And he forgot, for a while, about finance. Then, one day in 1960, William Sharpe presented himself at Markowitz's office door. Sharpe was a RAND staffer and economics doctoral student at the University of California at Los Angeles. UCLA was such a haven for rigorous, mathematical, operations researchy economics that it was sometimes hard to tell where the university left off and where the temple of operations research that was RAND, just down Wilshire Boulevard in Santa Monica, began. Sharpe was working on a dissertation and getting nowhere on it. He began searching for a new topic, and a UCLA professor who knew Markowitz brought the two together. Markowitz warmed to the affable young man, and he soon suggested a research project for him.

Markowitz's approach to portfolio selection had called for calculating the covariances of every security—how the members of each possible pair were expected to move in relation to each other. Even with the rapid advances in computing since 1952, this task was monumental. Calculating a single portfolio could eat up tens of thousands of dollars in computer time. Markowitz put Sharpe to work devising a simplified system. Sharpe came up with a measure of the covariance between an individual security and the stock market as a whole—rather than comparing each separate security to every other security as Markowitz's model had. It was, Sharpe wrote, the simplest model of the market he could build "without assuming away the existence of interrelationships among securities." What's more, he added, "there is considerable evidence that it can capture a large part of such interrelationships."[25]

This research became the first part of Sharpe's doctoral thesis, and it was later published as an article in the operations research journal *Management Science.* A one-hundred-security analysis that took thirty-three minutes on an IBM 7090 using Markowitz's methods needed only thirty seconds Sharpe's way. There was another gain from the new technique: Almost everyone who had considered diversification before Markowitz assumed that the risks of different securities were independent from each other. In *The Theory of Investment Value*, John Burr Williams wrote that he didn't consider risk in his calculations because he assumed that any prudent investor would be so well diversified that the riskiness of individual securities didn't matter. Markowitz didn't think this assumption could be right, but it was nonetheless possible under his approach to assemble a portfolio of stocks with covariances that added up to no risk at all. With Sharpe's model, there was simply no way to get risk down to zero while owning stocks.

For Markowitz, that was the end of the story. A better, simpler method had been devised for selecting portfolios. But Sharpe had a dissertation to write. "I said, well, what if everyone does what Markowitz says they should do," he recalled. "What does that tell us about equilibrium?" From that assumption, Sharpe derived a theory of asset pricing nearly identical to Jack Treynor's. Money is worth more to a person when nobody else has any, so a security that doesn't drop as much as the overall market when times are bad is a valuable thing. It is so valuable, Sharpe reasoned, that rational investors would be willing to pay more for it (and thus accept lower long-term returns from it) than for a security that bounced around more than the market. The measure of a security's covariance with the market that Sharpe had devised in conjunction with Markowitz thus became the key to investment returns. In his dissertation, Sharpe represented it in equations with the capital letter B, which other scholars later transmuted into the Greek letter "beta."

When Sharpe submitted a paper outlining this asset pricing theory to the *Journal of Finance*, the reception was chilly. One reviewer objected that the underlying assumptions about investor behavior were absurdly unrealistic. Sharpe stubbornly resubmitted the piece, writing a letter that cited Milton Friedman's "Methodology of Positive Economics" and argued that it was the implications of his theory that mattered, not the assumptions. "I've since come to think that maybe that was a little extreme and the question was *which* implications," said Sharpe later. "But at least I made the argument that if this really does tell us something about expected returns, it's worth considering." The journal had changed editors in the interim. This time Sharpe's paper was accepted, and published in September 1964.[26]

In a footnote to the published article, Sharpe mentioned that after finishing it he had seen a draft of Treynor's similar but unpublished work. In 1965, Harvard Business School's John Lintner unveiled his own version of the capital asset pricing model. Lintner had a Ph.D. from Harvard's Economics Department, and was hired at HBS in the 1940s over the objections of some of the school's anti-theorist old guard. He did his best to fit in, becoming an outspoken critic of economics-based theories of corporate behavior like those of Modigliani and Miller. After talking to Jack Treynor about his asset pricing ideas, Lintner set out to show why Treynor was wrong. The idiosyncratic risks of individual companies did matter, Lintner believed, and so did the differing opinions of individual investors. But as he assembled equations to represent his arguments, the individual risks and opinions Lintner thought were so important kept canceling each other out, leaving his model dependent on a single measure of risk similar to that used by Treynor and Sharpe.[27] A year later, Jan Mossin of the Norwegian School of Economics and Business Administration, who studied at Carnegie Tech, followed with yet another derivation of the asset pricing model that connoisseurs claim is the most elegant of the lot.[28]

Four different scholars, all coming from different directions, arrived at the same grand theory of asset prices. Clearly, there was something to it—in theory. But would it hold up on the stock market floor?

CHAPTER 6

GENE FAMA MAKES THE BEST PROPOSITION IN ECONOMICS

At the University of Chicago's Business School in the 1960s, the argument that the market is hard to outsmart grows into a conviction that it is perfect.

IN THE 1960S, THE UNIVERSITY of Chicago was a lonely outpost. Its Hyde Park campus was a thousand miles from its chief East Coast rivals, hemmed in by the disintegrating, crime-plagued South Side. "This is a Fort Dearborn situation," declared a character in Saul Bellow's Hyde Park novel *Humboldt's Gift*. "And only the redskins have the guns and tomahawks."[1]

The economists at Chicago saw their isolation and even embattlement in a more positive light. They inhabited a different intellectual world from their counterparts at MIT, Harvard, Berkeley, and Stanford, and they were glad. The Chicagoans used pretty much the same theoretical tools that had swept the rest of the profession in the 1950s—albeit with somewhat less mathematical fervor after the Cowles Commission decamped for Yale in 1955—but they wielded them to different ends.

Years later, in an attempt to define what set Chicago economics apart, Chicago's Melvin Reder wrote that he and his colleagues believed in "tight prior equilibrium," while economists at other universities subscribed to "diffuse prior equilibrium."[2] What Reder meant with those infelicitous phrases was that Chicagoans attacked almost every economic problem with the starting assumption that, absent interference from the government, the market got things right. Their counterparts at other universities weren't so sure. Put another way, most economists of the day saw government as the solution to economic problems, while the Chicagoans were convinced that government was the problem.

The shorthand account of this divide involves a group of friends who studied together in Chicago in the 1930s and went to work in New Deal Washington, where they became disillusioned with government attempts to manage the economy. They returned to Chicago in the 1940s and 1950s to impose an indelibly libertarian stamp upon the place. Chief among them were Milton Friedman, his friend George Stigler, and his brother-in-law Aaron Director. Statistics professor W. Allen Wallis played a role too, although more as an administrator than a crusader.

Both Friedman and Stigler later said that the crucial turning point in their thinking came when they read Friedrich Hayek's *The Road to Serfdom*. Hayek had studied economics in Vienna in the 1920s and moved in 1931 to the London School of Economics—an originally socialist institution that had become a bastion of free market thought. During the war, LSE shifted its operations to Cambridge, where Hayek and John Maynard Keynes shared air raid warden shifts, became friends, and talked politics. Having experienced the socialist "Red Vienna" of the 1920s and watched the Nazi takeover of his homeland from afar, Hayek was appalled by the equanimity, even enthusiasm, with which Keynes and other English liberal intellectuals greeted the growth of government.

Hayek wrote *The Road to Serfdom* with a British academic audience in mind, and in Britain it did not penetrate much beyond that audience. At the urging of Director—who had gotten to know Hayek during a year spent at LSE—the University of Chicago Press published the book in the United States. It became a sensation, especially after *Reader's Digest* printed a condensed version in May 1945.

For decades, the political right in America had been a territory populated by rubes and businessmen. As Columbia English professor and literary critic Lionel Trilling put it, liberalism had become "not only the dominant but even the sole intellectual tradition" in the United States.[3] Yet here was an urbane intellectual arguing that the seemingly inexorable trend toward more government control of the economy was not just unnecessary but a mortal threat to freedom. It was a worldview-shifting revelation. For many others it was Ayn Rand's 1943 bestseller *The Fountainhead* that had this effect, but economists understandably gravitated toward one of their own.

Subsequent events did not play out quite as Hayek warned in his book. "It is a fair reading of *The Road to Serfdom* to say that forty years more of the march toward socialism would lead to major losses of the political and economic freedom of individuals," Stigler wrote in 1988. "Yet in those forty years we have seen that continuous expansion of the state in Sweden and England, even in Canada and the United States, without consequences for personal freedom so dire as predicted."[4] Hayek soon put forward another argument that has held up far better—and was more directly applicable to the work of economists.

The problem with any government attempt to manage the economy, he wrote in a 1945 article titled "The Use of Knowledge in Society," is that there is no way for those in charge to know all that they need to know to do the job well. The knowledge required to make an economy run "never exists in concentrated or integrated form, but solely as the dispersed bits of incomplete and frequently contradictory knowledge which all the separate individuals possess," Hayek wrote. A shipper or a real estate agent or a commodities broker acts on "special knowledge of circumstances of the fleeting moment" that a government planner could never match.[5] The way that all these salt-of-the-earth types communicated their "special knowledge" to one another was through *prices*. Any attempt to regulate prices or business activity was doomed to thwart the movement of knowledge needed to make the economy run smoothly.

In 1947, Hayek organized a meeting of like-minded intellectuals from Europe and the United States. Friedman, Stigler, and Director all made the trip to the Mont Pelerin Hotel, on a hill overlooking Lake Geneva in Switzerland. "Liberals," they all called themselves, sticking to the nineteenth-century, pro-laissez-faire definition that was already being expropriated in the United States by the Left. Libertarians is what we would call them today.

Friedman later wrote that the Mont Pelerin meeting was "the beginning of my active involvement with the political process."[6] He had returned to Chicago to teach the year before, as had Director. Stigler made it a decade later. Hayek also moved to Chicago, but never really joined the "Chicago school" of economics he helped spawn. Instead it was Friedman who took the leading role. He built his reputation among his peers with theoretical work, as well as his famous methodology essay. But as the 1950s progressed he increasingly focused on issues of public policy.

While working in Paris for a few months in 1950 consulting for the U.S. agency that administered the Marshall Plan, Friedman wrote a memo that recommended ditching the Bretton Woods system of fixed currency exchange rates (devised in part by John Maynard Keynes, who had been almost ruined trading currencies in 1920). Friedman argued that free currency markets would not be the dens of speculative excess they were so often feared to be. "People who argue that speculation is generally destabilizing seldom realize that this is largely equivalent to saying that speculators lose money," he wrote, "since speculation can be destabilizing in general only if speculators on the average sell when the currency is low in price and buy when it is high."[7] As Friedman put it later, "It just seemed to me sensible that the only way you could make money was by buying low and selling high, and not the other way around. And if that's the case, then people who destabilize the market lose their shirt, and so they aren't going to be around for long."

The argument was presented without any empirical backup. Holbrook Working, remember, had found two decades before that speculators in agricultural futures markets did lose money. But along with a 1950 piece published in Chicago's *Journal of Political Economy* by UCLA's Armen Alchian, Friedman's currency paper staked out the intellectual territory to be occupied later by those who termed the market "efficient." Alchian's argument was even broader than Friedman's, applying not just to currency markets but all markets. "Those who realize *positive profits* are the survivors; those who suffer losses disappear," he wrote. The social Darwinistic overtones were no mistake: Alchian titled his piece "Uncertainty, Evolution and Economic Theory."[8] Not entirely coincidentally, *What the Social Classes Owe to Each Other* by William Graham Sumner, the social Darwinist Yale professor who had propelled Irving Fisher into economics, was republished in 1951. Ideas and attitudes that had lain dormant for decades were beginning their return to respectability.

Friedman soon became one of the most visible apostles of this revival. Two works published in the early 1960s established his reputation. His monumental *Monetary History of the United States, 1857–1960*—coauthored with economic historian Anna Schwartz and sponsored by the National Bureau of Economic Research—resurrected Irving Fisher's "dance of the dollar" as the chief explanation of business fluctuations and made the case that the Depression was not a natural outgrowth of industrial capitalism but the result of a massive screwup by the Federal Reserve. Then there was *Capitalism and Freedom*, a compilation of lectures that heralded the arrival of a bracing new voice on the broader American intellectual scene. "The great advantages of civilization, whether in architecture or painting, in science or literature, have never come from centralized government," Friedman began, before tossing out such incendiary proposals as abolishing the military draft and Social Security and replacing direct public funding of schools with vouchers.

Like Irving Fisher, whom he termed "my favorite economist," Friedman was moving away from equations and abstractions to address the general public on issues close to his heart. Unlike Fisher, he didn't come across as a nutty preacher. Sure, his policy arguments appalled some of his fellow economists. "Friedman is driven by the idea that whatever the government does is bad," scoffed Franco Modigliani.[9] But they left a deep impression on his students at Chicago. Taking a class with Friedman—a charming, friendly, even-tempered little man saying *outrageous* things—was often a life-changing event. "For many of us, the shock wave of Friedman's libertarian-conservative ideas forced a rethinking of our whole social philosophy," recalled economist and Friedman student Robert Lucas. "I tried to hold on to my New Deal politics, and remember voting for Kennedy in 1960 . . . But however we voted, Friedman's students came away with the sense that we had acquired a powerful apparatus for thinking about economic and social questions."[10]

STUDENTS AT CHICAGO'S GRADUATE SCHOOL of Business could take Friedman's economics classes, too, and it was testament to the interdisciplinary charm of the university that they did, in great numbers. As the 1960s progressed, though, one began to hear even bolder promarket arguments than Friedman's at the Business School itself. Friedman believed markets worked better than government. Some of Chicago's finance professors and their students came to believe that markets were *perfect*.

Chicago's Business School was founded in 1898, a decade before Harvard's, and it had never employed Harvard's approach to business education. The university prided itself on its origins as a research institution, not a training school for ministers like its Ivy League rivals. The Business School had always seen itself in the same light.

Its professors were meant to do original research, and to teach what they'd learned. It was the first Business School to grant doctorates. As Carnegie Tech and MIT broke new ground in business education and the Chicago Economics Department rose in prominence, though, Chicago's Business School fell behind. By the mid-1950s it was, in the judgment of then-professor James Lorie, "almost moribund."

In 1956, Lorie, who had been teaching marketing at Chicago since earning his doctorate there eight years before, was asked to help turn the school around. He was named associate dean of the Business School; W. Allen Wallis became the dean. The first act of the Wallis-Lorie regime was to ask the university for more money, which it got. The Ford Foundation, in the midst of a $35 million campaign to reform business education along the lines pioneered by Carnegie Tech, chipped in. Then the hiring began.

George Stigler was the first big catch, in 1958. Stigler had been at Columbia for a decade, and had made a name for himself exploring how information was disseminated through prices and how regulation created mixed-up incentives. While never the public figure that Friedman was, Stigler was if anything even more devoted than his old friend to the idea that markets got things right. "He came very close to being a Panglossian," said one early-1960s Chicago graduate student. "The story is that someone was walking across the Chicago campus with Stigler and said, 'There's a $20 bill.' Stigler replied, 'No, if it were a real $20 bill it would have been picked up already.' Stigler really did believe that."[11] (This joke is now applied generically to all economists.)

Stigler had only one foot in the Business School—his salary was split with the Economics Department. It was in 1961, the year Wallis and Lorie lured Merton Miller from Carnegie Tech, when the new era of business education at Chicago began. Miller brought his new amalgam of economics and finance, and combative tone. During a finance class one day in the early 1960s, he drew a vertical line on the blackboard, wrote "M&M" as a heading to the left of the line and "T" to the right. A student raised his hand and asked what the *T* stood for. "'Them,' Miller responded," the student recalled forty years later. "He was always at war with 'them.'"[12]

Such professors, and the chance to take economics classes with the increasingly famous Friedman, began attracting more and better students to the Business School. The most significant early arrival was Eugene Fama, an intense young alumnus (the first college graduate in his family) of Tufts University. Fama arrived at Chicago as an MBA student in 1960—steered there by professors who thought he was too intellectual for Harvard Business School. At Tufts, Fama had crunched numbers for a stock market newsletter published by one of his professors. He found lots of interesting patterns in stock prices, but noticed that they tended to disappear as soon as he had identified them. With this experience he gravitated toward the random walk work begun by statistics professor Harry Roberts. He also hooked up with wandering IBM mathematician Benoit Mandelbrot. His first published work was a Mandelbrot-guided exploration of the statistical distribution of stock price changes.

Fama stayed on for his doctorate, and under the influence of the newly arrived Miller he began to steer a course away from purely statistical work toward a research program shaped by economic theory. He still devoted the bulk of his 1964 doctoral dissertation, which was reprinted in full in the Business School's quarterly *Journal of Business*, to Mandelbrot's statistical ideas, but that wasn't the part to which people paid attention. What they read—especially after abridged versions appeared in the *Financial Analysts Journal* and *Institutional Investor*, two publications aimed at Wall Street practitioners—was the opening salvo in which Fama laid out the clearest explanation yet of why stock price movements should be random.

It was not that news relevant to stock prices could be relied upon to occur randomly, Fama wrote, or that investors' opinions were randomly distributed along a bell curve. Sometimes news would come in bursts, and investors would behave like sheep. But Fama argued that "sophisticated traders"—chart readers and fundamentalists alike—could be relied upon to attack any nonrandom patterns in the market and, in the process of making money off them, make them go away. That meant any chart-reading successes were of necessity fleeting, Fama wrote. This was not necessarily true of what he called "superior intrinsic-value analysis":

> In a dynamic economy there will always be new information which causes intrinsic values to change over time. As a result, people who can consistently predict the appearance of *new* information *and* evaluate its effects on intrinsic values will usually make larger profits than can people who do not have this talent.[13]

If there were enough of these "superior" analysts, though, their existence would "insure that actual market prices are, on the basis of all *available* information, best estimates of intrinsic values." Fama gave to this state of affairs the name "efficient market"—a term that, while used before in economics to denote a market in good working order, had never been defined quite this way. "In an efficient market," he wrote, "the actions of the many competing participants should cause the actual price of a security to wander randomly about its intrinsic value."[14] Just how *far* security prices wandered from those intrinsic values remained an important topic for further research. And Chicago's Business School was in the early 1960s assembling a database that would make the university the center of such research for years to come.

IT BEGAN WITH A PHONE call from Chicago alumnus Louis Engel, the head of advertising and marketing for Merrill Lynch. Engel was a former managing editor of *BusinessWeek* whose first significant act after joining Merrill in 1946 was to compose one of the great print advertisements of all time. Titled "What everybody ought to know . . . About This Stock and Bond Business," it ran more than six thousand words and took up a full page in the *New York Times*. It was a plainspoken soft sell that answered questions such as "What Do Stocks Cost?" and "How Do You Do Business with a Broker?" without mentioning Merrill Lynch until the very end. Four thousand inquiries came in the week the ad ran.[15] The ad also caught the eye of a publisher, who asked Engel to make a book out of it. He did, and *How to Buy Stocks* sold more than four million copies before his death in 1982.[16]

In 1960, Engel had an idea for an ad asserting that common stocks were an appropriate investment for regular folks. The Securities and Exchange Commission told Engel he couldn't make such a claim without evidence to back it up. He called the Chicago Business School for advice, and got Lorie on the phone. After discussing the matter with a few colleagues, Lorie concluded that a study of long-run stock returns along the lines of what Alfred Cowles had compiled in 1939 was in order. Engel agreed.

Lorie appointed himself director of the new Merrill-funded Center for Research on Security Prices, which soon came to be known almost exclusively by its acronym, CRSP (pronounced "crisp"). He chose as his number two Lawrence Fisher, an assistant finance professor with a Chicago economics degree and a reputation for being detail oriented, perhaps overly so. Fisher set to work compiling thirty-five years of price and dividend data on every stock ever traded on the New York Stock Exchange. It was an epic task, and it took more than three years of sleuthing, data entry, and fact checking to complete.[17]

What Fisher and Lorie reported in January 1964 was that someone who had bought all the stocks in the New York Stock Exchange every year from 1926 through 1960 and reinvested the dividends would have earned an average return—after brokerage commissions but before taxes—of 9 percent. This was no longer 1939, when Alfred Cowles reported similarly good news about stock returns and nobody listened. Wall Street had again caught the nation's fancy, and the Fisher-Lorie study got lots of attention. Unlike Edgar Lawrence Smith in 1924, Fisher and Lorie openly embraced the possibility that those 9 percent annual returns could be attained by monkeys with darts. The next year they even demonstrated it, randomly generating assorted portfolios that all performed well. "There is no evidence that mutual funds select stocks better than by the random method," Lorie said in May 1965.[18]

Up to this point, talk of the random walk had barely penetrated the national consciousness; it was just too mathematical and too arcane. But the demonstration that a dart thrower could obtain stock market returns of the sort that mutual funds crowed about was a revelation. *BusinessWeek* reported:

> For a sizable area of Wall Street—mutual funds, security analysts, investment advisers, and the like—the study should prove unsettling. Everybody in this area makes his money, to one degree or another, by selling his skill to less expert investors. Now, the Chicago study says that a random investment, one where no skill at all is applied, will prove profitable most of the time.[19]

Back on campus, the greatest significance of Fisher and Lorie's work was that it was all on computer tape. The first truly usable computers had begun arriving in university basements around 1960. At Chicago, it was an IBM 709. At first, "there was nobody else using it," Eugene Fama recalled. "It was me and a guy in the Physics Department." But that soon changed. The unspeakable drudgery of crunching numbers by hand was replaced with the far more manageable drudgery of programming a computer to do so, and stock market research quickly became a more attractive, popular pursuit. Arnold Moore, a Chicago grad student who had spent months gathering and manually crunching stock price data for his dissertation before leaving in 1960 with it still incomplete, got a call not long afterward from Fama. "You know, people are getting computers and putting all this data in them," Fama told him. "Somebody's going to do your dissertation in an afternoon if you don't hurry up."[20]

By the time Fama finished *his* dissertation, in 1964, and was asked to stay on as an assistant professor, a whole crowd of quantitatively minded, computer-savvy students was beginning to make waves. The ones who were to attain the most prominence were Michael Jensen, Myron Scholes, and Richard Roll.

Jensen and Scholes both enrolled in the Chicago MBA program in autumn 1962. Jensen was the son of a printer at the *Minneapolis Star-Tribune*, and had put himself through Macalester College by working a daily shift in a print shop. After trying and failing to get in to Harvard Business School, he got a Chicago scholarship and headed south with no real idea what was in store for him (other than a night-shift printing job at the *Chicago Tribune*). Scholes was an economics major from Ontario who was trying to delay going to work in his uncle's publishing business. He chose Chicago for the chance to take classes with Friedman and Stigler. Both men stayed on to get doctorates, and in 1964 their duo became a trio with the arrival of Roll. A bona fide rocket scientist, originally from Alabama, Roll had been sent to business school at the University of Washington by his employer, Boeing. His analytical skills so impressed one of his finance professors there that the man packed him off to Chicago to get a doctorate.

Roll already knew his way around a computer, and he got a job as Fisher's assistant at CRSP; Scholes and Jensen soon got up to speed as well. At another time, in another place, such skills and access to hitherto unavailable stock market data would have been put to use looking for ways to get rich. As this was the University of Chicago in the 1960s, they saw their goal instead as demonstrating how well the market worked. Most of the early random walk research had been aimed at puncturing the pretensions of the chartists. Now the investigation moved on to the deeper question of whether *any* information was enough to beat the market.

In 1967 Harry Roberts, the man who had launched Chicago's random walk effort, proposed that his colleagues sort out just what they meant by an efficient market. He suggested a taxonomy later refined by Fama. "Weak" efficiency was the old random walk hypothesis: You couldn't expect to beat the market using data on the market's past movements. "Semi-strong" efficiency meant that you couldn't beat it using any publicly available information. And "strong" efficiency described a market so perfect that even investors with access to private information couldn't outsmart it.

The Chicagoans were satisfied that weak-form market efficiency had been pretty well proven. When American University Ph.D. student Robert Levy begged to differ in the pages of the *Financial Analysts Journal* in 1967—claiming success for the "relative strength" method of piling in to stocks that have been doing markedly better than others in their peer group[21]—Jensen was dispatched to bat down his claims. This he did only partially, admitting that he could "not entirely explain all of Levy's results."[22] In a revealing glimpse into the Chicago worldview, Jensen wrote that if you tested enough different trading rules against the historical stock price data, you'd be sure to find some that beat the market. "But, and this is the crucial question, does this mean the same trading rule will yield superior profits when actually put into practice?" he continued. "Of course not."[23]

THE CONVICTION OF THE CHICAGOANS that the stock market approached a random sort of perfection only grew as the decade wore on. At first Lorie struggled to get scholars interested in using the market data that he and Fisher had collected at CRSP and asked his Chicago colleagues for help. Fama suggested to Jensen and Roll that they use the database to test how quickly the market reacted to new information. Together with Fisher, the trio examined price movements before and after stock split announcements. Stock splits were thought to signal management's optimism and often preceded dividend increases. The Chicago team found that markets usually sniffed out this optimism well before the split was announced publicly.[24] This approach became known as the "event study," and a subsequent one cooked up in a Chicago accounting workshop made the efficient markets case even more clearly. It concluded that 85 percent to 90 percent of the news in annual corporate earnings reports had already found its way into prices—through spadework by analysts, educated guesses by investors, and perhaps some trading by corporate insiders—*before* the reports were released.[25]

The event study became a staple of Chicago-style finance, with thousands of such examinations establishing beyond any reasonable doubt that yes, financial markets did a spectacular job of reflecting and transmitting new information—even well-hidden new information—by means of prices. Friedrich Hayek had made this case in 1946 for markets in general. He seems to have been on to something.

Ignored in all the excitement over event studies, though, was something that anyone with experience of the market knew well—that price movements also sometimes reflected false information, incorrect interpretation, and plain old mood swings. "Wall Street discounts the future," Charles Dow had written in 1899, "but its ablest leaders often get wrong by being too far ahead of the public."[26] This tendency would not show up in an event study. It required a "nonevent study," and the very assumption of efficient markets precluded that. If the market moved for no apparent reason, then it had to mean the market knew something that the researcher investigating it did not.

For his doctoral dissertation, Jensen settled upon another way of testing the efficiency of the market: measuring the performance of mutual funds. This had already been done in 1962 by a Wharton School team, which found that stock mutual funds as a group failed to keep up with the S&P 500.[27] Jensen had a new tool at his disposal: the relationship between market risk and return explored in the capital asset pricing papers published by Bill Sharpe in 1964 and John Lintner in 1965.

Jensen examined the performance of more than one hundred

mutual funds, and found that their returns, when adjusted for risk, significantly trailed those of the market. If one ignored all the fees and expenses charged by mutual funds and their brokers, the funds' performance looked a little less dismal, but it was still no better on a risk-adjusted basis than the market's. All the skill of the mutual fund managers and analysts, and all the money they spent gathering information, could only get them to par. Marveled Jensen:

> One must realize that these analysts are extremely well endowed. Moreover, they operate in the securities markets every day and have wide-ranging contacts and associations in both the business and the financial communities. Thus, the fact that they are apparently unable to forecast returns accurately enough to recover their research and transactions costs is a striking piece of evidence in favor of the strong form of the [efficient market] hypothesis.[28]

Following the precedent set by Fama a few years before, Jensen's thesis was published in full in the pages of Chicago's *Journal of Business* in 1969. Richard Roll did Jensen one better; his "Application of the Efficient Market Model to U.S. Treasury Bills" won the Irving Fisher prize for best economics dissertation in the nation. It was published as a book, complete with an admiring introduction by Paul Samuelson. "I was totally dumbfounded when that happened, because I wasn't even an economist," said Roll.

After years of looking down at the work being done at business schools, economists were taking notice. Merton Miller and Franco Modigliani—two economists moonlighting as finance professors—had begun the transformation of the discipline into something more like a science. In the late 1960s, full-time finance professor Eugene Fama set out to complete it.

Unlike so many of his Chicago colleagues, Fama was not driven by any obvious ideological bias in favor of free markets. His political leanings were—and remain—largely a mystery. But he was a stubbornly methodical researcher, and he wanted to follow the work that he and others at Chicago were doing to its logical conclusion. Upon joining the Chicago faculty, Fama had been dispatched to teach portfolio theory and asset pricing. Those were subjects he had never gotten around to looking into as a graduate student, so he introduced himself to the work of Harry Markowitz, and read the landmark papers of Bill Sharpe and John Lintner as they appeared. It was Fama who was first to demonstrate that these two seemingly different versions of the capital asset pricing model (CAPM) were actually saying the same thing. And it was Fama who determined that if his efficient market was to have any real meaning, it needed to be joined at the hip to CAPM.

Fama did the joining at the 1969 annual meeting of the American Finance Association. As published in the *Journal of Finance* the next year under the title "Efficient Markets: Theory and Evidence," his paper became—along with Harry Markowitz's portfolio theory, the M&M propositions, and the several CAPM papers—a core document of the new quantitative finance. Fama was trying to lend rigor to an enterprise that up to then had been marked mostly by enthusiasm. To argue that the market was hard to outsmart was one thing; to argue that it was right was another. Fama wished to assert that the market got prices right:

> The primary role of the capital market is allocation of ownership of the economy's capital stock. In general terms, the ideal is a market in which prices provide accurate signals for resource allocation: that is, a market in which firms can make production-investment decisions, and investors can choose among the securities that represent ownership of firms' activities under the assumption that security prices at any time "fully reflect" all available information. A market in which prices always "fully reflect" available information is called "efficient."[29]

Fama cited the bounteous evidence gathered in the previous decade indicating that the market was hard to predict and that it moved with lightning speed. "In short," he concluded, "the evidence in support of the efficient markets model is extensive, and (somewhat uniquely in economics) contradictory evidence is sparse." Before it could be said that markets got prices right, though, one needed to propose an economic theory of how prices were determined, and then test it against stock market data. The capital asset pricing model was the theory. Testing it, Fama wrote, was the next frontier.

The first two extensive empirical tests of what Fama called the "joint hypothesis" of efficient markets and CAPM were conducted soon afterward—one by Fama and a student, the other by Jensen, Scholes, and newcomer Fischer Black, an Arthur D. Little consultant turned Chicago finance professor. Both studies found the risk-reward tradeoff to be more complicated than envisioned in theory, but the results came close enough to the ideal to inspire more confidence than doubt.[30]

Around the same time, Fama joined forces with Merton Miller to write *The Theory of Finance*, the first textbook to tie together the different strands that had been developing over the previous two decades. The book was too austere and equation filled to be assigned to many MBA classes outside of Chicago. It was nonetheless a landmark. The discipline of academic finance had been reborn.

"In my first class with Merton Miller he explained the theory of efficient markets," recalled Rex Sinquefield, a former Catholic seminarian who started in the MBA program the autumn of 1970. "After about ten minutes it just hit me, this has got to be true. The idea for me was so powerful; I said to myself, 'This is order in the universe.'"

NOT EVERYONE WAS SO EASILY converted, of course. In 1966, several old-timers made impassioned speeches at the annual meeting of the American Finance Association (AFA) complaining that the *Journal of Finance* had been overrun by overly mathematical, overly theoretical articles. Their revolt was turned back by the organization's president,

Fred Weston of UCLA (who had been coeditor of the journal back when Harry Markowitz's portfolio selection article kicked things off in 1952). "The emerging problems and issues of finance make it unsatisfactory for us to expect that we can contribute to the improvement of economic and business decisions solely by generalization and judgment," Weston wrote in 1967.[31] Models and math were the future.

A final broadside came from Irwin Friend of the Wharton School, a veteran scholar who could do at least some of the new math but thought much of it nonsense. In his 1972 presidential address to the AFA, Friend denounced what he called the "mythodology" of new-style finance. His own tests of the capital asset pricing model had *not* delivered positive results, he said, and none of the tests of the efficient market hypothesis had examined whether the information contained in stock prices was truly useful for determining future earnings or risk. He concluded that "contrary to the impression yielded by the 'random walk' and related models of the market's performance, the market's ability to set up appropriate guidelines for channeling investment funds to their optimal use is not impressive, at least viewed in hindsight."[32]

Less than a decade later, similar arguments would be trotted out by younger scholars and begin a dramatic new chapter in the evolution of finance. But in 1972 they were seen as the dying roar of the old guard. "Good old Irwin, he got battered," recalled Michael Jensen. "What they were trying to defend wasn't very good."

A new paradigm had been accepted, and those who didn't want to work within it were no longer welcome. The concept of a paradigm, and especially a paradigm shift, has since become cliché, but in the early 1970s it was still fresh—and described well what was happening in finance. It was the brainchild of Thomas Kuhn, a physicist who had observed during a sabbatical year at Stanford's Center for Advanced Study in the Behavioral Sciences in the late 1950s that the assembled scholars—psychologists, sociologists, philosophers, an economist or two—were plagued by debates over fundamentals of a sort unheard of in the natural sciences. The problem, Kuhn explained in his 1962 book, *The Structure of Scientific Revolutions,* was that these fields hadn't quite developed into sciences yet. A true science, by Kuhn's definition, was a field of study in which the practitioners took a number of fundamental assumptions as given and spent their days solving tiny puzzles in ways consistent with those assumptions. Often the assumptions eventually turned out to be wrong, but all that puzzle solving was still useful. Scientists were able to accomplish so much in large part because they didn't waste their time arguing about the basics.

To some in the established sciences, Kuhn's account was a disturbing one, seeming as it did to accuse them of tunnel vision. Economists had a different reaction. They looked through Kuhn's list of the characteristics of a true science—agreement on fundamentals, unintelligibility to outsiders, communication by means of journal articles rather than books, a profound lack of interest in history—and recognized their own discipline as it had developed since World War II. No longer could economists be grouped with those quarrelsome psychologists or sociologists. They belonged to a real science. Within a few years, thanks to the generosity of Sweden's central bank, they even had an annual Nobel Prize to call their own.[33]

The new finance had sprung from the rib of this newly scientific economics. In economics, the core tenet was that people were rational. In finance, it was that financial markets were rational. This was, for a time, a spectacularly productive starting point. By making a simplifying assumption about the real world, finance professors were able to produce research that was enormously useful.

There's no denying, though, that they also came to suffer from tunnel vision. The narrow finance mindset was most famously expressed in a 1978 article by Michael Jensen, who after finishing at Chicago had helped transform the University of Rochester into a sort of Chicago-upon-Lake-Ontario. He began, "I believe there is no other proposition in economics which has more solid empirical evidence supporting it than the Efficient Market Hypothesis."[34]

THE CONQUEST OF
WALL STREET

CHAPTER 7

JACK BOGLE TAKES ON THE PERFORMANCE CULT (AND WINS)

The lesson that maybe it's not even worth trying to beat the market makes its circuitous way into the investment business.

IN 1959, A PAIR OF roommates at the University of Chicago came up with what they thought was a swell idea: Somebody should start a mutual fund that buys and holds the stocks in the Dow Jones industrials average. Edward F. Renshaw, an economist just finishing his Ph.D., and Paul J. Feldstein, an MBA student, were in no position to launch such a fund themselves.[1] They decided to share their idea for an "unmanaged investment company" with the world by submitting an article about it to the *Financial Analysts Journal*.

The piece, published in the journal's January–February 1960 issue, contained no references to efficient markets or random walks. It did mention Alfred Cowles's withering assessment of Wall Street forecasters from 1932, and said "the evidence that can be cited . . . indicates that the average return from professional advice and continued supervision is very low." The main argument, though, was that the mutual fund industry had grown so much that it was getting just as hard for investors to pick mutual funds as individual stocks. An unmanaged fund—based on the Dow simply because that's what investors were most familiar with—would provide a straightforward, low-cost alternative.[2]

For the two authors, that was the end of it. No one called them begging to bankroll their plan, and they got on with their lives. A few months later, though, a rebuttal of their article appeared in the pages of the *Financial Analysts Journal.* Its author was "John B. Armstrong"—a pseudonym, a footnote revealed, for "a man who has spent many years in the security field and wrote his Princeton senior thesis on 'The Economic Role of the Investment Company.'" His real name was John C. Bogle, and he was a rising young executive at Wellington Management Co., a Philadelphia mutual fund firm. He'd opted for the pseudonym (Armstrong was his maternal grandfather's last name) because he didn't want to get Wellington in trouble with the Securities and Exchange Commission.[3]

In his rebuttal, Bogle argued that the unmanaged fund was a solution in search of a problem. The four oldest mutual funds—Bogle didn't name them, but they were Massachusetts Investors Trust, Investors Incorporated (now called Putnam Investors), State Street, and Wellington—had all outperformed the Dow since 1930 with less volatility than the overall market, he wrote. Besides, the Dow wasn't unmanaged. The editors at the *Wall Street Journal* had made twenty-eight changes in the average since 1928. Finally, the unmanaged fund idea had been tried before in the form of "fixed trusts" that bought and held a preset list of stocks, and had faded from view.[4]

Bogle was arguing that investors were better off with an intelligently managed mutual fund than a haphazardly managed one. Historically speaking he had a point. Professional money managers owned only about 10 percent of the shares of the country's big publicly traded corporations in the 1950s (the figure had risen to 76 percent by the end of 2007). It wasn't unreasonable to think they could outsmart a bunch of amateurs. The funds Bogle cited were also run by crusty old sorts who remembered the great crash, giving them an innate understanding of risk. Even if they didn't beat the market, they could be said to be protecting their investors from some of its potential pitfalls.

But by 1960, the handful of funds that had survived the Depression was being muscled aside by a new generation. The mutual fund traits that Bogle valued most—conservatism, diversification, stewardship—were making way for a new ethos of performance obsession, specialization, and marketing. It would only get worse as the go-go 1960s progressed. It got so bad that a decade and a half later, none other than Jack Bogle launched the first index mutual fund. Much had to happen before he could get to that point, and the random walkers and efficient marketeers played a big part in getting him there. It was an unprecedented intertwining of academic theory and Wall Street reality. But that's getting ahead of the story.

THE MODERN MUTUAL FUND INDUSTRY was born in 1924 when a Boston stockbroker, appalled at how frequently amateur investors were fleeced and flummoxed by the stock market, decreed it was time for a new way to invest. The Massachusetts Investors Trust, which he founded, was to be a *mutual* fund, owned by those who put money into it. This was no mere legal fiction. MIT, as it came to be known, was a nonprofit entity run by a board that answered to the fund's investors. Other funds founded in Boston and elsewhere in the 1920s that later came under the rubric "mutual" were actually controlled by for-profit investment advisers. These funds did, however, share other traits with MIT: The price of a share was determined by the net value of the securities owned by the fund, and those security holdings were disclosed to shareholders on a regular basis. Managers were paid a percentage of assets under management, not a fee based on performance. Most important, the funds were open-ended: As money flowed in, the managers bought more stocks. When it flowed out, they sold.[5]

The birth of the mutual fund was a low-budget affair. MIT started with just $50,000. Down on Wall Street, brokerage houses were launching their own investment vehicles, closed-end trusts, with far more fanfare and cash. The first big one was the U.S. and Foreign Securities Corp., underwritten by Dillon Read, which raised $10 million in its initial offering. By 1929 there were hundreds of these trusts, with a total of $7 billion under management (about 8 percent of the stock market's total value).[6] They raised money in public offerings, bought stock with it, and after that they often kept shareholders in the dark while making their founders rich. Some trusts became virtual Ponzi schemes, borrowing money to buy back their own shares and drive prices upward.

After the crash, shares in many of these closed-end trusts were close to worthless. At MIT and the other open-ended funds there were losses, of course, but few wipeouts. By the end of the 1930s it was clear that the MIT model was a winner. In 1940 Congress enshrined the MIT way into law, with an Investment Company Act written largely by the fund's lawyers. Some closed-end funds lived on, but as regular folks gingerly began returning to the stock market in the 1940s, they voted with their pocketbooks for the open-ended MIT way of doing things.

The MIT formula was not one for trouncing the market. Other mutual funds had closed to new investors at various times as managers worried that performance would suffer as they grew too large. MIT never did that. The fund's goal wasn't so much to beat the market as to share in its gains, which MIT's trustees made easier by charging a minuscule management fee. Investors did have to pay a 7 percent brokerage charge to buy the funds in the first place (the brokerage firm that hawked the fund was the one dissonant for-profit note in MIT's investor-friendly symphony), but after that you owned the market at almost no cost. In a 1949 *Fortune* article on MIT, a competitor sniped that the fund was a fine investment "if all you want is a piece of the Dow Jones average." An MIT executive responded, "The Dow-Jones average is not a bad thing to own, since the small investor, sizing up the market for himself, seldom does as well as any of the accepted averages."[7]

This article, the first in-depth examination of the growing mutual fund industry in the national media, hooked Jack Bogle. Every Princeton University senior must write a thesis, and in late 1949 Bogle was a junior economics major searching for something to write about other than the default economics topic of the day, John Maynard Keynes. He was in the university's library, leafing through magazines, when he found his topic and his career.

The thesis that resulted contained two striking and somewhat contradictory assertions. One, mentioned almost in passing, was that "the funds can make no claim to superiority over the market averages." The other, to which Bogle gave a lot more buildup, was that a market in which mutual fund managers played a leading role would be nothing like the "beauty contest" described by Keynes—in which speculators spent all their time as "anticipating what average opinion expects the average opinion to be."

"Evidence . . . indicates that the investment company must stabilize rather than unstabilize the market, as its assets approach a size such that influence on it is appreciable," Bogle wrote. "Once this magnitude is reached, it will militate against Lord Keynes' dismal and socialistic conclusions."[8] Bogle was a crew-cut New Jerseyan of modest means (his father went bust in the 1929 crash) and, up to then, modest grades. He got an A+ on his thesis, and sent a copy to the Princeton alumnus who ran Wellington Management. That got him a job.

THE SMALL WORLD OF PROFESSIONAL investing that Bogle entered in 1951 really did possess something of the market-stabilizing character that he ascribed to it in his thesis. The investors who survived and thrived through the 1930s and 1940s were those who paid close attention to the underlying value of the companies whose shares they bought. One of them was Keynes: "My purpose is to buy securities where I am satisfied as to assets and ultimate earning power and where the market price seems cheap in relation to these," he wrote to a friend in 1942.[9] The success of this value approach to investing had made Keynes a rich man in the 1930s. As he never discussed it in public, it is justly identified instead with someone who did, Benjamin Graham.

When Graham graduated from Columbia College in 1914, the chairmen of the philosophy, mathematics, and English departments all asked him to stay on to pursue a doctorate. Columbia's dean felt Graham should get some real-world experience first, so he got the young man a job with a Wall Street broker.[10] There, working as a "statistician," Graham soon discovered that most Wall Streeters didn't understand the value of the data that Standard Statistics, Moody's, and the like were throwing at them. "In 1914 this mass of financial information was largely going to waste in the area of common-stock analysis," Graham wrote in his autobiography fifty years later. "The figures were not ignored, but they were studied superficially and with little interest ... To a large degree, therefore, I found Wall Street virgin territory for examination by a genuine, penetrating analysis of security values."[11]

Graham's first big coup came just a year out of college. The Guggenheim Exploration Co., which owned stakes in several major copper mines that were themselves listed on the New York Stock Exchange, announced that it was going to dissolve and distribute its holdings to shareholders. Graham did some arithmetic, and found the market was valuing these subsidiaries far higher than the parent company. He advised his firm's clients to buy Guggenheim shares and sell short the shares of its subsidiaries (that is, borrow shares from others and sell them in hopes that they could buy them back later for less). This is what's called arbitrage: Find the same thing selling at different prices in different places, buy it at the low price, and sell it at the high price. Those who followed Graham's advice made a killing.

Graham, who soon set up a money management operation of his own, was surely not the first to pursue these tactics. He was perhaps the first to write cogently about them in such publications as the *Magazine of Wall Street* and *Barron's* (he also wrote plays, one of which made it to Broadway but closed after four performances in 1934). In 1927, he began teaching a night class at Columbia in what he dubbed "security analysis." From the beginning Graham intended to turn his course materials into a textbook—existing investment texts were painfully dull and mostly about bonds. In 1934, with help from a young Columbia Business School professor named David Dodd who had been a student in that first class in 1927, Graham finished writing *Security Analysis*. The book rechristened "statisticians" as "analysts" and became the bible of the new profession.

Security Analysis was a guide to hacking through the thickets of earnings statements and balance sheets in search of value. As Graham put it later, in his book *The Intelligent Investor*, the "true investor" should think of himself as partner in a business with a manic-depressive fellow named "Mr. Market." Every day this Mr. Market offers to buy out the investor's stake or sell his own. Some days he offers a reasonable price, sometimes it's too high or too low. The job of the value investor is to have a good enough sense of what the business is worth to know when to cut a deal with Mr. Market and when to ignore him.[12] What many of Graham's readers seem to have missed through the years was just how seldom he thought an investor could be confident of outsmarting Mr. Market. "As far as the *typical* common stock is concerned—an issue picked at random from the list," he wrote in 1934, "an analysis, however elaborate, is unlikely to yield a dependable conclusion as to its attractiveness or its real value."[13]

Graham therefore focused on atypically cheap common stocks, those selling for significantly less than what he adjudged to be their "liquidating value." If a company was priced at substantially less than it could make by closing up shop and selling off all its factories, equipment, and security holdings, then its shares were probably a good buy. If all else failed, the company's owners could just shut it down and sell the pieces. It was, in a way, another form of arbitrage.

Graham came to refer to such companies as "cigar butts," and during the 1930s they were all over the place. It was an era that richly rewarded rational, patient investors, and they in turn slowly pushed prices back to rational levels. Over time, the numbers of such investors burgeoned—thanks in large part to the success of Graham's textbook and the influence of his Columbia class. In 1937 the New York Society of Security Analysts was founded, with twenty members. Ten years later it joined with similar associations in Boston, Chicago, and Philadelphia to form the Financial Analysts Federation (now known as the CFA Institute). The group launched the *Analysts Journal,* later to become the *Financial Analysts Journal,* and began requiring courses and tests to join its ranks.

It was all enough to make Graham nervous. He no longer had the market to himself, and had only himself to blame. When Nebraskan Warren Buffett graduated from Columbia Business School in 1951, Graham—who had given Buffett an A+ in his class—advised him to stay away from stocks, at least until after the next crash.[14] Buffett ignored him, and what followed over the next half decade "was by practically any statistical standard the greatest boom on record," wrote *New Yorker* stock market chronicler John Brooks in 1958. "In terms of sheer national madness, it probably has to take a back seat to the boom of the late twenties . . . Even so, it was pretty lively."[15]

As stock prices rose (the Dow Jones average finally surpassed its 1929 peak in 1955), Graham seemed ever more out of step with the times. "Graham and Dodd's *Security Analysis,* the erstwhile bible of the security analyst, had lost touch with the realities of the new 'new era' of common-stock valuation," a Princeton economics graduate student wrote in 1963—the first "new era" having been the 1920s. "The search for growth became the main preoccupation of the security analyst."

The grad student, former army officer and Smith Barney investment banker Burton G. Malkiel, went on to describe how this search for growth had led Wall Street to John Burr Williams and his dividend-discount model. The formula for calculating the present value of projected future dividends became part of every analyst's toolbox. Some of this shift to a more hopeful, forward-looking investing approach was warranted, wrote Malkiel. But when analysts factored fifty years of future growth into their calculations of the appropriate price for a stock, the formulas creaked under the weight of all that anticipation. When you are counting on dividends and earnings that far off in the future, the tiniest shift in projected interest rates means huge swings in stock values. The future is uncertain; the further into it you look, the less you know. This business of valuing securities, concluded Malkiel, was an "ephemeral process."[16]

Graham couldn't have agreed more. He had shut down his money management firm in 1956 and moved to Southern California. He was the first to admit that the circumstances that had allowed his methods to flourish in the 1930s and 1940s no longer applied. In a speech at the twenty-fifth anniversary of the New York Society of Security Analysts in 1962, he noted that the once-tiny society now had 2,945 members. "Neither the Financial Analysts as a whole nor the investment funds as a whole can expect to 'beat the market,'" he said, "because in a significant sense they (or you) *are* the market."

Then, sounding a bit like a Chicago economist, he continued:

> Analysts do in fact render an important service to the community in their study and evaluation of common stocks. But this service shows itself not in spectacular results achieved by their individual selections but rather in fixing at most times and for most stocks of a price level which fairly represents their comparative values, as established by the known facts and reasonable estimates about the future.

This statement was the essence of the efficient market hypothesis, as formulated loosely and reasonably by someone with actual market experience. It meant, Graham wrote, that the average analyst was best off simply accepting market prices as given, and spending his time and mental energy constructing portfolios that effectively balanced risk and return. Graham lectured occasionally at the UCLA Business

School, and followed developments there closely. He knew all about Harry Markowitz's efficient portfolios, and saw great merit in them as long as somebody could come up with better ways to measure the riskiness of individual stocks.[17]

BACK ON WALL STREET, WORRYING about risk was out of fashion. A money management industry that was finding it ever harder to beat the market had begun to make an obsession of doing just that. "Up until a very few years ago, you were safe as a fund manager if you bought the great blue chips, Alcoa and Union Carbide, Telephone and Texaco," declared journalist George A. W. Goodman (writing as "Adam Smith") in his classic portrait of 1960s Wall Street, *The Money Game*. "You couldn't be criticized even if they performed badly, because that would be like criticizing the United States of America."[18]

Now the blue chips were giving way to a new breed of corporations—fast-growing conglomerates such as Litton and LTV (Ling-Temco-Vaught), plus such technological marvels as Xerox, Polaroid, and Sperry Rand (a new incarnation, wonder of wonders, of Irving Fisher's Remington Rand). The most avid buyer of these companies, and the man generally credited with launching the 1960s obsession with "performance," was Shanghai-born, Boston-educated Gerry Tsai, known to one and all on Wall Street as "the Chinaman." Tsai had gone to work as an analyst in 1952 for Boston-based Fidelity Fund. Five years later he asked Fidelity boss Edward Crosby Johnson II for a fund of his own.

Johnson was a Boston lawyer who had been *given* Fidelity in 1943 by its previous boss, and he sensed before any of his old-line mutual fund peers that the days of stodgy trusteeship were over. He created a fund for Tsai, Fidelity Capital, which soon became famous for its frenetic trading and even more frenetic returns. It gained a stunning 50 percent in 1965.[19] Johnson put his son Ned in charge of another new fund called Fidelity Trend, which actually outperformed Tsai's fund (up 57 percent in 1965), although it never caught Wall Street's fancy in quite the same way.

Other mutual fund companies could not afford to ignore Fidelity's two young guns. "A number of fund managers I know describe their jobs very simply, all in nearly the same way," wrote Goodman. " 'My job,' they say, 'is to beat Fidelity.' "[20] Nobody was able to do that consistently, but many did beat the Dow in those giddy days. In 1965, the twenty-nine funds classed into the "performance" category by the brokerage firm Arthur Wiesenberger & Co.—the main source of mutual fund data at the time—recorded an average gain of 40 percent, compared with 15 percent for the Dow.[21]

How did fund managers trounce the market despite such intense competition? Mainly by loading up on the same extremely speculative, by now exorbitantly priced stocks that Tsai had begun buying in the late 1950s. When the market went up, as it did for most of the 1960s, those stocks went up even more. Was there any skill involved in such investing? Of course, said Wall Street's young guns. "The improved performance of certain institutions in the management of their funds is the natural outcome of better trained, more energetic, younger men in command," wrote one of them in the *Financial Analysts Journal* in 1966.[22] Old-timers weren't so sure. In an article in the same journal that year, one of the founding members of the Financial Analysts Federation fretted:

> Behind the ever more elaborate formulae for measuring rate of return—and they will become more elaborate as computers become more used—there is one vital problem: How much risk was incurred? By hindsight it makes no difference. More important, it is impossible to quantify. But that vital part in the equation exists and there is no point sweeping it under the rug.[23]

The old guard was right that risk shouldn't be ignored. But it's hard to win a quantitative argument by leaning on something that you contend is "impossible to quantify." In 1957, Jack Bogle had proposed a new performance measure that divided fund return by volatility,[24] the better to showcase Wellington's low-risk approach.[25] But most Wall Streeters didn't think volatility and risk were the same, and Bogle himself eventually stopped trying to fight the "performance" obsession. First, he persuaded his bosses to launch the all-stock Windsor Fund. Then, in 1966, just before taking over as Wellington's president, he arranged to merge it with a small Boston firm that ran one of the hottest performance funds of the day.

This left the field open to the practitioners of the new academic, quantitative finance. First to arrive was Jack Treynor of Arthur D. Little. In the late 1950s, Investors Diversified Services (IDS, now Ameriprise Financial), a Minnesota firm staffed by legions of door-to-door salesmen, passed Massachusetts Investors Trust and sister fund Massachusetts Investors Growth to become the country's biggest mutual fund complex. IDS wanted advice on what to do with all the money its salespeople were bringing in. It hired Arthur D. Little. Treynor and a colleague studied the ratings that IDS analysts gave to stocks, and the subsequent performance of those stocks, and found no correlation between the two. They reported this finding to IDS, but nothing came of it, apart from more consulting assignments from other money managers. As far as Treynor remembered, none changed their practices as a result of his recommendations.

After Treynor wrote his asset pricing paper and returned from his stint at MIT (the university, not the mutual fund), his boss at Arthur D. Little asked if there might be any practical application to the work he had been doing. Treynor suggested mutual fund performance measurement. "The effect of management on the rate of return on investments made in any one period is usually swamped by fluctuations in the general market," he wrote in a 1965 *Harvard Business Review* article. To better judge performance, he suggested, one needed to sift out those market fluctuations by dividing the fund's return by the measure of its sensitivity to market movements that later came to be known as "beta."[26]

Treynor began putting his new performance gauge to work for clients. At Yale University, the head of the endowment was getting pressure from alumni and administrators to jazz up his conservative investing style. "They said, 'Look at these people with great investment records, like the Chinaman,'" Treynor recalled. "'You should be emulating them.'" Treynor analyzed the record of Fidelity Capital under Tsai. "I found that his spectacular level of performance was due to his spectacular level of market risk," Treynor recalled decades later. He presented his conclusions to a room full of Yale trustees and alumni up from Wall Street. "I looked around that room and all I could see after my pitch was angry faces," he said. "Yale discarded my recommendation completely."

Years later, the "Treynor ratio" became a much-used measure of investment manager performance. Even better known is the "Sharpe ratio," a similar gauge—originally termed "reward-to-volatility"—that fellow CAPM pioneer Bill Sharpe introduced in a paper in 1966. Most famous of all is probably "alpha," devised by Michael Jensen for his 1968 Chicago Ph.D. dissertation on mutual fund performance. Alpha is a portfolio's performance minus the performance of a hypothetical benchmark portfolio of equivalent risk. This metric sounds complicated, but it delivers a wonderfully simple result. If you have an alpha of 1 percent, that's how much you *really* beat the market by.

None of these measures caught on immediately, and their inventors used them at first mainly as bludgeons with which to attack the mutual fund business and its pretensions. "We were all sticking it to Wall Street," said Sharpe. The inanity of the go-go years helped unite the efficient markets movement and attract new adherents. Economists with no connection to the earlier random walk research were nonetheless dubious that Wall Street's young stars could reliably trounce the market. Such claims smacked of that great economic impossibility: the free lunch.

Even Paul Samuelson took a stand. Testifying in 1967 before the Senate Banking Committee, which was considering new legislation to deal with the burgeoning fund industry, Samuelson declared that many mutual funds raked in huge fees for work of dubious value. He recalled seeing a secretary's fee-laden mutual fund contract years before and realizing that "there was only one place to make money in the mutual fund business—as there is only one place for a temperate man to be in a saloon, behind the bar and not in front of the bar." He also cited a recent Yale Ph.D. dissertation that showed randomly selected twenty-stock portfolios outperforming mutual funds, which prompted some disbelieving questions from Banking Committee chairman John Sparkman:

> THE CHAIRMAN: When you say twenty random stocks, are you referring to stocks that you just close your eyes and reach down and touch?
>
> MR. SAMUELSON: Yes. Precisely.
>
> THE CHAIRMAN: Or is some expert such as you picking them?
>
> MR. SAMUELSON: No. Random. When I say "random," I want you to think of dice or think of random numbers or a dart.

Samuelson closed on a conciliatory note. "I personally believe that there is something in performance," he said. "I think it is very hard to identify a performer, but I think there is something in performance."[27]

WHEN THE MOST FAMOUS PERFORMER of them all faltered, some began to have their doubts about even that. In 1966, after it became clear that not he but Johnson's son Ned would inherit Fidelity, Gerry Tsai left to start his own Manhattan Fund. He hoped to raise $25 million for the new venture; investors poured in $275 million the first day. The fund did well enough in its first full year in business, but seven months into 1968 it was down 6.6 percent, making it one of the worst-performing funds in the country. Tsai sold out to CNA Financial, an insurance company, for about $30 million, abandoned fund management, and moved into the CNA executive suite.[28]

This maneuver may have been evidence of consummate skill on Tsai's part. The next decade and a half was brutal for Wall Street and the mutual fund business. He had cashed out just in time. But the inability of Tsai or any of Wall Street's other headline-grabbing stars of the 1960s to sustain their market-trouncing performance seemed to confirm what the preliminary researches of Michael Jensen and Bill Sharpe and Jack Treynor had hinted. The supposed geniuses of the go-go years had simply been taking what were, in retrospect, harebrained risks. The scholarly consensus that *nobody* on Wall Street knew what he was doing began to harden. "Many academics have concluded that the value of investment advice is virtually zero," Burton Malkiel and a Princeton colleague wrote in 1968.[29]

This conclusion coexisted uneasily with the efficient market faith that, as a group, all these nitwit investors succeeded in setting the prices of stocks at or very near their intrinsic values. It was also, strictly speaking, not supported by the evidence. What had been demonstrated in the studies by Jensen and others was that the *average* value of the investment advice provided by the mutual fund industry as a whole was not just zero but less than zero. This was an important—and, to some, shocking—finding. It did not, however, preclude the existence of money managers with actual skill, or of investment vehicles better suited than the open-ended mutual fund to accommodate such skill.

The academic research and the mutual fund debacles did make clear, though, that the low-fee, "unmanaged" mutual fund suggested in 1960 by those two Chicago grad students was not a crazy idea. The first to propose it formally appears to have been Arthur Lipper III, whose brokerage firm rocked the industry when it began publishing *weekly* mutual fund performance data in 1967. Lipper asked the SEC in 1969 for permission to launch what he called a "stock average fund" that would hold the thirty Dow stocks. According to Lipper, the SEC never responded. Regulators weren't ready for such a bizarre idea quite yet.

Lipper wasn't the only Wall Streeter beginning to pay attention to the arguments of the random walkers. After launching the Center for Research in Security Prices at Chicago with a grant from Merrill Lynch, director James Lorie had promised to find other sources of money to keep the operation going. He had the smart idea in 1966 of holding a seminar where in exchange for $5,000 apiece, banks, insurance companies, and money management firms could send a couple of staffers to hear the latest in academic stock market research. Even firms dubious of the new finance were willing to make that small investment. The first seminar sold out, with thirty-six firms signing up. After that, the CRSP meetings became an influential twice-a-year event. Another brokerage firm, the now-defunct Goodbody & Co., set up a rival seminar series that it dubbed the Institute for Quantitative Research in Finance or Q Group. The typical attendee of both groups' seminars in the early days was an obscure young geek who'd been put in charge of a tiny quant division in some remote corner of an investment firm. Within a couple of decades many of those obscure young geeks had become rich and powerful.

The big-time Wall Street firm that came closest to going over to the side of the random walkers in the 1960s was Merrill Lynch. It's hard to envision today just how different Merrill was from the rest of Wall Street then. Its brokers were paid salaries, not commissions. It didn't just advertise; it advertised on *TV*.[30] It bankrolled some of the most important work in academic finance, from Holbrook Working to Harry Markowitz to CRSP. It hired Jack Treynor in 1966 as its putative quant czar. It put Chicago's Lorie on its board of directors. It enlisted Bill Sharpe to help launch a "beta service" that churned out historical measures of the sensitivity of individual stocks to market movements.

But even Merrill was too profitably wedded to the old ways to join the revolution outright. Treynor left in 1969 to edit the *Financial*

Analysts Journal—itself a landmark shift for such a mainstream Wall Street publication—and most of the firm's other quants cleared out in the early 1970s. "There was kind of a schizophrenia that said, 'This is important, but not important enough to be part of the mainstream,'" said Gil Hammer, who ran the Merrill beta service. "Merrill was out there to sell securities to clients."

It was thus left to firms that weren't already raking in millions selling securities to take the leap—firms such as Wells Fargo Bank in San Francisco. Wells Fargo had hired Smith Barney analyst and part-time computer geek Mac McQuown in 1963 to head a new Management Sciences Group charged with bringing modern, scientific thinking to all aspects of the bank's business. Its most visible accomplishment was Master Charge (now MasterCard), the multibank alternative to hometown rival Bank of America's BankAmericard (which later reinvented itself in Master Charge's image as Visa). It also pioneered the index fund.

Wells Fargo's CEO wanted to give his bank's retail customers access to the stock market free of the sales-pitch-laden, stock-by-stock approach of Wall Street brokerages. His dream shattered against the strictures of the Depression-era Glass-Steagall Act, which banned banks from getting into the brokerage business.[31] But McQuown's team had spent several years investigating the merits of an index-based mutual fund, and along the way became the nation's chief employer of moonlighting finance professors—most of whom McQuown had met at CRSP seminars. Myron Scholes and Michael Jensen were the first hires, followed by such present and future notables as Sharpe, Burton Malkiel, Barr Rosenberg of UC–Berkeley, and Fischer Black, a computer scientist who had succeeded Treynor at Arthur D. Little.

In 1971 the courts definitively closed the door to a Wells Fargo retail mutual fund. The Wells team was wondering what to do next when a recent Chicago graduate, whose family owned luggage maker Samsonite, came calling. Inspired by what he'd learned in class, the young man had persuaded his elders to invest some of the company's pension money in an index. When he asked his Chicago professors who might be willing to manage such an index fund, they steered him to Wells Fargo. Managing institutional funds wasn't against the Glass-Steagall rules, so the Wells crew put Samsonite's $6 million into every stock on the New York Stock Exchange, with an equal amount of money in each stock. The idea had been that an equal-weighted fund might outperform the straight index, but it soon became clear that keeping the weights equal required so much trading that the fund wasn't nearly as low-cost as envisioned.[32]

After several years of trial and error, Wells set up an S&P 500 fund for pension funds and other big institutional investors that held stocks according to their weight in the index. By the time the fund launched, though, Wells had two competitors: American National Bank in Chicago, where 1972 Chicago MBA Rex Sinquefield was the driving force, and Batterymarch, an upstart Boston firm that had been pushing the index idea since 1971 but didn't land its first customers until 1974.

RETAIL INVESTORS, MEANWHILE, HAD JUST lost the closest thing they had to an index fund: the low-turnover, low-fee Massachusetts Investors Trust. In 1969 the fund's trustees persuaded shareholders to vote to "demutualize," putting management in the hands of a for-profit adviser called Massachusetts Financial Services, or MFS. The fees MIT shareholders paid began rising soon afterward,[33] and the mutual fund industry no longer contained a single truly *mutual* fund.

It didn't, that is, until Jack Bogle came to the rescue. Bogle and the Boston money managers whose firm had merged with Wellington in 1967 had never gotten along well, and during the bear market of 1973 and 1974 the tension grew unbearable. The four Boston partners together controlled 40 percent of Wellington's shares to Bogle's 28 percent. They ousted him from the presidency.

As *mutual* funds, though, Wellington and Windsor still had a decision-making structure separate from that of their management company. This distinction is usually just a legal nicety, but the funds' boards had been appointed by Bogle and his predecessor, and the members were appalled by Bogle's firing. They balked when he suggested that they buy Wellington Management out from under its new management, but they did go for a compromise. The funds would declare partial independence, leaving fund management and distribution (done through an army of brokers who charged up-front "loads" to new investors) to Wellington Management, but putting "administration" in the hands of a new entity that, in keeping with the Napoleonic wars theme, would be named Vanguard, after Lord Nelson's flagship. At the time, "administration" didn't entail much beyond sending out annual statements to shareholders, but Bogle had a couple of ideas for getting around that limitation. One was that selling fund shares directly to investors, without a load, didn't really count as distribution. The other was that running an unmanaged mutual fund didn't count as management. The Vanguard board bought it. "It was," Bogle said later, "one of the greatest disingenuous acts of opportunism known to man."

That the opportunistic Bogle even thought to suggest an index fund, though—and that the board members didn't laugh him out of the room—owed a lot to some literary groundwork laid in the preceding years. Best known today is *A Random Walk Down Wall Street* by Princeton economist Malkiel, first published in 1973. Malkiel had been more a fellow traveler of the 1960s random walk movement than a leader. But his pre-grad-school stint on Wall Street, his dignified bearing, and his ability to translate academic jargon into English made him a far more effective ambassador to the outside world than, say, Gene Fama. The book was immediately hailed by *Forbes* as a classic. Paul Samuelson said it would become the "Dr. Spock of investment."[34] In fact it has held up much better than that; Spock's *Baby and Child Care* has become a quaint artifact of its time, while *Random Walk*, now in a ninth edition, is still current. The book's message was actually a bit less radical than the title implied. A *New York Times* business writer who read it expecting lessons in dart throwing professed to be disappointed that much of it was a guide to conventional value investing.[35] The first edition also couldn't recommend index mutual funds because they didn't exist yet. And Bogle himself didn't get around to reading the book until years later. But *Random Walk* undeniably played a big part in making index investing respectable, and Malkiel later ended up on Vanguard's board.

More directly on topic (and on Bogle's reading list at the time) was a 1974 essay by Paul Samuelson in the *Journal of Portfolio Management*, a wonky new publication for quantitatively inclined money managers, pension executives, and such.[36] Samuelson declared that "most portfolio decision makers should go out of business" and pleaded for someone, *anyone*, to launch an index fund for small investors.[37] A year later came a *Financial Analysts Journal* article by pension consultant Charley Ellis, titled "The Losers' Game," which reiterated a point that Ben Graham had made a decade before—professional investors now *were* the market, which meant that their performance must on average, after fees, trail the market.[38]

Bogle got SEC approval for the fund in 1976 but struggled to find a Wall Street firm willing to underwrite its launch. Then the magazine that had gotten him into the mutual fund business, *Fortune*, came through for him with a lengthy article by a recent graduate of the University of Rochester's Business School, headlined "Index Funds—An Idea Whose Time Is Coming."[39] After that, the money flowed.[40]

Now it's *possible* that the index fund would have been created even in the absence of these writings and of the efficient market hypothesis that helped inspire them. But it's hard to see how. The work of ivory tower scholars had launched a new school of investing, one that would survive and flourish in the decades to come. It was one of the great practical triumphs in the history of the social sciences.

• • •

AFTER THE LAUNCH OF THE Vanguard index fund, Paul Samuelson announced in his *Newsweek* column that he had celebrated the birth of his first grandson by buying the boy a few shares.[41] Ben Graham, just before he died in 1976, offered his own endorsement. In a Q&A with Charley Ellis in the *Financial Analysts Journal*, Graham defended index funds against their detractors on Wall Street and said that, in some matters, he now considered himself "on the side of the 'efficient market' school of thought now generally accepted by the professors."

This utterance has since been portrayed as an admission of defeat on the part of a tired old man, but it wasn't that at all.[42] Graham had been saying similar things for years. If you looked hard enough, you could even find hints of such sentiments in the 1934 first edition of *Security Analysis*. Meanwhile, in 1976, he still thought common stocks were "subject to irrational and excessive price fluctuations," and that those fluctuations provided occasional opportunities to value investors—especially individual investors because they could buy smaller stocks that were mostly off-limits to big institutions.[43] All he was trying to say was that there were *no easy pickings*.

CHAPTER 8

FISCHER BLACK CHOOSES TO FOCUS ON THE PROBABLE

Finance scholars figure out some ways to measure and control risk. More important, they figure out how to get paid for doing so.

IN LONDON IN 1952, STATISTICS professor Maurice Kendall saw the "graceful head" of the bell curve rising up "amid the uproar of the Chicago wheat pit." A few years after that, economist Paul Samuelson and physicist M. F. M. Osborne separately proposed that stock price changes followed a wandering, unpredictable path that nonetheless fit under the bell curve of the normal distribution. That is, you'd have lots and lots of small price changes—constituting the middle of the bell—a few slightly larger ones, and no huge ones. This was the random walk, with the emphasis on *walk*.

It was also extremely convenient. If stock price movements obeyed the normal distribution, all sorts of useful conclusions could be drawn. Harry Markowitz's equations for balancing risk and reward depended on stock price movements sticking to a bell curve. So did the investment-performance measures devised by Bill Sharpe, Mike Jensen, and Jack Treynor.

The only problem was that actual stock prices *don't* always follow a random *walk*. They do stroll about calmly if drunkenly much of the time—but not all of the time. Sometimes they plunge, as did the Dow Jones Industrial Average on October 28, 1929. The Dow usually moves in one-day increments of less than 1 percent. That day it dropped 13.5 percent, the next 11.7 percent. On October 30, it rose 12.3 percent.

In statistical terms these rare but significant events are called fat tails, because they are found at the tail ends of a statistical distribution and keep them from converging quickly with zero—as they would in a true bell curve. The tendency of fat-tail events to follow upon one another is called dependence.

IBM MATHEMATICIAN BENOIT MANDELBROT SAW fat tails and dependence in a chart of cotton futures prices at Harvard in 1960. Mandelbrot was a Polish Jew who had emigrated to France in 1936, spent what would have been his high school years hiding from the Nazis, and then got a doctorate in mathematics at the Sorbonne. It was a 1949 book by Harvard linguist George Zipf that first piqued his interest in strange statistical distributions. Pick a text and rank the words in it by how often each appears, then graph the result, as Zipf did, and you get a fascinating pattern. "The curve does not fall smoothly from most common to least common word," Mandelbrot observed. "It plunges vertiginously at first, then declines more slowly—like the profile of a ski jumper leaping into space, to land and coast down the gentler slope below."[1]

Such statistical distributions have become known as "power laws," because one variable is exponentially related to the other. These patterns, which allow far more room for outliers than the standard bell curve, had first been observed around the turn of the nineteenth century in the distribution of wealth,[2] and it was the statistics of wealth and income that Mandelbrot studied. Then he visited Hendrik Houthakker's Harvard classroom and saw that cotton futures prices fell into the same pattern as incomes and words. It wasn't just the ski jump line; the data was also "self-similar"—that is, charts of small snippets looked just like those of large swaths. Mandelbrot was later to find similar patterns in historical climate data along the Nile, the coast of Britain, and the ins and outs of tree bark. After he dubbed them "fractals" in 1982, he was hailed as a visionary, one of the progenitors of the new science of chaos and complexity that was transforming physics and other fields.

By then, though, Mandelbrot had long abandoned finance. At the beginning he had been warmly welcomed into the small but growing fellowship of random walkers. Gene Fama became his informal student. Harvard invited him to spend the 1964–65 academic year as a visiting professor of economics. He authored a paper that appeared not long after Samuelson's in 1965 showing mathematically that a random market would be a rational one.[3] "The first period was very nice," Mandelbrot recalled. "They were receptive, but with an ominous cloud."

The "cloud" was the frustration that developed among economists as they discovered how hard it was to work with Mandelbrot's power laws. In his depiction of security price movements, variance—the measure of how widely scattered the different data points are—was *infinite*. For scholars who were just getting acquainted with Markowitz's depiction of portfolio selection as a tradeoff between mean and variance, infinity was not helpful.

"Mandelbrot, like Prime Minister Churchill before him, promises us not utopia but blood, sweat, toil and tears," wrote random walk ringleader Paul Cootner in 1964. "If he is right, almost all of our statistical tools are obsolete . . . Surely, before consigning centuries of work to the ash pile, we should like to have some assurance that all our work is truly useless."[4] Such assurances were not forthcoming, and before long, finance scholars had ceased paying attention to Mandelbrot at all. "The reason people didn't latch on to that stuff is it's not that tractable," said Eugene Fama, who went from Mandelbrot disciple to Mandelbrot ignorer in a few short years in the 1960s. "It's not that easy to deal with those predictions in a systematic way." Physicist M. F. M. Osborne, who visited UC–Berkeley's Business School in

1972 to teach two finance courses, told his students that Mandelbrot's ideas about infinite variance were "a stew of red herring and baloney." Sure, there were jumps and dips in stock prices that couldn't be shoe-horned into a normal distribution, Osborne acknowledged. But for most purposes, it was OK to ignore them. The important thing was to figure out what you were measuring probability for:

> You ask what is probable and what is improbable, but definitely not impossible. For rainfall you take 99% of the occasions (days) when you average less than two inches of rain . . . That kind of information is significant for grazing or agriculture, for what kind of vegetation is likely to grow. The improbable situation, which may give much more than 1% of the total rain which may fall, is really concerned with a different caliber of problems. Are the roads going to be washed away, is it safe to build a house in certain locations if you want to live there for twenty or thirty years?[5]

The improbable-but-not-impossible was not something that bell curve statistics could address. But Osborne didn't see any point in reinventing statistics to handle it. When it came to rare events, he argued, one had to look outside the statistics of randomness and identify actual causes for the anomalies. This required judgment and experience, two areas in which finance scholars possessed no comparative advantage. They focused instead on the probable.

THE REWARDS FOR DOING SO were great in the 1970s, as the war between random walkers and professional investors began to settle into an uneasy but profitable truce. Hostilities still flared up from time to time, as on a mid-decade summer morning at Stanford Business School. On the first day of a weeklong seminar for money managers, a young accounting professor just arrived from Chicago (Bill Beaver) kicked things off with a ferocious attack on the idea that *anybody* could beat the market. By afternoon the money men were openly grumbling. Some threatened to leave. Asset pricing guru Bill Sharpe, who joined the Stanford faculty in 1970 and had helped organize the event, knew he needed to do something to stop the revolt.

Sharpe got up in front of the group and drew a line on the blackboard. "Here's the spectrum," he said:

Over here, markets are hyperefficient. Every piece of information is known and immediately embedded in market prices within seconds. Over on the other end, here's a market that's totally crazy. Prices bear no relation to value or anything. We all agree the market isn't over here, and it isn't over there, and the thing we need to talk about is, where is it? Bill Beaver believes it's pretty damned far over here; some of you may believe it's pretty damned far over there. But we've got to understand what it's like over there at that end in order to address the question and to get on with our lives.[6]

The money managers stuck around. They didn't want to be insulted, but they wanted advice. The stock market decline of 1973 and 1974 had been, in inflation-adjusted terms, worse than that of 1929 and 1930. It left Wall Streeters poorer, less confident, and far more willing to listen to new ideas.

At the same time, the investment business was in the midst of a transformation that made it especially receptive to the advice that the professors had to offer. Stock holdings had begun to migrate in the 1950s from individual portfolios to institutionally managed ones. Early on, mutual funds were the main drivers of this change, but in the 1970s—as stock mutual funds struggled—another group of institutions came to the fore. These were pension funds, which had been around in the United States since the nineteenth century but really took off after World War II. They were at first used as a way to circumvent postwar wage and price controls by giving workers benefits that weren't counted as wages, and soon became part of the social contract between large corporations and their workers. With General Motors leading the way, America's big companies began setting aside money and investing it to pay for future pension benefits. Together with foundations and university endowments, the pension funds had come to constitute a huge new pool of institutional money by the late 1960s.

The people in charge of this money seldom picked the stocks and bonds in their portfolios for themselves. In the early days they left the job to bank trust departments or insurance companies. Then, starting in the 1960s, a new breed of independent money managers began to bid for their business. As middlemen, the pension and endowment chiefs who hired these asset managers tended to focus less on the return end of the operation than on the risk. They followed the 150-year-old "Prudent Man" rule, a legal doctrine that instructed trustees of others' money to "observe how men of prudence, discretion, and intelligence manage their own affairs" and conduct themselves accordingly.[7]

This had long been interpreted to mean that trustees should stick the money in their charge in high-grade bonds and *maybe* a few blue-chip stocks. That approach was sorely tested in the 1960s, when imprudent investors seemed to be having all the fun and making all the money. It was tested even more in the 1970s, when neither bonds nor blue chips proved safe, leaving a big opening for the new approach to risk, return, and diversification that was introduced two decades before by Harry Markowitz. In this view it wasn't the riskiness of an individual stock or bond that mattered, but the way it fit in to a portfolio. By the mid-1970s, this approach had a name—modern portfolio theory—and was beginning to make slight inroads in the institutional investing world. Then Washington gave it a huge boost.

In the wake of several corporate bankruptcies that left pensions unpaid, Congress passed pension-reform legislation in 1974. The Employee Retirement Security Act has since gone on to have many interesting consequences. The first had to do with the standard of prudence laid down by the law and in subsequent regulations from the Department of Labor. No longer a legal concept based on tradition, prudence was redefined to mean following the scientific dictates of modern portfolio theory.[8]

IN THIS ACCOUNTING, RISK CEASED to be a vague, unquantifiable menace that could be tamed only with judgment. It was a number, variance, which could be estimated mainly by looking at past variance. This development was in one way curious: The same finance scholars who claimed that you couldn't predict future stock price movements by looking at past stock price movements were embracing the idea that future stock volatility could be predicted by looking at past stock volatility.

"Estimating variances is orders of magnitude easier than estimating . . . expected returns," reasoned Fischer Black, one of the most prominent of the 1970s risk engineers.[9] There was no economic law dictating that financial volatility had to be constant or predictable. But at least there wasn't any economic law that said it *couldn't* be. If the direction of stock prices could be predicted, there would be free lunch for all. If the volatility could be predicted, that just meant more work for finance professors.

There also was some empirical evidence that, even amid the leaps and plunges that so interested Mandelbrot, long-run stock price volatility displayed a certain constancy. In the early 1970s, Barr Rosenberg of UC–Berkeley looked back through a century of stock market data and found:

> If you cut it in half, basically the variance in the first half and the variance in the second half were the same. That's not by chance. That means that our particular society settles in with a certain amount of surprise being acceptable and indeed interesting. Too much is too much, too little is too little, so that's quite mysterious.

Rosenberg had been a Harvard student of John Lintner, the reluctant cocreator of the capital asset pricing model. Black was a computer scientist who discovered finance working alongside yet another CAPM cocreator, Jack Treynor, at the consulting firm Arthur D. Little. Together with Sharpe, the two outlined an approach to financial risk that has survived and mostly thrived to this day. They had varying views about market efficiency—Rosenberg didn't much believe in it; Sharpe and Black did, but saw it more as a continuum than an absolute truth. What all three shared was a conviction that, however correct or incorrect stock prices might be, the most straightforward and thus most teachable path to investing success lay in better understanding risk.

In this view, risk couldn't necessarily be captured or quantified *perfectly*, but that didn't mean it wasn't worth trying to quantify. To make sense of the fat tails in stock price data observed by Mandelbrot, for example, Rosenberg demonstrated in 1972 that one could account for most of them by cobbling together a series of different bell curves, and using economic data to predict when you were moving from one normal distribution to another. This may sound awfully complicated, but it was easier to work with than Mandelbrot's power laws.

Rosenberg never got around to publishing his insight, and a decade later another economist, Robert Engle, arrived independently at the same idea. Engle won a Nobel Prize for it in 2002. Rosenberg didn't have time to see the paper into print because he was building a consulting business upon his ideas. His firm, Barra, provided measures of beta—a stock's sensitivity to the movements of the overall market—that were enhanced with fundamental data on earnings, sales, industry sector, and the like.

"Barr's better betas" (also known as "bionic betas") were more palatable to active money managers than the bare-bones versions offered previously. Rosenberg himself was a uniquely effective proselytizer for portfolio theory among Wall Street's unconvinced. His belief that stock picking was far from pointless, coupled with a quiet confidence and charisma not found in a lot of finance geeks, propelled him to near cult-leader status in investing circles. "As Rosenberg speaks, a hush typically falls over the audience," claimed a 1978 cover story in *Institutional Investor.* "In the manner of sinners, heads are slightly bowed. Eyes are moist and a bit glassy. One can almost hear the murmurs of 'Amen, Brother' and 'Praise the Lord.'"[10]

People in the investment business wanted answers. Rosenberg seemed to have them. He wasn't alone. During the 1970s, young scholars with quantitative training were accorded spectacular power and influence by pension chiefs and other money managers in search of guidance. Among the most influential were two Chicagoans, Rex Sinquefield and Roger Ibbotson, who seemed to find an answer to the biggest question of all—where stock prices were headed. Sinquefield was the former seminarian and 1972 Chicago MBA who declared that the efficient market hypothesis was "order in the universe" and launched one of the first index funds. His roommate Ibbotson had entered the Ph.D. program in the Chicago Business School after getting an MBA from Indiana University in 1967 and struggling a bit in the business world.

While still a grad student, Ibbotson got a part-time job managing the university's bond portfolio. When it came to stocks, the Chicago approach encouraged formerly frenetic traders to buy and hold. Bond investing had long been all about buying and holding, but the high inflation of the 1970s made that untenable. Holding on to a bond paying 5 percent interest when inflation was 10 percent was equivalent to giving away money. Ibbotson, using analytical tools being developed or rediscovered on campus—Fred Macaulay's formula for duration had just been unearthed by two Chicago professors—began buying and selling bonds and running rings around the market.

Because of his bond job, Ibbotson was interested in possessing the sort of historical data on bond returns that his Chicago professors James Lorie and Lawrence Fisher had compiled for stocks. Sinquefield was in the midst of starting a stock index fund at American National

Bank, and he wanted updated stock market data. Fisher showed no interest in reprising his great labor of the early 1960s, so Ibbotson and Sinquefield took on the job themselves. It was to be Edgar Lawrence Smith all over again, the fourth great reconstruction of market history (after Smith in 1924, Alfred Cowles in 1938, and Lorie and Fisher in 1964). Then Fischer Black, who had recently joined the Chicago faculty as a finance professor, came up with a twist.

After getting a Ph.D. in applied mathematics (a.k.a. computer science) from Harvard in 1965, Black had gone to work at the Cambridge-based consulting firm Arthur D. Little. There Jack Treynor introduced him to CAPM and its simple linkage of market risk and reward. Black soon sought out the other two creators of the theory, paying regular visits to John Lintner at Harvard and getting his employer to fly Bill Sharpe to Chicago for a meeting in a hotel near O'Hare Airport (Michael Jensen was there as well) to discuss CAPM's implications for performance measurement. "The CAPM was . . . the final jump he needed to solve the problem of what to do with his life," wrote Black's biographer, economist Perry Mehrling. "From then on he knew what he had to do, and so he did it."[11]

When Black heard of Ibbotson and Sinquefield's plans to gather data on stock and bond returns, he saw a connection to asset pricing theory. He told Ibbotson that with data on risky stocks in one hand and data on risk-free government bonds in the other, he and Sinquefield could calculate the historical premium that investors received for owning stocks. It was wonderfully simple—all they had to do was subtract one from the other. Once they'd figured out this "equity risk premium," Ibbotson and Sinquefield could add it to the prevailing interest rate on government bonds to get what they called "the market's 'consensus' forecast" of its own future trajectory. It looked an awful lot like extrapolating the future from the past, and some critics at the time said as much. But if you bought the finance professors' understanding of risk, it was something more solid. It was, Ibbotson said later, "the first scientific forecast of the market."

Ibbotson and Sinquefield presented their findings at the May 1974 seminar of Lorie's Center for Research in Security Prices. Their audience consisted mostly of fellow quants, so they presented their forecast probabilistically, following a random walk to see how far actual returns might wander from the expected mean.[12] Just for fun, they also churned out a version geared more to the sensibilities of Wall Street, forecasting that the Dow Jones Industrials average, floundering in the 800s at the time, would hit 9,218 at the end of 1998. They also said it would get to 10,000 by November 1999.

That forecast turned out to be spectacularly on-target: At the end of 1998, the Dow was at 9,181, just thirty-seven points off the forecast. It hit 10,000 in March 1999, six months early. Back in 1974, of course, no one knew the predictions would be right. But there was enough interest in the data and the forecasts from brokers and institutional investors that Ibbotson—by this time a junior professor at Chicago—set up a side business of updating the stock and bond data every year.

The Ibbotson Associates yearbooks became part of the library of every serious money manager. Ibbotson also began publishing wall posters that showed how stocks beat bonds through the decades; they became fixtures in the offices of brokers and financial advisers. And the forecasts of double-digit annual stock market returns became, especially after they started coming true in the 1980s, accepted as an eternal investing verity—playing a major role in getting pension funds to shift from bond-dominated to stock-dominated portfolios.[13]

Ibbotson Associates became, along with Barr Rosenberg's Barra, a pillar of a new investing establishment, built not in the traditional big-money redoubts of New York and Boston, but in Chicago and even more so along the West Coast—where UCLA, UC–Berkeley, Stanford, Rand, and even NASA's Jet Propulsion Laboratory provided the talent. Other advisory operations founded or reinvented in those days along quantitative lines included Wilshire Associates and Russell Investments, both of which created new, broader stock market indices that became important benchmarks for money managers. Morningstar, founded by a Chicago MBA who wanted to bring similar tools to individual investors, came along a little later, in 1984. Bill Sharpe, while he didn't actually start a company of his own until the 1990s, was an influential consultant to pension funds and money managers.

It wasn't just the consultants and research shops. San Francisco's Wells Fargo Investment Advisors built upon its pioneering indexing work to become what was in 2008, under the name Barclays Global Investors, the biggest money manager on the planet. Number two, State Street Global, was a big indexer and asset allocator as well.[14] Every other money manager of any size in the world now uses at least some of the quantitative tools introduced in the 1970s by finance professors.

What's more, one 1970s quant tool made it far beyond the money management industry. Armed with Ibbotson's measure of the equity risk premium and Barra's (or some other firm's) measure of a stock's riskiness in relation to the overall market, one could now calculate any publicly traded company's cost of capital. This metric was the holy grail, the search for which had launched Merton Miller and Franco Modigliani on their 1950s assault on old-style finance. Now it was within anybody's reach. Calculating the cost of capital in this manner soon became standard practice for MBA students, investment bankers, consultants, and corporate finance executives.

THIS WAS THE FIRST GREAT wave of quantitative finance. In the early 1970s, a small band of soon-to-be-very-influential finance professors began readying the second. These scholars set aside big questions of risk and return to focus on how the prices of different securities related to one another. From that beginning, they proposed, they could answer all the questions that mattered about markets.

This quest began, mundanely enough, with the search for the formula for valuing an option to buy a share of stock. The typical option speculator thinks he knows something about the underlying stock that the rest of the market doesn't. When he buys an option, he is making a leveraged bet on the trajectory of that stock.[15] When one has no idea which direction a stock is headed but believes one knows something about its volatility, valuing an option is an entirely different matter. The more volatile the stock's movements, the more likely it is that an option on that stock will deliver a big payoff.

Louis Bachelier had understood this back in 1900, and he used his mathematical depiction of random short-term security price movements to build an option-valuation formula. His option equation delivered some clearly wrong results—in some cases it gave options a higher value than the underlying stock. But he had the general drift right, and found that option prices on the Paris Bourse moved in the direction his formula indicated.

Paul Samuelson was already thinking about options when he discovered Bachelier's thesis in the mid-1950s, and he thought even harder about them after that. He thought too hard, though, to get it exactly right. In 1965, in the same issue of the same journal that featured his "Proof That Properly Anticipated Prices Fluctuate Randomly," Samuelson published twenty pages of equations that unsuccessfully tried to prove an option-pricing theorem. They were followed by an even denser appendix by an MIT mathematician.[16] Samuelson hadn't been able to cut down the number of variables enough to solve the puzzle. Two other partial solutions published by economics graduate students in the 1960s suffered from similar limitations.[17]

As a member of the small community of finance quants resident those days in Cambridge, Fischer Black heard of this option-pricing puzzle, and set about trying to solve it. Not surprisingly, he looked for guidance to CAPM, in which risk is a stock's sensitivity to the fluctuations of the market and expected return is a function of that. Considered in this way, it didn't matter what the stock's expected return was. The return was already reflected in its price. All that mattered was volatility.

Black teamed up with Myron Scholes, who had just arrived from Chicago to teach finance at MIT's Sloan School, and the pair worked out the proof for an equation that valued an option using the price of the underlying stock, the exercise price of the option, the time until the option expired, the risk-free interest rate, and the variance of the stock. Black and Scholes figured all this out in 1969, and first presented it in public in 1970. It took three more years to get the formula published, in part because the Chicago economists who ran the *Journal of Political Economy* didn't understand why they should care about such an obscure and somewhat disreputable financial instrument.

At the time, options were created haphazardly by brokers and traded only over the counter. Warrants, the long-dated options sometimes created by corporations as a reward to bankers or as a sweetener for investors, were more respectable and transparent. But there just weren't all that many of them. This was about to change, though, and Chicago Business School professors Merton Miller and James Lorie were working on it, as members of a Chicago Board of Trade task force charged with figuring out how to make an options exchange work.

As the New York Stock Exchange boomed in the 1960s, Chicago's two agricultural futures exchanges languished, and both began looking for ways to expand beyond wheat futures and pork bellies. Inspired by a Milton Friedman complaint about being turned down by banks when he wanted to buy British pounds to bet on a fall in the dollar, the Chicago Mercantile Exchange was first to market with currency futures in 1972.[18] The older and larger Board of Trade proceeded more deliberately, but it finally launched the Chicago Board Options Exchange in April 1973.

By this time, Lorie and Miller had hired Fischer Black to teach finance at Chicago and were working to bring back Myron Scholes. They had also smoothed the feathers of their friends in the Economics Department to get the pair's paper published in the prestigious *Journal of Political Economy*. It hadn't made it into print yet when the new exchange opened, so student Roger Ibbotson suggested to Black that they buy an exchange seat together to use the still mostly secret formula to get rich. Black declined, telling Ibbotson that such information was better sold than used. Ibbotson bought the seat and made good money for about a year—until Black ruined everything by launching a service that provided volatility estimates for the stocks whose options were traded on the exchange. "Once they put it on the computers in the members' lounge, that pretty much killed the business," Ibbotson recalled.

That Ibbotson made money using Black-Scholes before Black ruined things indicated that the formula had merit. But the eerie correctness of traded options prices after Black started his volatility service was something else. Black-Scholes wasn't just predicting options prices. As the house formula of the brand-new options exchange, it was *setting* them.

The Black-Scholes model had become a self-fulfilling prophecy. A basic assumption behind the Black-Scholes model—that stock prices follow a bell curve random walk—was, as already noted, not quite right. This did not in itself render Black-Scholes invalid. As Milton Friedman had argued two decades before, a successful scientific model is invariably "descriptively false in its assumptions." The test of its value is whether it is any good at prediction, and by the mid-1970s Black-Scholes appeared to be *spectacularly* good at predicting options prices. This was the sort of evidence—akin to the crashing and burning of all those high-beta, go-go mutual funds in the late 1960s— bound to fill finance scholars with confidence that their theories were not just helpful approximations but eternal truths. Even though some of those truths were self-fulfilling.

The phrase "self-fulfilling prophecy" was coined by sociologist Robert K. Merton.[19] Merton also wrote about the vagaries of scientific credit and naming, mainly the fact that the right people often don't get credit for major discoveries. There was some of that at work with the options formula. Edward O. Thorp, a math professor at the

University of California–Irvine, had figured out the mechanics of it back in 1968. But he hadn't devised a proof of the formula—other than that when he used it, he made money. Plus, he kept it to himself. In scientific terms he didn't really deserve credit. Some have since argued that Bachelier's was the true breakthrough on options pricing, and everything else mere embroidery on his theme. Black and Scholes were undeniably the first, though, to give the formula grounding in economic theory.[20]

A more complicated case was that of Merton's son, Robert C. Merton. The junior Merton came in after Black and Scholes had figured out their formula and derived it again in a different, more mathematically elegant way. It was his approach, not theirs, that was to set the tone for the future development of mathematical finance. And since 1997, when Merton and Scholes shared the Nobel Prize in Economics—Black died the year before—most scholars have taken to calling the formula "Black-Scholes-Merton."

Merton had been playing the stock market since childhood. He studied engineering at Columbia, married a soap opera actress and *American Bandstand* dancer whom he met on blind date, then headed west to enter the Ph.D. program in applied mathematics at the California Institute of Technology. During his first year at Caltech, Merton went to a Pasadena brokerage most mornings at six thirty and traded until nine thirty, when he left for class. He decided that maybe he should be studying economics instead of computers.

Caltech was still a few years away from offering doctorates in economics, so Merton applied to six universities that did. He got in only to MIT, the one place where his hard-science credentials counted for more than his utter lack of economics training, and took Paul Samuelson's mathematical economics course his first semester there in 1967. Merton was smitten, and so was Samuelson, who hired the student as his research assistant and roped him in to his options quest.[21]

After Black and Scholes began making the rounds with their formula, Merton derived it in a way that made more logical sense to him.

The starting point in his version was that it was impossible to make easy arbitrage profits. Two portfolios with equivalent returns and risk profiles could be relied upon to sell for the same price, because if they didn't, somebody would take advantage of the mispricing and make it go away.

Franco Modigliani and Merton Miller had introduced this kind of proof to finance in their famous cost-of-capital paper in 1958. They showed that an investor could in theory replicate any level of corporate indebtedness simply by borrowing money himself, and concluded that a company's mix of debt and equity should have no effect on its value. Merton demonstrated that it was possible by borrowing money and buying stock with it to assemble a portfolio with returns identical to an option on that stock—assuming that you could adjust this position at no cost throughout the life of the option. Some exotic math (something called "Ito's lemma" played a key role) led from there to the same formula as Black and Scholes.

In this way, Merton was able to build a formula that relied only on the efficient working of the market. CAPM was an economic theory. Merton's version of the options formula was pure finance. "Neoclassical finance is a theory of sharks, and not a theory of rational *homo economicus*,"[22] is how a finance scholar put it years later. These sharks were the arbitrageurs who could be relied upon to attack risk-free money-making opportunities and make them disappear.

The predators who kept markets efficient did require a rarefied theoretical environment to thrive. Merton later dubbed it the "super-perfect market paradigm." In it there were no transaction costs, no worries about moving prices with one's buying or selling, and no market discontinuities—that is, markets were always open and prices only changed in small increments.[23] Louis Bachelier had envisioned such a market, too, but he had been unwilling to look more than an "instant" into its future. Over any longer period, his professor Henri Poincaré had surely warned him, the tendency of men to behave like ocean-jumping sheep stood in the way of rational theories of market behavior. Merton got around this by assuming that it was always possible, at any moment in time, to rearrange one's holdings to reflect changed market circumstances. This meant Bachelier's "instant" could be replicated again and again and again, into the indefinite future.

It was certainly an elegant solution, and Black and Scholes made Merton's proof the centerpiece of the long-delayed published version of their paper. Black's original CAPM–based proof was presented as "An Alternative Derivation." Black never entirely embraced Merton's approach, though. Trading in real markets, he worried, was anything but continuous or smooth.

This wasn't a matter of right or wrong. Both approaches were, like all theories, unrealistic simplifications. Merton's had more appeal to the mathematically minded students who had begun to populate finance graduate programs. It also lent itself better to building models to price securities other than stock options—and those models, for mortgage-backed securities, for interest-rate and currency swaps, for all manner of other exotic financial instruments, have gone on to transform financial markets around the world.

Merton-style finance also steered its adherents toward a different understanding of risk. In the version of finance built upon the capital asset pricing model of Treynor, Sharpe, Lintner, and Black, risk could be manipulated and controlled and reduced, but never entirely eliminated—not even in theory. In the no-arbitrage version pioneered by Merton, the right combination of securities could eliminate risk entirely.

Enough such securities could also bring about something akin to economic perfection. To provide for economic equilibrium in the face of economic uncertainty, Kenneth Arrow had proposed in the 1950s that there needed to be securities for sale representing every possible state of the future. That seemed a purely theoretical ideal at the time, of course. By the mid-1970s, though, one of Arrow's students, Steve Ross, was proclaiming that—thanks to option-pricing theory—the financial world was moving in that direction.

Ross had majored in physics as an undergraduate at Caltech, and then studied economics at Harvard with Kenneth Arrow. He landed a teaching job at the University of Pennsylvania, and discovered options theory when Fischer Black gave a seminar on campus. Ross took to the topic with enthusiasm, and was soon explicitly tying it to his mentor's theoretical work on economic equilibrium. He and two other scholars came up with a new and more practical option-pricing formula based in part on the idea of Arrow's "state securities."[24] And he argued that this work was leading the world ever closer to the theoretical economic perfection envisioned by Arrow and Gerard Debreu. "Although there are only a finite number of marketed capital assets, shares of stocks, bonds, or as we shall call them 'primitives,'" Ross wrote in 1976, "there is a virtual infinity of options or 'derivative' assets that the primitives may create."[25]

Ever since the Great Depression, the dominant regulatory approach to taming financial risk had been to restrict what financial institutions and investors were allowed to do, to reduce the number of financial bets that could be made. This regime was already under sustained assault by the 1970s from both the political right and economic reality. Ross wasn't arguing from the right, or even from practical reality. He was a former Marxist who had abandoned physics in part because he was strongly opposed to the Vietnam War and didn't want to see his work exploited for military ends. Yet here he was arguing for the freedom to create infinite varieties of new financial instruments—because equilibrium theory said it would bring the economic world closer to perfection.

THE RISE OF THESE DERIVATIVES, as Ross called them, became one of the great financial stories of the next quarter century. Chronicling it adequately would require a book of its own. But one early derivative product in particular deserves a closer look—as a prototype of what was to come, and what could go wrong. It was called portfolio insurance, and it was an attempt to hedge away the risk of the stock market.

Merton and Scholes, who had become good friends at MIT, were the first to market such a product, launching a mutual fund in the mid-1970s that, by buying both stock options and government bonds, provided some insurance against stock market drops. But individual investors bold enough to be playing the market in the mid-1970s didn't seem interested in insurance policies, and the fund flopped. Pension fund managers were another matter. They were trustees, worried about losses and lawsuits and perfectly willing to sacrifice potential gains in order to avoid bad news. Toward the end of the decade, a couple of UC–Berkeley finance professors, together with a veteran financial entrepreneur, figured out how to sell them on portfolio protection.

In the early 1970s, then-governor Ronald Reagan had cracked down on spending—and thus faculty pay—at California's public universities. In high-priced Berkeley, this turned professors' thoughts to moonlighting. Barr Rosenberg was the first great success at it. One night in mid-decade his friend and fellow finance professor Hayne Leland cloistered himself in his study, committed to devising his own money-making idea before he emerged. Leland remembered a comment that his brother, a money manager, had made after the stock market collapse of 1973 and 1974. "Gee, it's too bad people couldn't buy insurance against the losses." He thought about it, and realized that his brother was talking about a put option—an option to sell a stock at a preset price. Put options on the entire market weren't available for sale, but the whole point of Merton's version of Black-Scholes was that one could simulate an option with a combination of stocks and debt. Leland enlisted his colleague Mark Rubinstein, the coauthor with Ross of what is now called the binomial option-pricing model, and the two mapped out an approach.

They didn't get anywhere close to bringing it to market, though, until they met John O'Brien. O'Brien, whose early career provides a sort of guided tour of the nascent quant scene, had been an engineer at Rand in the 1960s when his division was spun off as a for-profit private company and he was put in charge of figuring out the new firm's employee pension plan. He hired Bill Sharpe—then teaching in Southern California at UC–Irvine—to give him advice. Deciding that there was a business in the kind of advice Sharpe had to offer, O'Brien hooked up with a Chicago brokerage firm for which he devised a "beta service" that rivaled the one Sharpe designed for Merrill Lynch. He then founded a small brokerage firm, with offices on Wilshire Boulevard in Los Angeles, that advised pension funds on how to pick money managers and allocate their investments. O'Brien Associates, as it was called, also launched its own all-market stock index, the O'Brien 5,000.

In 1971, O'Brien became worried that his little firm would not survive the looming deregulation of brokerage commissions. He sold out to his more optimistic number two, Dennis Tito, and took a job with a larger brokerage, A. G. Becker of Chicago, that did performance measurement for money managers. It was a bad decision. The old firm thrived as Wilshire Associates, with Tito making enough money to pay his way into orbit years later as the first-ever space tourist. The O'Brien 5,000 became the Wilshire 5,000. And O'Brien began looking for a way to make up for that blown opportunity.

He found it at a 1979 seminar at Berkeley where Leland and Rubinstein spoke about portfolio insurance. The three soon teamed up as Leland O'Brien Rubinstein, or LOR, and began selling insurance policies not long thereafter. The banishment of risk could now begin.

CHAPTER 9

MICHAEL JENSEN GETS CORPORATIONS TO OBEY THE MARKET

The efficient market meets corporate America. Hostile takeovers and lots of talk about shareholder value ensue.

THE EFFICIENT MARKET HYPOTHESIS IS a theory of financial markets, and its initial impact was on financial markets and those who make their living off them. But the securities traded on markets are generally connected to the real world. Among the most direct of those connections are those between stocks and corporations. And starting in the 1970s, the efficient market idea began to find its way into corporate America.

The first modern corporations were special cases, created by acts of parliament in the seventeenth-century Netherlands and United Kingdom to enable specific endeavors adjudged to promote the common good. That's not always what they promoted. The South Sea Company collapsed in such a bubble of speculation in 1720 that the British parliament banned the creation of such entities—characterized by dispersed shareholders whose liability for the company's debt was limited to the value of their shares.

In 1776, Adam Smith argued that the "joint-stock company," as the corporation was then known, had proved an unmitigated disaster. "The directors of such companies, . . . being the managers of other people's money than of their own, it cannot well be expected, that they should watch over it with the same anxious vigilance with which the partners in a private copartnery frequently watch over their own," he wrote in the *Wealth of Nations*. "Negligence and profusion, therefore, must always prevail, more or less, in the management of the affairs of such a company."[1]

During the industrial revolution that began just after Smith's death, it became apparent that his analysis was off. No small group of partners had enough money to finance a canal or a railroad or an electric-light factory, and even if they did, they were unlikely to possess the expertise needed to get the job done. Legislators in Britain and the United States recognized this limitation, and in the mid-1800s relaxed the laws governing the creation of limited liability corporations. Forming one now required not a legislative act but the signing of a few documents.[2] Corporations grew, and thrived.

By the 1920s corporations had grown and thrived so much, in fact, that scholars began to focus again on the separation of ownership and control that had so concerned Adam Smith. This time they weren't worried that corporations would fail, but that corporate managers wouldn't do right by shareholders. As stock market fever spread to the masses during that giddy decade, the owners of big companies became ever more dispersed and ineffectual as a voice in steering management—and managers and their lawyers ever more adept at finding ways to keep cranky outside investors from posing a threat.

"The power of corporate managements is becoming practically absolute, while social controls upon this power remain almost embryonic," wrote New York lawyer and part-time Columbia professor Adolf Berle Jr. in 1927. Berle (pronounced "burly") had no problem with managers making all the important business decisions, but he thought there needed to be checks on executives' ability to interfere with the rights of outside shareholders (by such means as issuing special, more powerful classes of stock to insiders). He held out hope that investment banks, stock exchanges, and the new species of institutional investor—insurance companies, mutual funds, and so on—could speak for outside shareholders and keep management in line.[3]

A few Wall Street professionals embraced this role. Benjamin Graham waged a noteworthy campaign from 1926 to 1928 to force the Northern Pipeline Co. (a product of the court-ordered 1911 breakup of Standard Oil) to sell off its massive bond holdings and distribute the proceeds to shareholders. "Old Wall Street hands regarded me as a crackbrained Don Quixote tilting at a giant windmill," he wrote later. Graham eventually won over the Rockefeller Foundation, Northern Pipeline's biggest shareholder, and got what he wanted.[4] Few other professional money managers possessed his patience.

In 1927, Berle got a grant—from another Rockefeller-linked foundation—to study the matter of corporate control in greater depth.[5] He hired his former summer camp buddy Gardiner Means, who was working on an economics Ph.D. at Harvard, to help. The two holed up in an office at Columbia Law School and set to work. Five years later, having toiled through the last of the Roaring Twenties euphoria, the great crash, and the first desperate years of the Depression, they were done.[6] The result was *The Modern Corporation and Private Property*, a book that combined Berle's observations about the separation of ownership and control with page after page of statistical evidence gathered by Means that showed just how powerful the two hundred largest American corporations had become—they controlled 49 percent of nonbank corporate wealth at the time. The market euphoria of the late 1920s and subsequent crash had disabused Berle of his earlier notion that investment bankers or big investors might force corporate managers to do the right thing. And corporations had become so large and powerful that Berle and Means believed competitive forces alone couldn't keep them in check. The only remedy, they concluded, was for control of big corporations to "develop into a purely neutral technocracy, balancing a variety of claims by various groups in the community and assigning to each a portion of the income stream on the basis of public policy rather than private cupidity."[7]

The immediate response to the book was rapturous. The *Nation* declared it to be "epoch-making" while the *New Republic* called it "epoch-shattering." In the *Yale Law Review,* Jerome Frank—later the chairman of the Securities and Exchange Commission—wrote that it "will perhaps rank with Adam Smith's *Wealth of Nations* as the first detailed description in admirably clear terms of the existence of a new economic epoch." In one of the few reviews that did not make use of the word "epoch," historian Charles Beard announced on the front page of the book section of the *New York Herald-Tribune* that it might be "the most important work bearing on American statecraft" since the *Federalist Papers.*[8]

Not surprisingly, *The Modern Corporation and Private Property* landed on the reading table of Democratic presidential candidate Franklin Delano Roosevelt. After FDR beat incumbent Herbert Hoover in 1932, he made Berle a member of his original "brains trust" of ivory-tower advisers. Means joined the administration, too. Berle didn't last as a presidential adviser (writing letters to Roosevelt with the salutation "Dear Caesar" can't have helped[9]), and neither he nor Means ever wielded great personal clout in New Deal Washington.[10] But their ideas were in the air as Congress approved the Securities and Exchange Acts of 1933 and 1934, creating the SEC and modern securities law.

What's more, executives at large corporations did, tentatively during the hard years of the 1930s but wholeheartedly once the nation entered World War II, come around to the idea that their jobs involved a certain amount of what Berle and Means called "public policy rather than private cupidity." Big companies accepted ever more government involvement in their activities—and ever more responsibility for their employees' well-being as they expanded their pension plans and began offering health insurance.

And why not? Giants like General Electric and General Motors seemed as substantial and permanent a part of the economic landscape as government itself.[11] When just-retired GM president Charlie Wilson, President Eisenhower's pick for defense secretary, was asked during his Senate confirmation hearing in 1953 which way he would decide if there was a conflict between the interests of his former employer and those of the nation, he famously replied, "I cannot conceive of one because for years I thought what was good for our country was good for General Motors and vice versa. The difference did not exist. Our company is too big. It goes with the welfare of the country."[12]

BY THIS TIME, THE IDEA that great corporations might be subject to economic laws dreamed up in a bygone era of independent shop owners and entrepreneurs seemed laughable to most of America's intellectuals. The mockery had begun at the turn of the century with Thorstein Veblen's tirades against free market economists and the capitalists they celebrated.[13] It continued less caustically in Berle and Means's book, and achieved more rigorous form with the theory of "monopolistic competition" advanced by Edward Chamberlin in his Harvard Ph.D. thesis in 1927 and the theory of "administered price" that Gardiner Means proposed in a government memo in 1935.[14] The gist of both hypotheses was that the large American corporation could set prices at will and effectively foist its products upon consumers. In a series of bestselling books in the 1950s and 1960s, Harvard economist John Kenneth Galbraith brilliantly popularized this view. Galbraith, the last great representative of the literary, institutionalist tradition in American economics that had begun with Veblen, likened American corporate executives to Soviet apparatchiks: the bureaucratic administrators of a vast system geared toward overconsumption and waste.[15]

In the 1950s, economists were busy dismissing the institutionalist approach from their discipline, but most shared Galbraith's views on corporate America. The main center of opposition to Galbraith's arguments could be found on the South Side of Chicago. The fiercest critiques came not from the University of Chicago's Business School or even its Economics Department, but from the Law School.

The leader of the counterrevolution was Aaron Director. Perhaps because he was older, and had spent more time in Washington (where he worked in the Treasury Department), Director was the first member of Milton Friedman's circle to turn openly skeptical of government. When his sister Rose, yet another product of the Chicago economics program, informed him in 1938 that she was marrying Friedman, Aaron wrote back, "Tell him I shall not hold his very strong New Deal leanings—authoritarian to use an abusive term—against him."[16] As a student at Chicago, Director had dazzled in class and in conversation but never completed a dissertation. Writing just wasn't his thing. Several of his Chicago teachers wanted to bring him back to the fold in the 1940s, but he had no doctorate and no plans to get one. As one doesn't need a Ph.D. to be a law professor, the economists persuaded the Law School to hire him in 1946.[17]

Director initially taught a single class, Economic Analysis, but he soon branched out. He led a class in antitrust law with Edward Levi, the Law School dean and a noted expert on the subject, that became legend. According to students who were there, Levi would spend the first four days of the week explaining existing antitrust law, after which Director devoted the fifth to explaining why none of it made any economic sense. At first Levi bridled, but eventually he was won over by Director's relentless economic logic.

So were the students. "A lot of us who took the antitrust course or the economics course underwent what can only be called a religious conversion," said Robert Bork, who studied law at Chicago in the early 1950s. "It changed our view of the entire world."[18] Many of Director's students went on to make his economics teachings the focal point of their careers. An academic movement had been launched.

Director's main message was that things happened in the business world for a reason, and that when one looked hard enough one would usually find Adam Smith's invisible hand at work—even at General Motors. "In each of the various practices he has analyzed (tie-in sales, patents, resale price maintenance, etc.) he has sought the profit-seeking reason that led businessmen to adopt the practice," wrote Chicago economist and kindred spirit George Stigler. "Sometimes the reason was the exercise of monopoly power, but other times an important efficiency was achieved by the practice."[19] As a result, Director argued, there was far less need for antitrust laws, or consumer protection regulations, than was commonly believed.

A separate school of thought, launched in the late 1950s and early 1960s by two Chicago products teaching at the University of Virginia, James M. Buchanan and Gordon Tullock, dovetailed perfectly with Director's arguments. Public choice, as it came to be known, taught that regulators and lawmakers were economic beings acting in their own self-interest—meaning that they couldn't really be relied upon to do what was best for the economy.[20] Combine that with law and economics, and you had an all-encompassing explanation of why regulation was bad and free markets good.

MILTON FRIEDMAN WAS NOT A full-fledged member of his brother-in-law Aaron Director's law-and-economics team. He was too busy with other work. But as he made the transition from scholar to media star in the 1960s, Friedman took on the responsibility of presenting his Chicago colleagues' ideas to the still largely hostile outside world. In 1970 he explained in the pages of the *New York Times Magazine* the Chicago view of the role of corporations in American life. The news peg was the rise of "Campaign GM," a movement led by consumer activist Ralph Nader to place three representatives of "the public interest" on the giant automaker's board of directors. Nader would push this theme throughout the 1970s, arguing that, because corporations had been created by government action, they ought to be held to high standards of civic responsibility.

Friedman had a different take. "There is one and only one social responsibility of business—to use its resources and engage in activities designed to increase its profits so long as it stays within the rules of the game, which is to say, engages in open and free competition without deception or fraud," he wrote. Corporate executives who purported to strive toward some higher goal were not only cheating their shareholders but "undermining the basis of free society."[21]

Friedman had made this argument before in his book *Capitalism and Freedom*, but this time it reached many more readers—different readers. These were shocking arguments for an establishment-liberal *Times* subscriber to wake up to on a September Sunday morning, and the magazine's letters page soon filled with outraged rebuttals. One said, "Friedman's defense of pure Adam Smith is like Billy Graham's defense of the literal truth of Genesis." A Harvard MBA student declared that Friedman was "a symbol of the mind which continues to propagate the *status quo*, ignoring the ever clearer handwriting on the wall."[22]

In fact, the handwriting on the wall was Friedman's (and Billy Graham's, come to think of it). Galbraith's depiction of a static economic landscape ruled by corporate apparatchiks contained much truth in the 1950s and 1960s. In the 1970s, though, the American economy was beginning to look more like something out of an economics textbook. Upstart competitors from overseas, aided by the advent of the shipping container—which wiped out most of the cost of overseas transport—began taking on American giants and winning.[23] No longer were executives at U.S. Steel or General Motors able to set prices at will and dole out products to captive consumers as they saw fit. They had to swim or sink in a truly competitive market.

Director and his disciples had been right that even big corporations couldn't flout economic laws. In throwing out this dirty intellectual bathwater, though, they ignored a crucial element of Berle's argument that had not lost relevance with the passage of time—the separation of ownership and control that had gotten Berle (not to mention Adam Smith) all worked up about corporations in the first place. Never fear, though. It was about to be rescued and reinvented by Michael Jensen, along with his University of Rochester colleague William Meckling.

The university where Jensen and Meckling taught was a private school of previously modest ambitions that emerged in the 1960s as one of the richest in America. The reason for Rochester's sudden wealth was that it had invested heavily in the shares of two local companies, Eastman Kodak and Xerox. The latter firm in particular had become a stock market sensation, going from obscurity to one of the most valuable corporations in America in half a decade on the strength of its new copying machine.[24] In 1962 the chairman of the university's board of directors—who also happened to be chairman of Xerox—lured W. Allen Wallis away from Chicago's Business School to be Rochester's new president.

Wallis promptly began hiring Chicago economists. He tapped Meckling, a Friedman student from Chicago who had been working at Rand and at the Center for Naval Analysis, as dean of the Business School. Meckling in turn hired Jensen to jump-start his finance program. The success of an endowment run like a go-go mutual fund had thus enabled Rochester to hire a scholar who had made his academic reputation demonstrating that the go-go funds' success was illusory. Jensen did not dwell on this irony. He and Meckling were once asked to look over the school's investment strategy, but neither was impolitic enough to suggest major changes.

Inspired by Friedman's *Times* article, Jensen and Meckling decided to write a paper on "the antisocial responsibility of business" for a summer conference in 1971. They thought it would be a simple matter to translate Friedman's journalistic arguments into the language of economics. It wasn't. "We started looking at it as economists," Jensen recalled. "We saw that competition between businesses wouldn't guarantee an optimal result, because the people running businesses had their own motives." Friedman had noted this problem in his article as well, stating that a company's owners were "principals" and its managers "agents," and that problems always ensued when agents took on responsibilities beyond those of looking out for their principals. But while Friedman simply argued that executives *shouldn't* behave that way, Jensen and Meckling looked more closely at the executives' incentives.

They reprised Berle's argument about the separation of ownership and control, but they gave it a different name—"agency costs"—and represented it with a bunch of equations that would have confounded Berle (who died in 1971). They also saw a way out of the fix that didn't involve government intervention: the efficient market. The stock market could be relied upon to "fully reflect all available information," and even some information that wasn't readily available. Companies whose executives failed to act in shareholders' interest would be punished with lower stock prices. The job of monitoring executives' behavior was thus left to Wall Street, and this monitoring—which reduced agency costs and made corporations behave more efficiently—provided a rational explanation for why mutual funds and brokerage firms expended millions of dollars analyzing stocks when it was impossible to beat the market. What made the securities analysts' exertions worthwhile, Jensen and Meckling argued, was the increased overall value of the stocks traded on the market.[25]

The concept of the efficient market had taken a big step. It is one thing to encounter a hypothesis within the science where it was developed—in its natural habitat, as it were. There, one can find caveats and doubts and people *who knew it when*. When such a theory is transferred intact to another discipline, a lot of that baggage is inevitably lost. The rational market idea had first made its way from theoretical economics into the empirical subdiscipline of finance, where it had lost in nuance and gained in intensity. Now it was voyaging into even more distant territory. Jensen and Meckling wanted to rely upon the stock market's collective judgment to resolve conflicts of interest that had plagued scholars, executives, and shareholders for generations.

Not that any of this caught on immediately. Big American companies reacted ponderously to the change in competitive environment brought on by the 1973–74 oil crisis and the less immediately obvious but even more significant rise of German and Japanese manufacturers. The stock market was of course much quicker to notice: Adjusted for inflation, the S&P 500 dropped even more from 1973 through 1977 than in the five years starting in 1929. The signals from the all-knowing market were clear. Corporate America needed to shape up. The question was how to get executives to pay attention.

ONE OPTION WAS PERSUASION. THIS became a specialty of Joel Stern, a blustery New Yorker who entered the Chicago MBA program the same year as Michael Jensen and Myron Scholes, but didn't stick around for a Ph.D. Instead, he went to work at Chase Manhattan Bank in New York, where he was assigned to a division that gave financial advice to corporate borrowers. When Stern arrived in 1964, that advice focused on helping corporations juice their reported earnings. Influenced by the arguments of his Chicago teacher Merton Miller, Stern was convinced that shareholders could see through such accounting machinations. The key was to judge all investments, acquisitions, and other spending decisions by the standard of Miller and Modigliani: Were they likely to deliver higher returns to shareholders than the shareholder could expect to make at similar levels of risk elsewhere in the market?

Over time, Stern found an audience for these ideas. In 1972 he wrote an opinion piece for the *Wall Street Journal* arguing that what really moved the market was not earnings or even expected earnings but "expected cash flow that is above and beyond the anticipated investment requirement of the business."[26] That's what the sole proprietor of a business cares about. Stern made the case that it's what shareholders in a big corporation are after as well. Stern's first *Journal* article led to others, and to a fortnightly column in the *Financial Times* of London. He became a regular guest on the new PBS show *Wall $treet Week*. He built his own fiefdom at the bank, a consulting division called Chase Financial Policy that assembled an impressive client list and succeeded in winning several CEOs over to Stern's way of thinking—notably Chuck Knight, who took over St. Louis–based conglomerate Emerson Electric in 1973 and with Stern's help transformed it into one of the most successful stock market performers of the last quarter of the twentieth century.

Other consulting operations with links to academic finance sprang up in the 1970s to dispatch similar advice. Marakon Consulting grew out of Wells Fargo's Division of Management Science. Alcar was the creation of Northwestern University accounting professor Alfred Rappaport and a colleague. In a 1981 *Harvard Business Review* article, Rappaport gave the approach a name that stuck: The most basic question for any strategic planner in business, he wrote, was "Will the corporate plan create value for shareholders?"[27] To figure out how to create this "shareholder value," Rappaport continued, one had to measure the expected return from any corporate investment against the cost of capital. To compute the cost of capital, Rappaport recommended using the Ibbotson-Sinquefield equity risk premium and Barr Rosenberg's measures of beta.

That was all fine and good, but corporate executives weren't going to focus on creating shareholder value just because they'd read about it in the *Harvard Business Review*. They needed incentives. Linking pay to stock prices was one way to do it, but that approach had fallen mostly out of favor in the 1970s. Options to buy corporate stock had been used widely in the 1950s and 1960s to reward executives and align their interests with those of shareholders. They were also a tax shelter—if executives held on to the shares they bought with the options, their gains were taxed not as income but capital gains, subject to a much lower rate. That tax advantage was steadily ratcheted back in the 1960s (the chief ratcheter was U.S. senator Al Gore Sr.) and removed entirely in 1976. Options virtually disappeared from the scene. Not that most executives minded—with stocks going downhill, they weren't clamoring to see their paychecks follow suit.

How could executives be made to pay attention to the verdict of the stock market? If they were worried that somebody might buy their company and throw them on the street, *that* might be a motivator. In the 1950s, takeover specialists—then known as "proxyteers," for their battles to win control over shareholder proxy votes—first became a significant factor on the American corporate scene. The most visible of the early takeover fights came in 1954, when former University of Georgia football star Lewis Wolfson launched a bid for control of poorly run retailer Montgomery Ward. Wolfson failed and corporate executives fought back, lobbying Congress to stop the barbarian onslaught.[28]

New Jersey senator Harrison Williams became the leader of the anti-takeover movement. "In recent years we have seen proud old companies reduced to corporate shells after white-collar pirates have seized control," he said on the floor of the Senate in 1965. "The ultimate responsibility for preventing this kind of industrial sabotage lies with the management and shareholders of the corporation that is so threatened. But the leniency of our laws places management and shareholders at a distinct disadvantage in coming to grips with the enemy."[29] How shareholders could be placed at a disadvantage by people who wanted to pay a premium for their shares was something of a mystery, but the threat to management was real, and corporate managers maintained a strong lobbying presence in Washington. Most critics of corporate America, meanwhile, came from the political left—people such as John Kenneth Galbraith and Ralph Nader—and weren't keen to embrace Wall Street raiders.

That left the field to Henry Manne, a 1952 graduate of the University of Chicago Law School. He had been through the usual conversion experience there, arriving with plans to become a labor union lawyer and emerging three years later a "confirmed free marketer." As a young legal scholar his interest in corporate governance did lead him down some interesting paths, among them some previously trod by Berle—a man his Chicago professors dismissed as a "nut." Manne corresponded with Berle and became an admirer of Wolfson and the other proxyteers, whom he saw as crucial to resolving Berle's ownership-and-control dilemma. After touching on this idea in several law journal articles, he attacked it head-on in the *Journal of Political Economy* in 1965 in what would become a landmark essay.

Mergers and takeovers among competitors had long been frowned upon in the legal literature because they reduced the number of participants in a market and thus reduced the number of choices for consumers. Manne argued that if you considered not just the market for a company's products but what he dubbed "the market for corporate control," such mergers began to look a lot better. "Only the take-over scheme provides some assurance of competitive efficiency among corporate managers and thereby affords strong protection to the interests of vast numbers of small, non-controlling shareholders," he wrote. "Compared to this mechanism, the efforts of the SEC and the courts to protect shareholders through the development of a fiduciary duty concept and the shareholder's derivative suit seem small indeed."[30] To believe this argument, Manne conceded at the time, you had to assume "a high positive correlation between corporate managerial efficiency and the market price of shares of that company."[31] Bad managers would be punished by lower stock prices, making it more likely their companies would be acquired. The people at the Chicago Business School had yet to deliver their "proof" of such market efficiency, but Manne could see it coming.

Senator Williams still got an anti-takeover law enacted in 1968, but Manne's ideas played a role in making the final Williams Act less draconian than what the senator had initially proposed.[32] The law made it impossible to launch a hostile takeover without warning, but it didn't make it impossible to launch a hostile takeover.

In the 1960s, takeovers—hostile and otherwise—were mostly the work of the companies Gerry Tsai loaded up on in his Fidelity Capital fund. Hot conglomerates such as LTV and ITT (International Telephone and Telegraph) used their high-priced stock to buy cheaper, less glamorous companies. In the bearish 1970s, such all-stock acquisitions didn't work anymore, but by the middle of the decade, stock prices had dropped so low that companies with extra cash began sniffing around for bargains. The $224 million all-cash hostile takeover of battery maker ESB (for Electrical Storage Battery Co.) by International Nickel in 1974 marked the beginning of a new era—notable because a blue-chip mining giant was doing the hostile bidding and a blue-chip Wall Street firm, Morgan Stanley, was representing it. Not many companies had that kind of money lying around. The advent of a takeover boom required the arrival of a financier.

Michael Milken was that financier. As an undergraduate at UC–Berkeley in the 1960s, Milken had come across a 1957 National Bureau of Economic Research study showing that low-grade bonds delivered better returns than high-grade ones. This made perfect capital asset pricing model sense: Bonds downgraded by S&P or Moody's had been deemed riskier than bonds that hadn't, so investors *should* reap a reward for buying them. While still in college, Milken began investing in these so-called junk bonds. When he went to work at the struggling brokerage firm Drexel Harriman Ripley after finishing his MBA at Wharton, he began building a business out of selling them.

The bonds Milken sold in the early days hadn't started out as "junk." They were securities of "fallen angels," companies that once seemed safe and secure but now weren't, of which there were many in the 1970s. In 1977, though, Drexel began *manufacturing* junk— underwriting bond issues that had low ratings and high interest rates from the start. With inflation moving into double digits, these "high-yield" bonds attracted investors, which meant that, despite a still-floundering stock market, it was now possible for even small operators to raise big money in the debt market. A new takeover era could begin.[33]

This time around, hostile takeovers would have articulate and influential defenders. The most strident invariably had ties to the University of Chicago,[34] but Manne had made sure it wasn't just Chicagoans who understood his argument. In 1971, while teaching at the University of Rochester, he began bringing in law professors from around the country for an annual summer economics institute. Later he started a similar program for federal judges. He also had the ear of the Reagan administration, which came to power in 1981. While hundreds of bills were introduced in Congress in the 1980s to rein in takeovers or junk bonds, none became law. When Reagan's SEC chairman began worrying loudly in 1984 about the dangers of takeovers, Treasury Secretary Donald Regan, the former CEO of Merrill Lynch, made the administration's position clear by stating that takeovers were "beneficial" as "they provide a means—sometimes the only feasible means—of policing management in widely held corporations."[35] A few months later, the annual Economic Report of the President included a whole chapter titled "The Market for Corporate Control"—written by a product of Chicago's Economics Department—that was simply an updated version of Manne's seminal 1965 article.[36]

The 1980s takeover boom did end eventually, shut down by state legislatures immune to Chicagoan reasoning, a U.S. attorney in Manhattan (Rudy Giuliani) intent on bringing down some big Wall Street names, and the crash of the junk bond market. But the power of Manne's arguments helped delay this fate for nearly a decade, during which buyout firm Kohlberg Kravis Roberts & Co., lone rangers Nelson Peltz and Carl Icahn, and others like them transformed the economic landscape. They accomplished this transformation with what to many seemed like great brutality and waste. By the late 1980s, many worried commentators were arguing that while Japan and Germany built up their industrial might, U.S. corporations were being forced by the takeover wave to shutter factories and load up on debt. The leveraged buyout artists were harming American competitiveness.[37]

MICHAEL JENSEN WAS CONVINCED OF the opposite—that the takeover wave was making America's economy stronger. And while Manne and others made their case in Washington and among those in the legal profession, Jensen preached the merits of takeovers to the most dubious audience possible—the present and future leaders of corporate America. This stance made him controversial, and about as famous as a business school professor can get. It also made him the main intellectual father of what became corporate orthodoxy and even a sort of national creed in the 1990s.

For all the success that the new ideas about efficient markets achieved on campus and within certain precincts of the investing world, they had yet to penetrate the real centers of economic power in America by the early 1980s. Index funds were still in their infancy. Few outside the investment business had noticed the growth and modern-portfolio-theory-guided transformation of pension funds. Wall Street itself was still far from the center of the economic world it would soon become. And while the theory-first, rational-market-based approach to business education that originated at Carnegie-Mellon and held sway at Rochester, Chicago, and MIT had spread to other schools,[38] it still hadn't cracked Harvard.

Harvard remained the biggest business school, the most influential with top business leaders, and the most resistant to economic theory. But it was going through an identity crisis. In 1971, business school deans polled by *MBA* magazine said it had been surpassed by Stanford in academic quality. A year later, Harvard had also fallen behind Chicago and MIT in the poll.[39] By the end of the decade even Harvard's administration had turned critical. University president Derek Bok wrote in his 1979 annual report that the Business School had become ingrown and was producing too little original research.[40]

Harvard Business School was thus interested in buying what Jensen was selling. For his part, he was getting a little tired of preaching to the converted up at Rochester. In 1984 he arrived on the Boston campus as a visiting professor. He soon signed on as a full-timer and created a course on organizational behavior, built around agency theory, that within a few years became the Business School's most popular elective. He also made full use of the pulpit granted him by a Harvard professorship. No longer was he making his arguments to his fellow finance geeks in the pages of the *Journal of Financial Economics*. His words were now in the *Harvard Business Review* and even the *New York Times*.

"The takeover market," Jensen told the *Times* in 1985, "provides a unique, powerful and impersonal mechanism to accomplish the major restructuring and redeployment of assets continually required by changes in technology and consumer preferences."[41] The problem with most corporate managers, he wrote a year later, was that they had a tendency to overinvest, to build firms larger than they needed to be. That was because growth stroked their egos and usually their paychecks. Hostile takeovers and other leveraged buyouts—even buyouts initiated by management—saddled companies with debt loads that altered managers' behavior. "In these cases, levering the firm so highly that it cannot continue to exist in its old form generates benefits," Jensen wrote in 1986. "It creates the crisis to motivate cuts in expansion programs and the sale of those divisions which are more valuable outside the firm."[42]

Jensen was making a more expansive argument than Manne ever had. It wasn't just that the threat of takeovers kept corporate managers from ignoring shareholders. Jensen's study of agency costs had convinced him corporate managers needed a single, unifying goal to do their jobs well—and the only one that made sense was economic value. If it turned out to be simpler to create that value for junk bond holders than shareholders, then so be it. It was all the same anyway, as Franco Modigliani and Merton Miller had demonstrated back in 1958.

Debt was good. Crisis was good. Management turnover was good. Precisely by forcing companies to get out of unpromising businesses and shut down underperforming factories, leveraged buyouts were making America more competitive. "By resolving the central weakness of the large public corporation—the conflict between owners and managers over the control and use of corporate resources—these new organizations are making remarkable gains in operating efficiency, employee productivity, and shareholder value," Jensen wrote in the *Harvard Business Review* in 1989.[43]

The idea that corporations should be run to benefit their owners was not new, having been bandied about—and repeatedly violated—since the dawn of the modern corporation. What *was* new was the conviction and all-encompassing nature of Jensen's worldview. To quote the grudgingly admiring words of one leftist critic:

> The great advantage of Jensenism is that, when combined with an uncritical acceptance of the efficient markets religion, it amounts to a unified field theory of economic regulation: all-knowing financial markets will guide real investment decisions towards their optimum, and with the proper set of incentives, owner-managers will follow this guidance without reservation.[44]

In the 1980s, this "Jensenism" was still a minority ideology. It wouldn't stay that way.

THE CHALLENGE

CHAPTER 10

DICK THALER GIVES ECONOMIC MAN A PERSONALITY

Human nature begins to find its way back into economics in the 1970s, and economists begin to study how markets sometimes fail.

THE ONLY POINT DANIEL KAHNEMAN was trying to get across was that praise works better than punishment. The Israeli Air Force flight instructors to whom the Hebrew University psychology professor delivered his speech that day in Jerusalem in the mid-1960s were dubious. One veteran instructor retorted:

> On many occasions I have praised flight cadets for clean execution of some aerobatic maneuver, and in general when they try it again, they do worse. On the other hand, I have often screamed at cadets for bad execution, and in general they do better the next time. So please don't tell us that reinforcement works and punishment does not, because the opposite is the case.

As a man trained in statistics, Kahneman saw immediately that *of course* a student who had just brilliantly executed a maneuver (and was thus praised for it) was less likely to perform better the next time around than a student who had just screwed up. Abnormally good or bad performance is just that—abnormal, which means it is unlikely to be immediately repeated. But Kahneman could also see how the instructor had come to his conclusion that punishment worked. "Because we tend to reward others when they do well and punish them when they do badly, and because there is regression to the mean," he later lamented, "it is part of the human condition that we are statistically punished for rewarding others and rewarded for punishing them."

Think back to Milton Friedman's billiards players, who didn't understand the complex physics behind their shot selection but acted as if they did. In billiards, the feedback one gets is immediate and informative. In flight training—or in investing, or in all manner of other endeavors clouded by statistical noise—that's not the case at all, which is what Daniel Kahneman had suddenly realized.[1]

Decades later, after he had won a Nobel Prize in Economics for his work, Kahneman described this moment with the flight instructors as "the most satisfying Eureka experience of my career." It was not an experience that he knew immediately what to do with. His own psychological research focused not on decision making but on technical matters like the dilation of people's pupils as they memorized long numbers. It wasn't until one day during the 1968–69 academic year, when Kahneman invited a younger colleague named Amos Tversky to speak to his students, that he began to figure out what to do with his insight.

Tversky was an almost-direct link to the ideas about decision making that had captivated economists in the late 1940s and early 1950s. Von Neumann and Morgenstern's expected utility and Savage's statistical axioms had captivated a few psychologists too. For decades, academic psychology in the United States had been stuck in a "behaviorist" rut of studying stimulus and response while ignoring cognition—what went on between the ears. For psychologists looking to break out of that rut and explore how decisions were made, the "statistical man" embraced by economists held great appeal.

For them it was just a starting place. Unlike the economists, who by the mid-1950s had—with few exceptions—accepted von Neumann-

Morgenstern as gospel truth and moved on, psychologists continued tweaking and testing. Among the most prolific of the tweakers and testers was Ward Edwards, Amos Tversky's academic mentor at the University of Michigan.[2] In one Edwards experiment, participants were shown two book bags full of poker chips. One was said to be filled mostly with black chips, the other with red. The test subjects were then given one of the bags, and told to draw chips from it. With each draw they assessed the probability that they'd gotten the mostly black bag or the mostly red one. These probability assessments generally moved in the right direction, but much more slowly than Savage's rules instructed.

Edwards concluded that his test subjects were rational if a bit "conservative." Upon hearing Tversky's account of the experiment, Kahneman recalled his flight instructor and drew a different lesson—that the poker chip grabbers were irrationally fixated on the color of the first chip they drew. Tversky was at first dubious, but when the two continued their discussion after class at a café in downtown Jerusalem he began to warm to Kahneman's contention that mankind's statistical reasoning might *not* accord with the models described in textbooks.[3]

To see how closely human decision making coincides with the rational model, one will devise tests likely to confirm that it more or less does. To see how far it diverges, one comes up with different questions to ask—which is what Kahneman and Tversky began to do, first devising a questionnaire that Tversky administered at a couple of conferences of mathematical psychologists. What he found, as Kahneman and Tversky detailed in their first paper together, "Belief in the Law of Small Numbers," was that even numbers-oriented psychology professors did not obey the rules of statistical inference. Instead, they attached great significance to early trends in their data. They assumed that whatever the first few subjects in an experiment did or said was representative of the population at large.[4]

This discovery set Kahneman and Tversky off on a series of similar experiments, all of which revealed gaps between the dictates of decision theory and the actual decisions made by even expert study subjects. In 1974 they brought their results together and published what amounted to a manifesto. "How do people assess the probability of an uncertain event or the value of an uncertain quantity?" they wrote. "People rely on a limited number of heuristic principles which reduce the complex tasks of assessing probabilities and predicting values to simpler judgmental operations. In general, these heuristics are quite useful, but sometimes they lead to severe and systematic errors." In other words, humans aren't constantly calculating statistical men, but they aren't idiots either. They follow shortcuts and rules of thumb that sometimes work, and sometimes don't.

There was no mention of economics in the paper, and no attempt by Kahneman and Tversky to tackle head-on the question of whether the heuristics and biases they had identified amounted to a challenge to the rationalist model of decision making. But Kahneman and Tversky chose to publish their article not in a psychology journal but in *Science*, a publication sure to reach scholars in other disciplines.

ECONOMICS HAD CONTINUED ON ITS ascent (or descent, if you prefer) into hyperrationality. For several decades the discipline had separated microeconomics, which was about selfish, rational people interacting in perfect markets, from macroeconomics, which was built around simple hydraulic models not based on any consistent theory of human behavior. It was an awkward coexistence, and it was probably inevitable that one day a mathematically inclined graduate student in economics would apply the elegant formulas he was learning in micro class to the inelegant problems of the business cycle.

It was also perhaps inevitable that this would happen at Carnegie Tech's Graduate School of Industrial Administration, that pioneer in imposing the scientific method on matters of money and human behavior. Economics maverick Herbert Simon was the instigator, in a backward sort of way. He had argued, decades before Kahneman and

Tversky, that because people don't have unlimited time and brainpower to devote to decision making they take shortcuts and follow rules of thumb. Humans don't "optimize," as the mathematical economists of the day theorized, but "satisfice" (a blending of "satisfy" and "suffice"). Simon was a major power at Carnegie Tech (in a unique arrangement, he served on the university's board of trustees even while teaching). The economists there had no choice but to listen to him, though they didn't have to like it. "I heckled the GSIA economists about their ridiculous assumptions of human omniscience," Simon wrote in his memoirs, "and they increasingly viewed me as the main obstacle to building 'real' economics in the school."[5]

In the late 1950s, Simon enlisted fellow faculty member Franco Modigliani and Modigliani's student John Muth to study the decision-making process in a paint factory in Pittsburgh. Simon led the project. The other two had no choice but to use his "satisficing" approach. As soon as it was over, Muth fought back. "It is sometimes argued that the assumption of rationality in economics leads to theories inconsistent with, or inadequate to explain, observed phenomena, especially changes over time," he wrote in 1959, citing Simon. "Our hypothesis is based on exactly the opposite point of view: that dynamic economic models do not assume enough rationality." Muth went on to propose not that every last individual or corporation made rational guesses about the future, but that when one averaged out the guesses about the future made by participants in an economy, they came to look a lot like the predictions of the most sophisticated economic models.[6]

This "rational expectations" hypothesis was more or less the same thing as the efficient market hypothesis, albeit it with broader reach and less evidence to back it up. It went nowhere at first, but as Keynesian economic policy faltered in the 1970s, several scholars who had passed through Carnegie Tech in the 1960s—notably Robert Lucas, the student once overwhelmed by "the shock wave of [Milton] Friedman's libertarian-conservative ideas" as a grad student at Chicago[7]—spread the word. Deirdre McCloskey, a former Chicago faculty member who has made a career of examining economists' rhetoric, described the shift in approach:

> In the Keynesian or monetarist models of the 1960s and before . . . the economic actor was perfectly astonished, the perfect rube: [Seizes newspaper.] "My word! The government has just reduced taxes in depression!" [Eyes bug out.] "Holy cow! The government has trimmed the growth of money after a long period of inflation! Gosh!" [Faints.] It would be trivially easy to manipulate such a dunce, from which grew the conviction in the 1940s and 1950s that it was trivially easy to manipulate the economy—to "fine tune" it, as the journalists said. The models of rational expectations in the 1970s went to the opposite extreme. They viewed the economic actor as a man of the world: "Oh, yes, a tax cut." [Yawns, lights cigarette in a golden holder.] "Hmm: I see that inflation has been going on for some months." [Settles into club chair.] "About time for the Fed to do its tight money act." [Calls broker, sips scotch; dozes off under his copy of *Barron's*.][8]

With astonishing rapidity, rational expectations became orthodoxy and the Chicago Economics Department—to which Lucas returned in 1974—its temple. "One cannot find good, under-forty economists who identify themselves or their work as 'Keynesian,'" Lucas wrote in 1980. "At research seminars, people don't take Keynesian theorizing seriously anymore; the audience starts to whisper and giggle to one another."[9] Even Paul Samuelson declared that if forced to choose between the "two extreme archetypes" of old-style Keynesianism and Lucas's rational expectations, "I fear that the one to jettison would have to be the ur-Keynesian model."[10] Lucas had taught himself mathematical economics the summer before he started graduate school at Chicago by working his way through the equations in Samuelson's *Foundations of Economic Analysis*. He portrayed his work as the logical continuation of Samuelson's relentless microeconomic reasoning into the realm of macroeconomics, a tribute Samuelson appreciated.

SAMUELSON DID NOT BELIEVE, THOUGH, that his relentless mathematical reasoning was adequate to the challenge of explaining economic reality. He was, recalled Joseph Stiglitz, a Samuelson favorite who got his Ph.D. from MIT in 1967, "quite good at identifying weaknesses in the perfect competition model and not taking it very seriously." Just identifying weaknesses wasn't enough for Stiglitz or his fellow student George Akerlof. "If you're going to say, 'This model does not provide a good description,' you need to provide a model that does provide a good description of what's going on," said Stiglitz. "George and I saw our job as graduate students as creating the models [of imperfect competition] that Samuelson was telling us about."

That's what they did, mostly by following a path blazed a few years before by Kenneth Arrow. Arrow was one of the most influential economists of the post–World War II era, right up there with (or maybe even ahead of) Samuelson and Milton Friedman. But he had nothing like their public profile. Instead, Arrow distinguished himself throughout his long career—spent mostly at Stanford but interrupted by an eleven-year stint at Harvard in the 1960s and 1970s—by his curiosity and his open-mindedness. No sooner had he helped define what a perfect market looked like, than he moved on to exploring why actual markets didn't look like that. One key reason, Arrow suggested in a landmark 1963 paper on the economics of health care, was that the parties to a transaction didn't always possess the same information.[11] Friedrich Hayek had argued that the dissemination of dispersed information was the greatest strength of markets, and it probably is. But when Arrow and others started looking closely at the economics of how information is gathered and disseminated, matters quickly got more complicated.

In a perfectly efficient market, information is presumed to flow like water—faster than water, actually. As soon as one person possesses it, it becomes known instantaneously to everyone through the mechanism of prices. But if that were the case, what incentive would anyone have to gather information? While teaching at Stanford in the mid-1970s, Stiglitz and a young colleague just out of Chicago, Sanford Grossman, asked this question. They came up with an interesting answer. "[P]rices cannot perfectly reflect the information which is available," they concluded, "since if [they] did, those who spent resources to obtain it would receive no compensation."

Grossman and Stiglitz proved, using a mathematical framework based on rational expectations and sprinkling their text with approving references to Hayek, that the strong form of the efficient market hypothesis could not be true. They also made the less obvious point that if information were inexpensive, there would in a market of rational investors be almost no trading, since all investors would have access to the same information and thus come to the same conclusions. Without expensive-to-unearth information or irrationality (or both), markets could not exist.

Grossman and Stiglitz said they were "attempting to redefine the Efficient Markets notion, not destroy it,"[12] and the reaction from most finance scholars was a shrug. "It was an obvious point," Richard Roll claimed later. "It didn't really need a paper." The overwhelming majority of research in finance in those days was no longer concerned with the question of *whether* markets were efficient. One just assumed that they were, and proceeded from there. The Grossman-Stiglitz result wasn't dramatic enough to stop finance scholars from doing that, so they ignored it.

Economists paid attention. Even as Chicago basked in its status as the center of the economics world in the 1970s, the wellsprings of a new economic mainstream bubbled up in Cambridge, Massachusetts. It wasn't just MIT and Harvard. In 1977, Wesley Mitchell's old National Bureau of Economic Research moved to Cambridge, reinvented by its new president, Harvard economist Martin Feldstein, as a place where top young scholars tried out the theories they'd just developed to examine real-world problems.

Many of the most prominent economists of the early twenty-first century emerged from this heady environment—Ben Bernanke, Paul Krugman, Larry Summers, Greg Mankiw, Glenn Hubbard, and many more.[13] These scholars all used lots of math, and usually built their theories around the rational, statistical economic man. Yet they were flexible and willing to follow both their reasoning and the empirical evidence to new, unexpected places. Rational expectations had taken the mathematical economics of the 1950s to its logical conclusion, and it turned out that not many economists were willing to go there. Some began heading in the opposite direction.

HERBERT SIMON, WHOSE QUARRELS WITH mainstream economists had helped inspire the rational expectations revolution, returned to the discipline in 1977. Kenneth Arrow was the responsible party, having campaigned to get Simon elected a fellow of the American Economic Association that year. This post gave Simon a prominent speaking slot at the AEA's annual meeting, which he used to talk about rationality and its limits. That presumably helped lead to his winning the next year's Nobel Prize in Economics, "for his pioneering research into the decision-making process within economic organizations."[14]

A year later, Daniel Kahneman and Amos Tversky built upon Simon's ideas and their experiments to launch their first head-on attack on economics and its reliance on von Neumann and Morgenstern's version of decision making under uncertainty. How do people really assess uncertain prospects? Kahneman and Tversky asked. First, they attach much importance to where things stand now, treating reductions in their current wealth significantly differently from reductions in future gains. Second, they regard remote probabilities and near-certain ones much differently from those in between. In graphic terms, the result was not a smooth curve representing the consistent trading off of risk and return, but a herky-jerky combination of different tradeoffs in different situations.[15]

Kahneman and Tversky published their article on "prospect theory" in *Econometrica,* the most mathematical of the major economics journals. It wasn't vague psychological theorizing but rigorous, equation-filled, and to a lay reader almost entirely unintelligible. It had just what it took to become a hit among economists who were getting more and more interested in asking subversive questions but didn't want to lose their chance at tenure by sounding too much like psychologists.

First and most eager among these economists was Richard Thaler. As a graduate student at the University of Rochester in the early 1970s, Thaler wrote a dissertation about the value of a human life. He measured how much people got paid to work in risky jobs such as logging or mining, compared these wages to the pay for safer jobs demanding similar skill, and with a little statistical work came up with a dollar amount for the value of avoiding death. This approach is called "revealed preference," and it was popularized by Paul Samuelson in the 1940s.

Thaler couldn't leave it at that. This was not an arcane technical matter, but life and death. He was curious, and he quizzed friends and acquaintances:

> I asked people two questions. First, how much would you be willing to pay to eliminate a one in a thousand risk of immediate death. Second, how much would you have to be paid to willingly accept an extra one chance in a thousand of immediate death . . . A typical answer was, "I wouldn't pay more than $200, but I wouldn't accept an extra risk for $50,000!" I came to two conclusions about these answers: (1) I better get back to running regressions if I want to graduate; and (2) The disparity between buying and selling prices was *very* interesting.[16]

Thaler ran his regressions well enough, earning not just a Ph.D. but a job as an assistant professor at Rochester's Business School, the territory of Bill Meckling, Mike Jensen, and many like-minded sorts. One professor even regularly regaled finance classes with cries of "The price is right! The price is right!" ("It was," recalled a student, "like a bad game show."[17])

Thaler could not, however, shake his curiosity about the choices people made. At a dinner party for colleagues during his first semester on the job in 1974, he served his guests a bowl of cashews as an appetizer. When it started looking like they might eat so much as to spoil their appetites, he removed it to the kitchen. The guests applauded this decision, but immediately began questioning its economic implications. They clearly wanted to eat the cashews, or they wouldn't have been eating them. But they just as clearly wanted to stop eating them, or else they wouldn't have been so happy when Thaler took them away. Thaler began compiling a list of such anomalous behavior on his office door, eventually building it into what he termed a "joke paper" on the "theory of economists' behavior." But it was just a joke.

Thaler's dissertation made him an authority on the economics of life and death. In the summer of 1976 he spoke on the subject at an academic conference on environmental risk in Monterey, California. Psychologist Baruch Fischhoff was at the conference, too, and afterward he bummed a ride with Thaler back up to the San Francisco Bay area. Fischhoff had just gotten his doctorate at Hebrew University, where he had been Kahneman's research assistant. During the car ride, Fischhoff told Thaler about the work Kahneman and Tversky were doing. Thaler was intrigued, and asked Fischhoff to send him some of it. The package that arrived a few weeks later included Kahneman and Tversky's 1974 *Science* article about heuristics and biases.

"When I read this paper, I could hardly contain myself," Thaler wrote. Suddenly, his less-than-serious collecting of decision-making quirks looked like a scientific pursuit, with a serious literature behind it. It was a psychology literature, not an economic one. Thaler soon learned from Fischhoff that Kahneman and Tversky were already at work trying to change that with their paper on prospect theory, and decided he wanted in. He found out that Kahneman and Tversky would be spending the next academic year at Stanford, and he arranged his own year-long sabbatical there. The three men became friends. They taught him psychology. He taught them economics.

Thaler's extracurricular activities did not impress his colleagues at Rochester. He tried to leverage a job offer from Cornell University into a promotion to associate professor at Rochester but was turned down. So he moved ninety miles down the road to Cornell. Thaler felt isolated there, but he was free to follow his interests. He explored how prospect theory could explain the behavior of Mr. H., who mows his own lawn even though his neighbor's son would be willing to do it for $8, but would not be willing to mow his neighbor's lawn for $20. Or the man who joins a tennis club and pays a $300 membership fee, then develops tennis elbow but keeps playing through the pain because, he says, "I don't want to waste the $300."[18]

With his former Rochester colleague, Hersh Shefrin, Thaler also explored the ramifications of his earlier experience with cashews before a dinner party. The lesson was that we are often of two minds, one that impatiently demands satisfaction now and another that rationally weighs present and future rewards. Thaler and Shefrin used a mathematical framework borrowed from agency theory to describe how these conflicting internal priorities interacted, and they described a real-world institution—the "Christmas club" stashes that people set up to deduct a preset amount from their bank accounts every month to save up for end-of-the-year shopping—that seemed to flow from it.[19]

Thaler began to find others interested in this new approach, which came to be called behavioral economics despite its roots in cognitive—not behavioral—psychology. Shefrin was the first convert and, like Thaler, soon left Rochester for a friendlier environment. In Shefrin's case it was Santa Clara University in California, where he and colleague Meir Statman began a productive collaboration examining the psychology of investor behavior. Thaler's Cornell student Werner De Bondt was another important early fellow traveler. Among established economists, George Akerlof was probably the most supportive, teaching a class together with Kahneman at UC–Berkeley for several years in the 1980s. A handful of adventurous young economists at other schools began following the study of less-than-hyperrational decision making in other directions.

Thaler's biggest triumph in those early days, though, was lining up psychologist and foundation executive Eric Wanner to be the intellectual movement's patron. Wanner ran the Russell P. Sage Foundation, a smallish foundation set up by the do-gooder widow of a turn-of-the-nineteenth-century robber baron. The foundation's chairman in the mid-1980s was Citicorp CEO John Reed, who had been frustrated with the inability of orthodox economists to see the third world debt crisis of the early 1980s coming and supported efforts to shake up the discipline. The Sage Foundation paid for conferences and workshops, handed out grants to young researchers, and even sponsored a regular behaviorist "summer camp" for graduate students and junior professors. The infrastructure of an intellectual movement was being constructed.

There were some questions early on about what kind of intellectual movement it would be. In the early 1980s, Thaler was briefly involved with a group called the Society for the Advancement of Behavioral Economics. George Akerlof and Herbert Simon were members of its first advisory board. It soon became apparent that most of those who signed up wanted to lay waste to the entire mathematical, hard-science apparatus that economists had built after World War II. Thaler didn't want to do *that*, and he later left the group—which lives on today as a low-profile organization with almost no impact on the economics mainstream.

"These guys did not want to blow economics apart," said Wanner of Thaler and the other economists who worked with the Sage Foundation. "They just wanted to show that there are lots of things about human decision making that aren't just noise around a rational mean but systematic irregularities." Colin Camerer, a 1981 Chicago Ph.D. and early Thaler ally, put it a different way. "In the 1980s, a lot of people went into behavioral economics because the math was too hard in regular economics. Thaler and I didn't want students like that," he said.

ANOTHER APPROACH TO ECONOMICS AROSE in the 1970s that was in some ways kindred to the behaviorists' work, although there was almost no contact between the two groups until decades later. If nothing else, they were linked by the disdain their methods had inspired in Milton Friedman. In his 1954 manifesto on economic methodology, Friedman dismissed the questionnaires of psychologists as too silly for economists to contemplate and the experiments of the hard sciences as impossible for them to replicate. Behavioral economics was all about reexamining that first judgment. The experimental economists aimed to overturn the second.

The economics of the laboratory had actually gotten its start just as Friedman was dismissing it, in the early 1950s in the Harvard classroom of Edward Chamberlin. Chamberlin had argued in his *Theory of Monopolistic Competition* that building economic theory around perfectly competitive markets was a mistake. To demonstrate the shortcomings of typical supply-and-demand models, each year the professor gave over the first day of his monopolistic competition class to an experiment in which students were designated as buyers or sellers and commanded to trade with one another. Each buyer was given a target price he wasn't supposed to go above, and each seller a target he wasn't supposed to go below. As the students went about the room making deals, their actions were dismaying for those who believed in perfect markets. Prices fluctuated wildly, and lots of "money" (there was no real money involved) was left on the table.[20]

For Chamberlin, that was the end of it: *Ha, ha, neoclassical economics is all wrong.* But a student who took his class in 1952, Vernon

Smith, saw greater potential in the experiment as an educational tool. As a Caltech graduate with a degree in electrical engineering, Smith was familiar with experimental science. His first teaching job out of Harvard was at lab-rich Purdue University, and in 1956 he reprised Chamberlin's experimental market for an introductory economics class. He made some crucial tweaks, using the rules of the New York Stock Exchange as a guide—transactions were anonymous and prices posted on a blackboard as the experiment proceeded—and repeating the affair several times to make sure the students understood what they were doing. What he found surprised him. Despite possessing only the bare minimum of information needed to trade, the students arrived at an equilibrium result straight out of Alfred Marshall's *Principles of Economics.*

Smith kept tinkering with these experiments in class, then wrote a paper about his results that, after four rejections, was published in Chicago's *Journal of Political Economy* in 1962. He left the idea alone for a while after that, only to revive it during a stint as a visiting professor at Caltech in the mid-1970s. The science and engineering hotbed had created an Economics Department of sorts,[21] and Smith's former Purdue colleague Charles Plott was one of its early hires. Together, they began to see the laboratory not just as an educational device but as a serious means of verifying economic theories. Smith and Plott hatched test after test, developing an experimental-economics ethos that has lived on at Caltech and a few other campuses, the most important element being that participants must compete for real monetary rewards. These weren't the questionnaires and what-if scenarios used by other social scientists, but actual markets—albeit artificial ones populated almost exclusively by college students.

The study of finance was replete with experimental possibilities. When one designs a market experiment, it's possible to know with certainty the intrinsic, fundamental value of the securities being traded. More often than not, in the markets designed by Smith, Plott, and others, prices converged toward that value—but not always. Bubbles developed; markets failed. Much depended on the rules that governed the market, and the greatest impact of experimental economics has been on market design.

Plott had even grander ambitions. During an academic year spent at the University of Chicago in the late 1970s, he asked Eugene Fama for advice on testing his efficient market hypothesis in an experimental setting. "He said his theory has nothing to do with experiments," Plott recalled—it applied only to markets in the field. "But aren't the principles of economics general enough to apply to both situations?" Plott remembers wondering. Fama's take, decades later: "Experimental research is no substitute for empirical work on real market data."

It was against actual financial market data that the hypothesis would have to be tested. And in the late 1970s, it began to fail those tests.

CHAPTER 11

BOB SHILLER POINTS OUT THE MOST REMARKABLE ERROR

Some troublemaking young economists demonstrate that convincing evidence for financial market rationality is sadly lacking.

IN THE SPRING OF 1979, just after the publication of their "Prospect Theory" article, Daniel Kahneman and Amos Tversky visited Richard Thaler at the University of Rochester. Thaler arranged a dinner for his guests and, somewhat mischievously, seated Tversky next to efficient markets apostle Michael Jensen. The exchange that resulted, recalled Thaler's Rochester colleague Hersh Shefrin, who was also at the table, "kind of set the tone for the debate over the next fifteen years."

The psychologist could not resist springing one of his quizzes on the finance professor. Tversky asked Jensen to describe how his wife made decisions. Jensen regaled him with tales of her irrational behavior. Tversky asked Jensen what he thought of President Jimmy Carter. An idiot, Jensen said. And what about the policies of the Federal Reserve chairman? All wrong. Tversky continued listing decision makers of various sorts, all of whom Jensen found wanting. "Let me see if I've got this straight," Tversky finally said. "When we talk about individuals, especially policy makers, they all make major errors in their decisions. But in aggregate, they all get it right?"

Jensen's response was "Well Amos, you just don't understand."[1] Errors and irrationalities of the sort Tversky asked about simply *didn't matter*. It was the market as a whole that got things right, not its individual participants. Cold-blooded professional investors could be relied upon to pounce on any financial market irregularity—"arbitrage opportunity," in the finance lingo—and make it disappear. That was what made markets so great. In a democracy, an irrational majority could dominate. In a free financial market, even a tiny rational minority would invariably prevail.

The most famous statement of this viewpoint was made a few years later by Chicago's Merton Miller. The occasion was a Chicago conference on "the behavioral foundations of economic theory"—motivated, its organizers said, by "the growing body of evidence" documenting "systematic departures from the dictates of rational economic behavior."[2] It attracted a crowd of all-stars from both sides of the rationalist divide, among them Miller.[3] In a paper reprinted several times and cited endlessly, the Chicago professor allowed that cognitive psychology might explain why some individual investors and individual corporations did what they did. But such explanations weren't what finance was about. "That we abstract from all these stories in building our models is not because the stories are uninteresting," he argued, "but because they may be too interesting and thereby distract us from the pervasive market forces that should be our principal concern."[4] The market was rational. Who cared about individuals?

This was the scientific paradigm within which Miller had been working for decades. All research proceeded from the assumption that "pervasive market forces" invariably pushed security prices toward their correct, fundamental values. This had been well established empirically back in the 1960s, after all. Or had it?

THE 1970 BOOK *Predictability of Stock Prices*, by Clive Granger and Oskar Morgenstern, reads as a sort of alternate-universe version of Eugene Fama's far better known distillation of the efficient market hypothesis. Granger and Morgenstern had been members in good standing of the 1960s random walk fellowship. They were also big-time economists. Granger went on to win a Nobel Prize in Economics, for unrelated work, in 2002. Morgenstern was coauthor (if not quite cocreator) of the von Neumann-Morgenstern model for decision making under uncertainty that dominated economics and finance.

Yet Granger and Morgenstern did not see the findings of the previous decade in the same light that the finance professors did. To start, they declared that "probably the most perceptive account of stock market behavior so far" was not some academic journal article but *The Money Game* by journalist George A. W. Goodman (writing under the pseudonym Adam Smith). In that entertaining 1967 bestseller, Goodman devoted a full chapter to the random walk, but declared that he didn't buy it, arguing instead "that in the long run future earnings represent present value and that in the short run the dominant factor is the elusive *Australopithecus*, the temper of the crowd."[5] Granger and Morgenstern did not disagree. "The random walk hypothesis does not say that price changes are unpredictable: it says they are not predictable using (linear) combinations of previous price changes," they wrote. "It is conceivable that one could introduce other variables which did have some predictive values."[6]

More to the point, they argued that it was nonsense to say stock prices reflected intrinsic values. These intrinsic values of stocks "are supposed to reflect fundamentals of their companies, such as capital equipment, inventories, unfilled orders, profits," they wrote. "Most of these items, and the values attached to them, will hardly fluctuate as fast and far as the stock prices do. It is . . . a subterfuge going back at least to Adam Smith and David Ricardo to say that market price will always oscillate around the true (equilibrium) price. But since no methods are developed how to separate the oscillations from the basis, this is not an empirically testable assertion and it can be disregarded."[7]

Fama had proposed that the way to test the efficient market hypothesis was to see if stock price movements obeyed the dictates of the capital asset pricing model, but this was only a relative test. It might reveal whether stock price movements made sense in relation to each other and the overall market, but it was no help in showing whether the overall market was correctly priced or not.

The mostly forgotten other father of the efficient market hypothesis, Holbrook Working, had tried to devise a more fundamental accounting. He got some crucial help along the way from the Chicago Mercantile Exchange, the nation's onion farmers, and the U.S. Congress. The Merc, which had started out as the Chicago Butter and Egg Board, lost its butter futures business in the 1930s with the advent of federal dairy subsidies. Onion futures were launched in the late 1940s to replace that lost income. The struggling Merc remained dominated by a handful of traders, and in 1957 a couple of them cornered the market in onion futures, and prices skyrocketed. Onion farmers who should have sold high and pocketed the money were swept up in the excitement and *bought* futures. It ended badly.

"Onions ended up selling for less than the price of the burlap bags in which they were delivered," recalled Leo Melamed, a trader who later went on to run the exchange. "The onion farmers of America were outraged. They had lost money on their crops as well as their futures contracts." The angry farmers lobbied their representatives in Washington to rid them of onion futures trading, and in 1958 a federal ban was enacted that remains on the books today.[8]

For the Merc, this debacle was the impetus for a big cleanup, and then a spectacular burst of innovation and reinvention led by Melamed that began with the creation of pork belly futures contracts in 1961 and continued through the introduction of financial futures based on currencies, interest rates, and stock market indices in the 1970s. For Working, the ban on onion futures was a prime opportunity to test the efficiency of futures markets. He figured that by comparing the volatility of onion prices in the presence and in the absence of futures trading, he could get a sense of whether futures markets steered prices toward their correct levels or simply added volatility.

Working initially looked at the behavior of onion prices before and after onion futures trading began in the 1940s and found that prices had been less volatile during the futures trading years.[9] This result was encouraging, but it was the postban studies, undertaken by other agricultural economists along the lines set out by Working, that could offer more compelling evidence. The first, in 1963, showed more price volatility after the ban than before—supporting the thesis that futures markets made pricing more calmly rational.[10] But in 1973, yet another study found that onion prices over the entire course of the 1960s, a decade void of onion futures trading, were the least volatile on record.[11] There may have been other factors at work: better transportation, better weather, better onions. But there was no clear evidence from the onion fields to support the presumption that speculative markets got prices right.[12]

That last study was published in a Department of Agriculture technical bulletin. Few nonagricultural economists noticed it, and the entire topic disappeared from sight for a while. Some economists remained dubious of the conviction that the rationality of markets was a closed case. As MIT's Franco Modigliani told an interviewer in 1982:

> I accept, by and large, the random walk hypothesis as a good approximation, but with the understanding that it is consistent with fairly long-lasting disequilibrium. In the short run you can get trapped into a situation in which no gain can be made, even though it is not one of fundamental equilibrium. The stock market is now way off, but I wouldn't advise anybody to rush in. I expect that some years from now it will be three times higher, but it can get a lot worse before it gets better.[13]

Modigliani wasn't saying he could predict the movements of the stock market with money-making accuracy (although anyone who bought stocks in 1982 and held on did make a killing). He was saying he was confident the market could be wrong for long—unpredictably long—periods of time. That was a statement with which most economists of his generation, including Paul Samuelson and even Milton Friedman, would agree. None of these men devoted any of their serious scholarly work to fleshing out these ideas about financial market error.

THAT WOULD BE THEIR STUDENTS' job. While Joe Stiglitz led the way in looking for theoretical flaws in the perfect market worldview, another product of Samuelson and Modigliani's MIT was to take on the efficient market hypothesis where it counted—in the data. Robert Shiller, who got his doctorate from MIT in 1972, was a sophisticated statistician and a crack computer programmer. He combined those skills with a seemingly naive eagerness to apply them to questions so simple that they could seem childlike, brazen, or even downright lunkheaded.

In his dissertation and his early work as a professor at the University of Pennsylvania, Shiller focused on whether real-world interest rates behaved in accordance with the theory of rational expectations. His answer to that question was mostly, although certainly not entirely, affirmative. He then moved on to the stock market.[14]

Irving Fisher and John Burr Williams had taught that stock prices represented the discounted value of future dividends. Shiller set out to test this assertion in the most straightforward possible way. He compared the movements of the S&P 500 to subsequent changes in dividends paid by S&P 500 companies. The stock prices turned out to be *vastly* more volatile than dividends. What Shiller had devised was in effect a nonevent study. He was looking for cases where nothing of consequence happened, but prices nonetheless moved.[15]

Shiller's graduate school classmate Robert Merton had a ready retort: Of course stock prices were more volatile than dividends, because corporate managers went out of their way to keep dividend payments steady. Why they did that was a question for which finance professors had no good answer, but Merton *was* right that there was another way to look at the discrepancy.

Financial market prices are just about the cleanest, hardest-to-manipulate data in all of economics. If they were more volatile than fundamentals like dividends, earnings, revenue, or book value, Merton argued, maybe the problem was with the fundamentals:

> If . . . the rationality hypothesis is sustained, then instead of asking the question "Why are stock prices so much more volatile than (measured) consumption, dividends, and replacement costs?" perhaps general economists will begin to ask questions like "Why do (measured) consumption, dividends, and replacement costs exhibit so little volatility when compared with rational stock prices?"[16]

It was a clever bit of argumentation, and one that should elicit at least some sympathy from anyone familiar with the sausage making involved in producing economic data or corporate earnings reports. It couldn't disguise that Merton and his colleagues in finance had no new evidence with which to sustain their "rationality hypothesis." Merton trotted out the usual litany of event studies and 1960s random walk work. Yet they weren't enough to establish that stock prices were *rational*. Shiller's evidence wasn't enough to establish that they were irrational, either. But it was enough to throw the whole matter in doubt. His brazen, childlike, even lunkheaded question had hit its mark, and he knew it.

The leap from observing that it is hard to predict stock price movements to concluding that those prices must therefore be right was, he declared at a conference in 1984, "one of the most remarkable errors in the history of economic thought. It is remarkable in the immediacy of its logical error and the sweep and implications of its conclusion."[17] One professor in the audience came up afterward and worriedly advised Shiller to remove these incendiary words from the published version of his paper. Another, with a better sense of how to make one's mark in the world, said, "No, no, don't take it out."[18] Shiller left them in.

Shiller was teaching at Yale by this time, and he had acquired an equally brazen ally up Interstate 95 at Harvard, the precocious Lawrence Summers. As the nephew of both Paul Samuelson and Kenneth Arrow, Summers had the most impressive pedigree of any economist, ever.[19] Seen as the brightest star in the dazzling constellation of smart young economists in Cambridge, Massachusetts, he worked within the economic mainstream. He did have an argumentative streak, and a mischievous one, and the dubious claims of the efficient marketeers drove him to exercise both.

Like Shiller, Summers had a knack for combining advanced mathematics with provocative rhetoric. As an example of the former, he constructed a model of an alternate financial universe in which investors weren't rational and prices didn't reflect fundamental values—and showed that, over a fifty-year observation period, there was no way to differentiate it statistically from a rationally random market. Only with one thousand years of data could you tell them apart.[20] As for the latter, you can't do much better than his witheringly funny putdown of the entire discipline of finance, delivered at—of all places—an annual meeting of the American Finance Association.

Summers began his talk by describing a world in which economists devote their careers to studying ketchup. Some, he said, study it as part of the broader economic system. Others are "ketchup economists located in the Department of Ketchup where they receive much higher salaries than do general economists." The general economists worry about factors that might affect the supply of and demand for ketchup—the cost of tomatoes, consumer incomes, and so on—and try to measure whether ketchup price fluctuations are in line with these fundamentals. The ketchup economists "reject out of hand much of this research on the ketchup market," Summers said. "They believe that ketchup transactions prices are the only hard data worth studying."

The research program of these ketchup economists consists largely of looking for—and not finding—ways to make excess profits in the ketchup market. Two-quart bottles of ketchup always sell for twice as much as one quart bottles "except for deviations traceable to transactions costs," and you can't get a bargain on ketchup by buying and combining the ingredients yourself. "Indeed," he continued, "most ketchup economists regard the efficiency of the ketchup market as the best established fact in empirical economics." Then Summers got serious for a moment:

> The parallels should be clear. Financial economists like ketchupal economists work only with hard data and are concerned with the interrelationships between the prices of different financial assets. They ignore what seems to many to be the more important question of what determines the overall level of asset prices. It would surely come as a surprise to a layman to learn that virtually no mainstream research in the field of finance in the last decade has attempted to account for the stock market boom of the 1960s or the spectacular decline in real stock prices during the mid-1970s.[21]

Who let Summers deliver such a speech at a meeting of finance professors? Fischer Black, who was in charge of the 1984 meeting agenda, did. The two had gotten to know each other in 1979, when Summers began teaching at MIT after getting his doctorate at Harvard (he returned to Harvard in 1981). Black had left Chicago for MIT because his wife was homesick.

In 1979, Black still believed in the rational market. Summers goaded him about it. "THERE ARE IDIOTS. Look around," began one informal paper that Summers shared with Black a few years later. People who did not follow the teachings of finance—idiots—seemed not only to exist in abundance, but to move prices. They had such an impact that it sometimes seemed as if the idiots had a better chance of striking it rich than those who bought and sold strictly on real information—and certainly a better chance than those who listened to the finance professors and bought index funds. "How many finance professors are included in the *Forbes* 400?" Summers asked, referring to the annual listing of America's four hundred richest people. "How many of the people who are there believe the market is efficient?" Finance professors assumed that smart traders would eat the idiots' lunches and thus move markets back toward efficiency. But Summers didn't see why idiots couldn't continue to dominate the market for a good long while.

Black handed the paper back with comments scrawled in the margins. He didn't agree with Summers's conclusions that "we might all be better off without a stock market," and "flexible exchange rates are unwise." But he took a remarkably benign view of Summers's assessment of markets, if not his exact choice of words. "I call them 'noise traders,'" he wrote of Summers's idiots. "They trade on noise as if it were information."[22]

With that, Black went from leading efficient marketeer to unlikely champion of the theory's critics. Why the switch? "He was the most pure truth seeker I ever knew," Summers explained. "Utterly unvested in his prior thought, his friends, what people thought would make sense, anything."

The first tangible result of Black's new stance was the 1984 publication in the *Journal of Financial Economics* of an article by behaviorist mavericks Hersh Shefrin and Meir Statman that explained corporate dividend payouts in terms of the psychological quirks of investors—mainly the propensity to prefer a certain reward today to an uncertain one tomorrow.[23] The question of why companies even bother to pay dividends had occupied finance professors ever since Franco Modigliani and Merton Miller had declared in 1961 that the decision to pay out or hold on to earnings had no effect on a corporation's value. Black had written before about this "dividend puzzle,"[24] so the journal's editors sent the piece to him for review. To their chagrin, he gave it two thumbs up.

"This paper is brilliant," Black wrote. "It rings both new and true in my ears."[25] And so it came to pass that the first real attempt to apply the teachings of Kahneman and Tversky to finance was published—reluctantly—by the house journal of the efficient marketeers (the *Journal of Financial Economics* had been founded by Eugene Fama, Michael Jensen, and Robert Merton). It was a shock to many readers. Merton Miller's declaration that finance should focus only on "pervasive market forces" was in large part a reaction to it.

Black was just getting going. As president-elect of the American Finance Association in 1984, he was in charge of the program for its annual meeting. He made room for Summers's ketchup speech, and asked Hersh Shefrin to organize the AFA's first-ever session on behavioral finance. Hardly anybody showed up for it, but Black made sure two of the papers from the session subsequently reached a bigger audience in the *Journal of Finance*.

One of these papers marked economist Richard Thaler's first real foray into finance. He and student Werner De Bondt set out to test the psychological finding that "most people tend to 'overreact' to unexpected and dramatic news events." They assembled portfolios of the stocks that had been the biggest gainers over a three-year period, and portfolios of the biggest losers—the reasoning being that big gains or losses were usually the result of unexpected and dramatic events. From 1932 to 1982, they found, the "loser portfolios" had consistently outperformed the market over the subsequent three years, while "winner portfolios" trailed it. This was strong evidence of a market inefficiency—an inefficiency that seemed to have psychological roots.

A year later, it was Black's turn to give the presidential address at the meeting. It was titled simply "Noise," and it lasted just fifteen minutes. Noise, Black said, "makes financial markets possible, but also makes them imperfect." It is the noise introduced by uninformed traders that makes markets liquid and allows informed traders to make money. Without it, markets might become trapped in the predicament that Sanford Grossman and Joseph Stiglitz had described a few years before, where rational traders never actually traded because they all agreed on what prices should be. This noise, however, not only keeps prices away from their fundamental values. It makes it impossible to tell what those fundamentals are:

> [W]e might define an efficient market as one in which price is within a factor of 2 of value, i.e., the price is more than half of value and less than twice value. The factor of 2 is arbitrary, of course. Intuitively, though, it seems reasonable to me, in the light of sources of uncertainty about value and the strength of the forces tending to cause price to return to value. By this definition, I think almost all markets are efficient almost all of the time. 'Almost all' means at least 90%.[26]

It was a loose, pragmatic, Ben Graham-ish definition, befitting a man who a year before had left MIT for a job in New York at Goldman Sachs. The AFA presidential address two years later by Richard Roll—by this time also working on Wall Street—followed similar lines. Roll had examined U.S. stock markets from September 1982 through August 1987, and found he could explain less than 40 percent of stock movements using available data on economic conditions, industry dynamics, and news about individual companies. Either there was a lot of private information moving stock prices not reflected in the databases Roll consulted, or else manias and panics gripped investors from time to time. "It would be nice," Roll drolly concluded, "to have a method for detecting the difference."[27]

THESE REMARKABLE ADMISSIONS CAME FROM prominent scholars who had been closely associated with the efficient market hypothesis, but they had almost no immediate impact on the day-to-day practice of academic finance. Most finance professors ignored the Shiller-Summers broadside against the efficient market. Robert Merton sprang to the defense of the rational market hypothesis against Shiller's critique mainly because Franco Modigliani—presumably trying to bring more attention to the matter—asked him to do it. Merton's colleagues figured they had better things to do.

However absurd and reality denying that may seem from the outside, it's how science works. "Normal science, the activity in which most scientists inevitably spend almost all their time, is predicated on the assumption that the scientific community knows what the world is like," wrote Thomas Kuhn in *The Structure of Scientific Revolutions.* "Much of the success of the enterprise derives from the community's willingness to defend that assumption, if necessary at considerable cost." Attacks from outside are thus likely to fail. It is only when hard-to-explain anomalies start cropping up *within* the paradigm of a science that change is possible.

In finance, such anomalies had actually been cropping up from the beginning. Even in the heyday of the random walk, scholars found nonrandom patterns tucked away in the chaos of price movements. Many of these patterns disappeared under scrutiny, or weren't profitable when you factored in trading costs. A few held up.

Some of the earliest and most durable were discovered by Victor Niederhoffer, who arrived at the Chicago Business School in 1964. A perennial national squash champion, Niederhoffer let his smelly sports clothes pile up in his study cubicle and walked around campus with a monkey named Lorie—after his faculty adviser James Lorie—on his shoulder. While an undergraduate at Harvard, he had read M. F. M. Osborne's 1959 account of Brownian motion in the stock market and had struck up a friendly correspondence with the physicist. Niederhoffer's fellow students at Chicago were obsessed with making economic arguments for market randomness; Niederhoffer and Osborne were far more interested in finding ways around that randomness.

Together and separately, the two men wrote several papers in the mid-1960s that documented evidence of market imperfections. Some were of the sort identified by Charles Dow two-thirds of a century before: Whichever direction the market or a particular stock was headed, it was more likely to keep heading in that direction than not. They also found predictable patterns in the other direction: After a decline of one-eighth of a point, a stock's next move was more likely to be up than down.[28]

Niederhoffer and Osborne were both careful in their statistical work, and the market predictabilities they found were not large. Niederhoffer's Chicago peers and professors received their evidence not so much as an affront as the kind of inevitable noise that if anything made their theories more credible.[29] As Fama put it in his famous 1970 efficient markets paper, the Niederhoffer-Osborne evidence was "statistically significant," but "is not a basis on which to conclude that the market is inefficient."[30]

These tiny irregularities, though, were just the beginning. As the years went by and computers moved from university basements to professors' desks, ever more anomalies were discovered. Some of the most interesting anomalies involved linkages between the stock price data provided by Chicago's Center for Research in Security Prices and the corporate financial numbers compiled since 1962 on Standard & Poor's Compustat computer database. When a corporation announced surprisingly high or low quarterly earnings, for example, the databases revealed that it took a while for its stock price to reflect this new information fully—a phenomenon that came to be known as earnings surprise, or earnings drift.[31] An even more persistent anomaly, and one that was more difficult to explain, was that cheap stocks outperformed expensive ones.

This discovery should not have been shocking. It was, after all, what value investors had said for generations. Roger Babson had advised investors to buy stocks with a price-to-earnings (P/E) ratio below ten and sell those above. Benjamin Graham, while his advice was a bit more complex, leaned in the same direction. The first significant empirical documentation that stocks with low P/E ratios outperform high P/E stocks over time was compiled by a Philadelphia bank vice president and published in the *Financial Analysts Journal* in 1960.[32] This history was easy enough to ignore, but in the late 1970s finance scholars using the latest data and techniques began to discover that, even accounting for risk, value stocks outperformed the market. The discipline, its members steeped in Kuhn's account of scientific revolutions, did not ignore the challenge to its paradigm.[33]

"In a manner remarkably similar to that described by Thomas Kuhn," Michael Jensen wrote in 1978, "we seem to be entering a stage where widely scattered and as yet incohesive evidence is arising which seems to be inconsistent with the theory." This sentence appeared in the introduction to a *Journal of Financial Economics* special issue on "Anomalous Evidence Regarding Market Efficiency"—just a couple of sentences away from Jensen's famous statement that "I believe there is no other proposition in economics which has more solid empirical evidence supporting it than the Efficient Market Hypothesis." Clearly, Jensen wasn't ready to give in just yet.

It was an article in the same issue by Ray Ball, an Australian accounting professor with a Chicago Ph.D., that showed the way forward. "As argued by Kuhn, no area of normal science can justify chasing all anomaly at the expense of more fruitful research," Ball wrote. He acknowledged that there was now so much anomalous evidence about earnings and stock prices that something had to give. That something, he argued, should not be the efficient market hypothesis but the model of risk and return embodied in the capital asset pricing model. It was time to accede to the reality that beta, the measure of a stock's sensitivity to the overall market's fluctuations, was not the only risk that mattered.[34]

The first new risk factor to be established was *smallness*. Chicago grad student Rolf Bänz examined fifty-three years of New York Stock Exchange data and found that small-capitalization stocks dramatically outperformed large ones. There was less information available about small companies, so investors had to be compensated for the "estimation risk" involved in buying them, Bänz argued. In the process, he also explained away much of the outperformance of value stocks, since small stocks as a group had lower P/E ratios than big ones.[35]

It was a reasonable enough thesis, but it soon began to unravel. Small stocks stopped beating the market after 1983—indicating that their previous outperformance may have been less a reward to "estimation risk" than a simple case of investors missing out on an opportunity and then jumping on it after someone (in this case Rolf Bänz) pointed it out to them.[36] It appeared to be a market inefficiency that, while it did finally go away, survived for decades.

In the meantime, more data trolling by finance professors revealed more phenomena difficult to explain within the efficient market paradigm. There was the case of winners becoming losers, and vice versa, identified by Thaler and De Bondt. There was the "January effect," in which stocks did especially well the first month of the year. And most of all there were those value stocks, which, continued study revealed, beat the market even when you controlled for the supposed small-stock effect.

FOR THE LONGEST TIME, THE author of the efficient market hypothesis was a mere spectator to these unsettling events. Eugene Fama did have a front-row seat—he was on Bänz's dissertation committee, for one thing. After the mid-1970s, though, he veered clear of serious research or writing on market efficiency. He did some work with his former student Michael Jensen on agency theory. He studied the impact of inflation on markets. He learned to windsurf—well enough that by the mid-1990s he declared himself to be "probably the best [windsurfer] in the world over age fifty."[37] He couldn't stay silent forever, though. And when Fama returned to the grand theory that had made his reputation, his data-driven, almost blindered approach brought a fascinating result. He didn't exactly repudiate the efficient market, but he managed to shake its foundations in a way that no one else could have done.

It started in 1991 with a look back, at the request of the editors of the *Journal of Finance*, at the landmark paper on the efficient market hypothesis that he had published two decades before. "Sequels are rarely as good as the originals," Fama began, and while the rest of his verdict was largely positive, it was far from triumphal. The efficient market hypothesis had "passed the acid test of scientific usefulness," he argued. "It has changed our views about the behavior of returns, across securities and through time." It had also changed Wall Street, helping bring about the rise of index funds, performance measurement, and the like. In a faint echo of what Michael Jensen had claimed in 1978, Fama wrote that "the past research on market efficiency is among the most successful in empirical economics, with good prospects to remain so in the future."

That was a different thing from saying that the market was perfectly rational or efficient, and Fama did not deny that some of the seeming certainties of earlier days had proved to be mirages. Sanford Grossman and Joseph Stiglitz had demonstrated, he acknowledged, that the strong form of the efficient market hypothesis could not be true. It had to be possible to beat the market using private information, or else no one would ever bother to spend money gathering information. The lesson from Bob Shiller and Larry Summers's 1980s broadsides, Fama continued, was "that irrational bubbles in stock prices are indistinguishable from rational time-varying expected returns." There was no way to be sure whether the market was irrationally volatile or not.[38]

But these still were, in Fama's view of the matter, side issues. As he had originally proposed it, the efficient market hypothesis held that stock price movements couldn't be predicted, except by means of the capital asset pricing model. According to CAPM, it was beta—a stock's volatility relative to the rest of the market—that determined how well that stock would perform over time. It was a simple tradeoff of risk and reward. Evidence had been piling up since the late 1970s against this combination of the efficient market and CAPM, but apart from a few outside-the-mainstream types, finance scholars shied away from challenging Fama's theory. Instead, they found ever-more-convoluted ways to blame the small-stock effect for every anomaly.

Fama didn't do that. He set out, together with a younger Chicago colleague, Kenneth French, to retest his original hypothesis. The results, which he described briefly in his 1991 paper and then laid out in full the next year in a blockbuster piece coauthored with French, weren't good. Fama and French examined market data from 1941 through 1990, and determined conclusively that beta just didn't cut it, at least not alone. "We are forced to conclude that [CAPM] does not describe the last 50 years of average stock returns," they wrote. Fama and French argued that it was beta's strong performance in just one decade, the 1940s, that had delivered positive results in the first round of CAPM tests in the early 1970s.

One of the most compelling pieces of evidence for the whole structure of efficient markets finance was, they seemed to be saying, just a data artifact. Coming as it did from Fama himself, this verdict had an impact that previous evidence of market patterns had not. "The Pope said God was dead," efficient market critic Robert Haugen of the University of California at Irvine wrote a few years later. "At least the God of CAPM."[39]

Fama was not at all ready to concede that the efficient market was dead, which meant that he needed a new risk model to replace CAPM. He and French found that both companies with low market capitalizations (small stocks) and low price-to-book ratios (value stocks) had delivered higher-than-normal returns between 1941 and 1990. Combined with beta, in fact, these measures seemed to "explain" most market behavior.

While beta made a lot of theoretical sense as a risk factor, and the small-stock effect at least a little, the outperformance of value stocks was much harder to explain in terms of risk. Not that Fama and French didn't try. "If stock prices are rational," they wrote, the book-to-price ratio must be "a direct indicator of the relative prospects of firms." A company with high book-to-price ratio was thus a risky company, which was why its returns to investors were high.[40] This amounted to saying that the same company was a riskier investment at $5 a share than at $20—a bizarre contradiction of the teachings of successful investors from Roger Babson and Benjamin Graham onward.

A year later, two other scholars established the existence of persistent "momentum" in stock prices. Over periods between three and twelve months, stocks that had been performing especially well continued to do so, and stocks that had been performing especially badly continued to do so. A similar case had been made back in the mid-1960s by American University Ph.D. student Robert Levy, and swatted away in the pages of the *Financial Analysts Journal* by Michael Jensen. Now it was back, and it was supported by far more extensive data.[41] It could not be dismissed.

Fama acknowledged that momentum was even harder to characterize as a risk factor than value. That didn't stop one of his students from tacking it on to the Fama-French model as another risk factor to take into account in judging investor performance.[42] And for that purpose, it wasn't so crazy—if you owed all your success to simple momentum or value strategies that any finance professor with a computer could replicate, maybe you weren't so brilliant after all. As an explanation of asset prices, though, it left an awful lot to be desired.

Fama had retested his original joint hypothesis of the efficient market and CAPM and found it wanting. Rather than jettison the efficient market, he ditched CAPM. But he failed to come up with a credible hypothesis to replace it. The Fama-French "three-factor model," as it came to be known, and the subsequent "four-factor model" that included momentum, weren't really economic theories. They were exercises in data mining, with dubious explanations tacked on after the fact. What's more, they were exercises in data mining that revealed several time-honored Wall Street strategies—dismissed by finance scholars since the 1960s as folklore or worse—to be consistent moneymakers. Hmmm, many of Fama's colleagues and students were already thinking, maybe there *was* something to that beating-the-market stuff after all.

CHAPTER 12

BEATING THE MARKET WITH WARREN BUFFETT AND ED THORP

Just because professional investors as a group can't reliably outperform the market doesn't mean that some professional investors can't.

IN MAY 1984, COLUMBIA BUSINESS School hosted a conference to commemorate the fiftieth anniversary of *Security Analysis*, the book hatched in Benjamin Graham's Columbia night school class in the late 1920s that had transformed Wall Street. The organizers invited two speakers to debate what Graham and coauthor David Dodd had wrought. One was Warren Buffett, a former Graham student who had begun to outshine his teacher. The other was finance professor Michael Jensen, who had declared a few years earlier that there was "no other proposition in economics which has more solid empirical evidence supporting it than the Efficient Market Hypothesis."

Jensen was aware that the Columbia audience was heavy on Graham fans, and he started off with a joking comment about feeling like a turkey at a turkey shoot. After that he didn't hold back. First he explained that years of academic research had shown analysis of publicly available data about securities to be close to worthless—at least as a means of beating the market. Then, to those who might object that some practitioners of Graham's art had achieved great success, he dismissed it as luck.

"If I survey a field of untalented analysts, all of whom are doing nothing but flipping coins," Jensen said, "I expect to see some who have tossed two heads in a row and even some who have tossed ten heads in a row."[1] This coin-flip analogy—popularized by Bill Sharpe at Stanford—had by this time become a staple of MBA education. After a few rounds, any group would produce a few apparent coin-flipping superstars. The implication was that the stock market worked pretty much the same way.

Buffett was ready for this argument. In a response that was reprinted in the Business School's alumni magazine a few months later and has been passed around, reprinted, and quoted countless times since, Buffett too described a coin-flipping contest. The entire nation would participate, with everyone staking a dollar on the first flip and the wagers rising with the winnings after that. After two hundred rounds of flipping, about 215 millionaires would remain. Many of these people would, Buffett said, become convinced of their own genius. Some would write books on the secrets of successful coin flipping; others would "start jetting around the country attending seminars on efficient coin-flipping and tackling skeptical professors with, 'If it can't be done, why are there 215 of us?'"

The professors could retort that coin-flipping orangutans would have achieved the same result, Buffett said. But what if, Buffett wondered—jumping from humans to primates in a leap that made no narrative sense but worked rhetorically—one took a closer look at where those coin-flipping orangutan millionaires came from?

> If you found that 40 came from a particular zoo in Omaha, you could be pretty sure you were on to something. So you would probably go out and ask the zookeeper about what he's feeding them, whether they had special exercises, what books they read, and who knows what else.

Buffett continued, "I think you will find that a disproportionate number of successful coin-flippers in the investment world came from a very small village that could be called Graham-and-Doddsville," he said. He then went through a list of nine investors—some former Graham students, some not—who had achieved inordinate success by following more or less the same principle: They sought out individual stocks that seemed especially cheap given the earnings or assets of the company, and otherwise ignored the swings of the market. "There will continue to be wide discrepancies between price and value in the marketplace," he concluded, "and those who read their Graham & Dodd will continue to prosper."[2]

If the debate had been scored by those on hand at Columbia, Buffett would have been the clear winner. The audience was biased, of course, but Jensen too was impressed. "One of the things I came away from that with was Warren Buffett was one of the smartest people I've ever met, and wise," Jensen said. "He could play on my turf without making mistakes . . . It's not by accident that he's worth billions."

Should that have been such a revelation? It was undeniably hard to separate the lucky from the skillful on Wall Street. It was also true, as Jensen's research demonstrated in the 1960s, that most mutual fund managers failed to beat the market after expenses. But to make the leap from these realities to claim that *all* successful investors were merely the beneficiaries of random chance had been, to quote Robert Shiller's condemnation of another such leap by the efficient marketeers, "remarkable in the immediacy of its logical error."

It was an error perhaps understandable in the context of the 1960s, when most of the big investing stars were little more than surfers of a bull market wave. Some surfed it more expertly than others—Fidelity's Ned Johnson springs to mind—but when the wave crashed, they all crashed, too. It was easy, and in most cases accurate, to dismiss these people's claims to investing brilliance as delusional. By the early 1980s, though, it was becoming apparent that there were people who knew how to make money no matter what the market was doing. There weren't a lot of them, they were hard to find, and even if you did find them they probably wouldn't take your money. But they did exist, and the two who were hardest to dismiss as lucky fools were probably Warren Buffett and a California math professor turned hedge fund manager named Ed Thorp.

BUFFETT'S SUCCESS HAD BEGUN TO cause head-scratching among finance professors long before his encounter with Jensen in 1984. Since ignoring Benjamin Graham's 1951 advice to avoid the stock market (at least until the next crash), Buffett had compiled a spectacular investing record. His story has been told at great length elsewhere. But a brief accounting of his rise, derived chiefly from Roger Lowenstein's book, *Buffett*, reveals some crucial elements.

Just as his mentor Graham had done when he set out on his own in the 1920s, Buffett structured his investment business as a partnership. The investors were limited partners who pocketed all the gains up to 6 percent a year, then received 75 percent of the annual gains after that, with Buffett getting the rest. If the partnership lost money, he didn't get paid. He told his investors nothing about the stocks he was buying and selling, and allowed them to move their money in and out only once a year, on December 31.

These were all characteristics of what is now called a hedge fund—although most of today's hedge funds charge an annual fee of 1 percent of assets (or 2 percent, or higher) in addition to the profit share. The name comes from Alfred Winslow Jones, who coined the term "hedged fund" to describe the way he invested—buying some stocks on margin (that is, with borrowed money) while simultaneously selling others short. Jones was a Harvard classmate of John Burr Williams who after stints as a sailor, diplomat, sociology graduate student, and *Fortune* magazine writer launched an investment partnership with four friends and $100,000 in 1949. Jones began accepting outside investments in 1952 under an arrangement similar but not identical to Buffett's—he kept 20 percent of net profits. He is now dubbed the father of the hedge fund. Neither the partnership structure he used nor the strategy of hedging his bets with short sales were in fact new, but his success led in the 1960s to the founding of numerous copycats calling themselves hedge funds (Jones deplored the dropped *d*). He does deserve some credit.

The incentives and possibilities faced by Jones and Buffett were markedly different from those of the manager of a mutual fund. The SEC did not (and still does not) allow mutual fund managers to share in investment profits. Instead, mutual funds charged customers an annual percentage of assets under management, an arrangement that rewarded asset gathering above all else. It certainly didn't hurt to beat the market, but the ultimate goal was to have more money to manage. Mutual fund investors could also add or withdraw money anytime, the funds' investment holdings were disclosed regularly, and there were tight restrictions on just what sort of securities the manager could buy (short selling was off the table). These rules, which have since been loosened slightly, helped inspire the investor confidence that made mutual funds the nation's predominant investment vehicle, but they didn't help managers beat the market. When stocks are cheap, investors are wont to desert; when they're expensive, they pour in new money.

Warren Buffett wasn't immune from these pressures. If he had a bad year, there was nothing to stop his investors from running for the exits on December 31. Year after year, he warned them that his "abnormal" performance couldn't continue, that an off year would come soon. But it never did. Buffett used the Dow Jones Industrials as his benchmark, and he beat the average every year that his partnership existed. Even in years when the Dow dropped, the Buffett partnership still managed double-digit gains. It was one of the great investing runs of all time.

Buffett at first stayed faithful to the teachings of Ben Graham. Most of his early successes were classic Graham "cigar butts": companies with a stock market value below what you could get by selling off their machines and real estate and office supplies. As stock prices rose and those tarnished gems became harder and harder to find, Buffett adapted. Under encouragement from a new friend he met at a party in Omaha, Los Angeles attorney Charlie Munger, he began tilting away from Graham and toward John Burr Williams. What mattered was the power to generate earnings over time—and Buffett could see that this earning power was generated not just by assets that showed up on the balance sheet but by intangibles like brands.

In the late 1960s, even the new-look Buffett couldn't justify the prices being paid for brand-name stocks. Proclaiming that the market had become "a game I don't understand," he shut down his partnership in 1969 and liquidated all its holdings but two, one of them a textile manufacturer turned hodgepodge holding company called Berkshire Hathaway. Successful mutual funds generally don't exit the game like this. Their incentives are about gathering assets, and a bull market is the best of times to do that. Buffett made money by making his partners money. He didn't see how he could do that anymore, and he got out.

BUFFETT'S INVESTORS NEEDED NEW PLACES to put their cash. One of them, neurologist Ralph Waldo Gerard, was dean of the graduate school at the brand-new Irvine campus of the University of California. UC–Irvine was also home to a math professor interested in money management, thereby entwining his remarkable story with that of Buffett.

In 1959, as an instructor at MIT, Edward O. Thorp had figured out how to beat the house at blackjack by counting cards. Crucial to his success was an IBM 704 in an MIT basement, which he used to analyze the changing probabilities as cards were removed from the deck. After presenting his findings at the January 1961 meeting of the American Mathematical Association, Thorp was profiled in several newspapers and swamped with mail from would-be gambling partners. He accepted the offer of a pair of New York area businessmen—

one of them Emmanuel Kimmel, whose New Jersey parking-garage business would later grow into entertainment giant Time Warner.[3] Kimmel flew Thorp to New York several Wednesdays in a row to practice the scheme, sending him back up to Boston each time, Thorp recalled, with a reward of $100 in cash and a salami.

During MIT's spring break, Thorp and his new partners traveled to Reno to try out his method. It worked, and Thorp wrote a book about it called *Beat the Dealer,* which became a bestseller and made the professor a minor celebrity. The book, still in print, continues to inspire new generations of card sharps (the MIT students in the book *Bringing Down the House* and movie *21* were Thorp acolytes).[4] But there were limits to how much Thorp could make at the gaming tables, especially with the casino bosses doing all they could to thwart him.

Thorp decided to put his skills to work where the odds were better and the potential payoffs bigger. He devoted the summer of 1964 to reading up on the stock market. Just as Paul Samuelson had fifteen years before, he concluded that the securities with the most potential for an analytical mind like his were not stocks themselves but warrants—options granted by a company to buy its shares at a set price.

The next year, when Thorp moved to UC–Irvine, he met an economist, Sheen Kassouf, who had devised a scheme for making money off warrants. Kassouf had noticed that out-of-the-money warrants (such as a warrant to pay $20 a share for a stock currently trading at $5) tended to trade at a steady price for months or years, only to collapse just before they expired. By selling such warrants short and buying the underlying stock to protect him in case the stock price suddenly rose, Kassouf made steady profits with seemingly minimal risk.

Kassouf had written his dissertation on warrants at Columbia. He did so under the supervision of Arthur Burns, Wesley Mitchell's protégé. Not surprisingly, he confined himself to empirical observation. Thorp refined Kassouf's findings with some of his mathematical ideas, and the two wrote a book about warrant investing, *Beat the Market,* that came out in 1967. It never approached the success of its blackjack predecessor, but it did catch the attention of the economists and finance scholars working on options pricing. Paul Samuelson wrote a review likening the book to "astrology."[5]

Not that this criticism bothered Thorp. "The book was what I expected it to be," he said, "an entrée to wealthy people." UC–Irvine's Dean Gerard was wealthy enough (thanks in part to his investment with Warren Buffett) to fit the profile. Gerard read *Beat the Market,* and arranged for Buffett—who vacationed on the coast near Irvine, to meet with Thorp. The two moneymen got along well, and Buffett told Gerard his money would be safe with the math professor. Thorp was even more impressed with Buffett. "He's really smart," he claims to have told his wife. "He's going to be the richest man in the United States someday."

Thorp and Kassouf talked about going into business together, but Kassouf wanted to partner with his brother (the Kassoufs later launched their own firm, Analytic Investment Management, which survives today). Thorp hooked up instead with Philadelphia stockbroker Jay Regan. Alfred W. Jones's "hedged fund," after flying under the radar for seventeen years, had garnered public notice for the first time in a 1966 *Fortune* article. His return to investors over the previous decade, the magazine reported, had been almost double that of the best-performing mutual fund (it still trailed Buffett's, but hardly anybody had heard of Buffett).[6] In the wake of the article, hundreds more hedge funds were launched.

Regan wanted to join these well-compensated ranks, and after vetting a few would-be money managers he settled on Thorp in 1969. Their partnership, initially called Convertible Hedge Associates and later redubbed Princeton-Newport Partners (Regan and his traders and salesmen were in Princeton, New Jersey, while Thorp and his handful of numbers jocks were in Newport Beach) set to work buying and selling options using the formula that would later be called the Black-Scholes model.

The final pieces of the options pricing puzzle had fallen into place in Thorp's head not long after *Beat the Market* was published. He relied not on theories of arbitrage or asset pricing, but on parsimony and trial and error. And he kept his formula secret. Princeton-Newport became the pioneer of black-box investing, the model for countless mysterious quantitative money management operations to come. It was also a success. As the market sputtered, and hedge fund after hedge fund closed, Princeton-Newport generated positive, usually double-digit gains every year.

After several years of this, Thorp got the notice in the mail that his secret formula was about to become public. It was a preprint of the Black-Scholes article, sent by Fischer Black, who professed in an introductory letter to be a "great admirer" of Thorp's work. After some initial puzzlement, Thorp realized that the Black-Scholes formula was the same as his. Not long after that, the easy options money had mostly disappeared. But Thorp displayed an uncanny ability to keep finding new sources of profit—and get out of them before they stopped working.

He was also willing to discuss his trades, at least after he'd made his money on them—something few of his black-box imitators have done since. This trade-and-tell act started with a *Wall Street Journal* front-page story in 1974, in which Thorp laid out in detail how he'd made an 8.5 percent profit in three weeks on underpriced Upjohn Co. options. "If you hedge properly, you can win on nine out of 10 trades," he told the *Journal* reporter. "I call it getting rich slow." Thorp relied heavily on computers programmed with his formulas to make his decisions for him.[7] But you didn't have to be a genius to understand the pricing discrepancies the computers found.

When the Chicago Mercantile Exchange launched trading in S&P futures in April 1982, speculators betting on the market's direction sent prices way out of whack with the actual S&P 500. This mispricing couldn't continue indefinitely: When the futures contracts came due, their payout was determined by the market price of the 500 stocks in the S&P index. Thorp began cashing in. When his computers told him futures prices were too high, Princeton-Newport sold the futures short and bought shares of 265 S&P stocks that Thorp's calculations told him were an acceptable proxy for the full 500. When the futures price was too low, the firm did the opposite. Princeton-Newport trading accounted for more than 1' percent of New York Stock Exchange volume on some days, and racked up huge brokerage fees. But over four months the profit came to $6 million.[8]

Another such windfall came out of the disassembling of Ma Bell. Just before the court-ordered breakup of the telephone monopoly was consummated, it was possible to trade shares of both the new regional Baby Bells and the old AT&T. Thorp's analysis showed that the old AT&T shares were cheaper than those of the Baby Bells. They were only a *little bit* cheaper, but Thorp saw the deal as such a sure thing that in 1983 he borrowed hundreds of millions of dollars to buy AT&T and sell the Bells short. It was the biggest trade in NYSE history, and it made Thorp and his investors $1.6 million.[9]

It also might sound familiar. Just a few months out of college in 1914, Benjamin Graham recommended that his brokerage firm's customers take advantage of the dissolution of the Guggenheim Exploration Co. by buying Guggenheim shares and selling short the overpriced shares of its subsidiaries. Thorp did the same at AT&T. His computers and mathematical formulas were something new, but his was also the time-honored way of the arbitrageur.

Wall Street had long been populated by firms that specialized in making money off of such tiny discrepancies as stocks trading at different prices in London and New York. These opportunities had been limited by technology and by law. "The arbitrageur's paradise is a place where cables cost five cents a word and all markets are both free and open," writer James Agee observed in *Fortune* in 1934. "He's a good bit this side of any such paradise, and he is getting no closer as the New Deal piles up restrictions and controls on the trader in U.S. markets."[10] In the 1970s and 1980s, the New Deal regulations were rolled back, communications costs dropped, and new derivatives markets provided countless cheap ways to place bets. Paradise was moving closer.

WELL BEFORE THIS, WARREN BUFFETT had reacquired his taste for investing. When he first began buying into Berkshire Hathaway in 1962, Buffett saw the textile company as a cheap stock. Not long after taking control in 1965, though, he began to treat it as a source of cash for him to invest elsewhere—and he soon added other cash machines (newspapers, insurance companies, a bank) to the mix. After Buffett shut down his partnership in 1969, the cash flow from these Berkshire enterprises gave him enviable freedom.

Buffett didn't do much with this freedom at first, preferring instead to consider other ways of occupying his time and intellect, such as public service. As the bear market drove stock prices down, the call of the market became too much for him to resist. "How do you feel?" a *Forbes* reporter asked him in October 1974. "Like an oversexed guy in a whorehouse," Buffett replied. "This is the time to start investing."[11] If Buffett had to raise money from investors to buy stocks, he would have gotten nowhere. It certainly wasn't as if investors were rushing to buy Berkshire. The company's stock price dropped from $87 to $40 over the course of the 1973–74 crash.

Buffett controlled a corporation that had its own cash, with an insurance investment portfolio upward of $100 million, plus several million a year in insurance and banking profits and $20 million that Berkshire raised by issuing bonds in 1973. He bought, and he bought, and had to ask no one permission—other than Charlie Munger, who began investing with Buffett in a side venture in the early 1970s and became Berkshire's vice-chairman in 1978. He was confident in his valuations, and he was perfectly positioned to ignore the lack of confidence displayed by the rest of the market.

By the late 1970s, Berkshire's stock had begun its epic rise. It was selling for just under $1,000 a share when Ed Thorp came across an article about Buffett. Until then he hadn't realized it was possible to invest alongside the man who had helped give him his start. Now he began acquiring Berkshire shares. "I bought and I bought and I bought," Thorp said. "I thought it was a good way to diversify what I was doing with Princeton-Newport Partners."

What *was* the secret of Warren Buffett's investing success? Part of it was his ability—attributable both to his temperament and to the structure of Berkshire Hathaway—to ignore the moods of the market and stay focused on his own judgments of what businesses were worth. A crucial metric for him was what he called "owner's earnings." That was the cash left over each year after expenses and capital investments, what Chicago-trained consultant Joel Stern dubbed "free cash flow." To judge whether these owner's earnings were adequate, Buffett figured them as a percentage of capital invested. This return on capital could then be compared to that of other companies in the same industry, or for the market as a whole. Buffett was—unlike his mentor Graham—dubious of dividends. They were taxed at a higher rate than capital gains, making them an inefficient way to distribute excess cash to shareholders.

Buffett was, in short, a creature sprung from the pages of Franco Modigliani and Merton Miller's famous papers of 1958 and 1961: a fully rational investor. When asked the key to his success, Buffett's alter ego Munger once responded, "I'm rational. That's it. I'm rational."[12] Thorp, too, was something out of a finance textbook—a classic arbitrageur. He jumped on relative mispricings within the market, and by doing so he helped make them disappear. Buffett and Thorp were also both random walkers, after a fashion. Neither claimed to be able to predict the next move of an individual stock or the overall market. In a speculative world, they resisted the urge to speculate.

Modigliani and Miller and the thousands of finance professors who followed their lead assumed for the sake of simplicity and scientific progress that the random market was a perfect market, with prices set by such superrational investors as Buffett and Thorp. The great men themselves were able to make a living because prices *weren't* always determined that way. For Buffett's investments to work out, Mr. Market eventually had to catch on to the real value of the stocks he bought (unless he bought a company outright, in which case he could simply count the cash as it poured in). And for Thorp's mispricings to pay off, they eventually had to disappear. The difference between the worldview of Buffett and Thorp and that of rational market finance was chiefly one of time frame. The finance guys thought markets got things right immediately. The moneymen believed it could take a while.

Slowly, the academic finance guys began to catch on that maybe at least some of these moneymen were right. Paul Samuelson bought Berkshire shares, and called Buffett "as near to a genius as I have observed." Bill Sharpe described him as "a three-sigma event," a one in four hundred investor. That was a dismissive sort of praise. What could one possibly learn from such a rare bird? But in the 1980s a few rational market types, believing themselves to be at least two-sigma events, began trying to beat the market themselves.

PAUL SAMUELSON WAS, AS SO often, ahead of the crowd. In 1969, one of his former students—who had written his Ph.D. dissertation on *The Dynamics of the World Cocoa Market*—correctly warned his employer, Nestlé, that cocoa prices were about to skyrocket. On the strength of that call, Helmut Weymar signed up six traders, among them MIT professor Paul Cootner, and set about raising capital to start his own trading firm. Samuelson bought a 3.1 percent stake, for $125,000; Nestlé and a venture capital firm pitched in, too.

Commodities Corp., as it was called, initially tried to beat the market with economic models and fundamental research, and failed. In 1971, over the objections of Samuelson and Cootner, Weymar began experimenting with what was essentially chart reading. It was pure Charles Dow: Trends tend to continue. The firm melded fundamentalist and chartist approaches using computer models, and implemented a risk control system that gave traders on a winning streak a free hand but reined them in as soon as they began to lose money. It became a big success.[13] Samuelson, who never had a hands-on role, and Cootner, who died in 1978, played only bit parts in that story. The professors-turned-speculators of the 1980s were more hands-on.

"The most celebrated defector," the *Wall Street Journal* reported in a 1985 article headlined "Some 'Efficient-Market' Scholars Decide It's Possible to Beat the Averages After All," was UC–Berkeley's Barr Rosenberg.[14] Rosenberg wasn't really a defector. The success of his consulting firm Barra had made him the most prominent salesman of the academic approach to investing, but he had never preached that the market couldn't be beat—just that its risks could and should be quantified. Not long before launching Rosenberg Institutional Equity Management in 1984, he coauthored a paper titled "Persuasive Evidence of Market Inefficiency," which argued that one could reliably outperform the market by buying stocks with low price-to-book-value ratios and those that had just had a particularly bad month.[15] Rosenberg's firm set out to do just that.

Fischer Black's 1984 switch from MIT to Goldman Sachs was more surprising to those in academia, but he too had already been straying from the efficient markets gospel. Some of his work at Goldman involved devising products that the firm could sell—like its own version of portfolio insurance. He came up with trading strategies as well. "My biggest surprise is how many opportunities there are to take advantage of," he told a journalist in 1987.[16] Later, he declared that "markets look a lot less efficient from the banks of the Hudson than the banks of the Charles."[17]

More puzzling were the professors who still maintained in the classroom that the market was efficient, yet seemed to be in the business of beating it. Some, like Richard Roll and Stephen Ross, argued that they were simply building portfolios that efficiently balanced risks. But Roll and Ross Asset Management followed Ross's arbitrage pricing theory, allowing them to pick and choose which risks mattered to stocks—inflation, interest rates, the price of oil. They couldn't deny that there was judgment involved. Inspired by Rolf Bänz's findings on the small-stock effect, Rex Sinquefield and another Chicago MBA, David Booth, started Dimensional Fund Advisers to run index funds of small-cap stocks. When Eugene Fama and Kenneth French published their research on the outperformance of value stocks, Sinquefield and Booth (who in 2008 gave $300 million to the Chicago Business School, which was renamed in his honor) signed them up as advisers and launched a value fund that was hard to distinguish from the value funds run by efficient market nonbelievers.

The most fascinating case was that of Robert Merton and Myron Scholes. In the 1980s, a spectacularly successful proprietary trading operation emerged at the bond brokerage Salomon Brothers. At its head was Chicago MBA John Meriwether, who assembled a team of traders and quants led by one of the best Ph.D. students Merton ever taught, Eric Rosenfeld. The approach was similar to Ed Thorp's, but with bonds instead of stocks and a lot more swashbuckling. Rosenfeld lured Merton on board in 1988 as a "special consultant to the Office of Chairman." Scholes joined up two years later as a consultant to and later cohead of Salomon's derivatives business.

When Meriwether and Rosenfeld launched the most famous (and soon most infamous) hedge fund of the 1990s, Long-Term Capital Management, Merton and Scholes signed on as partners. Merton usually justified his presence in terms of the advice he could give about tradeoffs between risk and return. Scholes was less circumspect. During a road show to pitch the fund in 1993, a young trader at an insurance company scoffed, "No way you can make that kind of money in Treasury markets." According to the trader, Scholes replied, "You're the reason. Because of fools like you."[18] Scholes said he never called the man a fool but did give him a talking to.

His reasoning was that people with advanced quantitative skills could find opportunities that conventional money managers could not. It wasn't all wrong. By the early 1980s, several headhunting firms already specialized in luring disgruntled physicists, mathematicians, and engineers to Wall Street jobs. Many of these quants manufactured new derivatives or managed risk. Of the ones enlisted to beat the market, most were involved in Thorp-style arbitrage—finding two securities that seemed mispriced relative to each other, then using lots of borrowed money to bet the prices would move back in line. Others followed Barr Rosenberg's path into value investing—using a computer to locate hundreds of cheap stocks rather than the conventional handful. Ever-more-powerful computers also allowed money managers to troll through ever-more-plentiful price data in search of identifiable patterns and trends—a practice that was, by the end of the decade, beginning to gain academic respectability. Some quantitative managers mixed elements of all three approaches.

What linked all of these operations, other than the heavy use of computers and a heavy dose of secrecy, was a belief that the risks they faced could be managed, and managed quantitatively. Some risks could, it turned out. Some could not.

CHAPTER 13

ALAN GREENSPAN STOPS A RANDOM PLUNGE DOWN WALL STREET

The crash of 1987 exposes big flaws in the rational finance view of risk. But a rescue by the Federal Reserve averts a full reexamination.

HAYNE LELAND COULD SEE, ALMOST from the moment portfolio insurance popped into his head in the den of his Berkeley house, that there was a catch. The option-pricing formulas upon which he based the strategy depended on the portfolio insurer being a price taker. That is, prices were set by the "pervasive forces" of the market. The actions of an individual market participant were presumed to have no impact at all.

If Leland's idea hit it big enough, he realized, the actions taken by portfolio insurers trying to cut their clients' losses during a market swoon might drive prices down even more. "But I honestly thought, 'How long would it take and how big would we have to become before our trades affected the market as a whole?'" Leland recalled. "It turns out it was only seven years."

Leland O'Brien Rubinstein, or LOR, started selling portfolio insurance in 1980. The business began to take off after the Chicago Mercantile Exchange launched trading in S&P 500 index futures in 1982. Instead of meddling with clients' stock holdings, LOR could achieve almost the same effect by buying and selling market index futures. This made its offerings attractive to pension funds that put their money with multiple managers, and pension funds became the firm's most important clients. By October 1987, LOR directly managed $5 billion and licensed its trading software to money managers that controlled another $45 billion. Competitors—mostly Wall Street firms such as Goldman Sachs and Morgan Stanley—insured another $40 to $50 billion in assets.

And so, when the portfolio insurers' formulas all told them to sell the morning of October 19, 1987, that selling affected the market as a whole. What resulted was the worst single day in U.S. stock market history, with the Dow Jones average falling 508 points, or 23 percent, and the S&P 500 20 percent. Leland and his partners, John O'Brien and Mark Rubinstein, surely weren't *solely* responsible for the crash of 1987. But that they even might have played a significant role was an indication both of how far academic finance had come and how limited its seemingly sophisticated theoretical models were. A trio of finance geeks had *that* kind of power? And they used it to do *what*?

The crash emboldened critics of the efficient market hypothesis and threw its champions on the defensive. It came nowhere near resolving that debate, though. What it did conclusively demonstrate was that the definition of risk accepted among finance scholars—and, increasingly, on Wall Street—was inadequate. In this worldview, risk was seen as a natural phenomenon, a scatter graph of potential outcomes that could be kept within bounds and manipulated mathematically. It was usually assumed for the sake of convenience that the bounds were those of the bell curve, the enormously useful properties of which had paved the way for modern portfolio theory, risk-adjusted performance assessment of money managers, and the options-pricing models behind the work done at Leland O'Brien Rubinstein.

Without estimating what could go wrong (and, if possible, insuring against it), one cannot begin to make the long-term investments that undergird economic growth. Without quantification of risk, modern capitalism would be unimaginable.[1] Quantifying risk in financial markets, though, is far more fraught than estimating the likelihood of fire or burglary or death. Financial markets are not natural phenomena. They are man-made—made by men and women whose business is gazing into an uncertain, risky future. The act of managing risk in such an environment alters that environment, creating a never-stable feedback loop. The crash of 1987 was the first alarming demonstration of the inherent instability of mathematical risk-management models in finance. It was not to be the last.

Portfolio insurance involved a lot of fancy math, but the actual mechanics were jarringly simple. You sold stock (or stock futures) and shifted money into cash as the market dropped. That was it. "The less these companies are being valued at, says this approach, the more vigorously they should be sold," wrote an incredulous Warren Buffett after the crash. "As a 'logical' corollary, the approach commands the institutions to repurchase these companies—*I'm not making this up* [italics his]—once their prices have rebounded significantly."[2]

Buffett took care to ensure that both his strokes of genius and his occasional mistakes were not those of the majority of his fellow investors. That's what being a value investor was all about—seeking value that others could not see. Pension fund managers out to keep their jobs and avoid being sued didn't have so much of a problem with making the same mistakes as their peers. What they wanted to avoid were big, embarrassing, *unique* losses—and they were willing to give up potential gains to do so. Hence the appeal of portfolio insurance.

By the summer of 1987 that appeal was so great that Hayne Leland began to worry that LOR and other portfolio insurers posed a danger to the market. He proposed to O'Brien and Rubinstein that they stop selling policies. "John [O'Brien] had a very good reason why we shouldn't do that," Leland recalled. "He said, 'If we turn them down, they'll just go down the street to Morgan Stanley.'" Instead, the trio began looking for ways to inform the world that their trading was, as Leland put it, "information-free." That turned out to be extremely difficult. Modern financial markets are set up to keep investors' identities and intentions secret. Exchange rules barred LOR's brokers from announcing who they were trading for, and an LOR-backed attempt to change that went nowhere.

That's where things stood when the market began to fall on Wednesday, October 14. Why the decline? The most-cited reason was the larger-than-expected U.S. trade deficit announced that day. The dollar's value in world currency markets had been falling for two years, and the big deficit raised fears of a further decline—which in turn raised fears of inflation and higher bond yields, both often bad news for stock prices. The declines continued on Thursday and Friday. Friday's 108-point fall in the Dow was the biggest point drop ever (although far from the biggest percentage drop). On what news? Again, it was nothing hugely dramatic. Treasury Secretary James Baker commented on Thursday that he might favor a further fall in the dollar against the German mark, and a bill was introduced in Congress on Friday to restrict hostile takeovers.[3]

Whatever the reasons for this decline, it meant that on the morning of Monday, October 19, the portfolio insurers lined up to sell S&P 500 futures on the Chicago Merc to rebalance their clients' portfolios. There was no way for them to signal that their selling was the result not of reasoned evaluation but of pure reflex. The futures traders in Chicago surely had an inkling, but that message seems to have been lost on the way to New York.

The index arbitrage that Ed Thorp pioneered five years before was by this time an everyday affair. Whenever the price of S&P 500 futures in Chicago got out of whack with that of the actual stocks trading in New York, one of several big brokerages and money managers bought one and sold the other for a quick and easy profit—in the process bringing prices back in line. That Monday, the mass selling by the portfolio insurers in Chicago drove the futures price well below where stock prices dictated it should be. The index arbitrageurs set to work.

"If we were going to sell a futures contract, the Merrill Lynch futures guy would buy it, and immediately Merrill Lynch would send out ten runners to ten posts [on the New York exchange] and each would sell five stocks," O'Brien recalled. "And Morgan and Goldman were doing the same thing. So the guys at the NYSE were suddenly seeing the five biggest brokerages scurrying around the floor selling tens of millions of shares. People on the other side got worried. . . . There was such a level of confusion that by and large they just stopped bidding."

With the New York market partially frozen, the gap between the futures price and the posted stock prices grew even larger, causing even more sell orders in New York from the index arbitrageurs. That drove prices lower, which caused the portfolio insurers to sell even more futures. And on it went. LOR and its fellow portfolio insurers hadn't *caused* the crash—prices had to begin falling before they would pile on—but it felt to just about everyone on the trading floors of Chicago and New York that they had turned a market correction into an old-fashioned panic.[4] Leland and O'Brien mostly agreed. Rubinstein preferred the explanation offered up afterward by Fischer Black. Investors had decided *en masse* that the market was riskier than they'd thought the day before.[5]

BLACK'S EXPLANATION WAS NOT ONE that people outside the academy found helpful. *Why* had investors decided the market was riskier? Why did they decide on October 19? Nobody had a convincing answer. The news tidbits of the preceding week were perhaps unsettling, but they simply didn't add up to the biggest-ever stock market drop. "It's conceivable that a change in the well-informed forecast of future economic events moved the market as it did," Bill Sharpe told the *Wall Street Journal* just after the crash. "On the other hand, it's pretty weird."[6] He soon heard from his appalled mother, "Fifteen years of education, three advanced degrees, and all you can say is 'it's weird'?"

Within a few months, other rational marketeers regained their bravado: "The appropriate response to the October performance of the market is applause," Gene Fama declared. Fama's reasoning was that an inefficient market would have been one in which the price decline occurred slowly. The rapid adjustment (a.k.a. crash) was evidence of how quickly the market processed new information.[7] Left unanswered was what exactly that new information was. If your belief in efficient markets was strong enough, you didn't need to know. The omniscient market had been able to sense something that, even after the fact, individual scholars and investors were unable to pin down.[8]

Unbelievers wanted better answers than that. Most market players settled on the story offered by federal regulators after the crash—that mass selling by portfolio insurers and other computer-driven "program traders" had triggered a disconnect between the Chicago derivatives markets and the New York stock market that turned a stock decline into a rout. Whether this disconnect was the fault of the hyperactive futures traders in Chicago or the slow-moving specialists of the New York Stock Exchange depended on which regulator you were talking to.[9]

Academic critics of the efficient market hypothesis, not surprisingly, felt vindicated by the crash. The same *Wall Street Journal* article that quoted Bill Sharpe's puzzled postcrash musings featured triumphalist declarations from Larry Summers and Bob Shiller. Said Summers, "If anyone did seriously believe that price movements are determined by changes in information about economic fundamentals, they've got to be disabused of that notion by Monday's 500-point movement." Said Shiller, "The efficient market hypothesis is the most remarkable error in the history of economic theory. This is just another nail in its coffin."[10]

Shiller had recently become interested in using surveys to learn more about investors' moods, and had sent out three thousand questionnaires the week of the crash. He learned that 43 percent of institutional investors and 23 percent of the individuals surveyed experienced "unusual symptoms of anxiety (difficulty concentrating, sweaty palms, tightness in chest, irritability, or rapid pulse)" on October 19. Shiller speculated that anxious investors, "falling back on intuitive models like models of price reversal or continuation," set off a sort of feedback loop.[11] Richard Thaler argued that the crash reflected the psychological propensity to overemphasize recent experience in extrapolating about the future.[12] Investors had driven prices too high before the crash by assuming that price increases would continue. After the market turned, they sent prices even lower by assuming that the declines would continue.

These explanations still didn't address why the crash happened when it did. They certainly didn't win over anybody in the efficient markets crowd. That the market had lost a fifth of its value in one day couldn't be denied, though, and *that* was a problem.

IT WAS A PROBLEM BECAUSE, according to the statistical portrait of market behavior accepted in most of academia and much of Wall Street, October 19 could not have happened. Actually, that's not quite right. After the dust had settled, Mark Rubinstein and a UC–Berkeley colleague calculated the likelihood of such a market drop in a world of normally distributed price changes as being in the neighborhood of 10^{-160}. That is, it was something investors could expect to happen once every couple billion billion years. The universe has only existed an estimated 12 billion years; the New York Stock Exchange was, as of October 1987, 170 years old.[13] Either stock market investors were desperately, spectacularly, unimaginably unlucky that October day, or the bell curve did not come remotely close to representing the true nature of financial market risk.

This realization came quickly to some options traders. After October 19, options prices displayed what came to be called a "volatility smile." By turning the Black-Scholes equation around, one can calculate the implied volatility of any stock from the price of its options. Put options allow one to sell a share of stock at a preset price. After the 1987 crash, put options that were well out of the money (the stock was at $40, say, and the put allowed one to sell it for $10) traded at prices that, according to Black-Scholes, implied a similar crash every few years. Other options on the same stocks, though, continued to trade at prices that implied less extreme volatility. That was the smile—flat in the middle, rising at the edge. The Black-Scholes formula assumed that volatility would be constant, consistent, and normally distributed. That clearly wasn't the case, and the search for better models of volatility was now on in earnest.

One starting point was the statistical framework assembled twenty-five years before by Benoit Mandelbrot. Mandelbrot hadn't predicted black Monday. He hadn't written anything about finance in years. But anyone who had studied his market writings from the 1960s was far less surprised by events on Wall Street than those who had restricted their reading to standard finance textbooks. Mandelbrot was by this time also becoming famous. His reputation-making *Fractal Geometry of Nature* came out in 1982. The year of the crash, journalist James Gleick's bestselling book *Chaos* introduced him to a much wider readership.

After 1987, Mandelbrot's long-ignored ideas began to intrude upon the consciousness of Wall Street. It wasn't so much his probability formulas that caught on—he had only written them down, he said later, because at the time "random processes could only be investigated through formulas and theorems." Now, thanks to ever-faster, ever-more-powerful computers, there was an alternative. A trader with a computer could simulate countless potential future paths for security prices, exploring the shape and texture of market volatility in the spirit of Mandelbrot's fractals.[14]

This remained, however, a minority pursuit. Bell curve finance, with its neat-but-misleading depiction of markets that move in small steps rather than big leaps, proved remarkably resilient in the aftermath of its great embarrassment of 1987. The quick recovery of financial markets soon made the crash look more like an anomaly than a major disaster. It was also convenient to have simple, standardized answers to the questions: How do I measure the performance of a money manager? How should I allocate my investment portfolio? How do I price an option?

This unwillingness to give up on theories even when their underpinnings had been largely demolished was, like so many things about rational market finance, not entirely crazy. "Neoclassical finance is about building bridges and railroads," is how finance scholar and money manager Steve Ross put it. His point was that the relativistic and quantum revolutions of the twentieth century have shown much of Newtonian physics to be wrong, yet engineers still design buildings and bridges following Newton's laws and the overwhelming majority of them don't fall down.

As memories of the crash faded, the brand of finance assembled in Chicago and Cambridge, Massachusetts, in the 1950s and 1960s survived and even thrived. A major landmark came when the Nobel committee awarded the 1990 economics prize to Harry Markowitz, Merton Miller, and William Sharpe "for their pioneering work in the theory of financial economics." It was a first for finance. The choice, exulted a University of Rochester professor writing in the next day's *Wall Street Journal*, "finally acknowledges that the field of financial economics is a genuine science, in the same league with physics and mathematics."[15]

Seven years later, Robert Merton and Myron Scholes won the Nobel. Fischer Black had died in 1995; otherwise he surely would have shared in the prize. The option-pricing model the three put together had "generated new types of financial instruments and facilitated more efficient risk management in society," the Swedish Academy of Science declared in awarding the 1997 prize. In his acceptance speech in December, Scholes argued that because derivatives "provide lower cost solutions to financial contracting problems," they "enhance economic efficiency."

Merton too was bullish in his speech about the pricing models that he, Scholes, and Black had developed. He did slip in a circumspect note, though. "At times we can lose sight of the ultimate purpose of the models when their mathematics become too interesting," he said. "The mathematics of financial models can be applied precisely, but the models are not at all precise in their application to the complex real world."[16] To get back to those bridges and railroads, physicists and civil engineers have learned through experience over the years when it's safe to apply Newton's theories and when it's not. The ground in finance is constantly shifting. It's a lot harder than in civil engineering to know when your models will work, and when they won't. Before 1998 was over, Merton and Scholes would learn this truth in painful fashion.

WHILE PORTFOLIO INSURANCE PROPER HAD been largely discredited in 1987, the market for insuring against the vagaries of the market never went away. Before long, the big banks and investment banks were using options-pricing models to design and price private contracts called over-the-counter derivatives that enabled clients to hedge against (or bet on) financial risks. Now these instruments cover stock market moves and loan defaults, among other things, but in the first years after the crash the two main categories were interest-rate and currency derivatives.

In the early 1990s, these derivatives got a lot of bad press. Options, swaps, and futures of various kinds played key roles in the bankruptcy of Orange County, California, the collapse of venerable British merchant's bank Barings, and big losses at Procter & Gamble, Gibson Greetings, and Metallgesellschaft.[17] For the most part, these debacles could be blamed on the usual Wall Street mix of bungling, greed, and deceit. "For all the horror stories about derivatives," Merton Miller wrote in 1997, "it's still worth emphasizing that the world's banks have blown away vastly more in bad real estate deals than they'll ever lose on their derivatives portfolios."

Miller was a godfather to the modern derivatives business. He'd been instrumental in getting the original Black-Scholes paper published, his and Franco Modigliani's pioneering arbitrage proof paved the way for much of Robert Merton's work, and he was a longtime adviser to the Chicago futures and options exchanges. He moved to emeritus status at the University of Chicago in 1992, and in a second career as what he called a "professional keynote speaker" he defended the financial instruments whose ascent he had helped smooth. "Contrary to the widely held perception, derivatives have made the world a *safer* place, not a more dangerous one," Miller argued. "They have made it possible for firms and institutions to deal efficiently and cost effectively with risks and hazards that have plagued them for decades, if not for centuries."[18]

Steve Ross had predicted this happy result two decades earlier when he argued that the more different securities there were representing different potential states of the world, the closer we would get to the state of perfect economic equilibrium envisioned by his teacher Kenneth Arrow in the 1950s. One could see shades of Harry Markowitz in this argument, too. Give people more ways to invest in and hedge against the future, and they could decrease the riskiness of their portfolios.

One didn't even have to believe in the rational market to share in this worldview. "We need to democratize finance and bring the advantages enjoyed by the clients of Wall Street to the customers of Wal-Mart," Robert Shiller opined. "We need to extend the domain of finance beyond that of physical capital to human capital, and to cover the risks that really matter in our lives." Shiller proposed creating new derivatives that would enable people to hedge the risks of income loss, fluctuations in home prices, and falling GDP. He argued that these instruments "would remove pressures and volatility from our overheated stock market."[19] There was, however, a catch—two catches, actually.

First, modeling financial risk is hard. Statistical models can never fully capture all things that can go wrong (or right). It was as physicist and random walk pioneer M. F. M. Osborne told his students at UC–Berkeley back in 1972: For everyday market events the bell curve works well. When it doesn't, one needs to look outside the statistical models and make informed judgments about what's driving the market and what the risks are. The derivatives business and other financial sectors on the rise in the 1980s and 1990s were dominated by young quants. These people knew how to work statistical models, but they lacked the market experience needed to make informed judgments. Meanwhile, those with the experience, wisdom, and authority to make informed judgments—the bosses—didn't understand the statistical models.

It's *possible* that, as more quants rise into positions of high authority (1986 Columbia finance Ph.D. Vikram Pandit, who became CEO of Citigroup in 2007, was the first quant to run a major bank), this particular problem will become less pronounced. But the second obstacle to risk-free living through derivatives is much harder to get around. It's the paradox that killed portfolio insurance—when enough people subscribe to a particular means of taming financial risk, then that in itself brings new risks.

In the early 1990s, as banks and their customers struggled to get a handle on the risks posed by their derivatives deals, most turned to an approach called "value at risk," or VaR. This name was new—coined at J. P. Morgan in the 1980s—but it described what Harry Markowitz had dubbed "semi-variance" in 1959. It was the downside risk, a quantitative measure of how much a portfolio could drop on a bad day. It was possible to estimate a value at risk that took into account some of the wondrous and fat-tailed behavior of actual financial markets, but that required guesswork and judgment. To persuade a wary CEO to green-light a derivatives deal or convince a bank regulator that capital reserves were enough to cover potential losses, one needed a standardized VaR model like the RiskMetrics version peddled by J. P. Morgan.

Even a good VaR model yielded only a partial picture of the true risks facing a bank or corporation or investor, and there were those who found this alarming. "Measuring events that are unmeasurable can sometimes make things worse," said Nassim Nicholas Taleb, a derivatives trader who—after making a mint in the 1987 crash—emerged as the most outspoken VaR critic in the mid-1990s. "A measuring process that lowers your anxiety level can mislead you into a false sense of security." Take this argument to its extreme, though, and there's no point in trying to measure financial risk at all. A happy mean must exist between quantification and judgment—even if it's seldom attained in the real world.

Taleb's harder-to-argue-away concern was that widespread use of VaR made markets riskier. A drop in the price of a security raised the value at risk of a portfolio containing that security. If a bank or hedge fund was trying to keep the VaR below a certain level, it might then have to sell off other securities to push the VaR back down. That put downward pressure on the prices of those other securities, which in turn threatened to start the cycle over again. Just as selling by portfolio insurers trying to protect their clients from price declines had driven down prices yet further in 1987, VaR had the potential to exacerbate a downturn. "Our activities may invalidate our measurements," Taleb said early in 1998. "All . . . markets go down together."[20]

THE SAGA OF LONG-TERM CAPITAL Management, or LTCM, offers so many cautionary tales that it's hard to keep track of all of them. Listen to one of the former partners, or read the two fascinating books that chronicle the fund's downfall, Roger Lowenstein's *When Genius Failed* and Nicholas Dunbar's *Inventing Money*, and one comes away shaking one's head at the many hazards of hubris, of wealth, of leverage, of trusting one's bankers, of trying to make decisions in a partnership.[21] The hedge fund's fall might be evidence that markets are efficient: Its market-beating returns were the result of taking excessive risks. Or it might be evidence that they are not: LTCM failed because security prices diverged dramatically from their fundamental values.

The hedge fund had grown out of the proprietary trading desk at Salomon Brothers, and signed up Robert Merton and Myron Scholes as partners. It followed the approach of quantitative pioneer Ed Thorp: Find two securities that by all rights ought to be traveling in the same direction but weren't, and bet that they would converge. A longtime favorite of LTCM chief John Meriwether was the off-the-run treasury trade. Brand-new thirty-year treasuries often sold at markedly higher prices than identical securities issued six months before. When that happened, LTCM sold the new treasuries short, bought the "off-the-run" treasuries, and usually made an easy profit.

By the mid-1990s lots of other hedge funds and Wall Street trading desks were making similar trades. The only way to make much money off them was to leverage them with borrowed money. Take a trade that returns 2 percent a year. Borrow $9 for every $1 in capital, and that trade now delivers a 20 percent return on the initial $1 (2 percent of $10), minus interest charges. LTCM was far more aggressive than that, borrowing $24 for every $1 of capital as of early 1998.[22]

LTCM also made bets using over-the-counter derivatives, which were often a form of leverage themselves. The firm put much stock in its VaR models, which weighed the risks and correlations of different trades against each other. But unlike the trading desks of the big Wall Street firms, which by the mid-1990s had to answer to increasingly dubious risk management chiefs and CEOs, LTCM was able to set its own limits. The banks that loaned LTCM money and acted as its counterparties on derivatives trades should have been monitoring its risks, but it was such a successful, glamorous, profitable client that as a group they entirely failed to do so. When Goldman Sachs's head of risk management looked at LTCM's books just after it melted down, he was taken aback by two things: One was that the hedge fund had been making exactly the same bets as Goldman's in-house traders. The other was that the positions LTCM took were ten times bigger.[23]

LTCM ran into trouble in the spring of 1998. The Asian currency crises of the previous year had left investors jittery. The "spreads" between interest rates on risky debt and those on U.S. treasuries (which are seen to pose virtually no risk of default) widened. Betting that spreads would narrow to normal levels was LTCM's bread and butter. When they failed to narrow as predicted, the fund began losing money. Then one of those things happened that can never be adequately shoehorned into a risk model. Financial conglomerate Travelers bought Salomon Brothers, the firm that had given birth to LTCM. Salomon's proprietary desk traded in many of the same markets as LTCM. Travelers's strong-willed number two, Jamie Dimon, distrustful of the Salomon quants and the big position that they had built up in Russian government bonds, ordered that the trade be unwound. That made spreads widen even more.[24] Then the Russian government announced that it was defaulting on some of its debts.

The losses LTCM suffered were substantial, but not big enough to threaten its survival. LTCM's partners had figured that, after such a loss, they would be able to rebalance their portfolio and go back to work—poorer, but still in business. With other funds following similar strategies rebalancing at the same time, though, the prices of LTCM's holdings dropped even more. Plus, the only counterparties to whom LTCM could offload most of its derivatives holdings were its wary bankers and brokers. They all began cutting their exposure to the firm. LTCM's access to leverage disappeared, and with it its business model.

A few years after LTCM's collapse, Harry Markowitz went to see one of the fund's former partners lecture about what had happened. "I was pleased on the one hand to hear that all these fancy young kids, when push comes to shove, do mean-variance analyses," Markowitz said. They were still using the approach he'd dreamed up in the University of Chicago library in 1950. "But on the other hand, the process somehow failed them." What went wrong? "I'm assuming that the investor is a price taker, he's not going to go in and bother the market if he makes a transaction. These guys were just too big a piece of the market to assume that."[25]

FINANCIAL RISK IS NOT JUST about numbers and scatter charts and pervasive forces. The actions of individuals matter. Ed Thorp managed his way through the market minefield of the late 1980s almost perfectly—Princeton-Newport Partners turned a profit in 1987—only to be blindsided by Rudy Giuliani. When the U.S. attorney for the Southern District of New York targeted Michael Milken for prosecution, Thorp's Princeton partners got caught in Giuliani's web. They were charged with parking securities for Milken's Drexel Burnham Lambert. Thorp, while never accused of any wrongdoing himself, had to shut down his hedge fund.

The influence of Giuliani paled, though, beside that of the most important one-man risk factor of modern times, the chairman of the Federal Reserve Board. On October 20, 1987—the day after black Monday—the gears of global finance stopped moving. Stock markets need credit to function. The specialists of the New York Stock Exchange and the market makers of Nasdaq regularly acquire shares with no purchaser lined up. The idea is to keep trading going, and they do it with borrowed money. On the morning of the twentieth, though, worried banks began threatening to cut the securities firms off. If they had, trading would have become impossible, the markets would have closed, and the subsequent chain reaction might have taken the banks down too. Alan Greenspan, the newly appointed Fed chairman, made sure that did not happen.

In the 1920s, Irving Fisher's talk of a "permanently high plateau" for stock prices rested on the assumption that the Federal Reserve knew what it was doing, and would not allow a collapse of prices and of the banking system. It was an incorrect assumption. In 1987, the

Fed's chairman understood what Fisher had been talking about. Before markets opened on the twentieth, Greenspan issued a statement affirming the Fed's "readiness to serve as a source of liquidity to support the economic and financial system." Gerald Corrigan, president of the Federal Reserve Bank of New York, began calling the biggest lenders to securities markets and twisting their arms not to cut anyone off. If banks found themselves squeezed for cash, the Fed stood ready with fistfuls more. It took a little while, but by the end of the day the market was working again and stock prices were rising.[26]

Seven years later, in 1994, the Greenspan Fed showed itself to be a different kind of risk factor—shocking markets with an interest-rate hike aimed at reining in inflation. Several large hedge funds failed in the wake of that hard-to-model move. In 1998, the Fed returned to the role of risk damper. As LTCM's crash threatened to unleash a chain reaction of hedge fund and bank failures around the world, New York Fed president William McDonough gathered the hedge fund's lenders in a room and browbeat them into waiting to demand their money back, to allow for an orderly unwinding of the firm. It wasn't so much a bailout, as many critics at the time charged, as a time-out. But it was a maneuver that could probably only have been arranged by the central bank. The Fed also poured cash into the global financial system, spreads narrowed, and fears that Brazil was about to follow Russia into default were never realized. LTCM's miscalculations ended up causing a scare, but nothing like a disaster.

This raised a couple of interesting questions. The close calls of 1987 and 1998 had made the quantitative risk models that had emerged from rational market finance look bad. Would they have looked much, much worse if the Fed hadn't bailed markets out? On the other hand, if the Fed could be relied upon to save the world's financial markets whenever they threatened to freeze up, what was the problem?

The Fed's success in bringing markets back to life in 1987 and 1998 had political and regulatory implications. In the wake of the 1987 crash there was much talk of the need to tax financial market transactions to throw sand in the wheels of hyperactive markets. These proposals normally go by the name "Tobin tax," after economist James Tobin, who in the 1970s proposed such a levy on foreign currency transactions. John Maynard Keynes had already broached a similar idea in his *General Theory*, and in 1929 U.S. senator Carter Glass had briefly thrown markets into a tizzy with a plan for a 5 percent tax on sales of stock that had been held for less than sixty days.[27] In any case, interest in such measures faded quickly—in the United States, at least—as markets recovered and then boomed in the 1990s.

Similarly, the 1998 LTCM debacle led Brooksley Born, chairman of the Commodity Futures Trading Commission, which regulates derivatives exchanges such as the Chicago Merc, to push for oversight of the burgeoning off-exchange (also known as over-the-counter) derivatives market. She was rebuffed by Greenspan and her fellow Clinton administration financial regulators, and late in 2000 Congress passed—and President Clinton signed—legislation barring regulation of over-the-counter derivatives. The market was working, the reasoning went. Why get in the way?

THE FALL

CHAPTER 14

ANDREI SHLEIFER MOVES BEYOND RABBI ECONOMICS

The efficient market's critics triumph by showing why irrational market forces can sometimes be just as pervasive as the rational ones.

IN 1985, MIT GRADUATE STUDENT Andrei Shleifer assembled what he thought was compelling evidence against the efficient market hypothesis. He found that, starting in September 1976—the month after Vanguard launched the first retail index fund—new stocks being added to the S&P 500 went up relative to the rest of the market. Nothing else had changed about these businesses. Their intrinsic value had not grown. In an efficient market, such things weren't supposed to happen.[1]

Shleifer presented his conclusions at the annual meeting of the American Finance Association. As is customary, another scholar was assigned to critique his paper. In this case, it was Myron Scholes. When Shleifer finished, Scholes got up and said:

> This paper reminds me of my rabbi back in Palo Alto. My rabbi, when he gives his sermon on Saturday, he always begins with a little story about something that happened to his family back in the shtetl, and then he generalizes from that little episode to some big moral about the whole world. That's what this paper reminds me of. It's rabbi economics.[2]

It was a criticism similar to Merton Miller's line about the need to focus on "pervasive forces" rather than anomalous quirks. Young Shleifer took it to heart. "He was right," he said years later. "It *is* important to focus on pervasive market forces." It became Shleifer's quest to figure out just what the pervasive market forces were that allowed prices to go wrong and stay that way.

He had other quests, too. Shleifer "shaped the basic paradigm" in the study of corporate governance, the economics of transition (from communism to market economies), and macroeconomics. At least, that's what one of his former MIT professors said when Shleifer won the John Bates Clark Medal in 1999 as the top American economist under forty.[3] Shleifer also ran a U.S.-government-funded operation that advised the Russian government on economic matters in the early 1990s, and his conduct there later landed him in legal trouble and played a role in his mentor Larry Summers's early exit from Harvard's presidency. But that's another story.[4] Shleifer's challenge to the efficient market hypothesis was eventful enough on its own.

WHEN EUGENE FAMA RESPONDED TO the evidence against his joint hypothesis of the efficient market and the capital asset pricing model by jettisoning CAPM in favor of a clunky, multifactor "risk" model, some in finance were disappointed. "They don't want to hear about theory," complained Fischer Black of Fama and his coauthor Kenneth French, "especially theory suggesting that certain factors or securities are mispriced."[5]

Two efficient market skeptics from the University of Illinois soon offered such a theory to explain the Fama-French results. Using different statistical techniques and a longer data sample, Louis K. C. Chan and Josef Lakonishok found that beta actually worked well in explaining stock market behavior from 1926 through 1982. It was only after 1982 that it ceased to fit the data. Chan and Lakonishok proposed that what changed the results after 1982 was the rise of investment strategies built around CAPM—indexing, asset allocation, beta-based performance measurement, and the like. The behavior of investors had changed, which in turn had changed the nature of investment returns. The practical triumph of the capital asset model had weakened its predictive power. Starting in the late 1970s, Chan and Lakonishok found, stocks that belonged to the S&P 500 index dramatically outperformed the rest of the market. Only 2 percent of the equity investments of the top two hundred pension funds were indexed to the S&P in 1980, they pointed out. By 1993 it was close to 20 percent.[6]

This was more rabbi economics. In the pervasive-forces, efficient-market view of the world, the fashions of the investment industry weren't supposed to impact prices. Two securities representing claims on the same assets *had* to sell for the same price, the reasoning went, because if they didn't, arbitrageurs would get rich selling one and trading it in for the other—in the process driving the prices back together. It was not so much an argument that prices are correct in some fundamental way as that they are relatively correct. But if all securities are priced correctly relative to each other, then prices should be right on the macro level as well.

That was the assumption—and it was an assumption that survived the self-inflicted demise of Fama's original efficient market hypothesis, despite the fact that it was shockingly untested. It was easy enough to see how arbitrage worked in the kinds of transactions that attracted arbitrageurs: When Ben Graham bought shares of Guggenheim Exploration and sold those of its constituent companies short, or when Ed Thorp bought the companies in the S&P 500 and sold the index futures short, each was dealing with mispricings contractually obligated to disappear in the near future. Things could still go wrong—as they did with S&P 500 futures on October 20, 1987. But they usually wouldn't.

When a security has no set expiration date or means of conversion into another security, it's not so obvious how one is supposed to profit from the knowledge that the price is wrong. With the exception of cases where companies are about to be merged or otherwise removed from trading, the stock market is made up of securities conspicuously lacking in expiration dates. So how was it again that arbitrageurs are supposed to force stock prices back into line in the short term?

Nobody had a good answer. Believers in the rational market often cited Milton Friedman's 1951 plea for floating exchange rates or the 1950 paper by UCLA's Armen Alchian that said inept economic actors would be weeded out by a Darwinistic process. Irrational traders would lose money and disappear from the scene, the thinking went, to be supplanted by rational ones. But this claim was basically just folklore. No one had ever offered a scientific explanation—let alone evidence—of how arbitrage was supposed to work on a market-wide scale. The arbitrage argument was rabbi economics too.

This is what Andrei Shleifer set out to demonstrate. Shleifer had arrived in the United States as a fifteen-year-old in 1976, having fled the Soviet Union with his parents with help from the Hebrew Immigrant Aid Society. The Shleifers ended up in inner-city Rochester, New York, and two years later a Harvard recruiter on the prowl for minority students stumbled across this Russian math whiz and urged him to apply. Shleifer got in, and majored in mathematics at Harvard. But he soon became enamored of economics. It must have been in the air. Two other occupants of his freshman-year dormitory suite also went on to get economics Ph.D.s.

During his sophomore year, Shleifer decided he wanted a summer job in the field. He heard that MIT professor and recent Harvard Ph.D. Larry Summers was in the market for a research assistant. He went to the library, made copies of a few of Summers's papers, and gave them a careful reading. Then he headed across town to the professor's office. "He kind of barged in. Maybe he knocked," Summers recalled. "He said, 'Those papers on unemployment, they're good but there are five mistakes.'" Charmed by the familiar combination of chutzpah and smarts—all delivered in a thick Russian accent—Summers offered Shleifer a job.

Shleifer enrolled in grad school at MIT just as Summers returned to Harvard, but the professor remained his crosstown mentor, and he enlisted Shleifer on his side of the battle over market rationality. Summers had argued that "idiots," renamed "noise traders" by Fischer Black, often made more money on the market than rational investors. Shleifer and Summers, together with Shleifer's freshman-year suitemates Brad DeLong and Robert Waldmann, tried to explain how this seeming injustice might be possible.

The quartet started with the assumption that the most important characteristic of noise traders was overconfidence, meaning that they were surer of their judgments than they had any right to be. These too-sure-of-themselves types traded a lot, and in the process they produced bigger market swings than was rational. From these beginnings it was possible to come up with plausible (if far from irrefutable) explanations of Robert Shiller's findings on excess market volatility, among other things. The first piece of noise trader research came out as an exquisitely timed National Bureau of Economic Research working paper in October 1987, the month of the stock market crash. More followed, strewn purposefully by the four authors among the major journals of finance and economics.

Getting articles like that published became a lot easier after 1987. The stock market crash was one obvious reason. Another was the appointment that year of Ohio State's René Stulz as editor of the *Journal of Finance*. The Swiss-born, MIT-trained Stulz was no peddler of unconventional ideas in his own work, but his dozen years in charge of the *Journal of Finance* were marked by a dramatically more open editorial policy than under his predecessors. No longer did it take the special intervention of Fischer Black to get a paper that mentioned psychology or questioned market efficiency into the pages of the discipline's flagship journal.

To a senior professor voting on whether to give a young colleague tenure, an article in the *Journal of Finance* was an article in the *Journal of Finance*, even if one disagreed with it. "He's the big hero," said Shleifer of Stulz. "He's the person who brought this field out of the forest. He just said, 'This is fine; we'll publish these papers,' and other journals began to follow in his lead.'" It certainly worked out for Shleifer. In 1990, just four years out of graduate school, he had already published four articles in the *Journal of Finance*, five in the *Journal of Political Economy*, a score in other respectable journals, and he was at age twenty-nine a tenured professor of finance at the University of Chicago's Graduate School of Business. With that, a generation of younger scholars received the clear signal that it wouldn't hurt their careers to bash the efficient market.

THE NOISE TRADER WAS BENJAMIN Graham's Mr. Market— sometimes willing to pay too much for a business, sometimes too little. Most people in academic finance were still convinced that the arbitrageurs of the world (the Benjamin Grahams) rapidly pushed prices back to where they belonged. Shleifer wasn't convinced, but he still needed an economic explanation for why arbitrage *didn't* always work. Summers had checked out by this point—he moved to Washington in 1991 to be chief economist of the World Bank and then stuck around in a succession of increasingly important jobs (including, eventually, the top one) in the Clinton Treasury Department. Shleifer returned to Harvard that same year. While he soon established himself as mentor to a steady stream of brilliant young graduate students, they weren't ready to start coauthoring papers with him. So he worked with older efficient market skeptics such as Richard Thaler and Josef Lakonishok, and with his contemporary Robert Vishny.

Shleifer and Vishny had gone to grad school together at MIT, and then taught finance together at Chicago's Business School. They got on well with Fama, but had their run-ins with Merton Miller. "He thought people who believed in behavioral finance were commies," said Shleifer. In fact, both Shleifer and Vishny were believers in free markets and in rational, greedy "economic man." Their very first paper together was a look at the salutary effects of leveraged buyouts that could have sprung from the computer keyboard of Michael Jensen. They both believed that financial markets did a pretty good job of getting prices right. They just didn't think the market did a *perfect* job.

The pair teamed up with Lakonishok and Thaler to examine "window dressing" by money managers. They documented, by looking at data from 769 pension funds, that managers sold poorly performing stocks near the end of each quarter and especially at the end of the year. That's when pension sponsors are most likely to take a close look at their funds' holdings, and managers presumably didn't want to be asked too many embarrassing questions about out-of-fashion stocks.[7] It was a clear case of professional money managers taking actions—in an entirely rational effort to hold on to their jobs—that the hypothetical rational investor would not.

That was published in 1991. Three years later, Lakonishok, Shleifer, and Vishny became professional money managers themselves, launching a firm that invested in value stocks. LSV Asset Management, which by 2008 had grown into the 158th-largest money manager on the planet, with $73 billion in its coffers, bought and sold in a disciplined, quantitative fashion that tried to exploit quirks such as window dressing.[8] Shleifer and Vishny, meanwhile, remained intrigued by the pressures that caused this behavior.

The defining characteristic of the modern professional investor is that he manages someone else's money. For such a professional, going against the sentiments of Mr. Market often means going against the sentiments of his clients. If he makes a contrarian bet, and it doesn't pay off quickly, he might be in big trouble. "It is the long-term investor, he who most promotes the public interest, who will in practice come in for the most criticism, wherever investment funds are managed by committees or boards or banks," John Maynard Keynes had written in the 1930s. "For it is in the essence of his behaviour that he should be eccentric, unconventional and rash in the eyes of average opinion."[9] As a result, Keynes argued, believing that such long-term investors would set market prices rationally was a pipe dream.

Market pros were aware of these pressures to go with the flow. The standard hedge fund setup, in which investors agree to lockups of a year or sometimes longer and are given only infrequent updates on a fund's holdings, was an attempt to wrest a modicum of maneuvering freedom for managers. Yet finance scholars, despite the attention they lavished on the incentives and conflicts faced by corporate managers, long ignored the potential that money managers might be beset by similar "agency problems."

Robert Haugen, a University of California at Irvine professor who considered himself an intellectual descendant of Benjamin Graham, appears to have been the first to attempt to address this oversight, in the mid-1980s. But Haugen was seen as a cantankerous outsider, and he made his points in a *book*.[10] It took an equation-riddled journal article by Shleifer and Vishny to get finance scholars to pay attention.

That article was titled "The Limits of Arbitrage," and it was published in the March 1997 issue of the *Journal of Finance*. It was precisely when the market was at its craziest, Shleifer and Vishny argued, that those who tried to end the craziness by placing bets against it would have the hardest time keeping their customers or borrowing money. "When arbitrage requires capital, arbitrageurs can become most constrained when they have the best opportunities, i.e., when the mispricing they have bet against gets even worse," they wrote. "Moreover, the fear of this scenario would make them more cautious when they put on their initial trades, and hence less effective in bringing about market efficiency."[11]

With that, it ceased to be possible to assert blithely that arbitrageurs kept prices in line with fundamentals. One had to have some answer for the concerns raised by Shleifer and Vishny, and nobody did. Theirs was a quintessentially Chicagoan theory. It did not rely on psychology or sociology or any other suspect discipline. It was a case of assuming that money managers—just like corporate executives or government bureaucrats—were economic creatures subject to complex incentives, and seeing where that led.

Shleifer and Vishny proposed that the limits to arbitrage made value investing work. It wasn't that there was anything especially risky about value stocks themselves, as Fama and French had argued, but that it was professionally risky for money managers to plunk down too much money on unpopular investments. Value stocks are, by definition, unpopular. A year after the paper came out, the arbitrageurs at Long Term Capital Management met their Waterloo. Shleifer and Vishny got lots of credit for "predicting" LTCM's demise, but the meltdown of the hedge fund wasn't really what they had had in mind. It was what came next, in the final crazy years of the 1990s stock market boom, that truly demonstrated the limits to arbitrage.

THANKS TO THE RAPID INTERVENTION of the Federal Reserve, U.S. stock markets recovered quickly from the 1987 crash. Within a year the major indices were back at precrash levels, and they continued to rise from there. The disastrous years after 1929 had taught several generations of Americans to avoid stocks. In contrast, the experience after 1987 gave birth to a profitable new mantra: Buy on the dips. The market dropped in 1990 as a recession slammed corporate profits, but it didn't see another down year until 2000. It was the greatest bull run ever.

There were real economic forces behind this stock market boom. The corporations whose shares traded on U.S. exchanges emerged from the 1990–91 recession lean and competitive. What followed were several years of what came to be called the "Goldilocks economy"—because, like Baby Bear's porridge, it was neither too cold nor too hot. GDP was growing fast enough to keep corporate profits rising but not so fast that inflation (and by extension a Fed crackdown to halt it) was a threat. The Goldilocks era gave way to an even more remarkable time when growth reached levels that many economists assumed would spark higher inflation, but for some reason did not.

That was a fundamentals-based recipe for higher stock prices, but it coexisted with and was hard to separate from a dramatic change in public attitudes about the stock market evinced by that belief in buying on the dips. Roger Ibbotson's data yearbooks and historical charts were a factor in the attitude shift. So was an acclaimed 1994 book by Wharton School finance professor Jeremy Siegel, *Stocks for the Long Run*.

Siegel's book was yet another in the long line of stock vs. bond comparisons begun in 1924 by Edgar Lawrence Smith and continued most recently by Ibbotson and Sinquefield. The main new twist was that Siegel extended his data all the way back to 1802. He also did not ignore the disconcerting parallels to Smith, and to Irving Fisher. He gave Fisher—in particular his October 1929 pronouncement that "stock prices have reached what looks to me to be a permanently high plateau"—a prominent place in his narrative. "Time did eventually justify stock levels in 1929," Siegel wrote. "But the time frame was far longer than Irving Fisher, or for that matter anyone else, believed."[12]

The book was full of such frank common sense, and Siegel went out of his way to state and restate that when he said long run, he really meant *long* run. As his plain-talk routine became a staple of the financial news channels, investing conferences, and stockbroker training sessions, though, it lost in nuance. The core message, after all, was simply that owning stocks was a good idea. Siegel became "the intellectual godfather of the 1990s bull market," as one journalist put it.[13]

A good friend of Siegel's, Robert Shiller, began worrying in the mid-1990s that this bull market had gotten out of hand. Siegel and Shiller had met while waiting in line for their physicals when they arrived for graduate school at MIT in 1968. Siegel became a reasonably orthodox finance professor—his first job out of MIT was at the University of Chicago Business School—and while Shiller made a career of challenging that orthodoxy they remained close.

After the 1987 crash, Shiller had turned away from the stock market to focus mostly on real estate. Wellesley College economist Karl Case had enlisted him in an effort to find out whether there was excess volatility in house prices—that is, whether real estate was prone to bubbles, too. They discovered that there were big problems with the then-available data on real estate prices, and began assembling data series of their own. Those grew into a successful business, and the Case-Shiller indices are now the most-watched indicators of home prices in the United States.

By the mid-1990s, though, stock prices had risen so dramatically that Shiller couldn't ignore them. He updated a 1988 paper he'd written with his former student John Campbell showing that high price-to-earnings ratios usually presaged periods of low returns. By July 1996, P/E ratios were so high that, according to the Shiller-Campbell model, the market was likely "to decline over the next ten years and to earn a total return of just about nothing."[14] In early December, with the market up another 20 percent just since July, Shiller and Campbell, a professor at Harvard, traveled to Washington to share their worries with the Federal Reserve Board. At lunch afterward, Shiller continued discussing his fears with Fed chairman Alan Greenspan.

Three days later, in a speech that would become famous, Greenspan asked, "How do we know when irrational exuberance has unduly escalated asset values?" Shiller hadn't used the phrase in his presentation, and Greenspan wrote later that he'd been planning the speech for months and had thought of its trademark phrase in the bathtub. The coincidence of the professor's visit and the chairman's gloomy warning nonetheless entered stock market mythology.

The words "irrational exuberance," stripped of the question mark, made headlines around the world. Markets swooned as speculators worried that Greenspan might be about to crack down by raising interest rates. In March 1997, after stock prices recovered and then some, the Fed tried a tiny rate hike. The market dropped for a while, then went back to rising—and Greenspan decided he was done trying to tame it. "In effect, investors were teaching the Fed a lesson," he wrote in his memoirs. "You can't tell when a market is overvalued, and you can't fight market forces."[15]

Greenspan got his economic philosophy from a grab bag of sources. He was the last prominent product of the school of business cycle research established by Wesley Mitchell—his initial Ph.D. adviser was Mitchell's protégé Arthur Burns—and he shared with Mitchell and Burns an almost tactile feel for economic statistics and business cycles. He was a follower of libertarian philosopher and novelist Ayn Rand, and he shared her distrust of meddling governments. His monetary policy ideas owed much to Irving Fisher. And since a mid-1970s stint as chairman of Gerald Ford's Council of Economic Advisers, he had become adept at sensing the winds of political Washington.

Put all that together, and what emerged in the late 1990s was the world's most prominent advocate for the idea that financial markets got things right. Greenspan was willing to accept that stock market bubbles could happen, but he also thought deregulation, globalization, and technological innovation were bringing about advances in economic productivity that the stock market might be sniffing out before the government's economists had. After his brief dalliance with "irrational exuberance," Greenspan went on to cite this putative productivity boom repeatedly in his speeches and congressional testimony. It wasn't quite a repeat of Irving Fisher. Greenspan never explicitly said high stock prices were justified. But it was similar in its calming effect. As the economy grew and grew, Greenspan was ascribed ever greater power and omniscience in the financial media and on Wall Street. If the Great Greenspan—journalist Bob Woodward had dubbed him Maestro—said the bull market had a basis in economic reality, it had to be true.

It was true, to a point. Economic data later showed that there was a sustained boom in labor productivity (that is, workers produced more per hour worked) beginning in 1995. In the decade following Shiller's 1996 forecast of stock market returns of "just about nothing," actual returns were slightly under historical averages but decidedly positive.[16]

• • •

FORECASTING THE MARKET IS HARD, and stock market bubbles tend to have some basis in economic reality. But that doesn't mean they aren't bubbles, and can't cause damage when they burst, which was really all that Shiller was trying to say. Orthodox finance scholars often seemed to bend over backward to miss this point. In 1991, professor and money manager Richard Roll—whose research in the 1980s had backed up Shiller's claim that markets were excessively volatile—followed up a Shiller presentation on market swings with a response that is still cited by efficient market stalwarts:

> I really wish Bob were right about markets being inefficient. Because if they were, and we could detect when the markets were overvalued or undervalued, we could sure do a heck of a lot better for our clients in the money management business than we've been doing. I have personally tried to invest money, my clients' money and my own, in every single anomaly and predictive device that academics have dreamed up . . . And I have yet to make a nickel on any of these supposed market inefficiencies.[17]

It was an interesting admission for a professional money manager to make, but Shiller had never claimed to be able to predict the market's movements with moneymaking precision (his 1996 forecast was loaded with enough caveats to sink a supertanker). Shiller's own market endeavors consisted of improving data and creating new securities with which people could hedge their risks. Just because market prices sometimes got way out of line with fundamentals didn't mean it was easy to make money off that knowledge.

Cliff Asness, a student of Eugene Fama who went on to a career in money management, was one of many investors who found this out in the late 1990s. Asness had written a dissertation under Fama on the subject of stock price momentum, and then he went on to manage money at Goldman Sachs. He quit Goldman in 1998 to start his own hedge fund, AQR Capital Management. AQR was very much the model of a modern quantitative operation, making billions of nickels off lots and lots of tiny bets on such market inefficiencies as momentum and earnings surprise. The core of Asness's approach, though, was value investing—which wasn't working in 1998 and 1999. Asness was griping to his wife about his struggles one day when she interrupted him. "Let me get this straight," she said. "I thought you said you make your money because people aren't completely rational. Yet now you're mad because they're *too* irrational?"[18]

This was a quandary faced by many rational investors during the final years of the end-of-millennium bull market. They were confident that prices were wrong. "Everybody knew there was a bubble," says money manager Jeremy Grantham, who from 1998 through 2001 made a practice of asking investment professionals at every conference he attended if they thought the price-to-earnings ratio of the S&P 500—in the high 20s in 1999—would soon drop below 17.5. Of seventeen hundred money managers polled, all but seven said yes. Betting actual money on such a drop, however, could be a career-killing move. "The market can stay irrational longer than you can stay solvent," goes a saying that was probably never uttered by John Maynard Keynes, but is often attributed to him.

A long line of value investors lost their jobs or at least a significant percentage of their clients in the last couple years of the 1990s or the first few months of 2000. The most famous victim was Julian Robertson, a hedge fund manager of the Alfred Winslow Jones model who closed up shop in March 2000, just before the market turned. Jeremy Grantham lost 45 percent of his assets under management. Even Warren Buffett's Berkshire Hathaway lost almost 50 percent of its market value between mid-1998 and March 2000, but Buffett was unique in having arranged his business so that didn't matter. He had all the cash he needed regardless of whether investors liked his strategy. Asness's late start and quantitative approach—which kept him from making big bets on one stock or the other—saw him through the crazy years.

He decried the insanity in writing, in a screed titled "Bubble Logic: Or, How to Learn to Stop Worrying and Love the Bull" that made the rounds of finance scholars and value investors in 2000.[19]

The billion-dollar valuations given to money-losing Internet start-ups could at least tenuously be rationalized as lottery bets. As Fama said, if just one of the dot-coms ended up as valuable as Microsoft, the prices of all of them would be justified. Such reasoning didn't hold, though, for Microsoft and other already established companies profiting from the tech boom. Asness focused his analytical attention on the most beloved of them all—Cisco Systems, the maker of the shovels and pickaxes of the Internet gold rush. Cisco had grown spectacularly over its sixteen years of existence. In March 2000, it wrested from Microsoft the crown of the most valuable company on earth, with a market capitalization of $531 billion.

Six decades earlier, John Burr Williams recommended that investors use his formulas to deduce "the particular rate of growth, the particular duration of growth . . . that is implied by the actual market price, and see in this way whether the prevailing price is reasonable or not. Thus the formulas become a touchstone for absurdity."[20] Asness did just that, and figured out that Cisco's share price implied annual earnings growth of 54 percent per year over the next five years. At least, that would be enough to satisfy investors happy with a 9 percent annual return on their investment. Cisco investors had grown accustomed to share price gains of 20 percent or 30 percent a year—not to mention that it was crazily optimistic to think Cisco could grow its earnings at 54 percent for the next five years, given that its earnings growth was already at 30 percent and slowing. "I think the case against Cisco as a long-term investment is reasonably strong given today's prices," Asness wrote. "However, it is not nearly as strong as the case against the entire Nasdaq 100. The entire Nasdaq 100 looks very much like a slightly less extreme version of Cisco, and while this analysis can certainly be wrong for one company . . . it gets much less plausible to assume this type of long-term growth for an entire index of 100 large companies."[21]

That optimism was one weird thing going on in early 2000. Another was the case of 3Com and Palm; 3Com was the perennial number two to Cisco in networking equipment. Palm was a wholly owned subsidiary that led the market in the new business of handheld computers. Palm was hot, 3Com not so much. In March 2000, 3Com took Palm public, selling 5 percent of its stake onto the market and announcing plans to spin off the rest of Palm to 3Com shareholders, at a ratio of just over 1.5 Palm shares for every 3Com share, before the end of the year. The 3Com shares thus represented 95 percent ownership of Palm plus full ownership of 3Com's other businesses, which were less fashionable but more profitable than Palm. They should have traded for well more than 1.5 times the price of Palm stock. Instead, they sold for less than Palm stock did.

"It took five months to correct," recalled 3Com CEO Eric Benhamou. "I was an insider so I couldn't take advantage myself, but it would have been easy to make billions of dollars exploiting the inefficiency of the market." Finance scholars of a rational market bent argued that it was actually hard for arbitrageurs to sell Palm short and buy 3Com because there were so few shares of Palm available. But that was exactly the point. There were, in real-world markets, limits to arbitrage that allowed hyperactive noise traders to drive prices to irrational levels and stay there for a while.[22]

Asness had evidence that it was hyperactive noise traders driving Cisco's share price upward as well. He once went on an Internet bulletin board devoted to Cisco stock talk and asked, "At what price would you guys say Cisco would be overvalued?" One enthusiast wrote, "If it fell 40%, I'd be out of here."

IT WAS IN MARCH 2000 that Cisco's share price and the market in general peaked. That month, Jeremy Siegel inoculated himself from future Irving Fisher comparisons with an op-ed in the *Wall Street Journal* arguing that the big tech stocks had become so expensive that they were "a sucker bet."[23] The Roger Babson of the 1990s boom, Siegel's friend Bob Shiller, did him one better. That very month saw the publication of the book that Siegel had been urging him to write for years: *Irrational Exuberance,* a guide for lay readers to the market's penchant for overenthusiasm.

These were two cases of exceptional—and lucky—timing. Not so well timed was *Dow 36,000,* a 1999 book by economist Kevin Hassett and journalist James Glassman that will go down with Fisher's "permanently high plateau" in the annals of embarrassingly bad market forecasts. Not surprisingly, Hassett and Glassman approached the subject from the perspective of rationalist finance. Stock prices had been rising, they argued, because the equity risk premium had been shrinking as investors realized that stocks weren't all that risky compared to bonds. It would keep shrinking until there was no premium at all, with the Dow Jones Industrials at the permanently high plateau of 36,000.

Things didn't work out quite that way, but the argument that the equity risk premium had shrunk caught the fancy of more sober scholars as well. For those who still believed in the rational market, it was a more palatable way to explain the high stock prices of the late 1990s than Shiller's tales of investor fashion and excess or Shleifer and Vishny's limits of arbitrage. "My own view is that the risk premium has gone down over time basically because we've convinced people that it's there," Eugene Fama said. Stock returns would be lower going forward, but the world hadn't necessarily gone mad.

If the equity risk premium could change over time, though, several long-accepted tools of quantitative finance were no longer of much use. The history-based Ibbotson forecasts of future stock returns and the cost of capital, for example, now appeared to be built on quicksand. Ibbotson himself opted to assume that there had been a one-time shift in the risk premium, but that it would be constant, if lower, going forward. He took the 10 percent annual return on stocks since 1925, and stripped out the tripling of the market's price-to-earnings ratio that accompanied it. "We think of that as a windfall that you shouldn't get again," he said. Dividends, earnings growth, and inflation remained as the drivers of stock returns. Ibbotson made a forecast of future inflation using current bond yields, assumed that dividend and earnings growth history would repeat themselves, and constructed a new equity risk premium from those elements.[24]

While the old Ibbotson-Sinquefield risk premium was based upon the wisdom of the all-seeing market, this new one was built on the same kind of earnings guesswork that investors had relied upon before anybody had ever heard of the efficient market hypothesis. It was just another Wall Street forecast, subject to disputation from anyone with different views about the future. The pervasive forces of the efficient market had proved too fickle to be relied upon.

CHAPTER 15

MIKE JENSEN CHANGES HIS MIND ABOUT THE CORPORATION

The argument that financial markets should always set the priorities—for corporations and for society—loses its most important champion.

ON MARCH 20, 2000, THE financial weekly *Barron's* ran a cover story pointing out that the dot-coms were running out of money. The article listed fifty-one Internet companies that would exhaust their cash reserves over the next twelve months—assuming revenue kept coming in and expenses kept going out at the same rate.[1] All this information was gleaned from financial reports that the corporations filed with the SEC and posted on the Internet. That is, it was already publicly available information. Yet the *Barron's* article was a sensation. "We were a little surprised by the response," said the head of the research firm that had gathered the data. "The report didn't show anything new, but I guess a lot of investors haven't been focusing on the risk factors of Internet companies, they've just been focusing on the rewards."[2] Over the following weeks they began to *obsess* over the risk. The prices of Internet stocks fell sharply.

The prices of Internet stocks had fallen before, only to recover. This time they didn't. The money-losing dot-coms had been living off their investors' generosity. A few used the windfall wisely and were headed toward a day when they would stop burning cash and start generating it. Amazon.com was on the *Barron's* list, for example, and it has since gone on to become one of the world's leading retailers. Many others were dead without more money from the stock market.

This wasn't necessarily evidence of investor irrationality: One could rationally (if optimistically) believe that drkoop.com, to cite one charming example, could count on continued cash infusions from investors for the two or three or ten years it would take to turn a profit. But it meant that the price investors placed on drkoop.com—that went from $45 a share in 1999 to under $1 in late 2000—could not be said to *reflect* its intrinsic value. The intrinsic value of these corporations reflected, in large part, how much more money investors could be expected to pump into them.

AFTER THE CRASH OF 1987, hedge fund manager George Soros had begun shopping around a vague concept that he called "reflexivity." The problem with academic financial theory, he told an audience of economists in 1994, was that in it "financial markets are envisaged as playing an essentially passive role"—valuing securities and then getting out of the way. In reality, Soros said, the way market participants interpret a market's behavior shapes that very behavior. The market's behavior in turn determines the economic reality that market prices are supposed to reflect.[3] Soros was referring to events like the 1987 crash or the collapse of the British pound in 1992—which he egged on mercilessly while earning himself and his fund's investors a reported $1 billion. But the rise of the U.S. stock market in the final years of the millennium was an even more vivid example. Investor perceptions created a new economic reality, a bizarro reality.

In the case of the dot-coms and their even more cash-hungry cousins the telecommunications start-ups, this amounted to an arguably positive if wasteful bout of enthusiasm. Trillions of investor dollars were lost, but they were used in part to build an infrastructure from which the global economy has since reaped benefits. "The U.S. economy has built almost every major wave of progress on the backs of a financial mania," said tech investor Roger McNamee at the height of the boom. "It's a particularly inefficient way of doing things, but it minimizes the time it takes to develop a new industry."[4]

For established, profitable companies caught up in the stock mania of the late 1990s, there was no positive spin you could put on it. Natural gas giant Enron and telco WorldCom both struggled to meet the expectations inherent in their stock prices, faked their earnings, and self-destructed. Entertainment conglomerate Time Warner sold out to a wildly overvalued Internet company, AOL, and vaporized $50 billion of its shareholders' money.[5] Even companies where management kept their heads struggled for years with the hangover from the late-1990s stock price party.

"Overvaluation triggers organizational forces that destroy value," Michael Jensen wrote, after it had all ended badly. "Like taking heroin, manning the helm of an overvalued company feels great at first. If you're the CEO or CFO, you're on TV, investors love you, your options are going through the roof, and the capital markets are wide open. But as heroin users learn, massive pain lies ahead."[6] Yes, this was the same man who had declared the efficient market hypothesis to have "more solid empirical evidence supporting it" than any other theory in economics, who had made the case that, if only corporate executives paid more heed to the stock market, America's companies would be more competitive. Now he was saying that too-high stock prices had led CEOs astray.

Jensen still claimed to believe the market was efficient—meaning, he said, "that we don't know whether stock prices are too high or low." That in itself was a major climbdown from "stock prices 'fully reflect' all available information," but even it didn't fully reflect Jensen's position. He sold almost all the stocks he owned in 1999, so convinced was he that the market had gone mad.

It had been a long, strange intellectual voyage. Jensen attributed some of it to the mellowing that comes with age, although even in his sixties he wasn't what any neutral observer would call mellow. He had also broadened his intellectual interests, becoming fascinated with the workings of the human mind.[7] Mostly it was that, however attached he was to his theories, Jensen paid attention to evidence.

JENSEN'S JOURNEY IS IMPORTANT BECAUSE so many people followed in his intellectual footsteps in the 1990s. Not just other finance scholars, but journalists, management gurus, CEOs, and politicians. At the beginning of the decade one still heard many voices—a majority, probably—objecting that short-term-obsessed Wall Street wielded too much power over American economic life. The argument was often framed in terms of national competitiveness. While U.S. companies had to answer to the fickle whims of the stock market, the reasoning went, their counterparts in Germany and Japan were controlled by banks that took a long-term view.[8]

The most vocal opposition to this conventional wisdom came from finance professors in the Chicago tradition. "American managers *are* more concerned with current movements in their stock prices than are Japanese managers. And rightly so," said Merton Miller in 1993. "Focusing on current *earnings* might be myopic, but not so for stock prices, which reflect not just today's earnings, but the earnings the market expects in all future years as well."[9] Making a similar argument a few years earlier, Jensen allowed that the "main banks" of the Japanese keiretsu—corporate alliances linked by cross-shareholding—had once played a useful steering role, but he said big Japanese companies were now so awash in cash that their managers were "increasingly unconstrained and unmonitored." They were beholden neither to the stock market nor to credit markets. The inevitable result, he said, was that "Japanese companies will make uneconomic acquisitions and diversification moves, generate internal waste, and engage in other value-destroying activities."[10]

Jensen wrote this in 1989—before the Japanese stock market

peaked, before the bubble economy deflated, well before it became clear to everybody and his brother that many of Japan's big companies and banks had been engaged in "value-destroying activities" for years. His words also preceded the fall of the Soviet empire, and the post-reunification economic struggles of Germany.

If the validity of a theory is to be judged by the correctness of the predictions it generates, the theories of Jensen and Miller looked not only good but prescient by the mid-1990s. The Japanese economy fell into depression, most of Western Europe floundered, and the Soviet Union collapsed. The stock-market-obsessed United States and United Kingdom thrived. One could no longer point to any significant, successful alternatives to the Anglo-American way of financial capitalism.

And so, even as the on-campus debate over market efficiency began to turn in favor of the skeptics, the popular and political view of financial markets headed in the opposite direction. "The ever-rising Dow was the ideological trump card that allowed the faithful to dismiss doubters with an almost mathematical certainty," wrote leftist pundit Thomas Frank in his book *One Market, Under God.* "Just as efficient markets theory holds that stock markets process economic data quickly and flawlessly, American commentators came to believe that stock markets perform pretty much the same operation with the general will, endlessly adjusting and modifying themselves in conformity with the vast and otherwise enigmatic popular mind."[11]

Unlike in the previous decade, this belief became a bipartisan one in the 1990s. Global, too. By the turn of the millennium one could hear business thinkers in Germany, Japan, and even France echoing Jensen's arguments.[12] Even most of the academic critics of the efficient market hypothesis went along. Andrei Shleifer spent part of the decade telling the Russians to privatize. Bob Shiller tried to create new securities to allow investors to bet on economic events and house prices. Larry Summers, who in the late 1980s had promoted a transaction tax to slow trading on financial markets, became one of the world's leading defenders of free financial flows as the number two and then the number one at the Treasury Department. "Shiller, Summers, and the rest are on to something of more than statistical interest," lamented Doug Henwood, editor of the *Left Business Observer* and a sharp-eyed critic of Wall Street. "But they don't draw some of the more interesting conclusions their work suggests."[13]

AMONG THE LAST HOLDOUTS FROM this celebration of financial markets, apart from the likes of Doug Henwood and Thomas Frank, were the nation's chief executives. If there was one group of Americans who didn't trust the stock market, it was the men who ran the corporations whose shares were traded on it. Even there, though, attitudes were changing. A few CEOs began to embrace the ethos of shareholder value.

The two most prominent early adopters were Jack Welch at General Electric and Roberto Goizueta at Coca-Cola, both of whom took the helm at their companies in 1981 and set raising the stock price as their primary goal. In the early days, Welch sold off so many divisions and laid off so many employees in pursuit of this goal that he got the nickname "Neutron Jack," after the proposed nuclear bomb that left buildings standing but killed their inhabitants. Goizueta, a former research chemist, believed that good measurement was essential to business success. He hired Chicago MBA Joel Stern—who by this time had broken off from Chase Manhattan to launch his own consulting firm—to give him advice. Then he relentlessly focused the company on delivering cash flow that exceeded its cost of capital. "Management doesn't get paid to make the shareholders comfortable," Goizueta liked to say. "We get paid to make the shareholders rich."[14]

By the late 1980s this approach was working well for both Welch and Goizueta. GE not only had a rising stock price but was beginning to hire and grow again, and Welch was on his way to becoming one of the century's iconic corporate chieftains. Goizueta's strategy at Coke garnered the invaluable endorsement of Warren Buffett, who bought 7 percent of the company and took a seat on the board. In November 1988, *Fortune* magazine put Goizueta on its cover for the first time, can of Coke in hand and polka-dotted silk hankie poking out of the pocket of his impeccable suit. YES, YOU *CAN* MANAGE FOR THE LONG TERM, blared the cover headline, continuing, "You say Wall Street won't let you look past the here and now? Nonsense! You're just making lame excuses."

Inside the magazine, the article ran through the usual CEO complaints about the market's fickle ways, and then pronounced:

> The stock market ignores profits generated by accounting flim-flammery. It assesses long-term investments better than many CEOs and at times appears to be peering further into the future than most. Says Alfred Rappaport, professor of accounting and finance at Northwestern University's Kellogg School and a leading student of stock values: "You can't justify today's stock prices without looking at profits into the 21st century."[15]

It took a while for CEOs other than Welch and Goizueta to catch on to this idea. Many still had to be pushed. Corporate raiders did the pushing in the 1980s, but if they had remained the most visible agitators for shareholder value it never would have taken root in the popular imagination the way it did. With the possible exception of colorful Texan T. Boone Pickens, the LBO artists weren't made out to be folk heroes. Fortuitously, a new sort of investor activist was on the rise, more palatable to the media, individual investors, and lawmakers than the takeover guys ever were.

The new breed was born in 1984, when the corporation-raiding Bass brothers of Texas made a hostile bid for Texaco. The oil company's management fended off the takeover by buying back the 10 percent of the company the Basses had acquired at a $137 million premium over the market price. California's state employee pension funds, the nation's largest, owned about 1 percent of Texaco. State treasurer Jesse Unruh, who helped supervise them, was outraged. The way Unruh saw it, the "greenmail" payment to the Basses was a $137 million theft from the rest of the company's shareholders.

The traditional Wall Street means of expressing dissatisfaction with a company's management was to sell one's shares. Selling shares was not really an option for the California Public Employees Retirement System (Calpers), which had followed the advice of consultant Bill Sharpe and put more than half its assets in index funds. Many other pension funds were moving in the same direction in those days. Unruh—a former Democratic speaker of the state assembly and a legendarily capable behind-the-scenes operator—made the rounds of his counterparts in other states. In 1985 they founded the Council of Institutional Investors to stand up for their collective rights.

That same year, Robert A. G. Monks launched a company called Institutional Shareholder Services (ISS). Monks was a Maine businessman and two-time Republican U.S. Senate candidate appointed to a Labor Department post in the early 1980s. While there, he amended the Employee Retirement Income Security Act (ERISA) regulations to require pension fund managers to vote their proxies solely for the benefit of the fund's beneficiaries (and not, say, those of the corporation that funded it). The new rules created a market for disinterested advice on how to cast those votes, and Monks founded ISS to provide it.[16]

Michael Jensen was initially dubious of these activists. "The real danger of this group is that previously passive institutional investors might begin to react to political pressure," he said when the Council of Institutional Investors launched. "Will they sell investments in companies the teachers' lobby doesn't like, for instance?"[17]

He needn't have worried. Unruh's council had too diverse a membership (it soon branched out to include union and corporate pension funds as well as government ones) and Monks's ISS was too interested in signing up paying clients to push political causes. They focused instead on the two principles that everyone interested in shareholder rights could agree upon: All shareholders should be treated equally, and management's job was to deliver the highest possible returns to shareholders.

Less than two decades after Milton Friedman scandalized liberal readers of the *New York Times* with his argument that the job of corporations was to make money, union pension funds and liberal state politicians were joining hands to pressure CEOs to . . . make more money. Years later, as pension funds heeded their consultants' calls to diversify into new asset classes, many even began investing in the funds of 1980s corporate raiders that had rebranded themselves as "private equity" firms.

Unruh died in 1987, but Dale Hanson—hired away from Wisconsin's state pension fund that year to run Calpers—proved a more than capable successor as a shareholder activist. Hanson saw that his potential allies weren't just the other pension funds that belonged to the Council of Institutional Investors, but mutual fund companies such as Fidelity and Vanguard. The mutual funds had no interest in waging public battles with the corporations whose 401(k) business they were courting, but their burgeoning size (and in Vanguard's case, its indexing bent) made it ever harder for them to bail out of underperforming companies. If Hanson wanted to raise a little hell, they weren't averse to quietly supporting him.

It all came to a head during the economic downturn of the early 1990s. Many big American corporations struggled, as they had during previous recessions in the 1970s and early 1980s. This time around, institutional shareholders showed little patience with CEOs who couldn't deliver a quick turnaround. Monks, who had sold ISS and started an activist fund called Lens, tried to get himself elected to the board of Sears to express his frustration with the retailer's direction. He failed, but Sears soon made many of the changes he had recommended. At Calpers, Hanson began pressuring boards to remove underperforming CEOs. In 1991 and 1992, CEOs targeted by Calpers and other institutions were thrown out at Westinghouse, American Express, and General Motors.

What Adolf Berle had called for in the 1920s finally seemed to be coming to pass: Institutional investors had taken on the role of watchdogs. Even Jensen came around. "Active investors are important to a well-functioning governance system," he said in his presidential address to the American Finance Association in January 1993, "because they have the financial interest and independence to view firm management and policies in an unbiased way."[18] *Fortune*, a reliable barometer of shifting opinion within corporate America, declared on its cover that same month that "The imperial CEO has had his day—long live the shareholders."[19]

WITHIN A FEW YEARS, THESE declarations of shareholder triumph had come to seem awfully naive. It was true that CEOs' jobs had become far less secure. They had ceased to be kings. That didn't mean they had become powerless. Many of them reacted to their new status—entirely rationally, it should be added—by ditching the noblesse oblige and becoming dictators, aware that they might be deposed in a putsch at any moment. They grabbed as much treasure as possible before that happened.

From the crash of 1929 through the 1970s, CEO compensation had stagnated. Workers' pay rose much faster than that of top executives. The most obvious reason for this stagnation was the tax code. Top marginal tax rates were punishingly high, topping 90 percent in the 1950s and early 1960s. Beyond a certain level there was no point in getting paid more. Top executives wanted perks like country club memberships and pensions and job security, not pay hikes of which they would see only 10 percent.

The Reagan tax cuts of 1981 changed all that. The 1986 tax reform, which brought the top rate down to 28 percent, changed it even more. CEO pay began to rise sharply, so sharply that it began to attract criticism in the media and from politicians. Its main defenders could be found—big surprise—on a couple of college campuses on the Great Lakes. A group of these scholars met at the University of Rochester in 1984 and arrived at the consensus "that executive salaries are determined by the market, and that changes in compensation are strongly related to company performance." That's how Michael Jensen and Kevin J. Murphy, who had just arrived at Rochester after writing a dissertation on executive compensation at Chicago, described it in an opinion piece they wrote for the *New York Times*. As there was competition for executive talent, the paychecks that resulted must be close to right.

At least, that was the starting assumption. Jensen had an endearing habit of digging in to the actual data, and when he and Murphy subsequently analyzed fifteen years of CEO pay at 250 big companies, they found almost no correlation between pay and performance. "Is it any wonder then," they wrote in the *Harvard Business Review* in 1990, "that so many CEOs act like bureaucrats rather than the value-maximizing entrepreneurs companies need to enhance their standing in world markets?"[20] These may have been the most influential of the many influential words Jensen wrote. Of course CEOs shouldn't be paid like bureaucrats, everyone from shareholder activists to compensation consultants to journalists to corporate board members to CEOs themselves agreed. They should be paid for *performance*.

Measuring executive performance has its complications, of course. What's the relevant time period—a quarter, a year, five years, ten? What's the right metric—profits, cash flow, free cash flow minus the cost of capital? The efficient market cut right through all that. Millions of investors weighed the present against the future and each investment against every other possible investment, and incorporated all of this into the stock price. What better gauge of performance could there be?

As almost always with this efficient market theorizing, there was something to this argument. But while the stock market delivers the best, most all-encompassing verdict on a CEO's success, it only does so reliably years after the fact. That's one reason why there was a long history of building delays into stock-based compensation, forcing executives to hold on for years before they could cash in. This history was thrown aside during the 1990s, due to the rise of the nonqualified stock option.

Granting executives options to buy stock in their company was not new. The practice came into widespread use in the 1930s, when struggling companies tried to lure and motivate competent managers with option grants. With cash in short supply and little public demand for stock, this approach was frugal and sensible. As Congress raised income tax rates in the 1930s, options provided an attractive alternative to cash pay for executives in high tax brackets—because options were taxed at the lower capital gains rate, not as income. The Supreme Court put an end to that in 1945 by deeming option gains ordinary income, then taxed at a top rate of 94 percent. Congress came to the rescue with "restricted" stock options that were taxed as capital gains—provided that executives held on to their shares for at least two years after exercising them. The permitted grants were modest in size, and in the mid-1970s, legislators revoked the tax break.

Then came the tax cuts of the 1980s. Congress resurrected the tax-advantaged restricted stock option (now called the "incentive stock option") in 1981. Far more important was the reduction in tax rates on the highest incomes. Unrestricted, plain-vanilla options were no longer such a bad deal. They were a better deal, actually, because those who exercised them could immediately turn around and sell the stock they'd bought. That removed all practical limits on how many of them an executive could get. And as the options grants got bigger, another quirk came into play: They were free, or at least appeared to be in the quarterly earnings reports provided to shareholders.

Even in the 1930s, astute investors knew this accounting was misleading. In 1936, Benjamin Graham wrote a parody press release, purported to be from U.S. Steel, in which the company announced that it would henceforth pay employees with stock options and stock options alone. "The almost incredible advantages of this new plan are evident from the following," Graham wrote:

A.   The payroll of the Corporation will be entirely eliminated, a saving of $250,000,000 per annum, based on 1935 operations.

B.   At the same time, the effective compensation of all our employees will be increased severalfold. Because of the large earnings per share to be shown on our common stock under the new methods, it is certain that the shares will command a price in the market far above the option level of $50 per share, making the ready realizable value of these option warrants greatly in excess of the present cash wages that they will replace.[21]

In the 1980s, the deal was even better than that. Because the IRS taxed employee options gains as income, the companies that granted the options could deduct these gains from their taxable income as a compensation expense. The options weren't just free to the company, they were a cash cow.

It was obvious to accountants that there was something wrong with this picture. They just didn't know how to fix it. The options were clearly compensation, and the way compensation (whether cash, cars, or stock) is accounted for is to expense it. The difficulty was that the standard executive option had a strike price equal to the stock price on the day it was granted. If a company's stock price was $20, one would get an option—usually good for ten years—to buy a share of stock for $20. On the day of the grant, one couldn't make a profit exercising the option, so the accountants deemed it worthless. Valuing the option when it was exercised, the way the IRS did, was so different from the way all other compensation was handled that the accountants never seriously considered it. Options remained free.

The options-valuation formula of Fischer Black and Myron

Scholes offered an alternative. It took a while, but in the 1980s the Financial Accounting Standards Board (FASB, usually pronounced "fazbee"), which determines what constitutes generally accepted accounting principles, took notice and began drafting a new standard that incorporated Black-Scholes. In 1993, the board made the proposal formal: Employee stock options would be valued when granted using the Black-Scholes model, and this amount counted as a charge against earnings.

Corporate America, which was then just coming around en masse to options, protested. In Silicon Valley, where options grants penetrated most deeply into the workforce, tech workers held an anti-FASB rally in 1994. "Give stock a chance!" shouted Kathleen Brown, then California's treasurer and a gubernatorial candidate, to cheers from the crowd. "Don't stop the engine of economic growth that has absolutely fueled this California economy!" At a public hearing at the FASB's headquarters in Connecticut, CEO after CEO argued that options had no value, and that expensing them would hurt the economy. When a FASB member explained to Home Depot chairman Bernie Marcus that academic studies had shown changes in accounting standards to have no effect on stock prices, Marcus retorted, "You're trying to confuse me with logic here. It's not going to work. I deal with the emotional side of the street. I deal with Wall Street."[22]

The shareholder activists who had struck such fear into executives just two years before were sidelined in this debate. With Silicon Valley a hotbed of options grants, California state politicians all opposed FASB's plan, so Calpers wasn't going to take a stand. The mutual funds didn't want to, either. Companies that bombarded their employees with options—Microsoft, Cisco, Home Depot—had the hottest stocks. Who'd want to look that gift horse in the mouth?

About the only vocal supporters of the FASB in its time of trial were Warren Buffett and Charlie Munger. Their political clout was limited, and, under intense pressure from Congress, the FASB backed down.[23] Options didn't have to be expensed, the FASB conceded, but companies did have to include an estimate of the Black-Scholes value of the options they granted in a footnote to their annual reports. The options party could proceed—and some other parties too. "Once CEOs demonstrated their political power to, in effect, roll the FASB and the SEC, they may have felt empowered to do a lot of other things too," Buffett said later.[24]

THE FINANCE PROFESSORS HAD MOSTLY been on the FASB's side. It was their option-pricing formula, after all.[25] But they didn't get too worked up. If the options data were disclosed in annual reports, the stock market would sort it out. The professors appear to have been right about that—when options costs finally were moved onto earnings statements in 2006, they had no noticeable effect on stock prices. Viewing accounting only in terms of its stock price impact, though, was a classic finance-scholar mistake. The place where the options accounting standard mattered most was within the corporation. Companies manage what they measure, and most executives and boards failed to manage the granting of options in a sensible way.

To reward performance and not just dumb luck, many finance scholars and compensation experts argued, executive options should have exercise prices indexed to the overall market or to other stocks in a company's industry. That way CEOs wouldn't be rewarded for a market boom or punished for a slump. If their company outperformed its peers, they'd make a killing. If it didn't, they wouldn't. Those kinds of options came with accounting complications that meant they had to be charged against earnings, and thus companies avoided them. Instead they gave their CEOs millions upon millions of plain-vanilla, at-the-money options. In the bull market of the 1990s, that made a few superstar CEOs into billionaires (Coke's Goizueta was the first hired hand to attain that status) and a lot of mediocrities into centimillionaires.

The SEC tried to crimp this excess by demanding better disclosure of executive pay, but that backfired as boards of directors strove to en-sure that their CEOs' pay beat the mean (the reasoning being that, if you wanted an above-average CEO, you had to offer above-average pay). Congress weighed in, too, with a 1992 law removing the cor-porate tax deduction from all compensation above $1 million a year, unless it was performance based. Options were the ultimate perfor-mance-based compensation. The law just caused corporations to give out even more.

What kind of performance were these options rewarding? In Black-Scholes and every other option-pricing formula, the value of an option increases with the volatility of the underlying stock.[26] CEOs were thus being paid to make their company's stock price more volatile—that is, to take more risk. Some argued that more volatility was a good thing, given that big-company executives had historically tended to be risk averse. But it may not have been what many share-holders had in mind with pay for performance.

Giving CEOs a shot at options billionairedom also had the ef-fect of making many of them intensely, obsessively interested in their company's stock price. That's what shareholders wanted, right? It's an interesting question, because different shareholders have different time frames. For the professional investors with whom executives were most likely to come in contact, that time frame was getting shorter and shorter. Up until the mid-1960s, when the mutual fund business first exploded, the average holding period in a professionally managed fund was seven years. By the late 1990s it was less than a year. Annual portfolio turnover exceeded 100 percent.

Professional money managers focused ever more intensely on quarterly earnings reports. "The fascination of investment managers with quarterly earnings is not terribly puzzling," wrote Alfred "Share-holder Value" Rappaport. "In fact, it is perfectly rational in a market dominated by agents responsible for other people's money but also looking out for their own interests."[27] These were the limits of arbi-trage: Keeping one's job as a money manager often required behavior far different from that of the hypothetical rational investor of financial economics.

That was one reason to focus on quarterly earnings. Another, as demonstrated by years of research by finance professors, was that a company's stock price tended to drift upward after quarterly earnings were announced that were higher than the market expected, and drift downward if the market was disappointed. By the 1980s it was possible to gauge with some precision what the market expected, as first the brokerage firm Lynch, Jones & Ryan and later First Call and Zacks collected the earnings forecasts of Wall Street analysts and consolidated them into "consensus" estimates. Investors began pursuing earnings-surprise strategies, thereby accentuating the immediate impact of a consensus-beating or -trailing earnings report. By the mid-1990s, the consensus forecast—or "the number," as it was often called—had become the single most important benchmark of short-term corporate performance.[28]

The number had its virtues. It offered a one-stop shop for busy investors trying to judge how a company was doing. One didn't have to worry about accounting changes or one-time charges, because those were already reflected in the number. The number also addressed a big complaint that finance scholars of the 1960s and 1970s had about Wall Street research. Most analyst reports were "logically incomplete and valueless," the University of Chicago's James Lorie and his student Mary Hamilton had complained in 1973. They failed to "determine or even consider whether the price of the stock already reflects the substance of the analysis."[29] Now an analyst knew he'd look stupid if he didn't make some reference to where he stood in relation to the consensus.

It was because the consensus number was so good that it became dangerous. Executives had always cared a lot about earnings. The consensus number for the first time provided a clear, realistic, universally agreed-upon target, while the growth in stock-based compensation provided a big incentive to meet that target. If a company's earnings came in below the target, the stock price—and with it top executives' wealth—went down. If they beat the number, they got richer. Rational executives did what it took to beat the number.

The most popular approach involved manipulating the consensus estimate. There were two ways to do it: Sometimes companies or entire industries persuaded the analysts who covered them to use a metric other than earnings. This alternative was usually chosen because earnings were negative, or volatile. The heavily indebted cable television industry, for example, adopted the convention of reporting earnings before interest, taxes, depreciation, and amortization, or Ebitda. The other way to change the consensus number was to "talk it down"—lead analysts to make earnings estimates easy to beat. This practice was sometimes portrayed as a virtuous one. It's far better to underpromise and overdeliver, after all, than to do the opposite. But negotiating earnings targets became a strange use of executives' and analysts' time, especially as investors caught on and began to assume that any half-competent management ought to be able to beat a target that it had, after all, negotiated for itself. In the late 1990s, analysts began sharing "whisper numbers" that were higher than their official forecasts with favored money managers.

The temptation also grew to manipulate actual earnings. Companies went to great lengths to meet sales targets before the end of a quarter. They scheduled transactions so as not to upset the earnings trajectory. And when all else failed, they threw everything into the kitchen sink—piling up write-offs and "restructuring costs" in one bad quarter so future quarters would look better. The appearance of good financial health was placed above the reality.

SHIFTING EARNINGS FROM QUARTER TO quarter isn't a problem as long as a company's general earnings trajectory is upward. For most American corporations for most of the 1990s, the trend *was* upward. Then, in 1998, the profits corporations reported to the IRS stagnated while those reported to investors kept going up. Much of this discrepancy had to do with the billions of dollars of stock-option profits reported as an expense to the taxman but not to investors, but at Enron and at WorldCom and other companies that didn't go quite that wrong, the struggle to meet earnings targets in the face of disappointing sales brought deception as well.

Stock prices had become so high relative to earnings than any sign of slower growth could send them (and with them the CEOs' net worth) plummeting. "By definition, an overvalued stock is one where the management team will not be able to deliver performance that will justify those prices," said Michael Jensen after it was all over. Jensen spent much of the 1990s working part-time for the Monitor Group, a consulting firm founded by Harvard Business School professors in 1983, so he had a lot of contact with management teams in this predicament. His advice to them was to talk their stock price down, to persuade investors to sell. That usually didn't go over well.[30]

Executives did have another, more profitable means of driving their stock price down—selling shares. They could either sell their own, mainly by exercising their stock options and dumping the stock, or they could sell the company's, by issuing new shares. Both these actions increased the supply of stock available, putting downward pressure on the stock price. In 2002, two former students of Andrei Shleifer proposed that by issuing stock when prices were high and repurchasing it when they were low, corporate America was in fact playing the crucial arbitrage role that professional investors could not. What kept the market at least within sneezing distance of rationality was not so much shark-like professional arbitrageurs as self-interested CEOs.

The biggest problems developed at companies where executives deluded themselves into thinking their stock wasn't overvalued. The finance professors had of course been supporting this delusion for decades by arguing that the market set prices rationally. "There was no listening in either the academy or the boardrooms for this story," Jensen said afterward.

In the mid-1990s, Jensen had gotten into a telling debate with UCLA finance professor Michael Brennan. Brennan had been Myron Scholes's student at MIT in the late 1960s, and was president of the American Finance Association in 1989. He was part of the efficient market establishment, but he was nonetheless troubled by Jensen's view of how the corporation worked. "I reject the position, which is implicit in the simple agency model, that the decisions of corporate executives are motivated solely by their personal financial incentives," Brennan wrote in 1994. "Other, ethical considerations such as duty, responsibility, honor and a sense of fairness are important also."[31]

After stock prices began falling in 2000, it became clear that Brennan was on to something. The company that had been the most valuable in the world, Cisco Systems, saw its profits drop to zero and its stock price from $80 to $14. Yet it didn't lose its way. It had a CEO who had been through tough times before. It had a corporate culture, inculcated by the long-serving chairman, of adaptation and flexibility. By 2008, while its stock price was still miles from its 2000 peak, the company had tripled its earnings, to $8 billion a year. Intangibles mattered.

In 2001, management researcher and former Stanford Business School professor Jim Collins published a book about corporations that had risen from mediocrity to greatness. The criterion for success in *Good to Great* was exactly what any finance professor would have chosen—dramatically better shareholder return than the overall market. Collins picked eleven companies that had made this leap and sustained it for at least fifteen years. Then he looked at what had actually happened to enable them to make the leap. There were some interesting commonalities, but the incentive structure for executives wasn't one of them. "Some companies used stock extensively, some didn't," Collins wrote. "Some had high salaries, others didn't. Some made significant use of bonus incentives, others didn't." Even when he went outside the good-to-great eleven and compared them to other companies, there were no identifiable patterns to executive compensation. Economic incentives simply weren't the decisive factor.[32]

JENSEN, CHARACTERISTICALLY, DIDN'T GIVE UP there. In 1998, his daughter attended a Landmark Education course in San Francisco. Landmark was the descendant of Erhard Seminars Training, or est, the 1970s self-actualization phenomenon perhaps best known for the infrequency of its bathroom breaks. Both Landmark and est focused on fostering authenticity and clear communication.

Jensen's daughter, with whom he had long had a fraught relationship, called him after returning from her course and asked him to try it. He flew out to San Francisco, and was hooked. He began studying the organization. Eventually he met up with est founder Werner Erhard, and together they began exploring what was missing from Jensen's models of corporate behavior.[33] The missing link, they concluded, was integrity. Not integrity in some vague moral or ethical sense. Being "in integrity" means "honoring your word," Jensen said, which means that—to quote from a PowerPoint slide at one of his presentations—you either:

- Keep your commitments and promises on time or
- When you have failed to keep a commitment or promise you:
- Acknowledge that failure as soon as you realize it
- And clean up any mess you created for those who were counting on your commitments and promises.[34]

If those norms were observed within a corporation or in the broader environment of the financial market, Jensen argued, vastly more economic value would be created and sustained than is currently the case.

It's a reasonable argument. More important than the details, though, is who made it. Jensen had been the most influential exponent of the notion that financial markets knew best, and that financial-market-based incentives were the ticket to a more efficient, more prosperous world. Now he was acknowledging that those incentives weren't enough. If market participants failed to follow a particular non-market-determined norm—integrity—markets wouldn't work. The market couldn't govern itself.

CHAPTER 16

GENE FAMA AND DICK THALER KNOCK EACH OTHER OUT

Where has the debate over market rationality ended up? In something more than a draw and less than a resounding victory.

EVERY YEAR, STUDENTS AT WHAT since 2008 has been called the University of Chicago Booth School of Business—like their counterparts at just about every top business school and law school in the country—put on a humorous musical revue called the Follies.

Among the acts at the 2002 Chicago Business School show was a mock musical boxing match featuring students playing the parts of professors Gene Fama and Dick Thaler. The Fama portrayer, who had been lifting weights for weeks to resemble the athletic scholar more closely, sang "Efficient" to the tune of "Tradition," from *Fiddler on the Roof.* (And who has the right, as father of markets/To have the final word on risk?/Gene Fama, Gene Fama! Efficient!/Gene Fama, Gene Fama! Efficient!)

His markedly doughier Thaler counterpart performed a finance-oriented version of Aerosmith's "Sweet Emotion." (Investors are not simple rational actors/You can't explain with your fancy three-factors!/Bad news, when the markets are on fire,/Gonna make me some money, can't call me a liar/Sweet Emotion/Sweet Emotion.)

After all the singing was done, the two knocked each other

out. "With no clear winner tonight, the debate rages on," the fight announcer declared.[1] Yes, even after the deflating of the 1990s stock market bubble, even in the face of reams of new evidence and theory on the craziness of financial markets, students at Chicago *still* saw the debate over market rationality as a stalemate. On the other hand, at least they knew there was a debate. And they could take classes with Dick Thaler.

BY THE TIME THALER MOVED to Chicago from Cornell in 1995, he was well known among economists. One key reason was the regular column he wrote for the *Journal of Economic Perspectives*, a publication launched in 1987 by the American Economic Association to keep increasingly specialized economists up to date on developments in the far corners of the discipline. Joseph Stiglitz was one of the founding editors. Giving Thaler several pages of prime real estate every issue was, he said, "an attempt to broaden the horizons of the profession." Plus, Stiglitz added, Thaler knew how to write.

The Anomalies columns that Thaler turned in were masterful exercises in the gentle tweaking of long-held beliefs. Why did the January effect in stock prices persist? Why did the winners of auctions so often overbid? Why do so many Americans choose to make interest-free loans to the government (by allowing taxes to be overwithheld so they got refunds)? Thaler never claimed to be *sure* that the answers couldn't be found within the standard rationalist paradigm of economics, though the examples he described could not help but raise nagging questions.

Even such polite tweaking was too much for Merton Miller, and the emeritus professor's vehement opposition kept Thaler off the Chicago finance faculty. Others in the Chicago Business School wanted Thaler on board, and he was appointed a professor of behavioral science. There was nothing to stop a professor of behavioral science from teaching and writing about finance—which Thaler continued to do.

He even began practicing it, adding his name in 1998 to the door of a firm run by former Washington State University finance professor Russell Fuller. Before long, Fuller & Thaler Asset Management was managing several billion dollars according to strategies based on "the behavioral edge."

No longer a voice in the wilderness, Thaler was now a respected, *wealthy* professor at the school that still considered itself the head-quarters of the modern study of finance. In 2002, the Nobel Committee awarded another bit of legitimacy, giving half of that year's Nobel Prize in Economics to Thaler's close friend and mentor in psychology, Daniel Kahneman. (Amos Tversky had died six years before; the other half of the prize went to experimental economics pioneer Vernon Smith.)

Thaler greeted these milestones less as battlefield victories in an academic revolution than as the inevitable pruning of the excesses of post–World War II economics and finance. He even, on occasion, painted it as a return to Irving Fisher. At a session honoring Fisher at the 1997 meeting of the American Economic Association, Thaler described how the forefather of modern finance interviewed Germans in the early 1920s to get a better idea of how they reacted to high inflation, and factored fashion and self-control into his thinking about the current value of future earnings. "Fisher . . . helped introduce mathematics to economics," Thaler said, but his written work was studded with what looked an awful lot like behavioral research and reasoning. "Young economists are taught these modern concepts (equations, diagrams and the like) but rarely go back and read the surrounding text," Thaler complained. "It is time to stop neglecting the words and time to start updating our equations to include these behavioral factors."[2]

WHEN IT CAME TO THE study of individuals and the decisions they make, this behaviorist updating of equations was an unalloyed success. Most economists and finance scholars had never disputed that people sometimes made weird choices. The issue was that finance professors in particular couldn't see why it mattered. They studied prices, not people.

Many of these same finance professors had been giving *advice* to investors all along. They just never gave much thought to whether anyone would follow it. In the 1970s, when those on the receiving end were mostly professional pension fund managers, this lack of attention to how regular people made decisions about money was perhaps not such a big deal. By the 1990s, though, individuals were increasingly in charge of their own financial destinies.

In the United States, this transformation was largely the doing of the same 1974 Employee Retirement Income Security Act that turned so many of the nation's pension fund managers into Harry Markowitz–following quants. ERISA also forced corporate executives to come to terms with the massive cost of their pension commitments. These executives reacted rationally—by minimizing that cost. As a result, it's hard to find a company founded after the passage of ERISA with a traditional pension plan. New companies, and many long-established ones, shifted the risk to worker-directed plans, mainly the 401(k).

The unwieldy name refers to a section of the tax code that a benefits consultant in Pennsylvania figured out would allow employers to set up tax-sheltered investment accounts for their workers.[3] As a retirement savings vehicle, the 401(k) has its good points—retirement funds can easily be transferred from job to job, which isn't the case with pensions. It also opened up a staggering new set of opportunities for poor financial decisions.

"Your parents probably had very little idea where or how their pension funds were invested," journalist Thomas Friedman wrote in his bestselling 1999 survey of the globalizing, increasingly market-dominated economic landscape, *The Lexus and the Olive Tree*. "Now many workers are offered a menu of funds, with different kinds of returns and risks, and they move their money around like chips on a roulette table, rewarding the successful mutual funds and punishing the less successful."[4]

Friedman made this change sound empowering, and it may have felt that way for some. But it was about the dumbest investing strategy imaginable. Hot funds tend to cool off. Cool ones tend to rebound. One analysis of mutual fund inflows and outflows found that equity mutual fund investors—largely by "rewarding the successful mutual funds and punishing the less successful"—earned an average annual return of just 2.57 percent between 1984 and 2002, while the S&P 500 delivered 12.22 percent a year. During the greatest bull market of all time, they hadn't even kept pace with inflation.[5] Another study found that the investment performance of 401(k)s trailed those of professionally managed pension funds by almost two percentage points per year.[6] That may not sound like much, but set aside $10,000 a year for forty years and earn 6 percent per year on it, and one ends up with $1.5 million. Take two percentage points off that annual return, and the sum drops by $550,000.

Standard academic finance and economics left no room for this kind of self-defeating behavior. The prospect theory of Daniel Kahneman and Amos Tversky—and the outpouring of behavioral economic research that followed—was all about this behavior. Chasing hot funds, for example, was a classic case of what the behaviorists called the representativeness heuristic, as investors used a small sample of recent data to gauge—usually incorrectly—a fund manager's ability.

Kahneman and Tversky had both moved to the United States in the early 1980s, with Kahneman landing at UC–Berkeley and Tversky across the bay at Stanford. The media caught on to the significance of their work long before most people in academic finance did. Popular science magazine *Discover* introduced them to a broad readership in 1985. *Fortune* explored the meaning of their work for investors a year later. *Money* followed a few years after that.[7] There now are enough books explaining their ideas to lay readers to fill a bookshelf or two.[8]

It was only with the publication of a pair of articles in the *Journal of*

Finance in 1998 that the mainstream of academic finance took notice. The author was Terrance Odean, an aging hippie who had gone back to finish his undergraduate education at Berkeley in the late 1980s and fell under Kahneman's spell. Odean wanted to stay on for a Ph.D. in psychology, but Kahneman steered him instead into finance, in part because Odean had a family to support and business schools paid better salaries. While working on his Ph.D. at Berkeley's Business School (portfolio insurer Mark Rubinstein was his puzzled-but-supportive adviser), Odean got his hands on a trove of customer data from a discount broker. He discovered that these customers traded way too much, chased after stocks that had been performing well, and as a group made much less money than they would have if they had simply bought index funds. Notably, the men did worse than the women by all these measures. The articles Odean subsequently published about his findings were a sensation, getting him media coverage around the world and a tenured job back at Berkeley.[9] Not surprisingly, this brand of research gained in popularity among graduate students and young professors of finance.

Odean's work showed how people who *chose* to play the market behaved. Subsequent research by others explored the different decision-making flaws of the involuntary participants of 401(k) plans. The 401(k)ers were prone to "naive diversification"—that is, they spread their investments more or less equally among the different funds on offer. They were daunted by choice—the more funds were available in a 401(k), the fewer workers participated in the plan. Far too high a percentage of 401(k) assets was in company stock. Most workers saved nowhere near enough to ensure a comfortable retirement. And so on.[10]

WHAT WAS TO BE DONE? Orthodox finance offered no answers beyond education, which usually wasn't very effective. Richard Thaler had another idea, one that related back to that dinner party in Rochester in 1978, where he set a jar of cashews in front of his guests, then took it away. With a jar right there, Thaler's friends ate the nuts. But when Thaler removed it so his guests didn't ruin their appetites, they applauded. They were of *two minds*, and which mind won out depended on how the choice of eating cashews was presented.

It wasn't just people. In a 1967 experiment that Thaler learned about later, a Harvard psychiatry student had given pigeons a choice of pecking a red key to get food immediately, or leaving the key alone and getting even more food a few seconds later. The birds invariably opted for the immediate reward. But when a green key was added that, if pecked, would prevent the red key from ever appearing, a minority of pigeons learned to peck *it* instead—so they wouldn't be tempted by the red key and would end up with the larger helping of feed.[11]

In the far larger and more complex human brain, these battles between present and future could by the 2000s actually be observed, thanks to magnetic resonance imaging. MRI experiments conducted by psychologists and behavioral economists showed that the more advanced, uniquely human parts of the brain are most active when we choose for the long run, while more primitive sections are in charge when we choose gratification now.[12] The key to encouraging better financial decision making appears to be structuring choices to put the higher brain in charge.

When Thaler and his former Rochester colleague Hersh Shefrin wrote a paper on the subject in 1981, they discussed one such setup for humans that already existed: the "Christmas club" accounts that allow bank customers to deduct a preset amount from their accounts every month to save up for end-of-the-year shopping. In behaviorist lingo, this kind of practice came to be called "bundling," because it involved combining lots of spend-or-save decisions throughout the year into a single decision at the beginning of the year. The 401(k) was a mixed bag in this regard. It was a savings vehicle, with automated deductions from every paycheck along the Christmas club model. But most of the corporate sponsors of 401(k) plans did little else to encourage smart long-run choices. That was partly because they were afraid of being sued if they gave investing advice that turned out badly. It was also because employees, egged on by the financial media, were pushing for plans loaded with so many choices and so much user-friendliness that they discouraged good decision making.

The big but simple decision of whether to save enough for retirement was being unbundled into a complicated array of little choices: Do you want to participate in the 401(k)? How much of your income do you want to set aside? Which of these thirty-seven different mutual funds do you want to put the money into? For millions of Americans, the answer was: I don't want to deal with it.

In the mid-1990s, Thaler and a former student, Shlomo Benartzi of UCLA, hit upon a way to combat this impulse. They dubbed it SMarT, a not-quite-acronym for "save more tomorrow," and it involved getting 401(k) participants to agree to an automatic increase in their contribution rate every time they got a pay raise. By taking money that people hadn't earned yet, the plan bypassed the natural resistance to giving up something one possesses—known as the endowment effect. And by bundling the annual choice of how much to save into a single decision that held for years, SMarT put the long-run-oriented part of the brain in charge. At the company where the plan was first tested in 1998, the 50 percent of employees who chose to sign up for the SMarT plan saw their average savings rate go from 3.5 percent of income to 11.5 percent of income in just over two years.[13]

That kind of success didn't go unnoticed, and over the next decade the 401(k) was almost entirely remade along lines suggested by behaviorist research. Instead of a bewildering array of choices, plans were increasingly built around a sensible default option—a life-cycle fund, with an investment mix that changed over time as you aged, or a portfolio regularly rebalanced along Markowitzian lines. Harry Markowitz himself became involved with a company that gave such guidance to 401(k) participants. Bill Sharpe founded another one. Roger Ibbotson got into the business too. All came to appreciate—

and in Sharpe's case even participate in—behaviorist research into individual behavior.

Politicians noticed, too. The Pension Protection Act of 2006, the biggest change in pension law since ERISA, encouraged companies to guide their employees' savings and investment choices along behaviorist lines. When President George W. Bush made his unsuccessful push to replace part of Social Security with individual investment accounts, almost all the proposals centered on a simple, low-cost default option such as a life-cycle fund. "We've accepted the argument of behavioralists like Dick Thaler that people do dumb things," said William Niskanen, a former Chicago student of Milton Friedman and chairman of the Cato Institute, the libertarian Washington think tank.[14]

Thaler joined forces with Chicago law professor Cass Sunstein to apply his ideas beyond retirement savings. They dubbed their guided approach to choice "libertarian paternalism," and showed how it could improve lending regulation, Medicare prescription plans, public schools, and marriage.[15] Just as the law and economics movement that emerged from Chicago gave intellectual backing to the great deregulation of the 1970s through the 1990s, Sunstein became a leading proponent of a new behavioral law and economics movement that aimed to guide a rethink of law and regulation.[16] Sunstein's friend Barack Obama, a former part-time Chicago law professor, put together a presidential campaign platform replete with behaviorist ideas—and appointed Sunstein as his regulation czar after he was elected. Across the Atlantic, Conservative Party leader David Cameron became an outspoken fan of Thaler and Sunstein's work.[17]

BEHAVIORIST RESEARCH INTO ECONOMIC DECISION making had clearly "passed the acid test of scientific usefulness," as Gene Fama claimed of his efficient market hypothesis a few years before. Still, there remained nagging questions. If people were beset by behavioral flaws, for example, then how could politicians and bureaucrats—who were also people, and thus subject to behavioral flaws—be expected to competently steer their decisions?[18] Also, the bulk of finance research still revolved around markets and prices, not individual decisions. Did behavioral theory really offer any answers there?

The bounty of observed behavioral quirks was part of the problem. "There's only one theory of efficient markets," Merton Miller would say. "There are hundreds of theories of inefficient markets."[19] One could come up with a plausible-sounding behavioral explanation for just about every market phenomenon. But if they were all *different*, that didn't amount to much of a theory of market behavior.

The first modern behavioral theory of inefficient markets was that proposed by Thaler and his student Werner De Bondt in their 1984 study of "winner" and "loser" portfolios. They told a story of investors overreacting to past stock performance, but it wasn't a cleanly symmetrical story. The loser portfolios beat the market by 19.6 percent, while the winners only trailed it by 5 percent. Why would there be so much more overreaction in one direction than the other? Efficient market stalwarts professed to see, as they so often did, the small-stock effect at work.[20] An even bigger issue was that lots of subsequent behavioral research documented underreaction—investors taking irrationally long to process new information.

"If apparent overreaction was the general result in studies of long-term returns, market efficiency would be dead, replaced by the behavioral alternative of De Bondt and Thaler," Fama wrote in a 1998 critique. "In fact, apparent underreaction is just as frequent." The upshot, he concluded, was "a Pyrrhic victory for market efficiency."[21]

There was no denying that it was Pyrrhic. The efficient market that Fama described back in 1969 was "a market in which prices provide accurate signals for resource allocation: that is, a market in which firms can make production-investment decisions, and investors can choose among the securities that represent ownership of firms' activities under the assumption that security prices at any time 'fully reflect' all available information."

That was a market in which prices were *right*. Since then, Fama had been defining efficiency down. By the turn of the millennium, all he was really espousing was the old random walk. Or not even quite that since, as a one-time protégé of Benoit Mandelbrot, he knew as well as anybody that markets didn't really follow a random *walk*. He was simply saying that market movements were hard to predict. But Richard Thaler was saying that, too.

"It's possible to predict stock prices, but not with great precision," Thaler declared in a 2002 debate with Burton Malkiel. Malkiel didn't really disagree. Yes, there were bubbles, the Princeton economist said. It was just hard to make money off them.[22]

THAT WAS THE YEAR I stumbled across this story. I found a copy of *The Paradox of Asset Pricing* in a pile of books sent to my then-employer, *Fortune* magazine, for review. The book by Caltech economist Peter Bossaerts was too dense and mathematical to be reviewed in the magazine, but I was drawn in by the introduction. Bossaerts seemed to be saying, albeit in sentences that weren't a lot easier for me to understand than his equations, that it was now widely understood that the efficient market hypothesis was wrong.[23]

As a business journalist, I had heard CEOs and Wall Streeters confidently assert this through the years, and I was aware of Bob Shiller's assault on "irrational exuberance." But I had been under the impression that the efficient market was still a core tenet of academic economics and finance. Yet here was Bossaerts—a quant, a Caltech professor, and, I learned later, a student of founding father of modern finance Richard Roll. He wasn't attacking the efficient market hypothesis. He was just, almost wistfully, declaring that its moment had passed.

There was a magazine article in that, I thought. After doing a bit of research, I flew to Chicago. I caught a cab from Midway Airport, wandered around Hyde Park for a little bit, then headed to the collegiate Gothic building on the university's main quad where Gene Fama and Dick Thaler had their offices (the Business School has since relocated to a Rafael Viñoly–designed glass-and-steel complex a couple of blocks away).

I visited Fama first, passing big portraits of George Stigler and Merton Miller in the stairwell as I hiked up to his third-floor office. He was feisty. "I don't know that it's progressed beyond the level of curiosity items," he said of behavioral finance. The behaviorists, he said, had provided no alternate framework to replace the efficient market, which still formed the foundation of most of what was taught in finance class. "I don't know what asset pricing would look like in a world that really took behavioral finance seriously," he continued. "If you really think prices are incorrect, what are you going to tell me about the cost of capital?"

After an hour or so of that, it was down to Thaler's office, directly below Fama's. Thaler was more magnanimous and diplomatic, saying he agreed with "the man upstairs" on investment advice (buy index funds). But, he said, "The important intellectual debate is about whether stock prices are right as opposed to whether you can beat the market." And what about Fama's objections that without the assumption that prices are right finance would get really messy? "It's going to be a big mess," Thaler agreed. "Because human nature is a mess . . . It's a choice between being precisely wrong or vaguely right."

I followed Thaler to a lunchtime behavioral economics seminar. A Ph.D. student was trying to explain several aspects of the Shanghai apartment market in terms of Kahneman and Tversky's prospect theory. At one point, Thaler interrupted him. Maybe it's just supply and demand, he said. His behavioral economics was an addition to the economics of Adam Smith and Irving Fisher. It wasn't a replacement.

• • •

I WENT BACK TO NEW York and wrote my article. ("Is the market rational?" the headline read. "No, say the experts. But neither are you—so don't go thinking you can outsmart it.") It grew into this book, and during my years of working on it I've continued to struggle with what to make of the conflicting but not diametrically opposed worldviews of Fama and Thaler.

Along the way, I *have* become convinced that behavioral finance is more than just a collection of curiosities, or a self-canceling mix of overreaction and underreaction. The most consistent trait identified in behavioral research is overconfidence, which leads investors to think they know more about a stock's value than they actually do. Overconfidence is so valuable in other endeavors—finding a mate, starting a company, making a living as a TV stock market pundit—that there's no reason to think that it will ever die out. And in finance it helps explain such phenomena as excess volatility, momentum, and that there's enough trading to keep markets going.

Overconfidence doesn't get you to a theory of asset prices. It gets you to a theory of why asset prices overshoot their fundamental values—which in turn can coexist with a loose version of the efficient market hypothesis. "In an efficient market," Fama had written in 1965, "the actions of the many competing participants should cause the actual price of a security to wander randomly about its intrinsic value." That was still the basic idea, even among many of the behaviorists. It was just now apparent that this wandering can take security prices away from their intrinsic values for years on end.

It was apparent even to Fama. In 2007, he and Kenneth French published the most remarkable in their two-decade series of stock market investigations, a theoretical look at what would happen in a market with lots of "misinformed" investors. One of the core tenets of efficient market finance had been that a few smart arbitrageurs could undo the pernicious effects of a million boneheaded investors. But now Fama and French had come around—without quite admitting that they had—to the argument made a decade before by Andrei

Shleifer and Robert Vishny: Smart arbitrageurs could undo some of the damage wrought by the misinformed, but they couldn't undo all if it. "Offsetting actions by informed investors do not typically suffice to cause the price effects of erroneous beliefs to disappear with the passage of time," Fama and French concluded. "For prices to converge to rational values, the beliefs of misinformed investors must converge to those of the informed, so eventually there is complete agreement about old news."[24]

After reading an early draft of the paper, I called Fama and reminded him of what he had said to me a few years before—"If you really think prices are incorrect, what are you going to tell me about the cost of capital?" Now here he was arguing in print that prices could go wrong and stay there. What could he tell me about the cost of capital? Fama laughed, and said, "That's why I don't teach corporate finance anymore."

Other, less senior scholars didn't have that option. Malcolm Baker was an Andrei Shleifer protégé from Harvard's Economics Department who moved across the Charles River after getting his Ph.D. in 2000 to teach at Harvard Business School. Baker's research focused on the limits of arbitrage and the inefficiencies of financial markets. When he was assigned to teach a first-year finance class to a bunch of sure-of-their-own-genius MBA students, he saw no choice but to hammer them over the head with the efficient market. "You have to take into account where people are starting from," said Baker. "The first thing you should do is not to assume that the market is wrong. The first thing is to assume that it's right until proven otherwise."

This was the strange state in which I found academic finance in the early years of the new millennium. The creator of the efficient market hypothesis no longer believed that prices were right, while some of the efficient market's fiercest critics found themselves teaching in the classroom that . . . prices were right.

• • •

WHILE BEHAVIORISTS AND OTHER CRITICS have poked a lot of holes in the edifice of rational market finance, they haven't been willing to abandon that edifice. They haven't been willing to dispense with the equilibrium framework that Irving Fisher imposed on the field a century before. They spend their days studying disturbances and biases, but they still trust that Merton Miller's "pervasive forces" are out there somewhere, pushing prices at least in the general direction of where they belong.

Is that really as far as the rebellion is going to go? For as long as equilibrium has been part of economics, there have been those both within and outside of the discipline who have ventured that perhaps it isn't the best metaphor for economic activity. Economists in the Austrian tradition avoided equations not just because they were poor mathematicians, but because they thought equations failed to allow for the uncertainty and change inherent in economic life. The American institutionalists believed that more intensive empirical study could give them a better feel for evolving market realities. Even neoclassical titan Alfred Marshall pined in the pages of his *Principles of Economics* for an approach that more closely resembled that of evolutionary biology.[25]

These alternative approaches were sidelined because they never offered anything like the precision and clarity of equilibrium economics—precision that it had borrowed in part from nineteenth-century physics. So it was significant when, in the 1980s, the physicists came calling on economics again. In the intervening century, much about their science had changed. They'd been through the theory of relativity, then quantum mechanics. Now many physicists were becoming fascinated with what they called chaos—the study of how simple initial causes led to dramatic effects that, with the right nonlinear equations, could at least partially be predicted, like that butterfly flapping its wings in Brazil and setting off a hurricane in Texas.

In 1984, a group of physicists with ties to the Los Alamos National Laboratory launched the Santa Fe Institute, which they hoped would become an interdisciplinary research center where scholars from different backgrounds could explore chaos and complexity—a catchall term for all evolving, adaptive phenomena, including ones that can't be predicted. They identified Citicorp CEO John Reed as a potential benefactor. Reed had been irked that his bank's economists failed to foresee the bad-debt debacle of the early 1980s, and was looking for better ways of seeing around financial corners. He was already supporting behavioral economics as chairman of the Russell Sage Foundation, and agreed to back the Santa Fe Institute if it focused on economics as well.

As Mitchell Waldrop tells it in his 1992 book, *Complexity*, the physicist charged with getting the Santa Fe economics effort started called a high school acquaintance, economics Nobelist James Tobin, to ask for advice. Tobin told him the effort sounded like something Kenneth Arrow would go for. The ever-curious Arrow agreed, and signed on with the Santa Fe Institute as economics adviser.

In 1987 the institute hosted its first conference on "The Economy as an Evolving Complex System" and invited a bunch of economists, among them Larry Summers. There were a few testy moments. The physicists were perturbed by the economists' unwillingness to give more weight to irrationality and feedback effects in their models. Summers complained that the physicists suffered from a "Tarzan complex,"[26] constantly beating their chests about how dense economists were. The economists' resentment only grew as, for years, the Tarzans got all the positive press. Economist Paul Krugman claimed to identify a tendency among journalists and other nonscientist intellectuals that he called "Santa Fe syndrome," which meant disdaining all mathematical models unless they're "confusing and seem to refute orthodoxy."[27]

It didn't help when initial hopes that the equations of the chaos theorists could be used to predict economic phenomena were quickly dashed.[28] Physicists struggled with the reality that sentient beings are harder to work with than, say, subatomic particles. "I think overall the physicists didn't have much of an impact," said Steven Durlauf, a University of Wisconsin economist who was involved with Santa Fe for a decade. "They didn't come up with very interesting models. They had very stupid agents."

These "agents" were the actors in computer simulations that became a favorite research tool at Santa Fe. Not all of them were stupid. Brian Arthur, a Stanford development economist who was recruited to Santa Fe by Arrow, once paid a visit to Citibank's foreign exchange desk in Hong Kong. He saw that the traders there relied on "seat-of-the-pants technical trading methods" such as chart reading and trend following, but quickly discarded approaches that didn't work and tried new ones. They weren't rational expected-utility maximizers out of von Neumann and Morgenstern, but they weren't dumb, either. They learned. Back in Santa Fe, Arthur and several colleagues populated an artificial stock market on a high-end NeXT workstation with such characters, and ran millions of trading sequences.

They found that when their agents adjusted their trading strategies slowly, the markets settled into an efficient equilibrium. When the agents adapted quickly—repeatedly changing strategies to react to others changing theirs—the artificial market became a much more interesting place. Bubbles and crashes happened, momentum strategies turned a profit, and price movements looked like those in a real financial market.[29] But even that volatility didn't lead to *crazy* prices. "The deviations we were getting from rational expectations were not huge," Arthur recalled. "They were Holbrook Working–style deviations." Arthur made that connection—which few economists today would—because he was a former employee of Stanford's Food Research Institute, Holbrook Working's longtime stomping grounds.

The agents in Arthur's simulation were also, in their primitive way, "anticipating what average opinion expects the average opinion to be," as Keynes had put it sixty years before. "All there is, is heuristics, hunches, and subjective guesses," said Arthur. "It's not that there's an optimal solution to the market under realistic assumptions, and people deviate away from it. It's a shift from assuming that there's an objective world out there to saying that the world is created subjectively."

Around the same time Arthur was running his market simulations, a trio of physicists started a money management firm in Santa Fe, the Prediction Company, that aimed to take the lessons of chaos and complexity to actual markets. They were the subject of a gushing book—*The Predictors*, by Thomas Bass—that portrayed them as bold innovators who transformed the investing world. That was an exaggeration. "I don't think anything we were doing was radically different," said one of the three, J. Doyne Farmer. They *were* awfully good with computers—setting up an automated system that sifted through the entire academic finance literature on market anomalies to identify the most promising—and the Prediction Company was a success.

After the founders sold out to a Swiss bank in 1999, Farmer turned to full-time study of financial economics at the Santa Fe Institute. He tried not to sound like a Tarzan. "The problems are hard," he said of economics. "It's a harder field than physics." Yet he remained convinced that economists were too stuck on deduction and equilibrium. Irving Fisher's metaphor for the market was a mechanical system of pumps and cisterns. Farmer looked instead to the shifting populations of predators and prey. Peaks in the prey population led to peaks in the predator population that in turn led to declines in the prey population, and so on. The system never settles into calm equilibrium. It oscillates.

Financial markets follow similar patterns, Farmer argued, as anomalies are ruthlessly hunted down until they disappear, only to give way to other anomalies—and eventually, to spring back into existence. Hedge fund managers often claim that, by hunting down and profiting from anomalies, they are making the market more efficient. But it may be that, while making particular inefficiencies disappear, they are only amplifying the oscillations of the overall market.

Would these ideas have any impact on finance and economics? Arthur doubted *his* would. Waldrop's book about Santa Fe, which portrayed him as a lonely hero out to show his blindered colleagues the error of their ways, "ended my career in economics," he said. Farmer went out of his way to reach out, coauthoring several papers with mainstream finance scholars and launching a new journal, *Quantitative Finance*, that included Robert Merton and Myron Scholes (along with Kenneth Arrow and Benoit Mandelbrot) on its advisory board. But his work has yet to really penetrate the academic mainstream either.[30]

Still, even as they resist the incursions from Santa Fe, economists have been taking steps away from their near-exclusive reliance on equilibrium. This transformation has been most dramatic in the study of long-term economic growth, which by definition can't really be about equilibrium. For that reason, the subject got short shrift from mathematical economists for decades. Now, by ditching the equilibrium while sticking with math, economists are finding better ways to describe the dynamics of growth and change. A key word in the new growth theory is "endogenous"—that is, arising from within. In an equilibrium, all disturbance must by definition come from outside. Explaining a spurt in economic growth requires a deus ex machina such as the discovery of the Americas or the invention of the electric motor. In new growth theory, the technological drivers of growth are depicted as the result of economic forces and decisions.[31]

Bringing this concept of endogenously generated change to the shorter-term fluctuations of the market is a more complex endeavor. In recent years a few economists and finance scholars have begun laboring on market models that do just that. These models tend to be populated by rational but half-informed actors who make flawed decisions, but are capable of learning and adapting. The result is a market that never settles down into a calmly perfect equilibrium, but is constantly seeking and changing and occasionally going bonkers. To name just a few such market models in the recent literature: "adaptive rational equilibrium," "efficient learning," "adaptive markets hypothesis," "rational belief equilibria."[32] That, and Bill

Sharpe now runs agent-based market simulations on his laptop to see how they play out.

CHANGE WOULD APPEAR TO BE coming. It's not here yet, though, and for now we have to make do with the muddle of neoclassical and behavioral and experimental and asymmetric-information economics and finance that we have. What practical lessons can be drawn from this muddle?

First, it *is* hard to beat the market. If you have money to invest, the only sensible place to start is with the assumption that the market is smarter than you. You don't have to stop there. But if you do come up with an idea for beating the market, you need a model that explains why everybody else isn't already doing the same thing that you are. Sometimes this model will fit in to the efficient market framework— say you're a petroleum engineer and you have good reason to believe Schlumberger has figured out some big advance in drilling technology that archrival Halliburton has not. That is, you possess nonpublic information. Other times a behavioral explanation might make sense. A certain stock is cheap because it's unfashionable. Or maybe it's the limits of arbitrage. Professional investors don't have the luxury of patience that you as an individual investor do. All the while, you need to watch out that your own behavioral quirks aren't leading you astray.

If you're picking somebody else to manage your money, the chances of finding a market-beating path are even harder. You're now paying a fee that cuts into your performance. Since retiring as CEO of Vanguard, Jack Bogle has published a series of studies on the determinants of mutual fund performance. The only measure that seems to have any predictive value is the management fee funds charge. The higher the fee is, the worse the subsequent performance.[33] Cost is thus a good all-purpose starting point in picking a money manager— one likely but not certain to lead one toward index funds. There are surely *some* high-cost money managers who more than earn their fees.

Maybe you can find one. But you can't just do it on the basis of past performance—you need to have some cogent explanation of why a particular manager can beat the market. Good luck.

For figuring out what your portfolio should look like, Harry Markowitz's model of balancing risk and reward—and looking for investments that aren't correlated with each other—remains an excellent starting point. The complication is that it's not past volatility and past correlations that determine investing success, but future volatility and correlations. That future can only be guessed. For trying to decide the mix of investments in a 401(k), this isn't the biggest deal in the world. In running a hedge fund that's leveraged twenty-five to one, expecting the future to be just like the past can be fatal.

It is when we get away from investing and start considering those affected by financial markets that broader questions of market efficiency come into play. It's not just whether one can beat the market, but whether one can rely on the prices prevailing on financial markets to be right. A popular concept in recent years has been the "wisdom of crowds"—the notion that groups can often make better-informed decisions than individuals. It's a valid enough idea, and the title of an excellent book by James Surowiecki, but the wording is misleading. Crowds—and markets—possess many useful traits. Wisdom is not one of them. It is as Henri Poincaré wrote a century ago:

> When men are brought together, they no longer decide by chance and independently of each other, but react upon one another. Many causes come into action, they trouble the men and draw them this way and that, but there is one thing they cannot destroy, the habits they have of Panurge's sheep.

Stock prices contain lots of information. Markets, as Friedrich Hayek argued, are the best aggregators of information known to man. Yet mixed up amid the information in security prices is an awful lot of emotion, error, and noise.

What does that mean? It means that managers of a publicly traded company should insulate themselves and their employees from day-to-day or even month-to-month stock price fluctuations. All the same, those prices shouldn't be ignored, because there is useful information in them. One way to sift out some of the noise is to focus more on relative prices than absolute prices. If your company's stock is lagging that of its chief competitor, that may be a signal that you're doing something wrong. If it fell 5 percent last week in the midst of a bear market, that may mean nothing at all.

The biggest and hardest questions have to do with what sort of role we as a society should give financial markets. For the past three decades the answer, backed by the theories of the rational market, has been to give markets an ever larger role—shoving aside other institutions such as governments and corporations. Now, though, we seem to have arrived at a turning point. It's not just that the rational market theories have fallen apart. Financial markets have fallen apart, too.

THE ANATOMY OF A
FINANCIAL CRISIS

THE INDUSTRIAL REVOLUTION GOT ITS start in England's Midlands in the late eighteenth century, and Manchester, just to the north, soon emerged as its throbbing, chaotic, dirty, stinky[1] heart. The small group of local businessmen and scholars who banded together in 1833 as the Manchester Statistical Society had what amounted to front-row seats at the creation of economic modernity. Thanks to that excellent view, the members of the Statistical Society were among the first to seriously examine some of the defining dilemmas of market capitalism. Among them was the question of what caused the business cycle—and in particular the periodic sharp downturns in financial markets that accompanied it.

William Langton, a banker who was the Statistical Society's driving force in its early decades, was the first to suggest that this cycle had to do with fluctuations in what he called the "fund of credit." Langton also asked a question that still resonates today: "Whether—allowing that the equalisation of wealth over the face of the earth is in the end a great benefit—this object be not more rapidly accomplished by such spasmodic action, than by the steady though slow progress of a cautious trade."[2]

It was a younger member of the society, banker and sometime poet John Mills, who took the first serious stab at explaining what brought on this "spasmodic action." In a paper he read to the society in 1867, "On Credit Cycles and the Origin of Commercial Panics," Mills made the case that "the malady of commercial crisis is not, in essence, a matter of the *purse* but of the *mind.*" It was, in particular, a matter of memory.

"[W]e know the tendency of the human mind to take from present conditions the hues of a forecasted future," Mills wrote. In the early years of a cycle—the "Post-Panic Period"—traders "have still a vivid remembrance of a 'black Friday' or some other day of equally sombre hue." Then comes the "Middle or Revival Period," when business is strong and optimism grows. After a decade or so of good times, most of the gloomy oldsters who remember the last crash are gone and "healthy confidence . . . has degenerated into the disease of a too facile faith." The "Speculative Period" has begun:

> The crowd of . . . investors in financial and industrial enterprises . . . do not, in their excited mood, think of the pertinent questions, whether their capital will become quickly productive, and whether their commitment is out of proportion to their means. The commercial and investing classes thus come under an enormous amount of obligation, dependent for its success upon the one precarious condition of a continuance of the existing scale of prices.

Then follows "Panic," in Mills's view not so much a phenomenon in its own right as the inevitable result of what went before.[3] This account has gone on to serve as the (usually uncredited) template for countless popular analyses of the market cycle. Economists, though, have struggled with it. Mills reported in 1871 that one economist had objected that his analysis was "'a Psychological study and not one of Political Economy'; and therefore, no doctrine of the latter science can be founded upon it."[4]

It's not clear who this economist was—from the context of Mills's remarks it seems unlikely that it was his friend and fellow Statisti-

cal Society member William Stanley Jevons, the pioneering mathematical economist. But four years later Jevons offered his famous
amendment to Mills's account: "that these moods of the commercial
mind, while constituting the principal part of the phenomena, may
be controlled by outward events, especially the condition of the harvests." The condition of the harvests were in turn determined, Jevons
hypothesized, by the eleven-year cycle of spots on the sun.[5]

That particular market hypothesis didn't hold up so well, but
economists kept looking for explanations of the market's ups and
downs that rested on something more solid than mass mood swings.
The standard neoclassical theories simply ignored the business cycle.
The mainstream economists such as Irving Fisher and John Maynard
Keynes who explored economic downturns tended to portray them
more as fixable divergences from the economic norm than as phenomena intrinsic to capitalism.

One cannot say they were wrong to do so. Fisher and Keynes devised genuinely useful tools for combating depressions. All Mills had
to offer back in 1867 as a remedy for panics was "the special Education of our trading classes in those scientific truths, bearing on the
creation and distribution of wealth."[6] Other economists who followed
in Mills's footsteps—such as Wesley Clair Mitchell—failed to come
up with anything much better.

It is apparent, though, that something important is lost when
Mills's observation about fluctuating attitudes toward risk is removed
from the analysis of the market. Keynes tried to incorporate it with talk
of "animal spirits" that affected economic activity, but the Keynesian
economics that arose in his wake busied itself with more mechanistic,
less psychological explanations for downturns.

Starting in the 1960s, economist Hyman Minsky began a long,
lonely effort to bring the animal-spirits side of Keynesianism back
into focus. Minsky was a product of Chicago (undergrad) and Harvard (doctorate), and taught at respectable places like UC–Berkeley
and Washington University in St. Louis. But he operated far out of

the mainstream. A few Wall Street thinkers were fascinated by his theories, but most academic economists ignored him.[7]

The most important theme of Minsky's work was similar to that of John Mills: Stability breeds instability. Sustained good times inevitably bring financial practices that are dangerously unstable. Wrote Minsky in 1978:

> In particular during a period of tranquility . . . there will be a decline in the value of the insurance that the holding of money bestows. This will lead both to a rise in the price of capital assets and a shift of portfolio preference so that a larger admixture of speculative and even Ponzi finance is essayed by business and accepted by bankers.[8]

Ponzi finance, in Minsky's taxonomy, involved making loans that couldn't be paid off out of the anticipated *income* of the borrower. Only if the price of the asset against which the loan was made kept going up would things turn out well. Just like the pyramid schemes of the turn of the early twentieth century Boston fraudster Charles Ponzi, this kind of thing by definition has to end badly. In 2003 or so, Ponzi finance came to dominate the U.S. housing industry. It ended badly.

THE HOUSE PRICE BUBBLE OF the new millennium began, as most financial bubbles do, with a solid grounding in economic reality. Prices rose through most of the 1990s as the economy grew, and they rose fastest in places—coastal California, coastal Florida, metropolitan New York—where building enough new housing to keep up with demand was, for reasons of geography and local politics, a challenge.

In the aftermath of the stock market bust, Alan Greenspan and his colleagues on the Federal Reserve's open-market committee worried that the United States might fall into a deflationary spiral. As good disciples of Irving Fisher, they brought short-term interest rates down to 1 percent and kept them there from mid-2003 to mid-2004 to stave off that dire possibility. The lack of any inflation threat, and high demand from overseas for fixed-income securities, kept rates on long-term debt down as well. Rates on both adjustable and fixed-rate mortgages hit historic lows.

These were the fundamental reasons for an above-trend increase in house prices, but eventually those rising house prices became a self-fulfilling prophecy. They rose so fast along the coasts that, even with low interest rates, fewer and fewer people could afford homes under traditional underwriting standards. Lenders desperate to keep volumes from dropping began to push exotic loans that allowed borrowers to pay nothing but interest, or started them out with superlow teaser rates, or otherwise got large sums of money into the hands of people who previously never could have borrowed that much.

Such subprime and unconventional loans weren't entirely new, but they had been a smallish business dominated by banks, thrifts, and credit unions that kept the loans on their books and thus had incentive to keep a close eye on the risks. The slicing and packaging of mortgages into debt securities—which first became common in the 1980s, thanks in part to option-based mathematical models that made it easy to price them—was only applied to high-quality, conventional mortgages. This market was dominated by two government-created giants, Fannie Mae and Freddie Mac.

Late in 2003, Fannie and Freddie pulled back, stung by accounting scandals and barred from buying most subprime mortgages or any loans bigger than the conforming loan limit set by regulators—$322,700 in 2003. Wall Street firms eagerly filled the void. They bought the mortgages from brokers and other mortgage lenders and packaged them into mortgage-backed securities. Perversely, Fannie and Freddie *were* allowed to buy these, and acquired tens of billions of dollars in subprime-mortgage-backed securities to meet affordable housing goals set by Congress. The Wall Street firms also repackaged mortgage securities into collateralized debt obligations (CDOs) that allowed them to transmute even the dodgiest subprime mortgages into triple-A debt. The new derivatives called credit default swaps, which allowed CDO packagers and buyers to offload some of their risks, allowed for even more credit creation. Backing up all this packaging and repackaging and derivatization were options-theory-based risk models that were, of course, only as good as the information fed into them. In many cases, because the securitization of these kinds of loans was so new, the models relied on only two or three years of historical data.

It was madness, and a lot of people knew it was madness while it was happening. "Lenders understand the risks, but they have little choice except to keep pushing the credit envelope," argued Mark Zandi, a widely read economic forecaster, in November 2005. "It is Gresham's Law at work: bad lenders are driving out the good. With the industry's now large capacity to produce mortgage loans, after years of soaring growth, all lenders must keep up with the most aggressive or risk quickly losing market share."[9]

Could this behavior be called rational? For the mortgage brokers and investment bankers arranging the deals, sure it could. The first were being paid to originate loans, the second to reconstitute them into marketable securities. The possible consequences of the bad loans were for later, the paychecks for now. The people who ran the mortgage banks and investment banks involved in this sorry business were going to be on the hook if the loans turned bad en masse, but that too was a hypothetical eventuality, while the battle for market share was very real. The same went for the decision makers at ratings agencies who lent their imprimatur to ever-less-transparent securities.

For the borrowers, it was more of a mixed bag. Many were flummoxed by the complexity of the loans. Some were consciously taking a risky-but-not-crazy flier on home ownership enabled by lax lending standards. Others were defrauded. Yet others were themselves frauds.

The investors who bought the mortgage securities—banks, hedge funds, pension funds, endowments, even governments—were perhaps the most interesting case of all. The warnings of Zandi and many others were there for all to read by late 2005. But investors kept buying. For the professional managers of those institutions, this thinking may have been rational. The high yields on mortgage securities and CDOs helped them meet their performance benchmarks and keep their jobs. As for the ultimate owners—bank shareholders, hedge fund customers, pensioners—could they really be expected to see through the many layers of risk piled atop the mortgage market? By comparison, the stock market bubble of the late 1990s had been a transparent, easy-to-grasp phenomenon.

Whatever the causes, the cumulative result was an irrational financial market, a market built to collapse as soon as house prices stopped rising. In the summer of 2006, prices peaked and started to fall. The giant, by now unspeakably complex edifice of mortgage securitization began to crumble. The world's financial system hasn't been the same since.

THE STOCK MARKET—THE ACTUAL SUBJECT of Eugene Fama's efficient market hypothesis—held up pretty well through the panic. Stock investors failed to foresee the troubles that would result from the mortgage mess, but they digested the bad news as it came out in admirably rational fashion. Stock prices fell, a lot, and volatility rose sharply, but stock markets never seized up and stopped functioning.

For just about everybody in finance besides Gene Fama, though, the concept of the rational financial market was about more than just stocks. Securities markets in general were believed to have near-magical properties of speed and randomness and correctness. The mortgage market had become a securities market. Yet it got things terribly wrong on the way up, and ceased to function on the way down.

This reign of error could be attributed in part to the inevitable perils of financial innovation. Almost every great financial market bubble and crash through history has involved some new financial product or technology that market participants, without experience to call on, vastly underestimate the risks of. From tulip bulbs in seventeenth-century Holland to CDOs built around subprime mortgages, newness has always been a danger sign. Nothing new there, except that quantitative risk modeling may have made people even more blind to the potential downside than usual.

"We were seeing things that were 25-standard deviation moves, several days in a row," said Goldman Sachs chief financial officer David Viniar in August 2007, after the firm's flagship hedge fund suffered sharp losses during the first dislocations in credit markets.[10] Viniar's point seemed to be that what had happened could not possibly have been predicted—a 25-standard deviation event should only occur every hundred thousand years. A better explanation may be that his risk models weren't very good.

In the housing market, such models replaced rules of thumb that had held sway for decades. Traditional ratios of loan-to-value and monthly payments to income gave way to credit scoring and purportedly precise gradations of default risk that turned out to be worse than useless. In the 1970s, Amos Tversky and Daniel Kahneman had argued that real-world decision makers didn't follow the statistical models of John von Neumann and Oskar Morgenstern, but used simple heuristics—rules of thumb—instead. Now the mortgage lending industry was learning that heuristics worked much better than statistical models descended from the work of von Neumann and Morgenstern.

Simple trumped complex. In 2005, Robert Shiller came out with a second edition of *Irrational Exuberance* that featured a new twenty-page chapter on "The Real Estate Market in Historical Perspective." It offered no formulas for determining whether prices were right, but it did feature an index of U.S. home prices back to 1890. That index, the first sixty years of which had been cobbled together for the first time by Shiller from a variety of sources, showed that inflation-adjusted house prices had in the past declined for decades on end. It also showed that the increase in prices since the mid-1990s was sharper than any on record.

That fall, a Fed economist and two business school professors published an article on house prices in the *Journal of Economic Perspectives*. They used regional data on the relationship between house prices and rents over the past twenty-five years to build a model that determined that in most of the country, prices were well within their historical bounds. In a dismissive nod to Shiller, they admonished those who argued that "high price growth" was "evidence *per se* that housing is overvalued."[11] It was true that Shiller's price history didn't prove anything, but his data did seem to indicate that using recent data to judge risk—because it's the best, most reliable data available—could be misleading. And it put Shiller yet again in the Roger Babson–like position of arguing that what goes up must come down—which it did.

As CREDIT MARKETS BEGAN TO unravel in the latter half of 2007, the once-obscure Hyman Minsky—who had died in 1996—suddenly became a star. He was cited incessantly by Wall Street strategists. His books returned to print. Mainstream economists began to acknowledge that there might be something to his ideas.[12] Even before then, in one of his valedictory speeches as Fed chairman in August 2005, Alan Greenspan struck a distinctly Minskyan tone:

> [The] vast increase in the market value of asset claims is in part the indirect result of investors accepting lower compensation for risk. Such an increase in market value is too often viewed by market participants as structural and permanent. To some extent, those higher values may be reflecting the increased flexibility and resilience of our economy. But what they perceive as newly abundant liquidity can readily disappear. Any onset of increased investor caution elevates risk premiums and, as a consequence, lowers asset values

and promotes the liquidation of the debt that supported higher asset prices. This is the reason that history has not dealt kindly with the aftermath of protracted periods of low risk premiums.[13]

This was a pretty accurate, if bloodless, description of what was to come. The Fed chairman also correctly identified mortgage markets as where the nasty aftermath was likely to begin. In a speech to the American Bankers Association in September 2005, he worried about "apparent froth in housing markets" and the risk that exotic mortgages could, "in the event of widespread cooling in house prices," expose borrowers and lenders to "significant losses."[14] He also worked with a Fed economist to document the huge sums flowing into the economy from home equity extraction, as homeowners refinanced at low rates and took piles of cash with them.[15] As soon as rates stopped falling and/or house prices stopped rising, this source of funding would dry up and the economy would take a big hit.

If Greenspan saw at least some of what was coming, why didn't he do anything about it? Mainly because he had taken the lesson from his "irrational exuberance" speech in 1996 that he was not smarter than the market. That, and there was a long tradition in economics that while cracking down on general price inflation was in the Fed's job description, squeezing the air out of financial market bubbles was not. This tradition dated at least back to early 1929, when the Fed raised interest rates in hopes of tamping down on what some Fed board members thought was excessive stock market speculation. Corporate leaders howled in protest, as did Irving Fisher. Princeton economist Joseph Stagg Lawrence offered the most eloquent critique. "The consensus of judgment of the millions whose valuations function on that admirable market, the Stock Exchange, is that stocks are not at present prices over-valued," he wrote. "Where is that group of men with the all-embracing wisdom which will entitle them to veto the judgment of this intelligent multitude?" Certainly not in Washington, Lawrence concluded.[16]

Even economists who weren't so convinced of the wisdom of investors frowned on the idea of central banks trying to stop the fun. "The remedy for the boom is not a higher rate of interest but a lower rate of interest!" wrote John Maynard Keynes in 1936. "For that may enable the so-called boom to last. The right remedy for the trade cycle is not to be found in abolishing booms and thus keeping us permanently in a semi-slump, but in abolishing slumps and thus keeping us permanently in a quasi-boom.[17]

This was the approach Greenspan—a man not usually identified as a Keynesian—chose to follow. He wouldn't try to deflate a bubble, but he would do whatever he could to ease the pain of the ensuing bust. It was a consciously asymmetric approach. It was also, as one Fed watcher put it, "a recipe for *serial* asset-price bubbles."[18] By allowing financial markets to run rampant on the upside, while intervening to soften the impact of every ensuing crash, the Fed was encouraging irresponsible behavior that would make subsequent crashes even worse.

For a small but persistently loud minority of market seers, the remedy was to let the market panic take its natural course, to teach bankers and investors and homeowners hard lessons about risk that too many had forgotten.[19] That may or may not be bad economics. Keynes's argument that government can leave everyone better off by averting outright depression has held up reasonably well over the past seventy years, although that's no guarantee it will forever. Letting panic and depression take its course is definitely bad politics, though, so it's not going to happen.

Where does that leave us? It leaves us with a need to find ways to temper speculative excess while acknowledging that we won't necessarily be able to distinguish speculative excess from an entirely sustainable boom. Financial regulation will be part of that. A rediscovery of ethics and of integrity—as defined by Michael Jensen and Werner Erhard or as defined by the dictionary—will play a role too, one hopes. So will memory, as John Mills of Manchester would surely point out.

Memory, or "the tendency of the human mind to take from present conditions the hues of a forecasted future," as Mills put it, played a crucial role in the story told in this book. The efficient market hypothesis, the capital asset pricing model, the Black-Scholes option-pricing model, and all the other major elements of modern rationalist finance arose toward the end of a long era of market stability characterized by tight government regulation and the long memories of those who had survived the Depression. These theories' heavy reliance on calmly rational markets was to some extent the artifact of a regulated, relatively conservative financial era—and it paved the way for deregulation and wild exuberance. Now we seem to be headed in reverse. Who knows what world-changing financial theories that will inspire.

THEN AGAIN, MAYBE THEY WON'T be all *that* different. In early September 2008, well into the financial crisis but before the Lehman Brothers bankruptcy transformed it into an outright panic, I took the train from New York to New Haven to pay a visit to Robert Shiller, who had just published a short book called *The Subprime Solution*. [20]

Shiller's office was on the ground floor of the just-restored mansion on Hillhouse Avenue that housed the Cowles Foundation for Research in Economics (Shiller was a Cowles research fellow). When I arrived, he took me down to the basement to make use of the espresso machine. While the machine whooshed, our eyes were both drawn to the bearded man in the large black-and-white photo on the opposite wall.

"That's Irving Fisher," Shiller said. "Do you know who he is?"

Well, yeah, I said. In fact, as I read through Shiller's book on the train up to New Haven, I had marveled at how much his proposed solutions to the financial mess reminded me of Irving Fisher. Several Shiller suggestions—new economic measures, improved databases of financial information—were nearly identical to proposals Fisher had made a century before. Even Shiller's new ideas—such as the continuous workout mortgage, in which the terms altered every year depending on developments in local housing prices, unemployment rates, and the like—had a distinctly Fisherian feel to them.

When I told Shiller this, he seemed a bit nonplussed. He knew all about Fisher's bad 1920s market advice and his economic theories, but he didn't know so much about Fisher's reams of financial inventions and would-be inventions.

Back upstairs in Shiller's office, we continued the discussion. Fisher's belief in better data and better financial instruments squared pretty well with his economic theories. But Shiller had been arguing for decades that even well-designed markets populated by well-informed investors were prone to manias and panics—which made his belief in progress through financial innovation a bit paradoxical. At least, that's what I told him.

"I don't think it's a paradox," he responded. "These are inventions that have to be human-engineered, and inventions can get people in trouble. When they first invented airplanes, there were a lot of crashes. I think it's really the same thing."

That reminded me of a headline I had seen in *The Onion* the previous year: "AMA: Plastic Surgery 'Only A Few Years Away' From Making Someone Look Better."[21] Shiller laughed at that, adding that he had read that medicine had crossed that threshhold of doing more good than harm sometime around 1865.

What about finance? "I think finance is way ahead of medicine in 1865, because finance is a huge net positive for the economy," Shiller said. "The countries that have better-developed financial markets really do better." So just because financial markets aren't perfect doesn't mean they're not useful? "Right. I think that we're less than halfway through the development of financial markets. Maybe there's no end to it."

AFTERWORD

ON MAY 28, 2010, VIEWERS of the CNBC morning show *Squawk Box* were treated to a rare and somewhat strange phenomenon: a television appearance by Eugene Fama. After introducing him as "the father of modern finance," host Joe Kernen asked the Chicago professor whether the financial crisis had exposed deep flaws in capitalism and perhaps shown that "the efficient market hypothesis doesn't work."

After some initial confusion ("What exactly do you mean by that?"), Fama launched into a concise explanation of efficient market theory and its relation to capitalism:

> It says prices reflect all available information, so that it's difficult if not impossible to beat the market. Now efficient markets and capitalism are very closely interrelated, because one of the founding principles of capitalism is that prices provide good signals for the allocation of resources, and that's basically the principle of efficient markets.

However, this doesn't mean markets always turn out to be right, Fama said. "They can't predict what's basically unpredictable." And so after a crash or a financial crisis, he explained, "people tend to do what I call condemning markets based on twenty-twenty hindsight."

But if financial markets were persistently wrong, Fama argued, then "there should be lots of evidence that people can time markets, and do much better than simply buying and holding the market. In fact, there is no such evidence. . . . When you turn around and actually test market efficiency, for all practical purposes it works very well."

Umm, not quite. For *some* practical purposes, the efficient market hypothesis works very well. For others, it's worse than useless. As an all-encompassing worldview, it gets an awful lot wrong. That this is true of just about every all-encompassing worldview is not a satisfactory defense. And conflating all criticism of efficient market theory with criticism of capitalism—which, to be fair, Kernen started, not Fama—isn't helpful.

WHEN I SET OUT TO write this book, I didn't have a particular ideological axe to grind about efficient markets. Sure, I had my biases (cognitive and otherwise), but I was mainly interested in reporting and telling a story. After the book came out, though, I had to take sides. Actually, I guess I must have taken sides before that, when I signed off on *The Myth of the Rational Market* as the title. But I tried very hard to be fair in the book (and the general reaction I got from the Chicago campus, at least, was that I succeeded). It was only in the summer of 2009, when the book was published, that I had to start offering my own opinions to interviewers from newspapers, radio, and television. *Has the efficient market theory been proved wrong?* my interrogators wanted to know. *Is it to blame for the financial crisis? What does all this mean for financial regulation, and for capitalism in general?*

I can't say I came up with the clearest of answers. The fact that finance scholars spent decades ignoring the forces behind financial booms, busts, and crises does seem like a problem. But there were booms, busts, and crises long before anyone had heard of efficient markets or, for that matter, finance professors. Also, few people on Wall Street bought fully into the finance professors' worldview. So it's hard to argue for a strict cause-and-effect relationship. Plus, this book is in part the story of how academic finance and economics began to make room for dissident scholars with new approaches to understanding the financial world. I wasn't going to say that these people were all ostriches with their heads in the sand. Finally, I don't know for sure what kind of financial regulation would be best, or just what amount of fettering capitalism needs to function optimally.

Others were less reticent, and less ambivalent. In the months after this book was published, they turned up the heat on the efficient market. The world had seen "a fairly complete train wreck of a predominant theory of economics and finance," said Adair Turner, chairman of Britain's financial regulatory agency, in a headline-grabbing interview in September 2009.[1]

"The economics profession went astray because economists, as a group, mistook beauty, clad in impressive-looking mathematics, for truth," economist Paul Krugman wrote in a lengthy apologia/broadside in the *New York Times Magazine* that same month.[2] *New Yorker* economics correspondent John Cassidy, in a book (*How Markets Fail*, published November 2009) that covers some of the same ground as this one, referred to efficient market economics as "utopian economics," and concluded, "In the world of utopian economics, the latest crisis of capitalism is always a blip."[3]

I can't say I disagree with any of that. But I still see a lot of value in the efficient market approach to economics and finance—as long as it's not the *only* approach. The critique of economists' role in the crisis that resonated the most with me was that of *Financial Times* econopundit Tim Harford. "I thought that the details did not much matter. Derivatives sounded like a sensible idea in principle, and that was all I needed to know," he wrote in the summer of 2010. "I wasn't paying enough attention. This is a failing that comes naturally to economists."[4]

THAT, IN THE END, IS the biggest problem with efficient market theory and many of the other creations of modern academic finance. They're all about *not* paying attention to the details. This approach can be helpful—remember Milton Friedman's argument that to be useful, scientific hypotheses have to be oversimplifications of reality. But relying on such theories exclusively, and failing to test them again and again against reality, can mean veering closer to superstition than science.

One such example of not paying attention to the details in finance has been the conflating of asset prices with prices for other things. As Fama put it in that CNBC interview: "One of the founding principles of capitalism is that prices provide good signals for the allocation of resources." Yes, prices for goods and services provide the essential information about supply and demand that allows capitalism to function. But prices in financial markets are different. They are the product not so much of supply and demand as of guesses about the future.

When the price of eggs goes up, people buy fewer eggs. When the price of a share of stock goes up, the speculator (or investor, or whatever you want to call her) often buys more.[5] Yes, there are cases where even goods markets get caught up in waves of fashion or hoarding, and even in financial markets prices eventually rise so high that they discourage buyers rather than encourage them. In general, though, the prices of goods and services markets give far less confusing signals to capitalists than financial market prices do.

None of this is to say that financial markets are useless. The prices prevailing on such markets give signals about the future, which are nice things to have, even if they turn out to be wrong much of the time. The price of eggs in a free market, though, is never "wrong." It simply is what it is. Financial-instrument prices are different. They're bets.

This matters even if, as Fama contends, there's no evidence that anybody can consistently outsmart these markets. That contention is itself an oversimplification: There's little evidence that *mutual fund managers*, the easiest group for finance scholars to study, can consistently beat markets. But there's ample anecdotal evidence, and some statistically defensible data in the case of hedge funds, that some savvy investors can harvest better returns than the market indices for decades on end.

That discussion can be a distraction, though. The observation that financial markets can get prices wrong matters regardless of its implications for investors. It matters to regulators determining how much leverage banks should be allowed to take on. It matters to corporate boards determining how much of a CEO's pay should come in the form of stock options. It matters to accounting-standards setters who are deciding how much weight to give market prices versus other measures. It matters to entrepreneurs determining how best to finance their dreams.

THERE'S ANOTHER ISSUE, TOO, ONE that I've come to understand through the work of business scholar Amar Bhidé.[6] The animating premise behind almost all of modern finance is that there is but one correct way to approach decisions involving investing and risk. Yet financial markets (and financial systems) work best when they consist of many participants with *different* ideas about the future. They break down when everyone thinks the same thing.

Finance scholars have long understood that if all stocks were owned by index funds, there would be no force driving stock prices toward their correct values—and reassured themselves that investing via index funds was but a minority pursuit. What they missed, though, is how other innovations inspired by academic finance— from portfolio insurance to the pricing models for mortgage securities—have had the same effect of taking judgment out of the hands of individuals and putting markets in the control of a senseless machine.

Individual judgment and initiative are the greatest drivers of the success of capitalism. The academic approach to finance that rose to prominence—and in some cases dominance—in the last few decades of the twentieth century was all about formulating rules and laws that everybody could follow. As supplements to individual judgment, and as checks on it, many of these new rules and tools of finance have turned out to be quite helpful. But as *substitutes* they bring disaster: They replace diversity and thought with mindless conformism. And while mindless conformism was characteristic of financial bubbles and panics long before there were finance professors, fostering even more of it has been the gravest sin of modern finance.

Cambridge, Massachusetts
September, 2010

1. "How to Tame Global Finance," *Prospect*, Sept. 2009.
2. Paul Krugman, "How Did Economists Get It So Wrong?" *New York Times Magazine*, Sept. 2, 2009.
3. John Cassidy, *How Markets Fail: The Logic of Economic Calamities* (New York: Farrar, Straus and Giroux, 2009), p. 346.
4. Tim Harford, "Confessions of an Armchair Economist," *Financial Times*, Aug. 4, 2010.
5. I owe this insight to Jack Bloom, who surely didn't originate it but made me take notice of it.
6. Amar Bhidé, "The Judgment Deficit," *Harvard Business Review*, Sept. 2010, and *A Call for Judgment: Sensible Finance for a Dynamic Economy* (New York: Oxford University Press, 2010).

CAST OF CHARACTERS

Kenneth Arrow Economist who in the early 1950s helped formulate, along with Gerard Debreu, the best mathematical model yet of how the invisible hand of the market worked, then spent much of the rest of his career examining situations where it didn't. Shared the economics Nobel in 1972.

Roger Babson Launched several market-data businesses in the early years of the twentieth century, then became a prominent value-oriented investment guru whose repeated warnings of a late-1920s stock market crash were dismissed by Wall Street (and by Irving Fisher).

Louis Bachelier French mathematician whose 1900 dissertation, written under the supervision of the great scientist Henri Poincaré, established that short-term financial market movements should be random. He used mathematical tools that presaged Albert Einstein's work to describe this randomness.

Fischer Black Computer scientist who was introduced to finance working alongside Jack Treynor at the consulting firm Arthur D. Little in the 1960s. Coauthor with Myron Scholes of the Black-Scholes option pricing model, later a partner at Goldman Sachs and an early supporter of behavioral finance research.

John Bogle After arguing against unmanaged index funds in 1960, the veteran mutual fund executive launched the first retail index fund at Vanguard in 1976.

Warren Buffett Student of value-investing legend Benjamin Graham at Columbia Business School who went on to great success as an investor. Outspoken critic of the efficient market hypothesis and the academic approach to finance.

Alfred Cowles III *Chicago Tribune* heir who, while convalescing from tuberculosis in Colorado in the 1920s, decided to research the effectiveness of various stock market forecasters. The 1933 paper in which he documented that most of the forecasts weren't very good was a landmark in stock market research, and led him—by way of Irving Fisher—to bankroll much early mathematical economic research.

Eugene Fama Finance professor at the University of Chicago who in the late 1960s formulated the efficient market hypothesis. Later, in a series of empirical studies with Kenneth French in the 1990s, he showed that the evidence didn't support his original hypothesis.

Irving Fisher Greatest American economist of the first half of the twentieth century, albeit now best known for his pronouncement that stock prices had reached a "permanently high plateau" in 1929. His work presaged most of modern finance.

Milton Friedman The leading figure of the postwar Chicago school of economics. Resurrected Irving Fisher's monetary theories, helped persuade economists to start with theories, not data, and became a leading proponent of free markets. Winner of the 1976 economics Nobel.

William Peter Hamilton Editor of the *Wall Street Journal* in the early decades of the twentieth century. Popularized and expanded upon the chart-reading Dow theory of his predecessor Charles Dow.

Friedrich Hayek Austrian economist whose anti-big-government book, *Road to Serfdom* (1944), inspired Milton Friedman and many other libertarians, and whose 1945 article, "The Use of Knowledge in Society," helped inspire the efficient market hypothesis. Moved to the University of Chicago in 1950 but never played a big role in the Chicago school. Co-winner of the 1974 economics Nobel.

Benjamin Graham Money manager who pioneered careful analysis of stocks and bonds and then, as a part-time professor at Columbia University and coauthor, with David L. Dodd, of the classic text *Security Analysis*, helped reshape Wall Street after the 1929 crash.

Alan Greenspan Product of Wesley Mitchell's institutionalist school of economics and protégé of libertarian author Ayn Rand who served as chairman of the Federal Reserve Board from 1987 to 2006. For most of his time in office he was acclaimed, but his beliefs that financial markets could regulate themselves and that the Fed should clean up after investment bubbles but not try to prevent them seemed discredited by the 2007–09 financial crisis.

Michael Jensen Product of the Chicago Business School of the 1960s who became the foremost apostle of the idea that corporate executives need to strive above all to increase their stock price and be paid accordingly, although he later had some doubts. Also originated "alpha," the risk-adjusted measure of investing skill that has become the chief benchmark of the hedge fund era.

Daniel Kahneman Israeli psychology professor who, together with colleague Amos Tversky, convinced economists to begin studying the sometimes self-defeating mental shortcuts people take in making judgments around money and the future. Co-winner of the 2002 economics Nobel.

John Maynard Keynes Product of Cambridge University's neoclassical economics department who in the 1930s partially upended neoclassical economics with new concepts to explain depressions. Also a successful investment manager and a skeptic of the rationality of financial markets.

Hayne Leland UC–Berkeley finance professor and, along with colleague Mark Rubinstein, creator of portfolio insurance—a financial product that may have helped cause the stock market crash of 1987.

Robert Lucas University of Chicago economist who popularized the theory of rational expectations, the economics version of finance's efficient market hypothesis. Winner of the 1995 economics Nobel.

Frederick Macaulay Student of Wesley Mitchell and skeptic of financial capitalism who presaged many of the developments of modern academic finance in his work in the 1920s and 1930s. May have been the first to compare stock market movements to the results of a coin flip.

Burton Malkiel Princeton economist and former Wall Street investment banker whose 1973 book, *A Random Walk Down Wall Street*, popularized the new academic approach to investing.

Benoit Mandelbrot Legendary Polish-French mathematician who was a key member of the group of scholars studying stock market random walks in the 1960s, but whose observations about the unpredictable nature of financial risk eventually drove him apart from the finance scholars.

Harry Markowitz As an economics graduate student at the University of Chicago in the early 1950s, he originated the statistical approach to weighing risk and reward in the stock market that came to be known as modern portfolio theory. Co-winner of the 1990 economics Nobel.

Jacob Marschak Harry Markowitz's dissertation adviser, research director of the Cowles Commission in its 1940s heyday as the most important breeding ground of modern mathematical economic theories. Helped convince economists to adopt John von Neumann and Oskar Morgenstern's expected utility theory.

Robert Merton Student of Paul Samuelson at MIT who helped solve the option-pricing puzzle with Fischer Black and Myron Scholes and went on to devise a hypermathematical, hyperrational approach to finance and risk management. Shared the 1997 economics Nobel with Scholes, was a partner with Scholes in the hedge fund Long-Term Capital Management, which unraveled in 1998.

Merton Miller Formulated, together with his Carnegie Tech colleague Franco Modigliani, a new theory-driven approach to finance with landmark papers on the cost of capital and dividends in 1958 and

1961. Then moved to the University of Chicago, where he became the feisty guiding light of the finance department from the 1960s until the early 1990s. Co-winner of the 1990 economics Nobel.

Wesley Mitchell Columbia economist, founder of the National Bureau of Economic Research, and longtime leader of the institutionalist school of economics that eschewed simple theories of economic behavior and favored empirical study.

Franco Modigliani Student of Jacob Marschak who coauthored two seminal finance papers with Merton Miller but never subscribed to the belief in rational markets that prevailed in finance. Winner of the 1985 economics Nobel.

Oskar Morgenstern Austrian economist who was frustrated with how the discipline dealt with uncertainty and linked up with mathematician John von Neumann at Princeton University to come up with a better approach. Later worked on early random walk research but was skeptical of the conclusions other random walkers jumped to.

M. F. M. Osborne U.S. Navy physicist whose research into stock market patterns, published in 1959, helped launch the random walk movement. Later collaborated with Chicago graduate student Victor Niederhoffer on research into nonrandom patterns in stock price movements.

Harry Roberts University of Chicago statistics professor whose own discussion of stock market randomness was published almost simultaneously with Osborne's in 1959. A mentor to Eugene Fama, he formulated the idea of separating the efficient market hypothesis into strong and weak forms.

Richard Roll Former aeronautical engineer who enrolled in the Chicago finance Ph.D. program in the mid-1960s and became a leading proponent of efficient markets finance. Authored two papers in the 1980s that called into question whether financial market movements really could be explained by rational market forces.

Barr Rosenberg UC–Berkeley finance professor who was the first of the quantitative finance crowd to strike it really rich in the 1970s.

His firm, Barra, provided sophisticated risk assessments to money managers battered by the decade's bear market. In the 1980s he went over to managing money himself.

Stephen Ross Student of Kenneth Arrow, co-originator of the binomial option pricing model. Argued that options and other derivatives were bringing the world closer to economic perfection. Founded a money management firm with Richard Roll.

Mark Rubinstein Coauthor with Stephen Ross of the binomial option pricing model. Cofounder with Hayne Leland and John O'Brien of the portfolio insurance firm LOR.

Paul Samuelson Greatest American economist of the second half of the twentieth century (although some might favor Kenneth Arrow or Milton Friedman). Finance was just a side interest for him, but he devised the first mathematical proof of the efficient market hypothesis and came close to solving the option-pricing puzzle. Recipient of the second Nobel prize in economics, in 1970.

Leonard "Jimmy" Savage Statistics professor whose axioms for assessing data under uncertainty informed the work of his Chicago student Harry Markowitz and helped define rationality for decades. Also coauthor of a seminal paper on expected utility with Milton Friedman, and rediscoverer of the work of French market theory pioneer Louis Bachelier.

Myron Scholes Classmate and friend of Michael Jensen and Richard Roll at Chicago. Devised the Black-Scholes option pricing model along with Fischer Black while teaching at MIT. Later a partner at the failed hedge fund Long-Term Capital Management, and co-winner of the 1997 economics Nobel.

William F. Sharpe While searching for a dissertation topic at UCLA in the early 1960s, he was introduced to Harry Markowitz and expanded Markowitz's portfolio teachings into a theory of market behavior, the capital asset pricing model. Later became one of the most important ambassadors to Wall Street of academic ideas about finance. Co-winner of the 1990 economics Nobel.

Robert Shiller MIT student of Franco Modigliani who showed in the early 1980s that stock prices jumped around more than could be justified by subsequent dividends. Became the most outspoken critic of the efficient market hypothesis, then warned in the late 1990s of irrational exuberance in stock prices and in the early 2000s of irrational exuberance in home prices.

Andrei Shleifer Protégé of Lawrence Summers who played a key role in explaining why arbitrage—which was supposed to keep prices in financial markets rational—didn't necessarily work in a market dominated by professional money managers.

Herbert Simon Economist at Carnegie-Mellon University who theorized in the 1950s that humans didn't optimize, as most of his colleagues assumed, but "satisficed"—that is, came up with simple but not always entirely rational solutions to his problems. Winner of the 1978 economics Nobel.

Joseph Stiglitz Student of Paul Samuelson and Franco Modigliani who, influenced by the work of Kenneth Arrow, showed how the efficient market hypothesis could not be—in theory at least—entirely true. Co-winner of the 2001 economics Nobel.

Lawrence Summers Nephew of Paul Samuelson and Kenneth Arrow. Author of sharp critiques of efficient market finance in the 1980s and early 1990s who went on to be Secretary of Treasury in the Clinton administration and top economic adviser to President Barack Obama.

Richard Thaler University of Rochester product who became Daniel Kahneman and Amos Tversky's first student among economists. Went on to be a founding father of behavioral economics and an influential professor at Chicago's Business School.

Edward Thorp Math professor at UC–Irvine who, after figuring out how to beat the house at blackjack and writing a bestselling book about it, figured out the formula for pricing options before Fischer Black and Myron Scholes did and became a pioneer of computer driven, black-box hedge fund management.

Jack Treynor As a consultant at Arthur D. Little in the late 1950s and early 1960s, he devised a capital asset pricing theory that predated and was nearly identical to William Sharpe's, but didn't publish it. Studied briefly with Franco Modigliani at MIT, influenced the work of Fischer Black, helped pioneer risk-adjusted measurement of investment performance.

Amos Tversky Psychology professor who partnered with Daniel Kahneman to prod economists to reexamine their assumptions about how people make decisions under conditions of uncertainty. His strong background in statistical decision theory (such as the Savage axioms) was crucial in giving these arguments credibility among economists.

John von Neumann Hungarian mathematician whose *Theory of Games and Economic Behavior*, coauthored with Oskar Morgenstern, had a huge impact on economics. The von Neumann-Morgenstern approach to making decisions under uncertainty shaped Harry Markowitz's portfolio theory and other aspects of quantitative finance.

Holbrook Working Stanford University agricultural economist who began studying the movements of futures prices in the 1930s, and in the late 1940s concluded that the apparent randomness of the market movements might be evidence that markets were doing a good job—making him a usually uncredited author of the efficient market hypothesis.

ACKNOWLEDGMENTS

WRITING THIS BOOK TOOK A lot longer than planned. During its gestation I went through four bosses and three book editors. That was partly just a reflection of the tumultuous state of magazine and book publishing in the 2000s, but it also indicates that these people have put up with a lot.

Let me thank first the bosses: At *Fortune*, Rik Kirkland gave me his blessing and a book leave, Eric Pooley gave me a work schedule intended to allow time for book writing, and while Andy Serwer was only my boss for about three days, I figure I had better thank him too. At *Time*, Rick Stengel also gave me time off and leeway in my work schedule, and must have kept wondering why the book wasn't finished yet. Well, it is now.

Then the book editors: First came Marion Maneker, who proposed that I write this book and signed me up to do it. Ethan Friedman got the thankless job of holding my hand through the difficult middle period (thanks, Ethan!), and finally Ben Loehnen edited the book, line by line, in the process bulldozing through narrative roadblocks that had held me back for months. This book wouldn't exist but for the efforts of all three.

Happily, I didn't go through multiple agents or wives while working on the book. My agent, Elyse Cheney, stuck with a project that sometimes seemed to be going nowhere, while my wife, Allison Downing, stuck with a husband who often seemed to be going nowhere. As for our son, Joey, who has lived more than half his life with this book in the background, well, I owe you, kid. Although those Pokemon packs covered part of the debt, right?

On to less guilt-ridden thanks: Jim Impoco edited the *Fortune* article that grew into this book, and Jim, Eric Gelman, and Jim Aley edited subsequent articles that shaped the narrative. Along the way, all of them made major contributions in helping me figure out what about this subject might be interesting to a general reader.

Long before then, it was my siblings who taught me how to read and write, my parents who encouraged me to pick a career that interested me rather than one that necessarily paid well, Hans-Peter Martin who gave me the notion that journalism might be an acceptable choice, Bill Greider who introduced me to economic journalism, Rob Norton and John Huey who gave me the opportunity to do it for a living, Jeff Gordinier and John Wyatt who alerted me to the fact that Norton and Huey might be willing to do such a thing, and Carol Loomis who steered me toward investigating the intersection between financial theory and real-world practice.

Peter Petre was the first to read an early manuscript of this book, and his encouraging words helped keep me going. Later on, Jim Aley, Barbara Kiviat and John Troughton all read the manuscript and offered excellent suggestions for improving it—a few of which I actually followed.

Dozens of sources for and subjects of this book have been generous with their time and their thoughts, for which I am hugely grateful. A few have been so encouraging and helpful as to deserve special thanks: Cliff Asness, Michael Jensen, Bill Sharpe, Andrei Shleifer, Larry Summers, Joseph Stiglitz, Nassim Nicholas Taleb, and Richard Thaler. Peter Bernstein provided a wonderful model for this book with his *Capital Ideas: The Improbable Origins of Modern Wall Street*, and encouragement throughout the writing of it.

Finally, thanks to Matt Inman and Lelia Mander for shepherding this book through production and Richard Ljoenes for overseeing the excellent cover and putting my name in such big type.

A NOTE ON SOURCES

I AM A JOURNALIST, NOT a scholar, and this is a work of journalism, not a Ph.D. dissertation. But it is a book *about* scholars, and I hope students of finance will find it useful. So I've included endnotes pointing to all the academic literature discussed in the book, and to sources for quotes, anecdotes, and facts that I didn't get directly from interviews. I've also exiled some anecdotes and discursions to the endnotes for the sake of maintaining narrative flow.

I have not, however, included endnotes for every last bit of information taken from interviews. You can generally assume that direct quotes and bits of personal history not otherwise attributed are taken from interviews with the person in question. I've tried to attribute all secondhand quotes and anecdotes to the person who related them to me.

My interviews ranged from formal, tape-recorded sit-downs to quick phone conversations or e-mail exchanges (the only person on the list below with whom the contact was *only* via e-mail was Daniel Kahneman). Some were conducted for magazine articles. Some people I talked to again and again. What follows is a list that, while it doesn't include every last person with whom I had informative discussions about the topic of the book, attempts to include everyone whose contributions can be said to have shaped its narrative. Not that any of them should be held responsible for it, of course.

George Ainslie, Clifford Asness, Robert Arnott, Kenneth Arrow, Brian Arthur, Malcolm Baker, Nicolas Barberis, Eric Benhamou, Peter L. Bernstein, Peter Bossaerts, Richard Brealey, Michael Brennan, Claude Brinegar, Gary Brinson, Robert Burch, Colin Camerer, Stan Chamberlain, Elroy Dimson, Steven Durlauf, Charley Ellis, Eugene Fama, J. Doyne Farmer, Baruch Fischhoff, Eugene Flood, Gifford Fong, Kenneth French, Milton Friedman, Alan Greenspan, Al Gordon, Clive Granger, Jeremy Grantham, Richard Grinold, Gil Hammer, Harrison Hong, Hendrik Houthakker, Roger Ibbotson, Michael Jensen, Ronald Kahn, Daniel Kahneman, Richard Kruizenga, David Laibson, Josef Lakonishok, Dean LeBaron, Marty Leibowitz, David Leinweber, Hayne Leland, Baruch Lev, Stan Levine, Arthur Lipper III, Andrew Lo, James Lorie, Louis Lowenstein, Benoit Mandelbrot, Henry Manne, Harry Markowitz, Paul Marsh, Mac McQuown, Robert Merton, Arnold Moore, William Niskanen, Terrance Odean, John O'Brien, Charles Plott, S. J. Prais, Alfred Rappaport, Kenneth Reid, Jay Ritter, Richard Roll, Barr Rosenberg, Stephen Ross, Mark Rubinstein, Paul Samuelson, Myron Scholes, William Sharpe, Hersh Shefrin, Robert Shiller, Andrei Shleifer, Harindra de Silva, Rex Sinquefield, Meir Statman, Jeremy Stein, Joel Stern, Joseph Stiglitz, Lawrence Summers, Nassim Nicholas Taleb, Richard Thaler, Edward Thorp, Sheridan Titman, Jack Treynor, Wayne Wagner, Eric Wanner, Victor Zarnowitz.

As my research on this book progressed, I found myself more and more frequently accessing information (articles, papers, sometimes even book chapters) online and never looking at the paper or microfilm version. For many of these documents, especially articles from newspapers and magazines, no page numbers were given in the online version. It seemed perverse to me to go to the effort to track down those page numbers when most readers who look up the information are never going to use page numbers. So when I knew the page numbers, I included them in the notes. When I didn't, I didn't.

NOTES

Introduction: It Had Been Working So Exceptionally Well

1. House of Representatives Committee on Oversight and Government Reform, *The Financial Crisis and the Role of Federal Regulators*, 110th Cong., 2d sess., preliminary transcript, 37. Downloaded at http://oversight.house.gov/story .asp?ID=2256.

2. International Swaps and Derivatives Association Market Survey results, available at www.isda.org.

3. Alan Greenspan, "Financial Derivatives," speech to the Futures Industry Association, Boca Raton, Florida, March 19, 1999.

4. Alan Greenspan, testimony to House of Representatives Committee on Government Oversight and Reform, Oct. 23, 2008, available at http:// oversight.house.gov/story.asp?ID=2256.

5. Economist Bob Shiller cites this as the earliest clear statement of the efficient market hypothesis that he has been able to find. Robert J. Shiller, *Irrational Exuberance* (New York: Broadway Books, 2001), 172.

6. Raymond de Roover, "The Concept of the Just Price: Theory and Economic Policy," *Journal of Economic History* (Dec. 1958): 418–34.

7. George Rutledge Gibson, *The Stock Exchanges of London, Paris, and New York: A Comparison* (New York: G. P. Putnam's Sons, 1889), 6–7 (manias and panics), 121 (bucket shops).

Chapter 1: Irving Fisher Loses His Briefcase, and Then His Fortune

1. Edward Scharff, *Worldly Power: The Making of the Wall Street Journal* (New York: Plume, 1987), 2.

2. Robert Loring Allen, *Irving Fisher: A Biography* (Cambridge, Mass., and Oxford: Blackwell, 1993), 95. The preceding story about the theft is taken from Allen's book and Irving Norton Fisher, *My Father Irving Fisher* (New York: Comet Press Books, 1956). These two books are the source of all Fisher biographical information in this book, except as otherwise noted.

3. Henri Poincaré, *The Value of Science: Essential Writings of Henri Poincaré* (New York: The Modern Library, 2001), 402.

4. Louis Bachelier, "Theory of Speculation," in *The Random Character of Stock Prices*, trans. A. James Boness, ed. Paul Cootner (Cambridge, Mass.: MIT Press, 1969), 28.

5. Bachelier, "Theory of Speculation," 17.

6. Poincaré, *Value of Science*, 419.

7. Bachelier, "Theory of Speculation," 25–26.

8. This and all other biographical information on Bachelier is from Jean-Michel Courtault et al., "Louis Bachelier on the Centenary of *Théorie de la Spéculation*," *Mathematical Finance* (July 2000): 341–53. Poincaré's report on Bachelier's thesis, translated by Selime Baftiri-Balazoski and Ulrich Haussman, is also included in the article.

9. Richard Hofstadter, *Social Darwinism in American Thought*, rev. ed. (Boston: Beacon Press, 1955), 51–53.

10. William Graham Sumner, *What the Social Classes Owe to Each Other* (Caldwell, Idaho: The Caxton Printers, 1989), 107.

11. Adam Smith, *Wealth of Nations*, book 4, chap. 2, par. 4, 2.9 (Indianapolis: Liberty Fund, 1981). It's not clear Smith himself saw it that way, although many subsequent economists did. The actual quote from the *Wealth of Nations* is:

> As every individual . . . endeavours as much as he can both to employ his capital in the support of domestic industry, and so to direct that industry that its produce may be of the greatest value; every individual necessarily labours to render the annual revenue of the society as great as he can. He generally, indeed, neither intends to promote the public interest, nor knows how much he is promoting it. By preferring the support of domestic to that of foreign industry, he intends only his own security; and by directing that industry in such a manner as its produce may be of the greatest value, he intends only his own gain, and he is in this, as in many other cases, led by an invisible hand to promote an end which was no part of his intention.

12. William Stanley Jevons, "The Progress of the Mathematical Theory of Political Economy, with an Explanation of the Principles of the Theory," *Transactions of the Manchester Statistical Society*, sess. 1874–75, 15. Along with Jevons, a self-taught jack-of-several-trades teaching economics at the University of Manchester, the other leaders of the "marginal utility revolution," as it came to be known, were Carl Menger of the University of Vienna and Léon Walras, a Frenchman teaching at Switzerland's University of Lausanne. There were antecedents in 1850s Germany and even 1730s Switzerland, but they weren't rediscovered until later.

13. Harris E. Starr, *William Graham Sumner* (New York: Henry Holt, 1925), 522.

14. Irving Fisher, *Mathematical Investigations in the Theory of Value and Price* (New Haven: Yale University Press, 1925). Reprinted in Reprints of Economic Classics, *Mathematical Investigations in the Theory of Value and Price and Appreciation and Interest* (New York: Augustus M. Kelly, 1961), 44.

15. William J. Barber, "Irving Fisher (1867–1947): Career Highlights and Formative Influences," in *The Economics of Irving Fisher: Reviewing the Scientific Work of a Great Economist*, ed. Hans-E. Loef and Hans G. Monissen (Cheltenham, UK: Edward Elgar, 1999), 4.

16. These are wholesale prices paid on the Chicago Board of Trade, courtesy of the National Bureau of Economic Research's historical database (www.nber .org/databases/macrohistory/contents/).

17. Irving Fisher, *Appreciation and Interest*, Publications of the American Economic Association (New York: Macmillan, 1896; New York: Augustus M. Kelly, 1961). Citation to Augustus M. Kelly edition, 37.

18. Quoted in Bruno Ingrao and Giorgio Israel, *The Invisible Hand: Economic Equilibrium in the History of Science* (Cambridge, Mass.: MIT Press, 1990), 159.

19. William Goetzmann, "Fibonacci and the Financial Revolution" (working paper no. 03-28, Yale International Center for Finance, Oct. 2003).

20. The indicators included new building, crops, clearings, iron production, money, failures, and "idle cars." Roger W. Babson, *Bonds and Stocks: The Elements of Successful Investing* (Wellesley Hills, Mass.: Babson Statistical Organization, 1912), chart, 48–49.

21. Roger W. Babson, *Actions and Reactions: An Autobiography of Roger W. Babson* (New York: Harper & Brothers, 1935), 147.

22. William Peter Hamilton, *The Stock Market Barometer* (New York: John Wiley & Sons, 1998), 27.

23. This is detailed in Irving Fisher, assisted by Harry G. Brown, *The Purchasing Power of Money: Its Determination and Relation to Credit, Interest and Crises* (New York: Macmillan, 1911), 332–37. In the book Fisher says William Stanley Jevons and Alfred Marshall had both broached this idea in the past.

24. An example: In early 2007, Microsoft had a market cap almost five times that of fellow Dow Jones Industrial United Technologies. But because its stock price was in the twenties while United Technologies' was in the sixties, it had less than half the impact on the movements of the average.

25. "Stock Price Index Numbers," *Standard Daily Trade Service* 30 (Oct. 25, 1923): 222. (The piece doesn't mention Fisher by name, but its reference to "various well known economists and statisticians" had to be aimed mainly at him.)

26. I have not found this suggestion in Fisher's own work, but it appears in a newspaper summary of his ideas, and I find it hard to believe that the reporter came up with it on his own. "Novel Suggestion to Curb the High Cost of Living," *New York Times*, Jan. 7, 1912, SM4.

27. Fisher, *My Father*, x.

28. Letter to Irving Norton Fisher, June 17, 1925. Cited in Barber, "Irving Fisher," 14.

29. Irving Fisher, Edwin Walter Kemmerer, Harry G. Brown, Walter E. Clark, J. Pease Norton, Montgomery Rollins, G. Lynn Sumner, *How to Invest When Prices Are Rising* (Scranton, Pa.: G. Lynn Sumner & Company, 1912).

30. Edgar Lawrence Smith, *Common Stocks as Long-Term Investments* (New York: The Macmillan Company, 1924), 29.

31. It was called Investment Managers Company, and later became Irving Investors Management Company, affiliated with the Irving Trust. After the publication of the book he also became a regular on the convention speaking circuit. "In these travels," he told his Harvard classmates in 1930, "I have shot no big game nor been intrigued by any Geisha girls, but I *have* run across some *strange fishes*." Harvard Class of 1905, *Twenty-Fifth Anniversary Report* (Norwood, Mass.: Plimpton Press, 1930), 589–90.

32. Irving Fisher, "Will Stocks Stay Up in 1929?" *New York Herald Tribune*, Dec. 30, 1928, Sunday Magazine, section 12, 1–2, 28–29.

33. John Burr Williams, Ph.D., *Fifty Years of Investment Analysis: A Retrospective* (Charlottesville, Va.: Financial Analysts Research Foundation, 1979), 6.

34. "Babson Predicts 'Crash' in Stocks," *New York Times*, Sept. 6, 1929, 12.

35. "Fisher Sees Stocks Permanently High," *New York Times*, Oct. 16, 1929, 8.

36. Irving Fisher, *The Stock Market Crash and After* (New York: Macmillan, 1930), 14–15.

37. Irving Fisher, "Statistics in the Service of Economics," reprint of speech delivered Dec. 29, 1932, *Journal of the American Statistical Association* (March 1933): 10.

CHAPTER 2: A RANDOM WALK FROM FRED MACAULAY TO HOLBROOK WORKING

1. "He was a cool 300 pounds and always smelled deliciously of tobacco and alcohol. He was bawdy, fun-loving and fascinating." Peter L. Bernstein, e-mail message to the author.

2. *Journal of the American Statistical Association* (June 1925): 248–49; the specifics of how Macaulay put together his chart come from Benjamin Graham and David L. Dodd, *Security Analysis* (New York: McGraw-Hill, 1934), 608n.

3. Geoffrey Poitras, "Frederick R. Macaulay, Frank M. Redington and the Emergence of Modern Fixed Income Analysis," in Geoffrey Poitras and Franck Jovanovic, eds., *Pioneers of Financial Economics*, vol. 2 (London: Edward Elgar, 2007), 60–82.

4. Investor Allen Bernstein hired Macaulay as his partner, not so much to make investment decisions as to reassure investors with his academic credentials and his non-Jewish surname. Peter L. Bernstein, e-mail message to the author.

5. Willford I. King, "Technical Methods of Forecasting Stock Prices," *Journal of the American Statistical Association* (Sept. 1934): 323–25.

6. Frederick R. Macaulay, *Some Theoretical Problems Suggested by the Movements of Interest Rates, Bond Yields and Stock Prices in the United States Since 1856* (New York: National Bureau of Economic Research, 1938), 11–12.

7. "It is only after a long course of uniform experiments in any kind, that we attain a firm reliance and security with regard to a particular event. Now where is that process of reasoning, which, from one instance, draws a conclusion, so different from that which it infers from a hundred instances, that are nowise different from that single one? This question I pose as much for the sake of information, as with an intention of raising difficulties. I cannot find, I cannot imagine any such rea-

soning. But I keep my mind still open to instruction; if any one will vouchsafe to bestow it on me." David Hume, *The Philosophical Works of David Hume*, vol. 4, sec. 4, An Enquiry Concerning Human Understanding" (Aalen, Germany: Scientia Verlag, 1964), 30.

8. Thorstein Veblen, "Fisher's *Capital and Income*," *Political Science Quarterly* (March 1908): 112.

9. Lucy Sprague Mitchell, *Two Lives: The Story of Wesley Clair Mitchell and Myself* (New York: Simon & Schuster, 1953), 241.

10. Solomon Fabricant, *Toward a Firmer Basis of Economic Policy: The Founding of the National Bureau of Economic Research* (Cambridge, Mass.: National Bureau of Economic Research, 1984).

11. Bruce Caldwell, *Hayek's Challenge: An Intellectual Biography of F. A. Hayek* (Chicago: University of Chicago Press, 2004), 150–51.

12. Peter Bernstein, quoted in Poitras, *Pioneers of Financial Economics*, 207.

13. Eli Ginzberg, "Wesley Clair Mitchell," *History of Political Economy* 29 (1997): 3. Reprinted in Wesley Clair Mitchell, *The Backward Art of Spending Money* (New Brunswick, N.J.: Transaction Publishers, 1999), ix–xxxv.

14. Thorstein Veblen, *The Engineers and the Price System* (New York: Viking, 1921).

15. John Maynard Keynes, *The General Theory of Employment, Interest, and Money* (San Diego: Harcourt Brace Jovanovich, 1953), 156.

16. "I feel no shame at being found still owning a share when the bottom of the market comes," Keynes wrote to a director of the National Mutual Life Assurance Society, of which Keynes was chairman, during a bear market in 1938. "I do not think it is the business, far less the duty, of an institutional or any other serious investor to be constantly considering whether he should cut and run on a falling market, or to feel himself open to blame if shares depreciate on his hands . . . An investor is aiming, or should be aiming primarily at long-period results, and should be solely judged by these." *The Collected Writings of John Maynard Keynes: Vol. XII*, ed. Donald Maggridge (Cambridge, UK: Cambridge University Press, 1983), 38.

17. The most important work of this genre was probably *Value and Capital: An Inquiry into Some Fundamental Principles of Economic Theory*, published in 1939 by John Hicks of the London School of Economics.

18. "Succumbing to Keynesianism," *Challenge* (Jan.–Feb. 1985): 6. Also in *The Collected Scientific Papers of Paul A. Samuelson*, vol. 5, ed. Kathryn Crowley (Cambridge, Mass.: MIT Press, 1986).

19. Macaulay's *Who's Who* entry shows him leaving Montreal's prestigious McGill University just before graduation and then finishing up, years later, at Colorado College in Colorado Springs. There's no proof that TB was involved, but why else would he have done a thing like that?

20. "Close of a Busy Life," *Chicago Tribune*, Dec. 21, 1889.

21. This was Robert Rhea, who described his acquaintance with Cowles in his newsletter *Dow Theory Comment*, mailing no. 9, Jan. 18, 1933. "He is a Dow theory skeptic," wrote Rhea, "and for years he has devoted his time to the task of attempt-

ing to assemble business statistics of past years into a forecasting device, an effort which will bear no fruit if the Dow theory is sound."

22. Murray Teigh Bloom, *Rogues to Riches: The Trouble with Wall Street* (New York: G. P. Putnam's Sons, 1971), 27.

23. The full text of *Theory of Interest* is available online at the Library of Economics and Liberty, www.econlib.org.

24. According to various Cowles Commission reports, attendees at the summer conferences, which ran from 1935 through 1940, included economists Ragnar Frisch, Trygve Haavelmo, Nicholas Kaldor, Oskar Lange, Wassily Leontief, Abba Lerner, Paul Samuelson, and Joseph Schumpeter; statistician-geneticist R. A. Fischer; statistical quality control pioneer Walter Shewhart; statisticians Corrado Gini (of "Gini coefficient" fame), Harold Hotelling, and Jacob Wolfowitz (who fathered a famous son named Paul); and mathematicians Karl Menger and Abraham Wald.

25. Alfred Cowles III, "Can Stock Market Forecasters Forecast?" *Econometrica* (July 1933): 324.

26. *New York Times,* Jan. 1, 1933, 7.

27. Alfred Cowles III, Herbert E. Jones, "Some A Posteriori Probabilities in Stock Market Action," *Econometrica* (July 1937): 280–94. Holbrook Working was later to point out that even this meager result was misleadingly positive because of flaws in Cowles and Jones's statistical technique.

28. Alfred Cowles III and Associates, *Common Stock Indexes,* 2d ed., (Bloomington, Ind.: Principia Press Inc., 1939).

29. Irving Fisher, in "Our Unstable Dollar and the So-Called Business Cycle," *Journal of the American Statistical Association* (June 1925): 199, approvingly cites Holbrook Working, "Prices and the Quantity of Circulating Medium, 1890–1921," *Quarterly Journal of Economics* (Feb. 1923): 228–56.

30. Adam Smith, *Wealth of Nations*, book 4, chap. 5, part B (Indianapolis: Liberty Fund, 1981), 527.

31. Henry Crosby Emery, *Speculation on the Stock and Produce Exchanges of the United States* (New York: Columbia University, 1896).

32. Holbrook Working, "Financial Results of the Speculative Holding of Wheat," *Wheat Studies of the Food Research Institute* (July 1931): 405–37.

33. Holbrook Working, "Cycles in Wheat Prices," *Wheat Studies of the Food Research Institute* (Nov. 1931): 2.

34. Karl Pearson and Lord Rayleigh, "The Problem of the Random Walk," *Nature* (July 27, Aug. 3, Aug. 10, 1905).

35. The name has often been rendered in English as the Conjuncture Institute, but this seems an overly literal translation. Kondratiev is also sometimes spelled Kondratieff. His 1926 monograph *Long Cycles and Economic Conjuncture* can be found in *The Works of Nikolai Kondratiev*, vol. 1 (London: Pickering & Chatto, 1998).

36. G. Udny Yule, "Why Do We Sometimes Get Nonsense-Correlations Between Time-Series?—A Study in Sampling and the Nature of Time-Series," *Journal of the Royal Statistical Society* (Jan. 1926): 1–64.

37. Eugen Slutzky [sic], "The Summation of Random Causes as the Source of Cyclic Processes," *Econometrica* (April 1937): 105.

38. Cowles Commission for Research in Economics, *Abstracts of Papers Presented at the Research Conference on Economics and Statistics,* Colorado Springs, 1936, 99.

39. Holbrook Working, "A Theory of Anticipatory Prices," *American Economic Review* (May 1958): 190.

40. Holbrook Working, "The Investigation of Economic Expectations," *American Economic Review* (May 1949): 158–60.

41. Claude S. Brinegar, *A Statistical Analysis of Speculative Price Behavior* (Stanford: Food Research Institute, 1970). (Supplement to vol. 9, *Food Research Institute Studies.*)

CHAPTER 3: HARRY MARKOWITZ BRINGS
STATISTICAL MAN TO THE STOCK MARKET

1. W. Allen Wallis, "The Statistical Research Group, 1942–1945," *Journal of the American Statistical Association* (June 1980): 322–23.

2. A. D. Roy, "Safety First and the Holding of Assets," *Econometrica* (July 1952): 431–49. Some have also seen hints of Markowitz's portfolio selection ideas in two earlier papers authored by Marschak: H. Makower, J. Marschak, "Assets, Prices and Monetary Theory," *Economica* (Aug. 1938): 261–88; and Jacob Marschak, "Money and the Theory of Assets," *Econometrica* (Oct. 1938): 311–25. But Markowitz said Marschak never even told him about the papers, which mention portfolio selection in passing as part of a larger model of economic behavior.

3. Oskar Morgenstern, "Perfect Foresight and Economic Equilibrium," *The Selected Economic Writings of Oskar Morgenstern* (New York: New York University Press, 1976), 172–73.

4. Morgenstern's chief mathematical mentor was Karl Menger, son of economist Carl, the great founder of the Austrian school and distruster of economic equations. During Irving Fisher's European tour of 1893–94, the elder Menger had told him that "later—say thirty years from now—the mathematical method will come in for the 'finishment' of the science." And it sort of did. William J. Barber, "Irving Fisher (1867–1947): Career Highlights and Formative Influences," in Hans-E. Loef and Hans G. Monissen, *The Economics of Irving Fisher: Reviewing the Scientific Work of a Great Economist* (Cheltenham, UK, Northampton, Mass.: Edward Elgar, 1999), 6.

5. E. Roy Weintraub, "On the Existence of Competitive Equilibrium: 1930–1954," *Journal of Economic Literature* (March 1983): 13.

6. It was left to others, such as John Nash of *A Beautiful Mind* fame, to develop a multiplayer theory of games better suited to modeling economic interactions.

7. John von Neumann and Oskar Morgenstern, *Theory of Games and Economic Behavior,* 65th Anniversary Edition (Princeton: Princeton University Press, 2004), 177–78.

8. Daniel Bernoulli, "Exposition of a New Theory on the Measurement of Risk," *Econometrica* (Jan. 1954): 23–36.

9. The story is Herbert Simon's:

> In the early 1950s, when I was on a faculty recruiting trip from Pittsburgh, I had dinner with Marschak one evening in the Quadrangle Club at the University of Chicago. The conversation turned to the selection of faculty. As he had assembled a spectacular group of stars in the Cowles Commission, I asked him what qualities he looked for in selecting staff. "Oh," said he, "I pick people with good eyes." I stared at him. Good eyes—what could he mean? I told him he was joking, but he insisted: He looked at their eyes. And then I began thinking of the clear dark Armenian eyes of Arrow, the cool blue Frisian eyes of Koopmans, and the sharp black Roman eyes of Modigliani. It was certainly true that they all had remarkable eyes.

Herbert A. Simon, *Models of My Life* (New York: Basic Books, 1991), 104–5.

10. Jacob Marschak, "Neumann's and Morgenstern's Approach to Static Economics," *Journal of Political Economy* (April 1946): 109.

11. Milton Friedman and Rose Friedman, *Two Lucky People: Memoirs* (Chicago: University of Chicago Press, 1998), 146.

12. Linear programming was independently developed by several others, including Leonid Kantorovich, who shared the 1975 Nobel Prize in Economics with Koopmans, and George Dantzig, who was Harry Markowitz's boss at Rand.

13. Who the broker was and what exactly he was doing there remains a great (and at this point probably unsolvable) mystery of financial history. Markowitz himself has no idea. Marschak's son Thomas says his father was not a big stock market player, but he did have a few investments. So it is possible the broker was waiting to see him. It's also possible the broker was waiting to see someone else at Cowles, or just making cold calls. In any case, the broker was there, and he and Markowitz got to talking.

14. Schumpeter worried that Williams's right-wing political views might get him into trouble with other members of the dissertation committee if he wrote about a more general economic topic. John Burr Williams, *Fifty Years of Investment Analysis: A Retrospective* (Charlottesville, Va.: Financial Analysts Research Foundation, 1979), 5–19.

15. John Burr Williams, *The Theory of Investment Value* (Burlington, Vt.: Fraser Publishing Co., 1997, exact copy of 1938 Harvard University Press version), 6.

16. Harry M. Markowitz, "Efficient Portfolios, Sparse Matrices, and Entities: A Retrospective," *Operations Research* (Jan.–Feb. 2002): 154.

17. Friedman and Friedman, *Two Lucky People*, 216.

18. Leonard J. Savage, *The Foundations of Statistics* (New York: Dover Publications, 1972), 16.

19. This can be found at the beginning of Chapter 15 of Twain's *The Tragedy of Pudd'nhead Wilson and the Comedy Those Extraordinary Twins*. At the start of Chapter 13 is Twain's most famous piece of investing advice: "October. This is one

of the peculiarly dangerous months to speculate in stocks in. The others are July, January, September, April, November, May, March, June, December, August, and February."

20. William Shakespeare, *The Merchant of Venice*, act 1, scene 1.

21. Harry M. Markowitz, "The Early History of Portfolio Theory: 1600–1960," *Financial Analysts Journal* (July/August 1999): 5–16.

22. Gerald M. Loeb, *The Battle for Investment Survival* (New York: John Wiley & Sons, 1996), 42.

23. Harry Markowitz, interview with the author. Discussion of semi-variance is in Harry M. Markowitz, *Portfolio Selection: Efficient Diversification of Investments,* Cowles Foundation Monograph 16 (New Haven: Yale University Press, 1970), 188–201.

24. The grad student was Henry Latane, and his paper was later published as "Criteria for Choice Among Risky Ventures," *Journal of Political Economy* (April 1959): 144–55. The chapter in Markowitz's book is titled "Return in the Long Run." And the whole saga is laid out in vastly more detail in William Poundstone, *Fortune's Formula* (New York: Hill and Wang, 2005), esp. 192–97.

25. As recalled by Mark Rubinstein.

CHAPTER 4: A RANDOM WALK FROM PAUL SAMUELSON TO PAUL SAMUELSON

1. Jürg Niehans, *A History of Economic Theory: Classic Contributions 1720–1980* (Baltimore: Johns Hopkins University Press, 1990).

2. Paul A. Samuelson, *Economics: An Introductory Analysis* (New York: McGraw-Hill, 1948), 570, 573.

3. Michael Szenberg, Aron Gottesman, and Lall Ramrattan, *Paul Samuelson: On Being an Economist* (New York: Jorge Pinto Books, 2005), 85.

4. The student, Richard Kruizenga, was chiefly interested in describing the securities and sketching their history. Samuelson wanted more. Recalled Kruizenga, "He had the ability to see what the real issue was, from an economist's standpoint: How do you value these things?"

5. Peter Bernstein's account in *Capital Ideas* (New York: Free Press, 1992) has Samuelson learning about the paper from Hendrik Houthakker. Samuelson didn't remember precisely when I interviewed him in 2004, but his and Houthakker's accounts both seemed to point toward Samuelson first encountering the article in the *Quarterly Journal of Economics* office.

6. M. G. Kendall, "The Analysis of Economic Time-Series—Part I: Prices," *Journal of the Royal Statistical Society, Series A (General)* 116, no. 1 (1953): 11–34 (the economists' responses are found on pp. 25–34).

7. M. F. M. Osborne, *The Stock Market and Finance from a Physicist's Viewpoint,* (Minneapolis: Crossgar Press, 1995), 12.

8. Osborne, *Stock Market and Finance,* 12.

9. Harry V. Roberts, "Stock-Market Patterns and Financial Analysis: Methodological Suggestions," *Journal of Finance* (March 1959): 1–10.

10. This is Arnold Moore's recollection.

11. James Gleick, *Chaos: Making a New Science* (New York: Viking, 1987). Both Houthakker and Mandelbrot confirm this account, although Houthakker would like the world to know that, contrary to an assertion in Gleick's book, he is younger than Mandelbrot.

12. Holbrook Working, "Note on the Correlation of First Differences of Averages in a Random Chain," *Econometrica* (Oct. 1960): 916–18.

13. C. W. J. Granger and O. Morgenstern, "Spectral Analysis of New York Stock Market Prices," *Kyklos* 16 (1963): 1–25.

14. "A Random Walk in Wall Street," *Fortune*, Feb. 1963, 204.

15. Paul A. Samuelson, "Paul Cootner's Reconciliation of Economic Law with Chance," in *Financial Economics: Essays in Honor of Paul Cootner*, William F. Sharpe and Cathryn M. Cootner, eds. (Englewood Cliffs, N.J.: Prentice-Hall, 1982), 105.

16. Adam Smith [George A. W. Goodman], *The Money Game* (New York: Random House, 1967), 156.

17. This story was related by Bill Sharpe, who heard Cootner tell it repeatedly. Repeated attempts to confirm it independently met with failure but, hey, it's a good story.

18. Hendrik S. Houthakker, "Systematic and Random Elements in Short-Term Price Movements," *American Economic Review* (May 1961): 164.

19. Robert E. Weintraub, "On Speculative Prices and Random Walks: A Denial," *Journal of Finance* (March 1963): 59–66.

20. Paul A. Samuelson, "Proof That Properly Anticipated Prices Fluctuate Randomly," *Industrial Management Review* (Spring 1965): 41–49.

CHAPTER 5: MODIGLIANI AND MILLER ARRIVE AT A SIMPLIFYING ASSUMPTION

1. Milton Friedman and L. J. Savage, "The Utility Analysis of Choices Involving Risk," *Journal of Political Economy* (Aug. 1948): 279–304.

2. I am thinking in particular of the introduction to Paul Samuelson's 1947 book, *Foundations of Economic Analysis* (Cambridge, Mass., and London: Harvard University Press, 1983), cited in chapter 4, and of Tjalling Koopmans's August 1947 screed, which is mentioned in the next note.

3. Tjalling Koopmans, "Measurement Without Theory," *Review of Economics and Statistics* (Aug. 1947): 167. It was a review of Arthur F. Burns and Wesley C. Mitchell, *Measuring Business Cycles* (New York: National Bureau of Economic Research, 1946).

4. Milton Friedman, "Wesley C. Mitchell as Economic Theorist," *Journal of Political Economy* (Dec. 1950): 465–93.

5. Thorstein Veblen, "Why Is Economics Not an Evolutionary Science," *Quarterly Journal of Economics* (July 1898). Reprinted in Veblen, *The Place of Science in Modern Civilisation and Other Essays* (New York: B. W. Huebsch, 1919), 73.

6. Milton Friedman, "The Methodology of Positive Economics," *Essays in Positive Economics* (Chicago and London: University of Chicago Press, 1953), 15.

7. Herbert A. Simon, "A Behavioral Model of Rational Choice," *Quarterly Journal of Economics* (Feb. 1955): 99–118.

8. Allais's 1950s papers were in French, so my source on this was Maurice Allais, "An Outline of My Main Contributions to Risk and Utility Theory," *Models and Experiments in Risk and Rationality*, Bertrand Munier and Mark J. Machina, eds. (Dordrecht: Kluwer Academic Publishers, 1994).

9. Arrow had studied with Harold Hotelling at Columbia and participated in an informal mathematical economics seminar that Jacob Marschak led during his New York years, then spent World War II trying to forecast the weather for the Army Air Corps. Debreu was a French mathematician who first encountered economic equilibrium theory in the 1940s and was immediately hooked.

10. The economist was Frank William Taussig, the leading American disciple of Alfred Marshall and his supply-demand charts. The story of the Business School's founding is recounted in Jeffrey L. Cruikshank, *A Delicate Experiment: The Harvard Business School, 1908–1945* (Boston: Harvard Business School Press, 1987), 34.

11. John Burr Williams, *Fifty Years of Investment Analysis: A Retrospective* (Charlottesville, Va., Financial Analysts Research Foundation, 1979), 23.

12. Peter Tanous, *Investment Gurus* (New York: New York Institute of Finance, 1997), 215.

13. A. D. Martin Jr., "Life Outside 500 Largest," *Alumni Bulletin* 5 (Aug. 1957). Quoted in Robert E. Gleeson and Steven Schlossman, "The Many Faces of the New Look: The University of Virginia, Carnegie Tech, and the Reform of American Management Education in the Postwar Era, Part II," *Selections: The Magazine of the Graduate Management Admission Council* (Spring 1992): 1–24.

14. Arjo Klamer, *Conversations with Economists: New Classical Opponents and Their Opponents Speak Out on the Current Controversy in Macroeconomics* (Totowa, N.J.: Rowman & Allanheld Publishers, 1984), 125.

15. Alfred P. Sloan Jr., *My Years with General Motors* (New York: Doubleday, 1990), 141.

16. Franco Modigliani, Merton H. Miller, "The Cost of Capital, Corporation Finance and the Theory of Investment," *American Economic Review* (June 1958): 280–81.

17. Merton H. Miller and Franco Modigliani, "Dividend Policy, Growth, and the Valuation of Shares," *Journal of Business* (Oct. 1961): 428.

18. Benjamin Graham and David L. Dodd, *Security Analysis* (New York: McGraw Hill, 1934), 23.

19. As recounted by my former *Fortune* colleague Shawn Tully, a Chicago MBA.

20. Tanous, *Investment Gurus*, 216.

21. Matthew 25:14–30. To give credit where it is due, I wouldn't have understood the parable if I hadn't had it explained to me in a sermon by the Rev. John A. Mennell at St. Michael's Church in New York.

22. Gerd Gigerenzer, Zeno Swijtink, Theodore Porter, Lorraine Daston, John Beatty, Lorenz Krüger, *The Empire of Chance: How Probability Changed Science and Everyday Life* (Cambridge: Cambridge University Press, 1989), 3–4.

23. A crucial intermediate step between Markowitz and Treynor was James Tobin, "Liquidity Preference as Behavior Towards Risk," *Review of Economic Studies* 25, no. 1 (1958): 65–86.

24. Jack L. Treynor, "Towards a Theory of Market Value of Risky Assets," in *Asset Pricing and Portfolio Performance; Models, Strategy and Performance Metrics,* Robert A. Korajczk, ed. (London: Risk Books, 1999).

25. William F. Sharpe, "A Simplified Model for Portfolio Analysis," *Management Science* (Jan. 1963): 281.

26. William F. Sharpe, "Capital Asset Prices: A Theory of Market Equilibrium Under Conditions of Risk," *Journal of Finance* (Sept. 1964): 425–42.

27. John Lintner, "The Valuation of Risk Assets and the Selection of Risky Investments in Stock Portfolios and Capital Budgets," *Review of Economics and Statistics* (Feb. 1965): 13–37. Interpretation and background can be found in Perry Mehrling, *Fischer Black and the Revolutionary Idea of Finance* (Hoboken, N.J.: John Wiley & Sons, 2005).

28. Jan Mossin, "Equilibrium in a Capital Asset Market," *Econometrica* (Oct. 1966): 768–83.

CHAPTER 6: GENE FAMA MAKES THE BEST
PROPOSITION IN ECONOMICS

1. Saul Bellow, *Humboldt's Gift* (New York: Penguin, 1996), 173.

2. Melvin W. Reder, "Chicago Economics: Permanence and Change," *Journal of Economic Literature* (March 1982): 1–38.

3. Lionel Trilling, *The Liberal Imagination* (New York, Viking, 1950): 5.

4. George J. Stigler, *Memoirs of an Unregulated Economist* (New York: Basic Books, 1988), 146.

5. F. A. Hayek, "The Use of Knowledge in Society," *American Economic Review* (Sept. 1945): 519, 522. Acolytes of Hayek's Vienna teacher Ludwig von Mises would have me point out that von Mises made pretty much the same arguments two decades earlier. But they didn't happen to appear in English in a publication read by virtually every American economist.

6. Milton Friedman and Rose Friedman, *Two Lucky People: Memoirs* (Chicago: University of Chicago Press, 1998), 159.

7. Friedman, *Essays in Positive Economics* (Chicago and London: University of Chicago Press, 1953), 176.

8. Armen A. Alchian, "Uncertainty, Evolution, and Economic Theory," *Journal of Political Economy* (June 1950): 211–21.

9. Arjo Klamer, *Conversations with Economists: New Classical Opponents and Their Opponents Speak Out on the Current Controversy in Macroeconomics* (Totowa, N.J.: Rowman & Allanheld Publishers, 1984), 120.

10. Robert E. Lucas Jr., "Autobiography," from *Les Prix Nobel. The Nobel Prizes 1995,* Tore Frängsmyr, ed. (Stockholm: Nobel Foundation, 1996). Also available at http://nobelprize.org.

11. William Niskanen, interview with the author.

12. Joel M. Stern with Irwin Ross, *Against the Grain: How to Succeed in Business by Peddling Heresy* (New York: John Wiley & Sons, 2003), 17.

13. Eugene F. Fama, "The Behavior of Stock Market Prices," *Journal of Business* (Jan. 1965): 39.

14. Eugene F. Fama, "Random Walks in Stock Prices," *Financial Analysts Journal* (Sept.–Oct. 1965, repr. Jan.–Feb. 1995): 76.

15. Julian Lewis Watkins, *The 100 Greatest Advertisements: Who Wrote Them and What They Did*, 2d rev. ed. (New York: Dover Publications, 1959), 164–65.

16. This and other biographical information on Engel comes from David Bird, "Louis Engel Jr., Ex-Merrill Partner, Dies," *New York Times*, Nov. 8, 1982, D15.

17. This tale of CRSP's founding is derived almost entirely from an interview with James Lorie.

18. "Study Shows 'Random' Stock Investment from '26 to '60 Had 3-to-1 Chance of Profit," *Wall Street Journal*, May 25, 1965, 10.

19. "It's easier to win than lose," *Business Week*, May 29, 1965, 122.

20. Arnold Moore, interview with the author. Moore finished his dissertation in 1962, and it was published as "Some Characteristics of Changes in Common Stock Prices," in *The Random Character of Stock Prices*, Paul Cootner, ed. (Cambridge, Mass.: MIT Press, 1964), 139–61.

21. Robert A. Levy, "Random Walks: Reality or Myth," *Financial Analysts Journal* (Nov.–Dec. 1967): 69–77.

22. Michael C. Jensen, "Random Walks: Reality or Myth—Comment," *Financial Analysts Journal* (Nov.–Dec. 1967): 84.

23. Jensen, "Random Walks," 81.

24. Eugene F. Fama, Lawrence Fisher, Michael C. Jensen, Richard Roll, "The Adjustment of Stock Prices to New Information," *International Economic Review* (Feb. 1969): 1–21. It took the paper years to get to print because Fama was set on publishing it somewhere other than the Chicago Business School's *Journal of Business*, where all his previous papers had ended up, and it was a struggle to find another journal willing to take it. (At least, that's how Jensen remembers it.)

25. Ray Ball and Philip Brown, "An Empirical Evaluation of Accounting Income Numbers," *Journal of Accounting Research* (Autumn 1968): 159–78.

26. "Review and Outlook," *Wall Street Journal*, May 19, 1899, 1.

27. Committee on Interstate and Foreign Commerce, *A Study of Mutual Funds, Prepared for the Securities and Exchange Commission by the Wharton School of Finance and Commerce*, 87th Cong., 2d sess., H. Rep. 2274.

28. Michael C. Jensen, "Risk, the Pricing of Capital Assets, and the Evaluation of Investment Portfolios," *Journal of Business* (April 1969): 169.

29. Eugene F. Fama, "Efficient Capital Markets: A Review of Theory and Empirical Work," *Journal of Finance* (May 1970): 383.

30. To be more specific, in "The Capital Asset Pricing Model: Some Empirical Tests," published in Michael C. Jensen, ed., *Studies in the Theory of Capital Markets* (New York: Praeger, 1972), Black, Jensen, and Scholes found that low-beta stocks had higher returns than predicted by the original CAPM, but that the relationship

between beta and returns seemed to fit an asset-pricing model in which borrowing limits and costs were taken into account. Meanwhile, Fama and James D. MacBeth, in "Risk, Return, and Equilibrium: Empirical Tests," *Journal of Political Economy* (May–June 1973), concluded that "although there are 'stochastic nonlinearities' from period to period," they could "not reject the hypothesis that in making a portfolio decision, an investor should assume that the relationship between a security's portfolio risk and its expected return is linear" as CAPM implied.

31. J. Fred Weston, "The State of the Finance Field," *Journal of Finance* (Dec. 1967): 539–40.

32. Irwin Friend, "Mythodology in Finance," *Journal of Finance* (May 1973): 257–72.

33. It's actually the Sveriges Riksbank Prize in Economic Sciences in Memory of Alfred Nobel, not an actual Nobel Prize, but it's administered by the same folks as the other Nobels.

34. Michael C. Jensen, "Some Anomalous Evidence Regarding Market Efficiency," *Journal of Financial Economics* 6, nos. 2/3 (1978): 95–101.

CHAPTER 7: JACK BOGLE TAKES ON THE PERFORMANCE CULT (AND WINS)

1. Renshaw, the economics Ph.D., went on to teach at the University of North Carolina and SUNY–Albany. MBA student Feldstein, who ended up staying on at Chicago for a doctorate, became a health care economist and taught at the University of Michigan and UC–Irvine.

2. Edward F. Renshaw and Paul J. Feldstein, "The Case for an Unmanaged Investment Company," *Financial Analysts Journal* (Jan.–Feb. 1960): 43–46.

3. Bogle said in an interview that he was afraid that if Wellington's name was attached to the article, the SEC might charge the firm with improper advertising.

4. John B. Armstrong, "The Case for Mutual Fund Management," *Financial Analysts Journal* (May–June 1960): 33–38.

5. The broker's name was Edward G. Leffler, and this account is drawn from a history of mutual funds published in *Investment Companies 1965: Mutual Funds and Other Types*, 25th annual ed. (New York: Arthur Wiesenberger & Co., 1965), 7.

6. Estimated stock market value of $89.7 billion from Ellen R. McGrattan, Edward C. Prescott, "The 1929 Stock Market: Irving Fisher Was Right," Federal Reserve Bank of Minneapolis, Research Department Staff Report 294, Dec. 2003, 3.

7. "Big Money in Boston," *Fortune*, Dec. 1949, 116–21, 189–96. There's no byline, but *Fortune*'s records show that it was written by Hedley Donovan, who went on to succeed Henry Luce as editor of Time Inc. The second quote was a paraphrase by Donovan of a statement by an MIT executive.

8. John C. Bogle, "The Economic Role of the Investment Company," reprinted in *John Bogle on Investing: The First 50 Years* (New York: McGraw-Hill, 2001), 355, 440.

9. *The Collected Writings of John Maynard Keynes: Vol. XII*, Donald Maggridge, ed. (Cambridge: Cambridge University Press, 1983), 100, 82.

10. Benjamin Graham, *The Memoirs of the Dean of Wall Street*, edited and introduc-

tion by Seymour Chatman (New York: McGraw-Hill, 1996), 124–26. The peace activist was Sir Norman Angell.

11. Graham, *Memoirs of the Dean*, 142.

12. This is detailed in Chapter 8, "The Investor and Market Fluctuations," of Benjamin Graham, *The Intelligent Investor: A Book of Practical Counsel*, 4th rev. ed. (New York: Harper & Row, 1973).

13. Benjamin Graham and David L. Dodd, *Security Analysis* (New York: McGraw-Hill, 1934), 299–300.

14. Roger Lowenstein, *Buffett: The Making of an American Capitalist* (New York: Main Street Books, 1996), 45.

15. John Brooks, *The Seven Fat Years: Chronicles of Wall Street* (New York: Harper & Brothers Publishers, 1958), 1.

16. Burton G. Malkiel, "Equity Yields, Growth, and the Structure of Share Prices," *American Economic Review* (Dec. 1963): 1026.

17. Benjamin Graham, "The Future of Financial Analysis," *Financial Analysts Journal* (May–June 1963): 65–70.

18. Adam Smith [George A. W. Goodman], *The Money Game* (New York: Random House, 1967), 211.

19. John Brooks, *The Go-Go Years* (New York: Weybright and Talley, 1973).

20. Adam Smith, *The Money Game*, 18.

21. *Investment Companies 1966: Mutual Funds and Other Types* (New York: Arthur Wiesenberger & Co., 1966), 118. The actual title Wiesenberger gave to the category was "Objective: Maximum Capital Gain."

22. John M. Birmingham Jr., "The Quest for Performance," *Financial Analysts Journal* (Sept.–Oct. 1966): 93–94.

23. Albert Young Bingham, "Relative Performance—Nonsense," *Financial Analysts Journal* (July–Aug. 1966): 102.

24. There are many different ways to measure volatility. The one used by Bogle, which was calculated by Arthur Wiesenberger & Co. for its mutual fund data yearbooks, took the percentage change in the price of a fund over a given period and divided it by the percentage change in the Dow Jones Industrial Average.

25. Gene Smith, "Funds are Rated by New System," *New York Times*, Dec. 8, 1957. Bogle is identified merely as a "mutual fund economist" in the article—again staying anonymous because he didn't want to get Wellington in trouble with the SEC.

26. Jack L. Treynor, "How to Rate the Management of Investment Funds," *Harvard Business Review* (Jan.–Feb. 1965): 63–75.

27. Hearings before the Senate Committee on Banking and Currency, *Mutual Fund Legislation of 1967*, 90th Cong., 1st sess., 353–57.

28. Brooks, *The Go-Go Years*, 148–49.

29. William J. Baumol and Burton Malkiel, Comments on Proposed Rule 10b-10, March 21, 1968, available at www.sechistorical.org.

30. Joseph Nocera, *A Piece of the Action: How the Middle Class Joined the Money Class* (New York: Simon & Schuster, 1994), 116–18. Merrill switched to paying its brokers with commissions in the early 1970s.

31. *Investment Company Institute v. Camp*, 401 U.S. 617 (1971).

32. A much more extensive account of this can be found in Peter Bernstein, *Capital Ideas* (New York: Free Press, 1993).

33. John C. Bogle, "Remutualizing the Mutual Fund Industry—The Alpha and the Omega," address at Boston College Law School, Jan. 21, 2004.

34. From an advertisement for the book that ran in *New York Times* on Oct. 14, 1973, 173.

35. Vartanig Vartan, "Research vs. Rhesus," *New York Times*, Oct. 14, 1973, 181.

36. The founding editor was Peter Bernstein, who had recently sold his investment firm, Bernstein-Macaulay, to American Express. The firm had been founded in the 1930s by Bernstein's father, who had recruited economist Frederick Macaulay—the man who brought coin flipping to stock market research—to be his partner. The junior Bernstein went on to become an acclaimed historian of investing.

37. Paul A. Samuelson, "Challenge to Judgment," *Journal of Portfolio Management* (Fall 1974). Reprinted in Peter L. Bernstein and Frank Fabozzi, eds., *Streetwise: The Best of the Journal of Portfolio Management* (Princeton: Princeton University Press, 1997).

38. Charles D. Ellis, "The Loser's Game," *Financial Analysts Journal* (July/Aug. 1975).

39. Aloysius Ehrbar, "Index Funds—An Idea Whose Time Is Coming," *Fortune*, June, 1976, 144–54.

40. This account is based chiefly on interviews with Bogle and on John C. Bogle, *The First Index Mutual Fund: A History of Vanguard Index Trust and the Vanguard Index Strategy* (Valley Forge, Pa.: Vanguard Group, 1997).

41. Paul Samuelson, "Coping Sensibly," *Newsweek*, March 6, 1978, 88.

42. I'm referring mainly to the account in Roger Lowenstein's *Buffett: The Making of an American Capitalist.*

43. "A Conversation With Benjamin Graham," Financial Analysts Journal (Sept./ Oct. 1976): 20–23.

CHAPTER 8: FISCHER BLACK CHOOSES TO FOCUS ON THE PROBABLE

1. Mandelbrot tells the story of encountering Zipf's work in Benoit Mandelbrot and Richard L. Hudson, *The (Mis)behavior of Markets: A Fractal View of Risk, Ruin, and Reward* (New York: Basic Books, 2004), 150–59. The Zipf book mentioned is *Human Behavior and the Principle of Least Effort: An Introduction to Human Ecology* (Cambridge, Mass.: Addison-Wesley, 1949).

2. This field had been pioneered by Italian mathematical economist Vilfredo Pareto. Pareto made important contributions to equilibrium economics and Irving Fisher visited him during his European grand tour in 1894. He was appalled that Pareto's wife smoked, but the two corresponded regularly afterward and Mrs. Pareto translated Fisher's doctoral dissertation into Italian. Irving Norton Fisher, *My Father Irving Fisher* (New York: Comet Press Books, 1956), 65. Pareto observed around the turn of the century that in the various European countries he studied, 80 percent of the wealth was in the hands of 20 percent of

the people. This "Pareto's law" has since become a standby of pop sociology and business advice: 20 percent of customers generate 80 percent of sales; 20 percent of vehicles generate 80 percent of the pollution, 20 percent of the people in a company do 80 percent of the work. Fred Macaulay, in a 1920s National Bureau of Economic Research study of income distribution, did not see this proportion at work in the United States and cast doubt upon it being any sort of statistical law. George Udny Yule, meanwhile, was among the first to notice power law distributions outside of income data. J. C. Willis and G. U. Yule, "Some Statistics of Evolution and Geographical Distribution in Plants and Animals, and Their Significance," *Nature* (1922): 177–179.

3. Benoit Mandelbrot, "Forecasts of Future Prices, Unbiased Markets, and 'Martingale' Models, *Journal of Business* (Jan. 1966): 242–55.

4. Paul Cootner, *The Random Character of Stock Prices* (Cambridge, Mass.: MIT Press, 1964), 337.

5. M. F. M. Osborne, *The Stock Market and Finance from a Physicist's Viewpoint* (Minneapolis: Crossgar Press, 2d printing 1995, 1ˢᵗ printing 1977), 203, 214.

6. William F. Sharpe, interview with the author.

7. Peter L. Bernstein, *Against the Gods: The Remarkable Story of Risk* (New York: John Wiley & Sons, 1996), 248.

8. This story is told in great detail in Michael J. Clowes, *The Money Flood: How Pension Funds Revolutionized Investing* (New York: John Wiley & Sons, 2000).

9. Merton Miller, "The History of Finance," *Journal of Portfolio Management* (Summer 1999): 95–101.

10. Chris Welles, "Who is Barr Rosenberg? And what the hell is he talking about?" *Institutional Investor* (May 1978): 59–60.

11. Perry Mehrling, *Fischer Black and the Revolutionary Idea of Finance* (Hoboken, N.J.: John Wiley & Sons, 2005), 22.

12. When they finally published their results in 1976, the projection was for 13 percent nominal stock returns through 2000, with 95 percent confidence that return would be between 5.2 percent and 21.5 percent. (The actual nominal return turned out to be 15 percent.) From Roger G. Ibbotson and Rex A. Sinquefield, "Stocks, Bonds, Bills, and Inflation: Simulations of the Future (1976–2000)," *Journal of Business* (July 1976): 313–38. The "consensus forecast" quote is also from this article, while Ibbotson's line about it being the first scientific forecast of the market is from an interview with him and was first published in Justin Fox, "9% Forever?" *Fortune*, Dec. 26, 2005, 64–72.

13. Barry B. Burr, "Eyeing the numbers: Class comparisons opened the doors," *Pensions & Investment Age*, Oct. 31, 1988, 69.

14. This is based on the *Pensions & Investments*/Watson Wyatt World 500: The World's Largest Managers, published in the Oct. 13, 2008 issue of *P&I* and available online at www.pionline.com. Barclays Global Investors reported $2.08 trillion under management, State Street $1.98 trillion.

15. Stock A is selling at $5 a share, say, and the speculator is sure it's headed to $20. So he spends $1 to acquire an option to buy that stock for $10. It amounts to a lever-

aged bet on the stock's trajectory: If the stock does go up to $15, a $100 investment in the options nets $900 while $100 spent on the stock itself nets $300. If it only goes to $10, the stockholder still makes $100 while the options holder gets nothing.

16. Paul A. Samuelson, "Rational Theory of Warrant Pricing," *Industrial Management Review* (Spring 1965): 13–32; Henry P. McKean Jr., "Appendix: A Free Boundary Problem for the Heat Equation Arising from a Problem of Mathematical Economics," 32–39.

17. Case M. Sprenkle, "Warrant Prices as Indicators of Expectations and Preferences," *Yale Economic Essays* 1, no. 2 (1961): 178–231. Reprinted in Cootner, *The Random Character of Stock Prices* (1964); A. James Boness, "Elements of a Theory of Stock-Option Value," *Journal of Political Economy* (April 1964): 163–75.

18. Friedman's quote was spotted in a newspaper article by Merc chairman Leo Melamed, who later enlisted the economist's help in lobbying regulators to allow the Merc to offer such futures. This story is told in Leo Melamed, with Bob Tamarkin, *Escape to the Futures* (New York: John Wiley & Sons, Inc., 1996), 170–73.

19. Robert K. Merton, *Social Theory and Social Structure* (New York: Free Press, 1968), 477. (Quote found via Wikipedia.)

20. Espen Gaarder Haug and Nassim Nicholas Taleb, "Why We Have Never Used the Black-Scholes-Merton Option Pricing Formula" (working paper, Social Science Research Network, Jan. 2008, http://papers.ssrn.com/sol3/papers.cfm?abstract_id=1012075). It should be noted that Haug and Taleb think Black-Scholes-Merton's grounding in economic theory is a *bad* thing.

21. Paul A. Samuelson and Robert C. Merton, "A Complete Model of Warrant Pricing That Maximizes Utility," *Industrial Management Review* (Winter 1969): 17–46.

22. Stephen A. Ross, "Neoclassical Finance, Alternative Finance and the Closed End Fund Puzzle," *European Financial Management* (June 2002): 129–37.

23. Robert C. Merton, *Continuous-Time Finance* (Cambridge, Mass.: Basil Blackwell, 1990), 15.

24. John C. Cox, Stephen A. Ross, and Mark Rubinstein, "Option Pricing: A Simplified Approach," *Journal of Financial Economics* (Sept. 1979): 229–63.

25. Stephen A. Ross, "Options and Efficiency," *Quarterly Journal of Economics* (Feb. 1976): 76.

Chapter 9: Michael Jensen Gets Corporations to Obey the Market

1. Adam Smith, *The Wealth of Nations* (Indianapolis: Liberty Fund, 1981), 741.

2. In the United States the first all-purpose general incorporation statute was Connecticut's, enacted in 1837, although some states allowed easy incorporation of companies in particular industries before that. In the United Kingdom, Parliament allowed for general incorporation in 1844. Robert Hessen, *In Defense of the Corporation* (Stanford, Calif.: Hoover Institution, 1979). Hessen, it should be

noted, thinks these legal changes were mere formalities because businessmen had already figured out ways to circumvent the post–South Sea ban on corporations.

3. A. A. Berle Jr., "Management Power and Stockholders' Property," *Harvard Business Review* 5 (1927): 424. There is a train of revisionist legal scholarship, summarized in Stephen M. Bainbridge, "The Politics of Corporate Governance," *Harvard Journal of Law and Public Policy* (Summer 1995): 671–734, that argues that the separation of ownership and control was present long before the 1920s. Yet another argument, outlined to me by Henry Manne in an interview, is that Berle's claims were vastly premature and most corporations in the 1920s were still controlled by a few big shareholders. But I'm sticking with the standard account because the 1920s is when people like Berle began to notice and write about the separation of ownership and control.

4. Benjamin Graham, *The Memoirs of the Dean of Wall Street* (New York: McGraw-Hill, 1996), 199–211.

5. The recycling of monopoly oil profits was a major factor in American intellectual life in the 1920s. The Laura Spelman Rockefeller Memorial also bankrolled the Social Science Research Council, founded in 1923, which transformed the study of political science in particular, and was a big funder of the National Bureau of Economic Research. The Rockefeller Foundation subsumed the Spelman Fund in 1929 and continued funding those activities, as well as bringing to the United States many European scholars whose ideas and actions, as already noted in Chapter 2, helped transform the study of economics and finance.

6. The grant was from the Laura Spelman Rockefeller Memorial Fund. Jordan A. Schwarz, *Liberal: Adolf A. Berle and the Vision of an American Era* (New York: The Free Press, 1987), 51–56.

7. Adolf A. Berle Jr., and Gardiner C. Means, *The Modern Corporation and Private Property* (New Brunswick, N.J.: Transaction Publishers, 1991), 312–13.

8. Robert Hessen, "The Modern Corporation and Private Property: Revisited," *Journal of Law and Economics* (June 1983): 273.

9. Jonathan Alter, *The Defining Moment: FDR's Hundred Days and the Triumph of Hope* (New York: Simon & Schuster, 2006), 97. Another telling quote: "Of Berle Raymond Moley acidly noted that while he once may have been considered an infant prodigy, he continued to be an infant long after he had ceased to be a prodigy," from Christopher D. O'Sullivan, *Sumner Welles, Postwar Planning, and the Quest for a New World Order, 1937–1943*, available at www.gutenberg-e.org).

10. Berle was to exert significant influence over U.S. policy toward Latin America as assistant secretary of state from 1938 to 1944, but that didn't have much of anything to do with the New Deal.

11. "These show marked indications of immortality," wrote John Kenneth Galbraith of the two companies in *The Affluent Society* (New York: Mentor Books, 1958), 57.

12. Testimony to Senate Armed Services Committee, Jan. 15, 1953, quoted in "Excerpts from Two Hearings before Senate Committee on Defense Appointment," *New York Times*, Jan. 24, 1953, 8.

13. Most notably in *Theory of the Leisure Class* (New York: Macmillan, 1899) and *Theory of the Business Enterprise* (New York: Scribners, 1904).

14. Chamberlin's dissertation was later published and went through several editions: Edward Chamberlin, *The Theory of Monopolistic Competition* (Cambridge, Mass.: Harvard University Press, 1933). Means's report was published as U.S. Department of Agriculture, *Industrial Prices and Their Relative Inflexibility* (Washington, D.C.: U.S. Government Printing Office, 1935). Equally important was Cambridge economist Joan Robinson's *Economics of Imperfect Competition* (London: Macmillan, 1933), which I omit from the main text only because she (a) was British, and thus not directly involved in the American intellectual debate and (b) makes no other appearance in this book.

15. The books were *American Capitalism: The Concept of a Countervailing Power* (Boston: Houghton Mifflin, 1952), *The Affluent Society* (Boston: Houghton Mifflin, 1958), and *The New Industrial State* (Boston: Houghton Mifflin, 1967). The Soviet apparatchik parallel is explored in the last of these, while *The Affluent Society* focuses more on overconsumption and waste.

16. Milton Friedman and Rose Friedman, *Two Lucky People: Memoirs* (Chicago: University of Chicago Press, 1998), 81.

17. This was accomplished with funding from the conservative Volker Foundation of Kansas City, the same outfit that was to pay to send Director, Friedman, and Stigler to Mont Pelerin in 1947. Edmund W. Kitch, ed., "The Fire of Truth: A Remembrance of Law and Economics at Chicago, 1932–1970," *Journal of Law and Economics* (April 1983): 180–81.

18. Kitch, "Fire of Truth," 183.

19. George J. Stigler, *Memoirs of an Unregulated Economist* (Chicago: University of Chicago Press, 1988), 103.

20. James M. Buchanan and Gordon Tullock, *The Calculus of Consent: Logical Foundations of Constitutional Democracy* (Ann Arbor, Mich.: University of Michigan Press, 1962), is generally seen as the founding document of the public choice school, although Tullock credits earlier works by Scottish scholar Duncan Black.

21. Milton Friedman, "A Friedman Doctrine—The Social Responsibility of Business is to Increase its Profits," *New York Times Magazine*, Sept. 13, 1970, 32–33, 122.

22. *New York Times Magazine*, Letters, Oct. 4, 1970, 21, 63.

23. This seemed like an excellent opportunity to put in an enthusiastic plug for Marc Levinson, *The Box: How the Shipping Container Made the World Smaller and the World Economy Bigger* (Princeton: Princeton University Press, 2006).

24. Details on the Rochester endowment's investment policy are in Robert Sheehan, "The Rich, Risky Life of a University Trustee," *Fortune*, Jan. 1967, 169.

25. "We expect the major benefits of the security analysis activity to be reflected in the higher capitalized value of the ownership claims of corporations, and *not* in the period-to-period portfolio returns of the analyst." Michael C. Jensen and William H. Meckling, "Theory of the Firm: Managerial Behavior, Agency Costs and Ownership Structure," *Journal of Financial Economics* (Oct. 1976): 305–60. It took so long to get the paper published, according to Jensen, because Jensen

and Meckling's arguments were torn to pieces when they first presented them at a Chicago economics seminar in 1973. "There was this unspoken belief [at Chicago], never formalized but very strong, that competition between corporations would deliver an optimal result," Jensen said. "The paper challenged that." Several Chicagoans also objected that the principal-agent conflict had been amply and recently discussed in Armen Alchian and Harold Demsetz, "Production, Information Costs, and Economic Organization," *American Economic Review* (Dec. 1972): 777–95. I focus on the Jensen-Meckling paper instead because it is far more explicit in linking agency costs and the efficient market, and because Jensen subsequently built an illustrious career upon it.

26. Joel Stern, "Let's Abandon Earnings Per Share," *Wall Street Journal*, Dec. 18, 1972. Reprinted in Joel M. Stern with Irwin Ross, *Against the Grain: How to Succeed in Business by Peddling Heresy* (Hoboken: John Wiley & Sons, 2003), 171–77.

27. Alfred Rappaport, "Selecting strategies that create shareholder value," *Harvard Business Review* (May–June 1981): 139–49.

28. Diana Henriques, *The White Sharks of Wall Street: Thomas Mellon Evans and the Original Corporate Raiders* (New York: A Lisa Drew Book/Scribner, 2000), 150–58.

29. Cited in Daniel R. Fischel, "Efficient Capital Market Theory, the Market for Corporate Control, and the Regulation of Cash Tender Offers," *Texas Law Review* 57, no. 1 (Dec. 1978): 17.

30. Henry G. Manne, "Mergers and the Market for Corporate Control," *Journal of Political Economy* (April 1965): 113.

31. Manne, "Mergers and the Market," 112.

32. Louis Lowenstein, "Pruning Deadwood in Hostile Takeovers: A Proposal for Legislation," *Columbia Law Review* (March 1983): 251–52.

33. Both the Milken background and the rise of the takeover artists are recounted in Connie Bruck, *The Predators' Ball: The Junk Bond Raiders and the Man Who Staked Them* (New York: Simon & Schuster, 1988). Drexel was not the first firm to "manufacture" junk bonds; Lehman Brothers was, in 1977. But Drexel soon came to dominate the business.

34. Years later, after a federal judge had thrown Milken in jail for securities fraud, Chicago professor and soon-to-be law school dean Daniel Fischel wrote a book with the very unprofessorial title *Payback: The Conspiracy to Destroy Michael Milken and His Financial Revolution* (New York: HarperBusiness, 1995).

35. Fischel, *Payback*, 38. (Despite the incendiary title, it's a useful source of information.)

36. *Economic Report of the President, February 1985*, Washington, D.C.: U.S. Government Printing Office, 1995, 187–216. In an interview with the author, William A. Niskanen, then a member of President Reagan's Council of Economic Advisers, said he wrote the chapter.

37. The ranks of these critics were huge, but perhaps the most thoughtful was Columbia law professor Louis Lowenstein, a former corporate lawyer and executive who in a series of law review articles—most notably "Pruning Deadwood in Hostile Takeovers: A Proposal for Legislation"—and then the books *What's Wrong with*

Wall Street? (Reading, Mass.: Addison-Wesley, 1988) and *Sense and Nonsense in Corporate Finance* (Reading, Mass.: Addison-Wesley, 1991) systematically tore down many of the rational-market-based arguments of the takeover apologists. Lowenstein's son, journalist Roger Lowenstein, has become another well-known critic of the efficient marketeers.

38. The most important agent of this spread of ideas was probably Richard Brealey and Stewart Myers, *Principles of Corporate Finance* (New York: McGraw-Hill, 1981), which soon became the standard text on the subject, a required course in most business schools. Brealey was a professor at the London School of Business. He had come to the United States in the 1960s to work for Keystone Funds, fallen in with the Chicago Center for Research on Security Prices crowd, and authored some lucid works for investment practitioners on the new finance. McGraw-Hill asked him to write a corporate finance text, and he ended up collaborating with Myers, a Stanford Ph.D. who taught at MIT's Sloan School. Theirs wasn't the first corporate finance text to mention the efficient market hypothesis, but it was the first to be completely suffused by it.

39. William Wong, "Harvard West? Losing 'Minor' Image as a Business School, Stanford's Fame Rises," *Wall Street Journal,* Sept. 23, 1976, 1, 28.

40. Thomas McCraw and Jeffrey L. Cruikshank, *The Intellectual Venture Capitalist: John H. McArthur and the Work of the Harvard Business School* (Boston: Harvard Business School Press, 1999), 8.

41. Leonard Silk, "The Peril Behind the Takeover Boom," *New York Times,* Dec. 29, 1985, F1, F6.

42. Michael C. Jensen, "Agency Costs of Free Cash Flow, Corporate Finance, and Takeovers," Papers and Proceedings of the AEA annual meeting, held Dec. 28–30, 1985, *American Economic Review* (May 1986): 323–29.

43. Michael C. Jensen, "The Eclipse of the Public Corporation," *Harvard Business Review* (Sept.–Oct. 1989): 61–62.

44. Doug Henwood, *Wall Street* (London: Verso, 1998), 276–77. Henwood, by the way, is just about the only person who means Michael Jensen when he writes "Jensenism." The term generally refers to the controversial theories about IQ and heredity of psychologist Arthur Jensen.

CHAPTER 10: DICK THALER GIVES
ECONOMIC MAN A PERSONALITY

1. I owe this insight (the billiards connection, that is) entirely to Colin Camerer.

2. The apotheosis of this work was the "Skinner box," devised ca. 1930 by Harvard psychologist B. F. Skinner. Animals, usually pigeons or rats, were stuck in a box with a lever and a food dispenser. They then learned which actions were rewarded and which were punished, and generally reacted accordingly. Human behavior, Skinner argued, was the result of similar conditioning by society. In the 1950s, though, a few psychology students who wanted to do more than put pigeons and rats in boxes began looking into *how* people made choices.

3. Most of the information and all of the quotes in the foregoing paragraphs are from Kahneman's autobiography, *Les Prix Nobel 2002* (Stockholm: Nobel Foundation, 2003); also available at www.nobelprize.org.

4. I would repeat some of the questions Tversky asked, but they're phrased in the arcane language of statistics. Amos Tversky and Daniel Kahneman, "Belief in the Law of Small Numbers," *Psychological Bulletin* 2 (1971): 105–10. Reprinted in Daniel Kahneman, Paul Slovic, and Amos Tversky, *Judgment Under Uncertainty: Heuristics and Biases* (Cambridge, UK: Cambridge University Press, 1982), 23–31.

5. Herbert A. Simon, *Models of My Life* (New York: Basic Books, 1991), 144.

6. John F. Muth, "Rational Expectations and the Theory of Price Movements," *Econometrica* (July 1961): 315–35. The paper was first presented at an Econometric Society meeting in 1959.

7. The other two were Edward Prescott and Thomas Sargent.

8. Donald N. McCloskey, *The Rhetoric of Economics* (Madison, Wisc.: University of Wisconsin Press, 1985), 91. (Donald subsequently became Deirdre, which is another story entirely. Deirdre McCloskey, *Crossing: A Memoir* [Chicago: University of Chicago Press, 1999].)

9. Robert E. Lucas Jr., "The Death of Keynesian Economics," *Issues and Ideas* (University of Chicago), (Winter 1980): 18–19. Cited in N. Gregory Mankiw, "The Reincarnation of Keynesian Economics," *European Economic Review* (April 1992): 559.

10. Kathryn Crowley, ed., *The Collected Scientific Papers of Paul A. Samuelson*, vol. 5, (Cambridge and London: MIT Press, 1986), 291.

11. Kenneth J. Arrow, "Uncertainty and the Welfare Economics of Medical Care," *American Economic Review* (Dec. 1963): 941–73.

12. Sanford J. Grossman and Joseph E. Stiglitz, "On the Impossibility of Informationally Efficient Markets," *American Economic Review* (June 1980): 393–408, quote is from p. 405. The paper was first presented at an Econometric Society meeting in 1975.

13. Bernanke got his doctorate from MIT in 1979 and Krugman in 1977. Summers got his from Harvard in 1982, and had been an MIT undergraduate before that. A few others: former Federal Reserve governor Frederic Mishkin (MIT 1976); Bush administration economic advisers Glenn Hubbard (Harvard 1981), Larry Lindsey (Harvard 1985), and Greg Mankiw (MIT 1984); Clinton administration economic adviser Laura Tyson (MIT 1974); Columbia professor and globetrotting do-gooder Jeffrey Sachs (Harvard 1980); blogger/professors Brad DeLong and Tyler Cowen (both Harvard 1987); freakonomist Steven Levitt (MIT 1994), and so on.

14. The Sveriges Riksbank Prize in Economic Sciences in Memory of Alfred Nobel 1978, press release, Oct. 16, 1978.

15. Daniel Kahneman and Amos Tversky, "Prospect Theory: An Analysis of Decision Under Risk," *Econometrica* (March 1979): 263–92.

16. Richard H. Thaler, *Quasi Rational Economics* (New York: Russell Sage Foundation, 1991), xi–xii.

17. Justin Fox, "Is the Market Rational?" *Fortune*, Dec. 9, 2002, 120.

18. Richard H. Thaler, "Toward a Positive Theory of Consumer Choice," *Journal of Economic Behavior and Organization* 1 (1980): 39–60. Reprinted in Thaler, *Quasi Rational Economics*.

19. Richard H. Thaler and H. M. Shefrin, "An Economic Theory of Self-Control," *Journal of Political Economy* (April 1981): 392–406.

20. The best description of Chamberlin's experiment, and of the rise of experimental economics in general, is in Ross M. Miller, *Paving Wall Street: Experimental Economics and the Quest for the Perfect Market* (New York: John Wiley & Sons, 2002).

21. It's called the Social Science Faculty, and includes anthropologists, psychologists, political scientists, and legal scholars as well as economists.

CHAPTER 11: BOB SHILLER POINTS OUT THE MOST REMARKABLE ERROR

1. At least, that's how Thaler remembers it. The account is assembled from his recollections as well as those of Shefrin and Kahneman. Jensen professes not to recall the exchange at all, but he doesn't dispute that it happened and the views he held at the time are well documented.

2. Robin M. Hogarth, Melvin W. Reder, "Prefatory Note," *Journal of Business* (Oct. 1986): S181.

3. Others included Kahneman, Tversky, Thaler, Shefrin, and Shefrin's Santa Clara University colleague Meir Statman, as well as economists Kenneth Arrow, Robert Lucas, Herbert Simon, and George Stigler.

4. Merton H. Miller, "Behavioral Rationality in Finance: The Case of Dividends," *Journal of Business* (Oct. 1986): S467.

5. Adam Smith [George A. W. Goodman], *The Money Game* (New York: Random House, 1967), 158.

6. Clive W. J. Granger and Oskar Morgenstern, *Predictability of Stock Market Prices*, (Lexington, Mass.: D.C. Heath and Co., 1970), 3. According to Granger, the book's introductory chapter, which contains its most incendiary comments, was all Morgenstern's work, although he agreed with most of what Morgenstern had to say.

7. Granger and Morgenstern, *Predictability of Stock Market Prices*, 9, 22.

8. Leo Melamed, with Bob Tamarkin, *Escape to the Futures* (New York: John Wiley & Sons, Inc., 1996), 99.

9. Holbrook Working, "Price Effects of Futures Trading" (reprinted from *Food Research Institute Studies* 1, no. 1 [Feb. 1960]), in *Selected Writings of Holbrook Working*, Anne E. Peck, ed. (Chicago: Chicago Board of Trade, 1977), 45–71.

10. Roger W. Gray, "Onions Revisited" (reprinted from *Journal of Farm Economics* 45, no. 2 [May 1963]), in Peck, *Selected Writings*, 325–28.

11. Aaron C. Johnson, "Effects of Futures Trading on Price Performance in the Cash Onion Market, 1930–1968" (excerpted from USDA, ERS, Technical Bulletin no. 1470, Feb. 1973), in Peck *Selected Writings*, 329–36.

12. A recent summing up of the research on the question of whether derivatives mar-

kets add volatility can be found in Stewart Mayhew, "The Impact of Derivatives on Cash Markets: What Have We Learned?" (working paper, Terry College of Business, University of Georgia, 2000), available at http://media.terry.uga.edu/documents/finance/impact.pdf.

13. Arjo Klamer, *Conversations with Economists: New Classical Opponents and Their Opponents Speak Out on the Current Controversy in Macroeconomics* (Totowa, N.J.: Rowman & Allanheld Publishers, 1984), 223.

14. This work is described in chapter 13, "Bond Market Volatility: An Introductory Survey," of Robert J. Shiller, *Market Volatility* (Cambridge, Mass.: MIT Press, 1989), 219–36. The best known of his papers on the subject was "The Volatility of Long-Term Interest Rates and Expectations Models of the Term Structure," *Journal of Political Economy* (Dec. 1979): 1190–219. Reprinted in Shiller, *Market Volatility,* 256–87.

15. Robert J. Shiller, "Do Stock Prices Move Too Much to Be Justified by Subsequent Changes in Dividends?" *American Economic Review* (June 1981): 421–35. Reprinted in Shiller, *Market Volatility,* 105–30. Two Federal Reserve Board economists published a similar study with similar results—based on reported earnings rather than dividends—the same year. But they didn't give it nearly as attention getting a title, and it got substantially less attention: Stephen F. LeRoy and Richard D. Porter, "The Present-Value Relation: Tests Based on Implied Variance Bounds," *Econometrica* (May 1981): 555–74.

16. Robert C. Merton, "On the Current State of the Stock Market Rationality Hypothesis," *Macroeconomics and Finance: Essays in Honor of Franco Modigliani,* Rudiger Dornbusch, Stanley Fischer, and John Bossons, eds. (Cambridge: MIT Press, 1987), 117.

17. Robert J. Shiller, "Stock Prices and Social Dynamics," *Brookings Papers on Economic Activity* 2 (1984): 457–98. Reprinted in Shiller, *Market Volatility,* 8.

18. Paul A. Samuelson and William A. Barnett, *Inside the Economist's Mind* (Malden, Mass., and Oxford: Blackwell, 2006), 241. (The economist who urged Shiller to keep the line in was Yale's William Nordhaus.)

19. Summers's father was Samuelson's younger brother, but had changed his surname to avoid anti-Jewish discrimination. Arrow was Summers's mother's brother. Summers studied economics as an undergraduate at MIT, got his Ph.D. at Harvard and his first teaching job at MIT, and then he returned to become the youngest-ever tenured professor at Harvard, all the while writing a lot of working papers for the National Bureau of Economic Research.

20. Lawrence H. Summers, "Does the Stock Market Rationally Reflect Fundamental Values?" *Journal of Finance* (July 1986) 591–601. The piece was originally circulated as a National Bureau of Economic Research working paper in 1982.

21. Lawrence H. Summers, "On Economics and Finance," *Journal of Finance* (July 1985): 633–35.

22. Lawrence H. Summers, "Finance and Idiots," copy of undated paper with comments from Fischer Black, provided to the author by Andrei Shleifer.

23. Hersh M. Shefrin and Meir Statman, "Explaining Investor Preference for Cash

Dividends," *Journal of Financial Economics* (1984): 253–82. The *Journal of Finance* had actually run one behavioral finance article more than a decade before, but it was not by a finance professor and it occasioned little follow-up: Paul Slovic, "Psychological Study of Human Judgment: Implications for Investment Decision Making," *Journal of Finance* (Sept. 1972): 779–99. (Slovic was a research psychologist at the Oregon Research Institute who was later to work closely with Kahneman and Tversky.)

24. Fischer Black, "The Dividend Puzzle," *Journal of Portfolio Management* (Winter 1976): 5–8.

25. Black did complain that Shefrin and Statman had spelled his first name wrong—a recurring theme in Black's interactions with the world. But that seemed to be his only real problem with their work. In a subsequent letter to Shefrin, *Journal of Financial Economics* editor G. William Schwert professed to have "reservations" because the piece "seems to have no empirical implications." But he couldn't dismiss Black's positive verdict. May 1982 comments from Fischer Black and May 27, 1982, letter from G. William Schwert courtesy of Hersh Shefrin.

26. Fischer Black, "Noise," *Journal of Finance* (July 1986): 530, 533.

27. Richard Roll, "R²," *Journal of Finance* (July 1988): 541–66. Roll had investigated the question earlier for the orange juice futures market, with similar results: Richard Roll, "Orange Juice and Weather," *American Economic Review* (Dec. 1984): 861–79.

28. Victor Niederhoffer, M. F. M. Osborne, "Market Making and Reversal on the Stock Exchange," *Journal of the American Statistical Association* (Dec. 1966): 897–916.

29. I owe this observation to Baruch Lev, who wasn't referring to Niederhoffer's work in particular but remembered Merton Miller saying in class one day in the 1960s, "I will start to believe when I see the first study that contradicts market efficiency."

30. Fama, "Efficient Capital Markets," 398.

31. Victor Niederhoffer and Patrick J. Regan, "Earnings Changes, Analysts' Forecasts, and Stock Prices," *Financial Analysts Journal* (May–June 1972): 65–71. An even earlier account of the phenomenon was a chapter called "Earnings Changes vs. Stock Price Changes" in Burton P. Fabricand, *Beating the Street—How to Make Money on the Stock Market* (New York: David McKay, 1969). But none of the academic researchers appear to have noticed it.

32. S. Francis Nicholson, "Price-Earnings Ratios," *Financial Analysts Journal* (July–August 1960): 43–45.

33. The most important and controversial of the lot, because it directly posed the question of whether the value effect violated the efficient market hypothesis, was Sanjoy Basu, "Investment Performance of Common Stocks in Relation to Their Price-Earnings Ratios: A Test of the Efficient Market Hypothesis," *Journal of Finance* (June 1977): 663–82.

34. Ray Ball, "Anomalies in Relationships Between Securities' Yields and Yield-Surrogates," *Journal of Financial Economics* 6 (1977): 103–26. Preparing the groundwork for this had been Stephen A. Ross, "The Arbitrage Theory of Capital Asset Pricing." *Journal of Economic Theory* (Dec. 1976), 343–62, and Richard Roll, who

pointed out in 1977 that the theoretical "market portfolio" at the heart of the capital asset model was such a vast and amorphous thing (should it include gold, real estate, life insurance policies?) that its performance couldn't really be measured. Richard Roll, "A Critique of the Asset Pricing Theory's Tests, Part I: On Past and Potential Testability of the Theory," *Journal of Financial Economics* 4 (1977): 129–76.

35. Rolf W. Bänz, "The Relationship Between Market Value and Return of Common Stocks," *Journal of Financial Economics* (Nov. 1981): 3–18.

36. Floyd Norris, "Return of the Small Stock Conundrum," *New York Times*, Jan. 6, 1991.

37. Peter Tanous, *Investment Gurus* (New York: New York Institute of Finance, 1997).

38. Eugene F. Fama, "Efficient Capital Markets: II," *Journal of Finance* (Dec. 1991): 1575–617.

39. Robert Haugen, *The New Finance: The Case Against Efficient Markets* (Englewood Cliffs, N.J.: Prentice Hall, 1995), 65.

40. Eugene F. Fama, Kenneth R. French, "The Cross-Section of Expected Stock Returns," *Journal of Finance* (June 1992): 450.

41. Narasimhan Jegadeesh, Sheridan Titman, "Returns to Buying Winners and Selling Losers: Implications for Stock Market Efficiency," *Journal of Finance* (March 1993): 65–91.

42. Mark Carhart, "On persistence in mutual fund performance," *Journal of Finance* (March 1997): 57–82.

CHAPTER 12: BEATING THE MARKET WITH
WARREN BUFFETT AND ED THORP

1. Roger Lowenstein, *Buffett: The Making of an American Capitalist* (New York: Main Street Books, 1996), 317. All the information on Buffett in this chapter is, unless otherwise noted, from Lowenstein's book.

2. Warren E. Buffett, "The Superinvestors of Graham-and-Doddsville," *Hermes* (Fall 1984): 4–15.

3. For the full story on that, read Connie Bruck's *Master of the Game: Steve Ross and the Creation of Time Warner* (New York: Penguin Books, 1995), esp. 29–39.

4. Thorp also figured out in the early 1960s how to beat the house at baccarat and roulette, the latter by using a wearable computer—the world's first—that he and legendary MIT scientist Claude Shannon designed to predict the ball's path after it was dropped.

5. Paul A. Samuelson, "Review of *Beat the Market*," *Journal of the American Statistical Association* (Sept. 1968): 1049–51.

6. Carol J. Loomis, "The Jones Nobody Keeps Up With," *Fortune*, April 1966, 237, 240, 247.

7. Jonathan R. Laing, "Playing the Odds: Computer Formulas Are One Man's Secret to Success," *Wall Street Journal*, Sept. 23, 1974.

8. Andrew Tobias, *Money Angles* (New York: Simon & Schuster, 1984), 70–71.

9. William Poundstone, *Fortune's Formula* (New York: Hill and Wang, 2005), 175–77.

10. James Agee (the article is not bylined, but *Fortune*'s records indicate that Agee wrote it), "Arbitrage," *Fortune*, June 1934, 93–97, 150–60.

11. Lowenstein, *Buffett*, 161. The actual *Forbes* article, published Nov. 1, 1974, substituted "harem" for "whorehouse."

12. Carol J. Loomis, "The Inside Story of Warren Buffett," *Fortune*, April 11, 1988, 32.

13. Shawn Tully, "Princeton's Rich Commodities Scholars," *Fortune*, Feb. 9, 1981, 94–98. Commodities Corp. alumni include legendary (among the cognoscenti) traders David Tudor Jones, Bruce Kovner, and Monroe Trout.

14. George Anders, "Some 'Efficient-Market' Scholars Decide It's Possible to Beat the Averages After All," *Wall Street Journal*, Dec. 31, 1985, 11.

15. Barr Rosenberg, Kenneth Reid, and Ronald Lanstein, "Persuasive Proof of Market Inefficiency," *Journal of Portfolio Management* (Spring 1985): 9–17. Reprinted in *Streetwise: The Best of the Journal of Portfolio Management*, Peter L. Bernstein and Frank Fabozzi, eds., (Princeton, N.J.: Princeton University Press, 1997), 48–55.

16. Michael Schrage, "Nerd on the Street," *Manhattan Inc.*, Oct. 1987, 104.

17. Peter L. Bernstein, *Against the Gods: The Remarkable Story of Risk* (New York: John Wiley & Sons, 1998), 7. (The Charles, in case anyone is puzzled by the quote, is the river that runs between Boston and Cambridge, Massachusetts.)

18. Roger Lowenstein, *When Genius Failed* (New York: Random House, 2000).

CHAPTER 13: ALAN GREENSPAN STOPS A RANDOM PLUNGE DOWN WALL STREET

1. This is the gist of Peter Bernstein's book, *Against the Gods: The Remarkable Story of Risk* (New York: John Wiley & Sons, 1996).

2. Warren E. Buffett, Berkshire Hathaway 1987 Letter to Shareholders, Feb. 29, 1988. Available at www.berkshirehathaway.com/letters/letters.html. (Italics his.)

3. Most of this summary of events is taken from the January 1988 "Brady report": *Report of the Presidential Task Force on Market Mechanisms*, Washington, D.C.: U.S. Government Printing Office, 1988, 15–29. The Brady report is politic enough not to focus on the comments by Baker, who was still treasury secretary when it came out. They can be found in Peter T. Kilborn, "U.S. Cautions Bonn That It May Force the Dollar Lower," *New York Times*, Oct. 16, 1987, 1.

4. The Brady report concluded that about a third of the selling on October 19 was portfolio-insurance related.

5. Perry Mehrling, *Fischer Black and the Revolutionary Idea of Finance* (Hoboken, N.J., John Wiley & Sons, 2005), 271.

6. Barbara Donnelly, "Efficient Market Theorists Are Puzzled by Recent Gyrations in Stock Market," *Wall Street Journal*, Oct. 23, 1987, 7.

7. Gary Hector, "What Makes Stock Prices Move?" *Fortune*, Oct. 10, 1988, 69.

8. A few months after the crash, Richard Roll studied the behavior of twenty-three stock markets around the world on and before October 19 and concluded that the whole event was just "the normal response of each country's stock market to a worldwide market movement." Richard Roll, "The International Crash of October 1987," *Financial Analysts Journal* (Sept.–Oct.1988): 19.

9. The main reports were the above-mentioned Brady report and the SEC's *The October 1987 Market Break: A Report by the Division of Market Regulation* (Feb. 1988), which were both perceived by the Chicago exchanges as blaming them for the crash. Merton H. Miller summarizes the results of a Chicago Merc study that saw things differently in "The Economics and Politics of Index Arbitrage," keynote address, fourth annual Pacific Basin Research Conference, Hong Kong, July 6–8, 1992, in *Merton Miller on Derivatives* (New York: John Wiley & Sons, 1997), 26–39.

10. Donnelly, "Efficient Market Theorists Are Puzzled."

11. Robert J. Shiller, "Speculative Prices and Popular Models," *Journal of Economic Perspectives* (Spring 1990): 58.

12. Hector, "What Makes Stock Prices Move?" 72.

13. Jens Carsten Jackwerth and Mark Rubinstein, "Recovering Probability Distributions from Equity Prices," *Journal of Finance* (Dec. 1996): 2.

14. Benoit Mandelbrot, interview with the author.

15. Gregg A. Jarrell, "En-Nobeling Financial Economics," *Wall Street Journal*, Oct. 17, 1990, A14.

16. Myron S. Scholes, "Derivatives in a Dynamic Environment," and Robert C. Merton, "Applications of Option-Pricing Theory: Twenty-Five Years Later," in *Nobel Lectures, Economics 1996–2000*, Torsten Persson, ed. (Singapore: World Scientific Publishing Co., 2003). Also available at http://nobelprize.org.

17. In the case of Orange County, Treasurer Robert Citrin followed a strategy in the early 1990s of buying derivatives called "inverse floaters," which paid higher returns the lower that short-term interest rates went. From 1991 to 1994 this strategy paid off handsomely, bringing in profits of over $750 million—with almost no volatility. But Greenspan's Fed raised short-term rates because of inflation fears in 1994, and the value of the portfolio Citrin managed suddenly dropped by $1.7 billion.

18. Merton H. Miller, *Merton Miller on Derivatives* (New York: John Wiley & Sons, 1997), ix.

19. Robert J. Shiller, *The New Financial Order: Risk in the 21ˢᵗ Century* (Princeton: Princeton University Press, 2003), 1–2, 5.

20. "Roundtable: The Limits of VAR," *Derivatives Strategy* (April 1998): www.derivativesstrategy.com/magazine/archive/1998/0498fea1.asp.

21. The subsequent account of Long-Term Capital Management's fall is, except where otherwise attributed, taken from the two books: Nicholas Dunbar, *Inventing Money: The Story of Long-Term Capital Management and the Legends Behind It* (New York: John Wiley & Sons, 2000); Roger Lowenstein, *When Genius Failed: The Rise and Fall of Long-Term Capital Management* (New York: Random House, 2000).

22. Joe Kolman, "LTCM Speaks," *Derivatives Strategy* (April 1999): www.derivativesstrategy.com/magazine/archive/1998/0499fea1.asp.

23. Robert Litzenberger speech, Society of Quantitative Analysts.

24. Richard Bookstaber, *A Demon of Their Own Design: Markets, Hedge Funds, and the Perils of Financial Innovation* (Hoboken, N.J.: John Wiley & Sons, 2007), 97.

25. The LTCM partner whose lecture Markowitz attended was David Modest.

26. The most detailed description of Greenspan's and Corrigan's actions is in Bob Woodward, *Maestro: Greenspan's Fed and the American Boom* (New York: Touchstone, 2001), 36–47, but better accounts of the market's malfunctioning on the twentieth can be found in the Brady report and in James B. Stewart and Daniel Hertzberg, "Terrible Tuesday: How the Stock Market Almost Disintegrated a Day After the Crash," *Wall Street Journal*, 1, 23. (Stewart and Hertzberg won a Pulitzer for the piece.)

27. James Tobin, "A Proposal for International Monetary Reform," *Eastern Economic Journal* (July–Oct. 1978): 153–59; Keynes, *General Theory*, 160; "Glass's 5% Tax Plan Stirs Wall Street," *New York Times*, June 6, 1929, 6.

CHAPTER 14: ANDREI SHLEIFER MOVES
BEYOND RABBI ECONOMICS

1. Andrei Shleifer, "Do Demand Curves for Stocks Slope Down?" *Journal of Finance* (July 1986): 579–90.

2. This is Shleifer's recollection. Scholes doesn't recall the event but admits it sounds like something he would've said.

3. Oliver Blanchard, "In Honor of Andrei Shleifer: Winner of the John Bates Clark Medal," *Journal of Economic Perspectives* (Winter 2001): 189–204.

4. Shleifer ran an advisory office in Moscow that was affiliated with Harvard and funded by the U.S. Agency for International Development. USAID later charged that Shleifer had countenanced conflicts of interest as he, his number two, and their wives and girlfriends made investments in Russian companies while advising the country's government. Shleifer maintained that he had been in Harvard's employ, not USAID's, and that his behavior hadn't violated the university's less-stringent conflict-of-interest rules. But a federal judge didn't buy it, Harvard ended up paying a fine of $26.5 million, Shleifer paid $2 million, and the episode exacerbated faculty dissatisfaction with Summers, who ended up leaving Harvard's presidency in 2006. An epic, and almost virulently Shleifer-unfriendly account of the affair can be found in David McClintick, "How Harvard Lost Russia," *Institutional Investor* (Feb. 2006).

5. Fischer Black, "Estimating Expected Return," *Financial Analysts Journal* (Sept.–Oct. 1993): 36–38.

6. Louis K. C. Chan and Josef Lakonishok, "Are the Reports of Beta's Death Premature?" *Journal of Portfolio Management* (Summer 1993): 51–62.

7. Josef Lakonishok, Andrei Shleifer, Richard Thaler, Robert Vishny, "Window Dressing by Pension Fund Managers," *American Economic Review* (May 1991): 227–31.

8. "Pensions & Investments/Watson Wyatt World 500: The world's largest managers," *Pensions & Investments*, Oct. 13, 2008. Shleifer and Vishny had by this point both left the firm.

9. John Maynard Keynes, *General Theory* (New York: Harcourt, Brace, 1936), 157.

10. Amir Barnea, Robert A. Haugen, and Lemma W. Senbet, *Agency Problems and Financial Contracting* (Englewood Cliffs, N.J.: Prentice-Hall, 1985).

11. Andrei Shleifer and Robert W. Vishny, "The Limits of Arbitrage," *Journal of Finance* (March 1997): 37.

12. Jeremy J. Siegel, *Stocks for the Long Run*, 2nd ed. (New York: McGraw-Hill, 1998), 45.

13. Pablo Galarza, "It's Still Stocks for the Long Run," *Money*, Dec. 2004.

14. Robert J. Shiller, "Price-Earnings Ratios as Forecasters of Returns: The Stock Market Outlook in 1996," paper posted on Shiller's Web site, July 21, 1996, www.econ.yale.edu/%7Eshiller/data/peratio.html. The original paper was John Y. Campbell and Robert J. Shiller, "Stock Prices, Earnings, and Expected Dividends," *Journal of Finance* (July 1988): 661–76.

15. Alan Greenspan, *The Age of Turbulence* (New York: Penguin, 2007), 176–79.

16. J. Bradford DeLong and Konstantin Magin, "Contrary to Robert Shiller's Predictions, Stock Market Investors Made Much Money in the Past Decade: What Does This Tell Us?" *Economists' Voice* (July 2006).

17. "Volatility in U.S. and Japanese Stock Markets: Selections from the First Annual Symposium on Global Financial Markets," *Journal of Applied Corporate Finance*, Spring 1992: 4–35. (Roll's quote is on pp. 29–30.)

18. This is directly from Cliff Asness. A slightly different version of the story can be found in Joseph Nocera, "The Quantitative, Data-Based, Risk-Massaging Road to Riches," *New York Times Magazine*, June 5, 2005.

19. The October 2000 version is available for download at http://ssrn.com/abstract=240371.

20. Williams (1997), 188.

21. Clifford Asness, "Bubble Logic: Or, How to Learn to Stop Worrying and Love the Bull," partial draft of an unpublished book, June 1, 2000.

22. Owen A. Lamont and Richard H. Thaler. "Can the Market Add and Subtract? Mispricing in Tech Stock Carve-Outs," *Journal of Political Economy* (April 2003): 227–68.

23. Jeremy Siegel, "Big-Cap Tech Stocks Are a Sucker Bet," *Wall Street Journal*, March 14, 2000.

24. Justin Fox, "9% Forever?" *Fortune*, Dec. 26, 2005.

Chapter 15: Mike Jensen Changes His Mind about the Corporation

1. Jack Willoughby, "Burning Up: Warning: Internet companies are running out of cash—fast," *Barron's*, March 20, 2000, 29.

2. Greg Kyle, president of Pegasus. Quoted in Betsy Schiffman, "Going, Going, Gone: Business-to-Consumer Sector Goes Bust," Forbes.com, April 19, 2000.

3. George Soros, "The Theory of Reflexivity." Delivered April 26, 1994, to the MIT Department of Economics World Economy Laboratory Conference, Washington, D.C.

4. Justin Fox, "Net Stock Rules: Masters of a Parallel Universe," *Fortune*, June 7, 1999; Daniel Gross's book *Pop: Why Bubbles Are Great for the Economy* (New York: Collins, 2007), explores this argument in more detail.

5. This approximate number was arrived at by taking Time Warner's market cap before the merger with AOL was announced, $76 billion, and subtracting from it the value of the 45 percent of the company that those shareholders owned after the merged company's stock slumped in late 2002.

6. Michael C. Jensen, "Agency Costs of Overvalued Equity" (working paper 39/2004, European Corporate Governance Institute, May 2004).

7. He participated in an interdisciplinary project on "Mind/Brain/Behavior" launched in 1993 by Harvard president Neil Rudenstine, in which he worked alongside psychologists and neurobiologists to study "self-command."

8. Influential journalist James Fallows, after an extended stay in Asia, went so far as to call into question the entire neoclassical approach by attempting to resurrect the arguments of nineteenth-century German thinker Friedrich List. List, who remained influential in Asia, had tried to construct an economics based on national interest rather than individual utility. He is, it should be emphasized, a figure worthy of renewed interest whether you buy in to his economic ideas or not. He founded the German railway system, for one thing. Also, after moving to the United States in 1825 on the recommendation of his good friend the Marquis de Lafayette, he spent several very active years editing a newspaper in Pennsylvania, helping out with Andrew Jackson's presidential campaign, and playing a major role in U.S. economic-policy debates before returning home in 1831. William Notz, "Friedrich List on America," *American Economic Review* (June 1926): 249–65. Fallows's take on List can be found in James Fallows, *Looking at the Sun: The Rise of the New East Asian Economic and Political System* (New York: Vintage, 1995), 179–95.

9. Speech at the Second Mitsui Life Symposium on Global Financial Markets, May 11, 1993. Published as Merton Miller, "Is American Corporate Governance Fatally Flawed?" *Journal of Applied Corporate Finance* (Winter 1994): 32–39.

10. Michael C. Jensen, "Eclipse of the Public Corporation," *Harvard Business Review* (Sept.–Oct. 1989): 73–74.

11. Thomas Frank, *One Market Under God* (New York: Doubleday, 2000), 93–94 (in the UK edition).

12. I have a vivid memory of two Social Democratic members of parliament from Germany reciting Jensen's agency theory in great detail during a visit to *Fortune* in 1999 or so. Sadly, I haven't been able to find my notes.

13. Doug Henwood, *Wall Street* (rev. ed.) (London: Verso, 1998), 179.

14. Gary Hector, "Yes, You *Can* Manage for the Long Term," *Fortune*, Nov. 21, 1988.

15. Hector, "Yes, You *Can*."

16. Marc Gunther, "Investors of the World United," *Fortune*, June 24, 2002.

17. Fred R. Bleakley, "A Trustee Takes on the Greenmailers," *New York Times*, Feb. 10, 1985, 143.

18. Michael C. Jensen, "The Modern Industrial Revolution, Exit, and Control Systems," *Journal of Finance* (July 1993): 831–80, quote from p. 867. Jensen's change of heart was influenced by the work of Harvard law professor Mark Roe, who in a series of law review articles and then his book, *Strong Managers, Weak Owners* (Princeton, N.J.: Princeton University Press, 1996), made the case that Congress and the legal system had long undercut the power of institutional investors.

19. The repeated use of *Fortune* cover headlines in this chapter is in part the product

of having ready access to back issues of the magazine. But they also do a great job of capturing the conventional wisdom, or soon-to-be conventional wisdom of the business world.

20. Michael C. Jensen and Kevin J. Murphy, *Harvard Business Review* (May–June 1990): 138–53, quote from p. 138.

21. "U.S. Steel Announces Sweeping Modernization Scheme," by Benjamin Graham. Reprinted as appendix A to the 1990 Berkshire Hathaway shareholder letter.

22. The Brown quote was from a videotape of the rally loaned to me by the Financial Accounting Standards Board, and the Marcus quote in the transcripts of an FASB public hearing. Both were originally cited in Justin Fox, "The Next Best Thing to Free Money," *Fortune*, July 7, 1997, 60.

23. Connecticut senator Joe Lieberman led the charge.

24. Justin Fox, "The Next Best Thing to Free Money."

25. The one notable exception was Mark Rubinstein, cocreator of the binomial option-pricing model, who thought options should be expensed but hated the way the FASB did it. The standard set in stone the valuation of the option when it was granted, and didn't allow for any "trueing up" later on if it expired worthless or was exercised for a big gain.

26. Think of it this way. If a CEO gets a million options a year, and the company's stock stays at $10 for a decade, he makes no profit at all. If instead the price bounces from $10 one year to $20 and the next to $10 again, he makes $50 million while a buy-and-hold shareholder is stuck at zero.

27. Alfred Rappaport, "The Economics of Short-Term Performance Obsession," *Financial Analysts Journal* (May/June 2005): 65–79.

28. Alex Berenson has written an entire book about this phenomenon: *The Number: How the Drive for Quarterly Earnings Corrupted Wall Street and Corporate America* (New York: Random House, 2003).

29. "The most general implication of the efficient market hypothesis is that most security analysis is logically complete and valueless," is how Lorie and Hamilton began their passage on security analysis. In his Warren Buffett biography, Roger Lowenstein used this as evidence of the extremism of the efficient marketeers. But Lorie wasn't an efficient markets extremist (he was convinced his student Victor Niederhoffer could beat the market), and what he and Hamilton were trying to say was something Buffett and Benjamin Graham would both endorse: You shouldn't buy a company's stock because you like its prospects, you should buy it because you think the current market price is lower than those prospects warrant. James H. Lorie and Mary T. Hamilton, *The Stock Market: Theories and Evidence* (Homewood, Ill.: Richard D. Irwin Inc., 1973), 100.

30. I can testify to this from personal experience, having once invited Jensen to a *Fortune* magazine conference where he presented the idea to a room full of corporate executives.

31. Michael Brennan, "A Plain Man's Response to Professor Jensen" (unpublished paper, 1994). It followed an exchange between Brennan and Jensen in the *Journal of Applied Corporate Finance* (Summer 1994): 31–45.

32. Jim Collins, *Good to Great* (New York: HarperBusiness, 2001), 49.
33. Some of this story is told in David Warsh, "Beyond Coordination and Control Is
    . . . Transformation," *Economic Principals*, April 8, 2007.
34. Michael C. Jensen, "Putting Integrity into Finance Theory and Practice: A Positive Approach (Pdf of Keynote Slides)," first presented at the meetings of the
    American Finance Association, Boston, Mass., Jan. 6, 2006. Available at http://
    ssrn.com/abstract=876312.

CHAPTER 16: GENE FAMA AND DICK THALER KNOCK EACH OTHER OUT

1. Jason M. Heltzer, Evan M. Raine, "Rumble in Hyde Park," Follies 2002, University of Chicago Graduate School of Business (script given to the author by Jason Heltzer). Heltzer wrote another Fama-Thaler duet to the tune of "Confrontation" from *Les Miserables* that was, regrettably, never performed.
2. Richard H. Thaler, "Irving Fisher: Modern Behavioral Economist," *American Economic Review* (May 1997): 439–41.
3. The origin of the 401(k) is described in Michael J. Clowes, *The Money Flood* (New York: John Wiley & Sons, 2000), 188–89. The story of the rise of "investor nation" is told in depth in Joseph Nocera, *A Piece of the Action: How the Middle Class Joined the Money Class* (New York: Simon & Schuster, 1994).
4. Thomas L. Friedman, *The Lexus and the Olive Tree* (New York: Anchor Books, Random House, 2000), 58.
5. *Quantitative Analysis of Investor Behavior 2003*, Dalbar, Inc., July 14, 2003.
6. Chris Flynn, Herbert Lum, *DC Plans Under Performed DB Plans* (Toronto: CEM Benchmarking, 2006).
7. John J. Curran, "Why Investors Make the Wrong Choices," *Fortune*, Nov. 24, 1986; Clint Willis, "The Ten Mistakes to Avoid with Money," *Money*, June 1990.
8. Gary Belsky and Thomas Gilovich, *Why Smart People Make Big Money Mistakes and How to Correct Them* (New York: Simon & Schuster, 1999); Dan Ariely, *Predictably Irrational* (New York: HarperCollins, 2008); Jason Zweig, *Your Money and Your Brain* (New York: Simon & Schuster, 2007); and so on.
9. To get the records, Odean had to promise not to say *which* firm, and he won't. But everyone else in finance assumes it had to be Charles Schwab. Terrance Odean, "Are Investors Reluctant to Realize Their Losses," *Journal of Finance* (Oct. 1998): 1775–98. Terrance Odean, "Volume, Volatility, Price, and Profit When All Traders Are Above Average," *Journal of Finance* (Dec. 1998): 1887–934. Brad M. Barber and Terrance Odean, "Boys Will Be Boys: Gender, Overconfidence and Common Stock Investment," *Quarterly Journal of Economics* (Feb. 2001): 261–92.
10. A good summary of the evidence can be found in James Choi, David Laibson, Brigitte Madrian, and Andrew Metrick, "Saving for Retirement on the Path of Least Resistance," in *Behavioral Public Finance: Toward a New Agenda*, Edward J. McCaffrey and Joel Slemrod, eds. (New York: Russell Sage Foundation, 2006), 304–51.
11. George Ainslie, "Impulse Control in Pigeons," *Journal of the Experimental Analysis of Behavior* 21 (1974): 485–89.

12. Samuel M. McClure, David I. Laibson, George Loewenstein, and Jonathan D. Cohen, "Separate Neural Systems Value Immediate and Delayed Rewards," *Science* (Oct. 15, 2004): 503–7.

13. Richard Thaler and Shlomo Benartzi, "Save More Tomorrow: Using Behavioral Economics to Increase Employee Savings," *Journal of Political Economy* (Feb. 2004): pt. 2, S164–S187.

14. Justin Fox, "Why Johnny Can't Save for Retirement," *Fortune*, March 21, 2005.

15. Richard H. Thaler, Cass R. Sunstein, *Nudge: Improving Decisions About Health, Wealth, and Happiness* (New Haven: Yale University Press, 2008).

16. Cass R. Sunstein, ed., *Behavioral Law and Economics* (Cambridge and New York: Cambridge University Press, 2000).

17. Aditya Chakrabortty, "From Obama to Cameron, why do so many politicians want a piece of Richard Thaler?" *Guardian*, July 12, 2008, 16.

18. Edward Glaeser, "Paternalism and Psychology," *University of Chicago Law Review* (2006): 133–56.

19. Told to me by William Sharpe.

20. The first criticism is in Paul Zarowin, "Does the Stock Market React to Corporate Earnings Information?" *Journal of Finance* (1989): 1385–99, the second in K. C. Chan and Nai-fu Chen, "Structural and Return Characteristics of Small and Large Firms," *Journal of Finance* (1991): 1467–82.

21. Eugene F. Fama, "Market Efficiency, Long-Term Returns, and Behavioral Finance," *Journal of Financial Economics* (Sept. 1998): 283–306. Fama originally posted the paper in 1997 on the Social Science Research Network, an academic Web site run by Michael Jensen that has become the main forum for sharing work in progress in finance and several other disciplines. It was, as of March 2009, the most downloaded paper in SSRN's history.

22. "Is That a $100 Bill Lying on the Ground? Two Views of Market Efficiency," *Knowledge@Wharton*, Oct. 23, 2002, http://knowledge.wharton.upenn.edu/article.cfm?articleid=650.

23. Peter Bossaerts, *The Paradox of Asset Pricing* (Princeton, N.J.: Princeton University Press, 2002).

24. Eugene F. Fama and Kenneth R. French, "Disagreement, Tastes, and Asset Pricing," *Journal of Financial Economics* (March 2007): 667–89.

25. "The Mecca of the economist lies in economic biology rather than economic dynamics," Alfred Marshall, *Principles of Economics*, preface to the 8th ed. (Amherst, N.Y.: Prometheus Books, 1997), xx.

26. J. Doyne Farmer, "Physicists Attempt to Scale the Ivory Tower of Finance," *Computational Finance* (Nov./Dec.1999): 26.

27. Paul Krugman, "Ricardo's Difficult Idea," *The Economics and Politics of International Trade: Freedom and Trade*, Routledge Studies in the Modern World Economy, 10 (London: Routledge, 1998), 22–36. Also available online at http://web.mit.edu/krugman/www/ricardo.htm.

28. James B. Ramsey, "If Nonlinear Models Cannot Forecast, What Use Are They?" *Studies in Nonlinear Dynamics* 1, issue 2 (1996): 65–86.

29. W. Brian Arthur, John H. Holland, Blake LeBaron, Richard Palmer, and Paul Tayler, "Asset Pricing Under Endogenous Expectations in an Artificial Stock Market," in *The Economy As an Evolving Complex System II* (Reading, Mass.: Addison-Wesley, 1997), 15–44.

30. He does have some devoted fans off campus, such as Eric D. Beinhocker, author of *The Origin of Wealth: Evolution, Complexity, and the Radical Remaking of Economics* (Boston: Harvard Business School Press, 2006), and Legg Mason strategist Michael Mauboussin.

31. The definitive layman's account of the rise of new growth theory is David Warsh, *Knowledge and the Wealth of Nations: A Story of Economic Discovery* (New York: W. W. Norton, 2006).

32. On "adaptive rational equilibrium," see William A. Brock and Cars H. Hommes, "A Rational Route to Randomness," *Econometrica* (Sept. 1997): 1059–95; on "efficient learning," see Bossaerts, *Paradox*; on "adaptive market hypothesis," see Andrew W. Lo, "The Adaptive Markets Hypothesis: Market Efficiency From and Evolutionary Perspective," *Journal of Portfolio Management* 30 (2004): 15–29; on "rational belief equilibria," see Mordecai Kurz, "On Rational Belief Equilibria," *Economic Theory* 4 (1994): 859–76.

33. John C. Bogle, "An Index Fund Fundamentalist," *Journal of Portfolio Management* (Spring 2002): 31–38; "The Implications of Style Analysis for Mutual Fund Performance Evaluation," *Journal of Portfolio Management* (Summer 1998): 34–42.

EPILOGUE: THE ANATOMY OF A FINANCIAL CRISIS

1. "Here, as in most of the working-men's quarters of Manchester, the pork-raisers rent the courts and build pig-pens in them," Friedrich Engels wrote in *The Condition of the Working-Class in England in 1844.* "In almost every court one or even several such pens may be found, into which the inhabitants of the court throw all refuse and offal, whence the swine grow fat; and the atmosphere, confined on all four sides, is utterly corrupted by putrefying animal and vegetable substances."

2. T. S. Ashton, *Economic and Social Investigations in Manchester, 1833–1933: A Centenary History of the Manchester Statistical Society* (London: P. S. King & Son, 1934), 71–72.

3. John Mills, "On Credit Cycles and the Origin of Commercial Panics," *Transactions of the Manchester Statistical Society,* sess. 1867–68, 9–40.

4. John Mills, "Inaugural Address: On the Scope and Method of Statistical Enquiry, and on some Questions of the Day," *Transactions of the Manchester Statistical Society,* sess. 1871–72, 4.

5. "The Solar Period and the Price of Corn," read at meeting of British Association in Bristol, 1875. Reprinted in W. Stanley Jevons, *Investigations in Currency & Finance* (London: Macmillan and Co., 1884), 203.

6. Mills, "On Credit Cycles," 29. He suggests on the next page that Jevons be the one to do the educating: "[T]he Cobden chair of Political Economy at Owens College, at present so ably filled, might become a centre from which should radiate the remedial influences which I venture to suggest."

7. A notable exception was MIT economist Charles Kindleberger. But Kindleberger's 1978 history, *Manias, Panics and Crashes: A History of Financial Crises* (New York: Basic Books, 1978), which drew heavily on Minsky's theories, also seemed to draw far more readers from trading floors than economics seminar rooms.

8. Hyman P. Minsky, "The Financial Instability Hypothesis: A Restatement," *Thames Papers in Political Economy* (Autumn 1978). Reprinted in *Can "It" Happen Again: Essays on Instability and Finance* (Armonk, N.Y.: M. E. Sharpe, 1982), 106.

9. Mark Zandi, "Where are the Regulators?" Moody's Economy.com, Nov. 1, 2005, www.economy.com/home/article.asp?cid=18664.

10. Peter Thal Larsen, "Goldman pays the price of being big," *Financial Times*, Aug. 13, 2007.

11. Charles Himmelberg, Christopher Mayer, and Todd Sinai, "Assessing High House Prices: Bubbles, Fundamentals and Misperceptions," *Journal of Economic Perspectives* (Fall 2005): 67–92.

12. Justin Lahart, "In Time of Tumult, Obscure Economist Gains Currency," *Wall Street Journal*, Aug. 18, 2007, 1.

13. Alan Greenspan, "Reflections on Central Banking," speech given at the annual Jackson Hole symposium of the Federal Reserve Bank of Kansas City, Aug. 26, 2005.

14. Alan Greenspan, "Mortgage Banking," speech to the American Bankers Association Annual Convention, Palm Desert, California (via satellite), Sept. 26, 2005.

15. Alan Greenspan and James Kennedy, "Estimates of Home Mortgage Originations, Repayments and Debt on One-to-Four Family Residences," Finance and Economics Discussion Series, Divisions of Research and Statistics and Monetary Affairs, Federal Reserve Board, 2005–41; Greenspan and Kennedy, "Sources and Uses of Equity Extracted from Homes," Finance and Economics Discussion Series, Divisions of Research and Statistics and Monetary Affairs, Federal Reserve Board, 2007–20.

16. Joseph Stagg Lawrence, *Wall Street and Washington* (Princeton: Princeton University Press, 1929), 179.

17. John Maynard Keynes, *The General Theory of Employment, Interest and Money* (New York: Harcourt, Brace, 1936), 322.

18. Paul L. Kasriel, "Is Mishkin Mishuga About Asymmetric Monetary Policy Responses?" *Econtrarian* (Northern Trust Global Economic Research), Sept. 12, 2007.

19. Members of this minority include Peter Schiff, Jim Rogers, Marc Faber, and many more.

20. Robert Shiller, *The Subprime Solution: How Today's Global Financial Crisis Happened and What to Do About It* (Princeton: Princeton University Press, 2008).

21. "AMA: Plastic Surgery 'Only A Few Years Away' From Making Someone Look Better," *The Onion*, July 19, 2007.

INDEX